SOURCES IN WESTERN CIVILIZATION

The Seventeenth Century

THE

Sources in Western Civilization

GENERAL EDITOR, *Herbert H. Rowen*

RUTGERS UNIVERSITY

SEVENTEENTH CENTURY

EDITED BY

Andrew Lossky

UNIVERSITY OF CALIFORNIA, LOS ANGELES

THE FREE PRESS, NEW YORK

Collier-Macmillan Limited, London

Collier-Macmillan Canada, Ltd., Toronto, Ontario

Library of Congress Catalog Card Number: 67–10426

First Printing

ACKNOWLEDGMENTS

In the first place the author wishes to acknowledge his debt to the real authors of this volume — the nineteen persons of the seventeenth century from whose writings he has culled the selections that appear below. It is fortunate that the form of the *Sources in Western Civilization* does not permit extensive footnotes; otherwise the introductory essay would have been swollen to almost double its length with bibliographical and other references bearing witness to the author's indebtedness. To give an idea of its extent, the author will list, in alphabetical order, just a few of the historians who have influenced his selection of materials for this anthology or his interpretation of the seventeenth century sketched in the Introduction: E. N. Andreson, E. L. Asher, S. T. Bindoff, J. S. Bromley, G. N. Clark, M. H. Curtis, S. Drake, R. Ehrenberg, F. Ford, L. Gershoy, P. Geyl, R. M. Hatton, H. Hauser, H. Haydn, P. Hazard, E. F. Heckscher, H. Holborn, A. Hoxie, J. Huizinga, E. Israels, E. Labrousse, R. Mandrou, G. Mattingly, F. Meinecke, H. C. Meyer, Jr., D. Mornet, R. Mousnier, G. Pagès, R. H. Popkin, G. J. Renier, M. Roberts, H. H. Rowen, P. Sagnac, G. di Santillana, P. M. Sonnino, R. H. Tawney, M. A. Thomson, E. Troeltsch, G. Vernadsky, C. V. Wedgwood, J. B. Wolf, G. Zeller. This list would have to be trebled if one tried to make it complete. However the author cannot forbear from mentioning one more person: Mr. Geoffrey W. Symcox has not only translated five of the selections published here, but has proven to be an invaluable collaborator in the planning and preparation of this anthology. To all those who have aided him the author extends his gratitude. It would be unfair, however, if the reader were to conclude that the shortcomings of this volume should in any way be imputed to any of the persons listed by name or otherwise above: for these the author alone must bear responsibility.

A. L.

CONTENTS

viii

SOURCES IN WESTERN CIVILIZATION

The Seventeenth Century

Introduction

THE SEVENTEENTH CENTURY in Western Europe was born in chaos and ended in a semblance of order that ushered in the Age of the Enlightenment. The search for order is the main theme of European history in this period.

This search was, for most, an unconscious yearning for stability, but more thoughtful men sought to work out definite and explicit answers to the problems that beset them. It is only recently that historians have begun to investigate the realm of "climate of opinion" or "mood-thought" — that vast, incoherent body of beliefs underlying human activity, without whose concurrence no system, however ingenious, can achieve success. Unfortunately, the character of the sources for this new history is such that they cannot be satisfactorily represented in an anthology of documents. We must therefore limit ourselves to selections from the standard type of source, and in view of the main theme of the period, we must give primacy to intellectual history. This is not as simple as it may seem, for most of the seventeenth-century thinkers were rugged individualists who do not fit neatly into schools of thought. Any decision as to who among them are typical of their age must be strictly arbitrary.

The chaos at the beginning of the seventeenth century engulfed most aspects of life — religious, intellectual, artistic, economic, social, and political. It was further confounded because the attempts to introduce order were incomplete and uneven; the chaos in religious thought, for instance, began to be overcome earlier than that in the other domains. The elements of an orderly system thus emerged piecemeal, resulting in a bizarre, incongruous structure. The situation was made even more confused by the weakness of the enforcement mechanism of the state and of the other large social organizations. This effectively restrained even the most extreme organizers from conceiving a totalitarian state and society — the panacea of the utopians and the dream of the organization men in our own age.

4

The religious unity of the Western Church, with its libertarian overtones, had been shattered during the Reformation. By about 1560, the several fragments of Western Christendom had managed to arrive at a new definition of their respective doctrinal tenets, and in the process they lost much of their former elasticity and freedom of expression. This hardening of positions was largely responsible for the outbreak of a series of religious wars, which lasted for about eight decades and culminated in the first world war of modern times, commonly known as the Thirty Years War. In its brutality this war is reminiscent of the mores of the twentieth century. There is, however, a vital difference from the present day: in the course of the Thirty Years War most of the political leaders lost whatever control they had once exercised over their instruments of power, and the reversion to barbarism proceeded from utter disarray rather than from excessive organization [1].* Whatever the causes of this outburst of brutality, it administered a shock to many contemporary thinkers.

The beautiful and coherent structure erected by medieval scholastic philosophers, who had adapted the philosophy of Aristotle to the needs of Christian theology, no longer satisfied the needs of the New Learning or of the new society. The substitution by some Renaissance thinkers of Cicero and Vergil for Aristotle as the supreme authorities had also failed to bring the expected remedies. These failures led to the movement that has recently been dubbed the Counter-Renaissance; this term is designed to accommodate a variety of thinkers who do not fit among either the scholastics or the Ciceronians. Many of them stressed the importance of the experience of the senses as a source of certain knowledge, particularly in medical science. We meet such rebels against Aristotelianism fairly frequently in Spain in the sixteenth century; but by the early seventeenth century, their chief arena was Italy. Furthermore, there was a revival of Platonic thought, with its emphasis on the reality of logical entities, and especially on the idea of number. The Platonic mathematicians and the believers in experimentation based on sensory data were not one and the same group; but there were some thinkers, notably Galileo [3], and later Newton [6], who managed to combine these two approaches.

The same uncertainty reigned in the arts in the early seventeenth

* Bracketed numbers refer to the numbers of the selections printed in the text.

century. No one has yet succeeded in adequately defining baroque style. Probably the only point on which most people who have written about the baroque agree is that it reflects a certain imperfectly resolved tension. This is as much as saying that a baroque work contains an element of disorder in its composition, which is certainly true of the belles-lettres of the early seventeenth century, only partly true of the architecture, painting, and plastic arts, and quite untrue of the music of the period.

One of the manifestations of the intellectual and literary ferment of the age was the "war between the Ancients and the Moderns," waged throughout the seventeenth century. The defenders of the former maintained that the Ancients had laid the foundation of all sciences so well, and had attained such perfection in the arts, that nothing remained for Moderns to do but to work out the implications of what the Ancients had done and to imitate models of classical art. The modernists, while not denying the merit of the Ancients, maintained that their own age was in no way inferior, and that the canons laid down in classical antiquity were not necessarily sacrosanct. This in no way implies, however, that the modernists were perforce either more talented or more original than their opponents.

In the sphere of economic activity, the picture was also somewhat confused. There can be no certainty about economic relations if the concept of property is not clearly defined. Generally speaking, there are two main concepts of property that have been devised in the history of man. The one that was in vogue in ancient Rome and in Europe and America in the nineteenth century defines property as an absolute and exclusive possession of a physical object, carrying with it the right of use and abuse of this object. According to the other view, property is the possession of certain specific rights with regard to the object possessed, these rights being subordinated to the moral and customary law. Moral law forbids abuse of the object — that is, its use for ends contrary to those for which it is deemed to have been created; customary law defines the specific conditions under which every piece of property is held. Moreover, since no one has absolute possession, several persons, several groups, or even several sovereign states, can simultaneously possess the same object, such as a piece of land, in different respects. This second view was prevalent in medieval Europe. It was fully supported by the traditional teachings of the Christian Church, and it was still the concept commonly held by both Church and State in the seventeenth century.

In Renaissance Europe, simultaneously with a revival of the study of Roman law, and with the growing needs of a large-scale trading economy, there was a recrudescence of the Roman concept of property. It was taken up even by some members of the Roman Catholic hierarchy. For example, Adhemar Fabri, the fourteenth-century bishop of Geneva, issued a charter guaranteeing full freedom of usury in his bishopric. It appeared in the enclosure movement, practiced, on a modest scale, in sixteenth-century England. It was also evident in some of the dealings of the sixteenth-century financiers; but here we must add that the possession of money as a symbol of potential power always presented a difficulty to the moral philosopher, for whom the ultimate purpose of money was not as clear as that of a piece of land.

However, a formidable barrier to the onward march of absolute private property was erected by the Calvinists of the sixteenth century (though not by their descendants), by the Counter-Reformation Catholics, and, to a lesser extent, by the Lutherans. All of them denounced the spirit of secularism and unbridled gain and, whenever they could, passed legislation against its manifestations. It was not until the nineteenth century that the medieval sin of greed was firmly transformed into the modern virtue of thrift. This barrier of hostility to the establishment of absolute private property was reinforced by many of the members of the older nobility, who began to defend their social status and economic interest against the encroachment of the financier. Even the activities of mercantilist statesmen like Colbert in some measure put a limit to the growth of private property, inasmuch as they tended to vest the ultimate and absolute right of possession in the state rather than in the individual. Thus the progress of private property was rather effectively checked in most of Europe in the seventeenth century. The dikes held less firmly in England, where conditions were unsettled as a result of several revolutions. It is therefore all the more interesting to consider Locke's justification of the right of private possession by Natural Law, which, while it secures this right, also limits it [12].

There were two rival theories on the nature of trade in the seventeenth century. According to the traditional view, God has so set up the different parts of the earth as to make necessary an exchange of goods between them. The commerce thus engendered maintains peaceful intercourse among men, from which everybody must benefit materially and spiritually; it unites mankind and serves as a vehicle for the spread of the Church. This is not exactly the view of an ordinary shopkeeper, whose immediate aim, all too often, is to do in his rival next door and to engross as much of the trade as he can. It is to this latter outlook that the frame of mind known as "mercantilism" owes so much. Let us note, however, that the prosperity of the individual merchant interested a mercantilist theoretician or statesman not for its own sake, but only to the extent that it could contribute to the power of the state. Colbert [13] expressed the mercantilist hierarchy of values in a nutshell when he wrote to his cousin in 1666: "Trade is the source of finance, and finance is the vital nerve of war." In order to accumulate power, chiefly at the expense of one's neighbors, economic activity had to be regulated by the state.

Frequently we find that the extreme mercantilist point of view was advanced by men who had risen from the bourgeoisie, like Thomas Mun or Colbert, whereas members of the established nobility, such as Sully or Richelieu, tended to cling to the older belief that trade, like agriculture, was a divinely-inspired institution meant to benefit everybody and that it should be left as free as possible. In the seventeenth century, these men wrote long and rather dull treatises under such titles as *The Theater of Agriculture*, which purported to show that land, not money, was the source of real, stable prosperity. They were the spiritual ancestors of the eighteenth-century physiocrats, who likewise defended the values of the landed aristocracy.

It is remarkable that the more old-fashioned view of trade just described should have found many adherents in the Dutch Republic, commercially the most advanced of the seventeenth-century states [14]. True enough, the Dutch Republic had sprung from the resistance of privileged groups against the spirit of modernism, the encroachments of the central authority, and all that the emerging modern state stood for. However, the Dutch insisted on the beneficent, God-guided role of free commerce in human affairs much as a lion would have defended the freedom of the beasts of the jungle. This Dutch attitude sprang largely from confidence in their own economic power. When necessary, the States party, ever responsive to the interests of maritime trade, did not hesitate to send out the Dutch fleet, which it had built up to such great strength that it was able to defeat the combined naval forces of England and France in 1672. At other times, when it was necessary to destroy a rival, the Dutch merchants, with the full support of their government, engaged in a ruthless underselling and skulduggery that made Colbert envious.

One of the conditions necessary for the development of a money economy and of state finance is the belief that arithmetical figures denoting the quantity or measure of material things or of money have a real meaning in the life of an individual or of society. Without such an act of faith, which seems axiomatic to us, no budget could ever be drawn up, except, perhaps, for innocent amusement. In the early seventeenth century, this truth was not altogether self-evident to many men, who were in no way inferior to the succeeding generations in intellectual acumen, but who were more used to qualitative than to quantitative judgments and measures. By the second half of the seventeenth century, however, there was a wide-spread passion to measure and count the quantity of everything in the world. Not only did such great original thinkers as Galileo, Descartes, Newton, and Leibnitz contribute to this phenomenon, but also a host of lesser figures who wrote fairly popular tracts on the use of mathematics in just about everything. Colbert had been a practitioner in "political arithmetic" long before this term was invented by Sir William Petty in the 1690's to denote the new science of statistics. But at the beginning of the seventeenth century, Spain, the greatest power that Christendom had seen since the days of Rome, functioned without a state budget, and this did not prevent her from exercising political hegemony in Europe. The first state budget of the modern type was produced by Colbert in France in the 1660's. By 1700, there was hardly a country in Europe, however small, that did not follow this practice. Since so many "revolutions" have of late been invented to describe great new departures in human affairs, we might well speak of the "Mathematical Revolution" of the seventeenth century.

One of the most difficult aspects of the seventeenth century for the modern man to grasp is the social structure of the European states, for it has been beclouded by several conflicting mythologies. It is normal for every social group to evolve its own mythology, by which it seeks to arrogate to itself special charismatic properties that qualify it for natural leadership. Not all of these mythologies are of recent invention, nor is every myth a hypocritical cover for material interests. Let us consider a few examples of such myths. Many members of the nobility believed that they had inherited from their

ancestors special gifts for military leadership and for the responsibili-
ties of government and that these gifts had been further cultivated by
the right kind of upbringing [1]. Moreover, the nobles had a greater
stake in the realm than the others and were thus its natural guardians. The mythology of the ever-rising middle class, or bourgeoisie,
is even more extravagant: it is asserted that this class is the bearer of
all virtues and talents in all walks of life, the architect of material
well-being, and the mainstay of real culture (which, it is claimed,
can flourish only in cities). The bourgeoisie is contrasted with the
insolent, unproductive, spendthrift, and foppish aristocracy on the
one hand, and with the shiftless and brutish peasants and proletarians
on the other. This mythology of the middle class is of comparatively
recent origin and did not appear in full bloom until the end of the
eighteenth century, though some of its elements are much older. The
mythologies advanced on behalf of the peasants and of the city
proletariat are, if anything, even more fantastic than that of the
middle class, though peasant-worship (not necessarily practiced by
the peasants themselves) has a much longer pedigree than that of
the city proletarians, for it feeds on the cult of the noble savage, whose
roots go back to ancient Greece. Every class mythology claims for
its group the pre-eminent right to exercise power and to enjoy certain benefits and privileges that the group seeks either to obtain or
to defend if it feels itself threatened.

Both the bourgeois and the Marxian mythologies see society as
divided into two unequal groups — the privileged and the unprivileged. While there is much to be said for such a diagnosis in
the nineteenth century, it falls wide of the mark if we try to apply
it to the seventeenth. This does not mean, of course, that there were
no conflicts and no antagonisms between different social groups. But
if someone had tried to explain to a seventeenth-century audience
the plight of the unprivileged classes, it is most unlikely that anybody but the highwaymen and the outlaws would have understood
what was being said. The reason is that every individual and every
small group (such as a guild corporation in a city) possessed its
privileges and its "liberties" — that is, specific rights that could not
be forfeited except for felony. These privileges differed from person
to person, from corporation to corporation, from city to city, and
from province to province; thus there was no equality of privilege,
even between members of the same social class. There was even less
similarity between the privileges of a duke and peer on the one hand

and those of a sharecropper on the other. The former would include an exemption from certain taxes and immunities from some jurisdictions, the right to be addressed as "my cousin" by the king, the pretension to sit in the king's council by right of birth; the latter would include a claim to a specific share of the crops, to economic and judicial protection by his lord, and to membership in the village council. And yet the attitude of the sharecropper toward his privileges was identical with the attitude of the duke and peer toward his. The privileges of the sharecropper were just as inalienable as those of the duke, and in this respect the sharecropper and the duke were equal.

Some of the privileges were defined in special charters issued by the sovereign, but most of them had become established by custom and long possession. In view of the prevailing attitude toward privileges, it was virtually impossible to legislate social reform, except through the back door or in moments of general disaster, for anyone who tampered with established privileges was courting rebellion. Indeed, nearly all of the rebellions in the seventeenth century were sparked by real or presumed innovations from above; they were thus conservative in nature, and their ostensible aim was usually to defend what was considered to be the status quo. The art of government consisted chiefly in the ruler's not becoming so bogged down in the morass of various privileges as to be incapable of any decisive action. Only the strong could escape this fate; the others were paralyzed, as was the government of Spain in the second half of the seventeenth century — not through lack of talent but through insufficient will at the top. But before discussing various modes of government action, we should consider the main characteristics of several social classes.

In the seventeenth century, the nobility of every European country was a self-conscious class. It was organized to some extent, although this organization varied considerably from country to country and from province to province. The aristocracies of different countries, however, had a certain feeling of affinity, based in part on what still remained of the old code of chivalry, which had been universal for the whole brotherhood of knights. The self-consciousness of this class was heightened by their fear of the centralizing tendencies of the emerging sovereign states. They also contemplated with distaste the prospect of having their ranks swollen by a crowd of newcomers: men ennobled through holding administrative or judicial office or through an outright purchase of a patent of nobility. Normally a successful rise from prosperous banker or merchantman to well-entrenched nobleman took three generations; members of the judicature made the same transition in two generations. Most of the older nobles had come to accept this situation in principle: it provided them with a choice of eligible rich heiresses to marry. Moreover, without a steady influx of new families, the number of noble houses would have quickly dwindled, for wars and other disorders took their toll of the nobility; it has been estimated that, in the later Middle Ages, the average life-span of a military feudal family was five generations. Nevertheless, we can understand the social antagonisms which mass ennoblement by the fiat of the sovereign power could arouse. Louis XIV, for instance, sold 2,040 patents of nobility in the year 1696 alone. At best, a social upstart was liable to be the butt of many jokes, as was Molière's *bourgeois gentilhomme.*

Turning to the other classes of society, let us note that the clergy, despite its divisions, had a feeling of solidarity, and possessed an organization far more developed than that of the nobility. The ethos of the higher clergy — many of whom, though by no means all, were of noble descent — was not very different from that of the nobility. For most purposes, therefore, we can consider the upper clergy and the nobility as forming one group. The lower clergy formed a class apart from the others, however, many of its members retaining ties with the groups from which they had issued. As for the middle classes, their unit of consciousness and of organization was smaller than that of either the nobility or the clergy. Thus there was no French, German, or Spanish bourgeoisie, except as an abstract notion. But there were the city communities of Tours, Augsburg, and Segovia, each with its own professional corporations; to these cities and corporations, the burgesses — that is, the full-fledged members of the city community — were bound by ties of loyalty and interest. This fragmentation of the bourgeoisie, with its attendant provincialism, goes far to explain the political ineptness and comparatively poor showing of the "third estate" in most of the representative assemblies of the seventeenth century. The role of the House of Commons in England does not invalidate this generalization, for most of its members belonged not to the bourgeoisie but to the gentry. Even in the Dutch Republic, Venice, and Genoa — republics of merchants and bankers — the tone of social and political life was set by the regents or patricians, who were not themselves directly involved in trade operations. Their upbringing differed from that of the nobility only in that it laid less stress on military prowess. We can catch a glimpse of their outlook on life in the writings of De la Court [10]. As for the peasant, his sphere of consciousness was even smaller than that of the average bourgeois and seldom extended beyond the manor or parish in which he lived.

The notions of privilege and of property that we have briefly discussed bear a direct relation to the nature of office in early modern times. An office-holder regarded himself primarily not as a functionary of the state but as a privileged proprietor of his office. In the fifteenth and sixteenth centuries, the number of such officials was much increased, mainly because of the expanded administrative activity of the state. But the central powers were too weak to prevent this new class of officials from developing the mentality of the old feudal barons. Indeed, most of them came to regard their offices as fiefs, as personal property that was theoretically held in precarious tenure but that was in practice inalienable except for adequate recompense and could be forfeited only for felony. From this there was only one step to turning the office into a salable piece of property and to making it hereditary. A new nobility of office was thereby created.

One of the secrets of the vitality of the medieval monarchies had been their ability to create new offices, duplicating old ones that had become ossified, unresponsive, or recalcitrant. Under the dispensation of these times, however, an office could seldom be suppressed, and it would not be long before the new officials would become indistinguishable from the old ones. The administrative machine thus built was becoming ever more complex, unwieldy, and clogged with the debris of the past; it resembled Descartes's description of buildings and towns that had grown up in the course of several centuries [4, a].

During the turmoils of the sixteenth century, the office holders were able to entrench themselves. Furthermore, all the governments found themselves in such fiscal straits, especially in times of inflation, that they had to acquiesce in the proprietary aspirations and practices of the officialdom, provided that they could share in the sale and inheritance transactions by imposing a duty on them. The officials were quite willing to pay the modest sums demanded of them, for it made their positions and emoluments more secure. Only in England was this process held in check. But everywhere on the Continent by the early seventeenth century the sovereigns found themselves face to face with a class of new feudatories whom they themselves had called into being and who, like the old feudal barons, effectively limited the government's freedom of action. Moreover, despite some friction between the nobility of office and the old feudal nobility, the two groups soon began to intermarry. They frequently made common cause in defense of local institutions and customs against the encroachments of central authority. Thus, by 1600, an invigorated and turbulent noble class was flexing its muscles, ready to defend itself against all comers — if need be, by rebellion. This, in the days of divided loyalties, could be quite dangerous to the very existence of the state.

We need not imagine, however, that the central powers sat idly watching their own predicament. To deal with the barons and the recalcitrant officials, sovereigns possessed an old and tried weapon: commissioners, whether they were called *missi dominici*, intendants, or *commissarii*. The commissioner did not own his position; he had specific powers delegated to him which could be revoked at any time. Whether his functions were extensive or limited, a commissioner was responsive to the power that had created him and that could terminate his commission at any time. Needless to say, no love was lost between the commissioners and the officeholders. In France, for instance, many of the officeholders and members of the aristocracy employed the expression "minister of state" as a term of abuse right up to the collapse of the Fronde; a minister of state was the crown's closest adviser in matters of policy and was the highest of all the commissioners.

It was generally taken for granted that if the sovereign personally ordered his subject to do a certain thing, the subject was honorbound to carry out his master's wish, provided that the order did not violate divine or natural law. But from this it did not follow that the same obedience was due to the king's temporary agents or commissioners. Nowadays, when nearly all agents of the state are commissioners, and when we obey them all indiscriminately, it is hard for us to conceive of such a situation. Yet the establishment of the principle of obedience to the lowly agent of the central power is the crucial theme in the emergence of the modern state. Everywhere in Europe this development took a long step forward during the seventeenth century. By 1700, however, the process was by no means complete, and its final triumph did not come until the French Revolution. The chief reason for its advance in the seventeenth century was psychological: almost a hundred years of the turmoil and chaos of religious wars had produced a feeling of disgust with the "thousand tyrannies" (as Louis XIV called them) set up by local strong-arm men. The hankering for security, which only a strong central government could provide, produced a ground swell of royalist sentiment over most of the Continent in the second half of the seventeenth century.

Three conditions would have been necessary to translate this feeling of the majority into a revolution from above that would have established a full-fledged modern sovereign state. First, there had to be a total collapse of the existing class of officials. Second, there had to be revolutionary monarchs, ready to make full and fearless use of the sentiment in their favor. Third, the thinkers of the period had to work out the theoretical foundations and justifications of the new society, which, when vulgarized at the level of the uncritical public, would have helped to shape a climate of opinion favorable to the new state. Not one of these conditions was present in Western Europe in the seventeenth century.

The officeholders, somewhat shaken by their experience of chaos, became more orderly and obedient. They began to treat their sovereigns with more deference than before, but this did not amount to a complete change of outlook. As for the sovereigns, only Philip II of Spain had, in his youth, entertained visions of a streamlined, efficient, honest administrative machine, established in disregard of precedent and privilege and fully subservient to the will of a self-disciplined master. Philip's attempt to set up such a government in the Netherlands involved him in his most disastrous war, and he learned his lesson. Scarcely any of the seventeenth-century monarchs and statesmen were revolutionaries; for the most part they were cautious, rather conservative men, content to leave things as they were so long as they could have their way in special projects dear to their heart. This was true of Richelieu, Louis XIV, the Emperor Leopold I, the kings of Spain, and most of the other statesmen. Only the Emperor Ferdinand II, Olivarès, Colbert, and Peter the Great had more or less the same notions as the young Philip II. Ferdinand's efforts collapsed in the Thirty Years War; Olivarès and Colbert were not the sovereign masters of Spain and France; and Peter the Great partially succeeded only because Russian society had suffered a complete breakdown at the beginning of the seventeenth century and was still disoriented when he assumed power in the 1690's.

Of the theorists, only Hobbes [9] and, to a lesser extent, Spinoza, conceived of unlimited sovereign power in the state, but their writings were received with consternation by most of their contemporaries.

There was an intermediate class of servants of the state between the officeholders and the commissioners: men who undertook contractual obligations to the sovereign. Among them were the various tax farmers and the armed forces. The tax farmers advanced money to the government and received in exchange the right to reimburse themselves by collecting certain taxes for a number of years. This was the golden age for private enterprise in government finance: if the government was weak, as it usually was, only about one third or less of what the tax farmers collected reached the treasury; if it was strong, as it was in France during Colbert's administration, the government might receive over seventy per cent of the moneys collected. Since the governments were chronically in debt to the financiers, and since the latter often had connections in high places, the central powers were unable to deal effectively with this evil, except by occasional bankruptcies of the treasury, open or concealed; these were especially common in Spain. But this expedient had the disadvantage of impairing the credit of the treasury, so that future loans would have to be raised at even higher rates of interest. For instance, by 1670 the Spanish Crown had to pay about forty per cent annual interest on some of its loans. Only the Dutch Republic, Venice, and Geneva were able to maintain sound government credit and found it comparatively easy to finance their enterprises in the seventeenth century. In the 1690's, England joined this group of powers with the establishment of the national debt and of the Bank of England.

The sovereigns had much better success in the seventeenth century in dealing with their armed forces. Ever since the decline of feudal warfare, war was becoming increasingly a preserve for expert technicians who sold their services. A captain or a colonel received the king's pay and in return undertook to maintain a company or a regiment of which he was the virtual owner. When the colonel of one of Louis XIII's regiments died during the siege of La Rochelle, the king was forced to give the command to the fourteen-year-old son of the deceased, rather than to the person he deemed most suitable, for fear that the regiment would mutiny and disperse.

Private entrepreneurs raised, organized, and equipped their troops, and then hired out their services to the highest bidder. At the beginning of the seventeenth century, the Genoese banker Spinola was involved in equipping Spanish troops; he tried his hand at commanding them, turned out to be a first-rate tactician, and became a great commander-in-chief. Spinola happened to be very loyal to his masters in Madrid and Brussels, but the allegiance of someone like Bernard of Saxe-Weimar was doubtful. This brilliant general leased himself and his army to France when Richelieu decided to enter the Thirty Years War openly. Having won a great victory at Breisach in 1638, he went his own way, much to the consternation of the Cardinal. At the time of his death in 1639, Bernard bequeathed his entire army to a Swiss friend, who later sold the whole force to France outright. But, of course, the most famous of the military tycoons was Wallenstein. It was not only inconvenient, but dangerous, for the state to employ such commanders.

By the end of the seventeenth century the military situation changed radically. Everywhere in Europe (though not in the colonial world) war had become the preserve of the state, to the virtual exclusion of private entrepreneurs. The state asserted its power to make the appointments and to control the whole chain of command in the armies and navies. Offices that had carried with them the right to issue commissions were left vacant or otherwise curbed. Only in the artillery did the semi-civilian contractor continue to play an important part. In short, the career of Grimmelshausen's hero [1] was unlikely to be duplicated at the end of the seventeenth century, except among the privateers at sea.

The "military revolution," which finally transferred the waging of war from private hands into the hands of the state, owed much to the innovations in tactics started by Maurice of Nassau and the other Dutch commanders early in the seventeenth century, but it was consummated by Gustavus Adolphus, who introduced a new type of gun, the *fusil*, that was lighter than the old musket and could be reloaded much faster. With this weapon a far smaller Swedish force was able to deliver as much fire as the regular "Spanish square" formation. Moreover, since the Swedish formation was only four to six ranks deep instead of fifty, the direction of fire could be shifted much more quickly and easily than that of the Spanish square; this allowed a further reduction in manpower. Gustavus' army required a new type of discipline that had to be far more exacting than that of Wallenstein's hordes. Much of the responsibility for tactical success was shifted from the general to the subordinate commanders of smaller units, who were now expected to exercise initiative in a rational way, and yet be responsive to orders from above. As a result, all the European armies had to be overhauled in the middle of the seventeenth century. They became smaller, more professional, and more pliable than before, and the governments were able to take firm control of them. These smaller, better-disciplined armies could more readily abide by the rules of warfare. All the governments were determined not to experience the chaos of the Thirty Years War again, and they were quite successful in bringing warfare itself under control, in limiting it, and in making the game of death as "civilized" as it can be. The rules of the game held good for almost a century and a half, until the French Revolution.

One may well wonder how a government managed to command any obedience at all under the conditions we have described. Revolutionary solutions, as we have seen, were seldom attempted; when they were, they usually failed. Yet in most of Europe, there was much more obedience to central authority in 1700 than in 1600. The elaborate precautions that Louis XIV had to take in arresting Fouquet in 1661 {17, a] would no longer have been necessary for most sovereigns after 1700. How was this achieved? Richelieu lets slip a curious statement in the chapter of his *Political Testament* that deals with the venality of offices: It would be a crime, says the Cardinal, to introduce such practices in establishing a new republic, but "in an old monarchy . . . whose disorder, not without usefulness, forms part of the order of the state," the situation is different. The key phrase here is "not without usefulness." In other words, one unruly element can be used to check another.

The society that we have sketched was divided into many small groups and individuals; all the rights and pretensions of one group or individual had to be fitted in with those of other groups and individuals, in accordance with different codes, enactments, and customs, all having currency within the same country and administered by competing jurisdictions. Almost every person and family of any importance and almost every corporation was in a state of rivalry and chronic litigation with other persons, families, and corporations. The support that a king or his minister could throw behind one or the other litigant or jurisdiction might mean the difference between winning and losing a lawsuit. Moreover, in most countries any pending case could at any time be evoked from a lower court to be judged by the highest tribunal of the land — that is, before the king's council sitting in a judicial session.

By exploiting the local rivalries, by exerting little pressures here and there, by playing the game adroitly and relentlessly but without driving anybody to desperation, the sovereign and his commissioners could imperceptibly increase their actual power. The royalist sentiment of the common people and the preoccupation of the intellectuals with order came to their aid. But beside skill, imagination, and constant application, something else was needed for this game: a mass of detailed and accurate information on who was doing what, what his strong and weak points were, and where his interests lay. We need not be surprised that many of the governments in the second half of the seventeenth century went on a spree of gathering information on individuals and on local institutions, amassing statistical data, and even engaging in historical research in order to vindicate their claims.

The process by which royal power was increased is evident above all in France, in the lands of the Austrian Hapsburgs, and in some of the smaller states. It is less evident in England, which was shaken by revolutionary upheavals and which had less immediate need to increase the power of central authority because the Tudors had already made the crown quite strong. The seventeenth-century monarchs of Spain were weak, and the regeneration of monarchic administration did not really set in until the second decade of the eighteenth century. In the Dutch Republic, on the other hand, the maintenance of old-time privileges and institutions was the essence of the state itself; it was thus a living negation of the modern state. Yet at times even the United Provinces needed some authority to direct their federal action. The basic technique of exerting influence in the Dutch Republic was not unlike that used in the other states, but the situation was complicated by the fact that there were several sources of power in competition with one another: the Prince of Orange, the Grand Pensionary, the States of Holland, the City of Amsterdam, the East India Company, and least important of them all, the States General. When all these powers cooperated, as was usual in times of grave international crisis, all went smoothly and the Republic acted vigorously and effectively.

In the absence of the ultimate weapon of enforcement — the machine gun — no state could subsist without the support of public opinion. In the final analysis it was the pressure of one's family, colleagues, friends, and neighbors that made the individual comply with orders that he would not have carried out of his own accord. If he defaulted on his taxes, his neighbors would have to supply the deficiency. If he persisted in defying the powers that be, his whole community would be threatened with divine wrath — failure of crops, the plague, and other disasters. If he did not choose to renounce all his privileges, become an outlaw, and be hunted down, he would do well to conform. Thus, again, we come up against the all-important role of the small local groups and organizations in holding society together.

In shaping the opinion of a small local group, the parish priest or minister was the key figure. The Church was the only organization that penetrated to every locality and yet embraced the entire realm. It was usually the priest who had to explain to his parishioners the awful consequences of disobedience. If the government wished to make anything known to the illiterate inhabitants, the only effective way of doing so was to have the parish priest read the proclamation after the Sunday service. If a sizable number of people had stopped going to church on Sunday, the working of the government would have been seriously impaired. Since it was physically impossible for the central power to communicate with each parish priest individually, it had to do so through the bishop, or, in a Protestant country without episcopal organization, through a synod or similar organization. The importance of the clergy in secular affairs in the Middle Ages is well known. In early modern times, the clergy became less conspicuous in shaping high policy, but in the day-to-day administration of the State, especially on the local level, its role was if anything even more important than before.

The secular power could not remain indifferent to the religion of its subjects or to ecclesiastical appointments. Inevitably, the State was drawn into theological disputes, for the theology of a clergyman colored his entire outlook on life and on this depended his role in the State. Thus we need not be surprised that religious toleration, except as a temporary political expedient, could not be expected from the secular power. Wherever it was practiced, it was the measure of the government's weakness, or of the degree to which the government had emancipated itself from reliance on the ecclesiastical chain of command. In this connection Pufendorf's discussion of the relations between different faiths is of special interest [16].

It is important to remember, however, that a vast majority of seventeenth-century statesmen were sincere in their religious convictions. Assuredly they were also influenced by political, aesthetic, social, and economic motives, but to treat their religion as merely a hypocritical cover for political, economic, or other interests, is to misunderstand completely the temper of the age.

Earlier we have said that the quest for order was the principal theme of seventeenth-century history. This search was largely prompted by the desire to escape from the chaos that prevailed in most of Europe after the Reformation. However, it would be naive to attribute the discoveries of Galileo and the thought of Descartes or of Grotius only to the quest for order. The yearning to escape from chaos may have influenced their general interest in the problem of regularity in the universe, but it could not have produced the specific contents of their thought.

It is impossible in an anthology such as this to represent adequately the variety of thought that flourished in the seventeenth century. Regretfully, we must leave out such important and original figures as Suárez, Pascal, Spinoza, Bayle, Leibnitz, Althusius, Harrington, St. Francis de Sales, Molinos, and many others. Nor is it possible to do justice even to the thinkers represented here and to show the full complexity and richness of their thought. For instance, our understanding of the Newtonian system is defective if we forget that its author was a Christian mystic; likewise, we cannot fully comprehend the political thought of Locke without taking into account his epistemology and his defense of toleration based on grounds of theology, not of mere political expediency.

There were certain interests, and even some acts of faith, that most seventeenth-century thinkers shared in common. Nearly all of them believed that the world in its ideal state was an orderly place, governed by laws whose ultimate author was God and which could be discovered by human reason. It followed that if a concerted effort were made by all men of learning to uncover the true foundations of the world, a coherent body of knowledge would emerge which could guide mankind on the road to perfection and salvation. Hence we find the idea of an academy of science frequently cropping up in many places: in Federico Cesi's Lincean Academy [2], in Descartes' writings [4], in the various official and unofficial Italian, French, Dutch, and German academies, in the Royal Society in England, and finally, in Leibnitz' activities. It was not altogether fortuitous that

Leibnitz, in whom the rationalist philosophy of the century found its culmination, was himself the last man of learning who could with justice be described as a "one-man academy"; he became the spiritual father of the Prussian and of the Russian Academies of Science.

Men of the seventeenth century could plainly see that the world around them was neither orderly nor perfect. Many of them — Descartes, for instance — became obsessed with the idea of perfection; in its primary, ontological meaning, perfection was one of the main attributes of God; when applied to man, it was tantamount to salvation. As for the cause of the imperfect state of the world, there was virtual unanimity that it was brought on by unreasonable passions of man. Thus the nature and control of passions became the central preoccupation of the age. Nearly all of the major thinkers, men of letters and other artists, as well as frequenters of the salons, grappled with this problem. In this anthology, the reader will find it explicitly dealt with by Descartes, Félibien, Hobbes, Bossuet, Locke, Callières, and Pufendorf.

The novelty of manner and of style of some of the seventeenth-century thinkers produced the impression — and sometimes the self-delusion — that a totally new era in thought had begun and that, for the first time in the history of man, all would soon be brought under the sway of reason. Such a frame of mind was likely to produce a generation of serious, dedicated men capable of purposeful action; it was not generally conducive to a sense of humor, to an ability to see oneself in perspective and to laugh at oneself; it was also apt to exacerbate the war between the Ancients and the Moderns. And yet, paradoxically enough, most of the great seventeenth-century thinkers, with the important exception of Hobbes, were not revolutionaries. Very few of them built their systems with wholly new materials. In fact, in their most striking and lasting contributions, where their original genius was best displayed, they salvaged some of the elements from the debris of the Middle Ages, refurbished them, and gave them new life and vigor.

A good example of a self-conscious modernist is Descartes [4]. Having renounced all ties with scholasticism, and having proclaimed his determination to start his system from scratch, he proceeded to devise a method of logical reasoning based on an analysis of every entity down to its simplest component parts. But this method was precisely what the schoolmen had been practicing for several centuries before Descartes — only the schoolmen had used Aristotle,

Aquinas, and the Bible as their field of inquiry, whereas Descartes chose his own consciousness as his first field of analysis. Furthermore, Descartes' proof of the existence of God is but a restatement in terms of modern philosophy of the "ontological proof" of God's existence which St. Anselm had formulated in the eleventh century. Thus, despite all protestations to the contrary, the father of modern philosophy turns out to be a schoolman in disguise, though his field of endeavor was different from that of his predecessors.

Descartes' God could have created only an orderly universe, and he is therefore above all the Lord God of Mathematics, which is the most rational and therefore the most certain of all the sciences. In an ideal situation, it should have been possible to build a full picture of the world by a set of deductions from first principles, mathematics, and simple innate ideas. But man's intellect being too weak for such an enterprise, it was necessary to have recourse to experiments, that is, to sensory experience, and this is where error was apt to creep in. For this reason Descartes and his followers doubted the efficacy of the experimental method in building a full body of scientific knowledge. They contributed instead to the revival of interest in mathematics, and they fostered the "geometric spirit" that invaded the thinking and the arts of the seventeenth century. As examples we can cite Spinoza's *Ethics* "demonstrated in the manner of geometry," or the gardens of Versailles. The Cartesians stressed order in the ideal universe, and they liked order in society and in the State. To history they were at best indifferent and sometimes even hostile; the catalog of human errors in the past had little intrinsic value for them.

Quite different was the position of Galileo and the experimentalists. True enough, many of them — Galileo himself, for instance — believed in mathematics as a cardinal science, and in this they agreed with the Cartesian rationalists. Yet Galileo, a passionate man, let slip into *The Starry Messenger* [3, a] a phrase about "all the certainty of sense evidence." Many of his discoveries rested ultimately on sensory experience, even though in some of his writings he had much to say about the tricks that the senses play on us. We need not be surprised that to the more old-fashioned Aristotelians Galileo and his followers looked like dangerous anti-intellectuals, undermining the very foundations of science and reason. The more serious of Galileo's opponents, men who were not acting out of jealousy or pique, were neither ignoramuses nor obscurantists. Like Cardinal Bellarmine [3, d], many of them were ready to accept the Copernican theory as a mathematical hypothesis and no more, much in the same way that nineteenth-century physicists treated the concept of ether. The affair took an ugly turn when the administrative apparatus of the Roman Catholic Church stepped in on the side of the conservatives. The reason for this intervention is not far to seek: the Curia was understandably scared by political events and sought security in a general tightening of discipline. No "organization man" relishes a dispute over fundamental issues that might rock the boat; in times of crisis this can be dangerous. We should also note that the cause of the experimentalists in general was not helped by the fact that such notoriously disorderly characters as Gaston d'Orléans and Queen Christina of Sweden were known to pass their spare time staging experiments in chemistry.

The condemnation of Galileo had a stifling effect on experimental science in Italy. But the new science had already penetrated into France, the Dutch Republic, England, and parts of Germany, where the political climate was more favorable to the Galilean type of research. Many men of these countries who were interested in science made prolonged visits to Italy or maintained a steady correspondence with Italian scientists in the first half of the century. Thus we find a number of scientific societies springing up outside of Italy in the 1630's. In spite of their reservations about the experimental method, Cartesian rationalists took part in the work of these societies, the interest in mathematical measurement providing a link between men of different outlook and inclinations.

It was left to Newton to combine the Cartesian and the Galilean traditions into one harmonious whole [6]. Newton was not afraid to draw the ultimate conclusions from the belief that God had created an orderly, rational world, ruled by universally applicable laws. If this was so, then one could grasp these laws by observing their manifestations in individual instances, as well as by deducing them from first principles. This in no way implies that Newton distrusted or disparaged the deductive method of reasoning. He began his investigations with analysis, as the scholastics and Descartes had done before him; then he proceeded to experimental observation, using the inductive method; and finally, he capped his work off by using the deductive method to arrive at further results. To regard Newton as a simple experimentalist wedded to the inductive method is to do violence to him and to his system.

While the Cartesians, Galileans, and Newtonians were erecting their stately systems, there began to emerge a group of men who later became known as the skeptics. In this anthology they are represented by René Rapin [5]; but the greatest of them all was Pierre Bayle (1647–1706). The skeptics maintained that the true nature of God's creation was unknowable and that all systems conceived by the feeble mind of man were therefore false, or at least only partly true. They trained their guns on all systems of philosophy, and their favorite target was, of course, Descartes, the creator of the most comprehensive and formidable system of the century. Most seventeenth-century skeptics, including Rapin and Bayle, believed that their work of demolition would restore faith to its rightful position of pre-eminence. This opinion was not shared by many professional theologians, nor did the self-appointed disciples of the skeptics in the eighteenth century view their work in this light.

Among the seventeenth-century thinkers, Blaise Pascal (1623–1662) occupies a unique place. A brilliant mathematician, and also an experimentalist in physics, he did not doubt the validity of his rationalist assumptions or of his findings. Yet he was painfully aware of their limitations. Something entirely different was needed to probe the innermost recesses of the human heart, the nature of its intercourse with God, the mystery of the Creation, and the ways of divine grace and providence. Like Newton, Pascal was a solitary figure, with this difference: Newton's religion had an element of serene self-sufficiency in it, whereas Pascal, acutely aware of man's moral insufficiency and nothingness before God, suffered the sharpest pain. This was natural, for Newton's God revealed himself mainly in the elegance of orderly creation, whereas Pascal's God acted directly on human beings and yet remained inscrutable.

The seventeenth century also witnessed the establishment of scientific criticism of historical sources. The art of scholarly textual criticism had been practiced in Erasmian circles early in the sixteenth century. But by 1600 in most of Europe, it had almost become a casualty of the Reformation and Counter-Reformation; moreover, by mid-seventeenth century there were some skeptics who believed that nearly all documents, especially those of the earlier Middle Ages, were spurious. To the Cartesians and their successors — the classicists of the eighteenth century — historical inquiry, especially into the Middle Ages, was useless dabbling in barbarism. It was thus in a generally unfavorable climate of opinion that a group of the French Benedictines of the Congregation of St. Maur turned their attention to medieval studies, with a view to writing a critical history of their order and of its saints. In the process, they developed the science of palaeography and the art of scientific scrutiny of historical documents. Most prominent of the Maurists was Jean Mabillon (1632–1707). His treatise *De re diplomatica* (1681) established the canons of the science of diplomatics — the study of the form of documents — on such a firm foundation that they have not been altered to this day, in spite of the many new techniques that have been invented since. Without the labors of these Benedictine historians many medieval sources would have been lost through neglect. At the same time, a number of "antiquaries" were engaged in a parallel effort to find out all they could about the details of life in classical antiquity through an examination of artifacts as well as through literary sources. Their tradition, we must add, had not been interrupted since the early Renaissance. One of them, Ezechiel Spanheim (1619–1710), a German diplomat, did for modern numismatics what Mabillon had done for scientific criticism of written sources.

Among the other intellectual trends of the seventeenth century we should note the role of the Jesuits in keeping alive the belief in the "noble savage." The Jesuits, mainly on the authority of St. Paul's Epistle to the Romans, stressed the basic goodness of man's nature. They found a confirmation of their belief in the American Indian, who appeared to have the law of nature written in his heart and only needed some additional religious instruction to be saved. This mode of thinking found an echo among some of the early physiocrats and some ecclesiastics, like Archbishop Fénelon. It was one of the sources of the cult of the "noble savage" that burgeoned in the eighteenth century.

There were many other currents of thought, more or less in conflict with the ones we have described and with one another. To mention only a few: there were the Jansenists, the Molinists or "Quietists," the mystics like St. Francis de Sales, the Socinians, the Arminians, the Unitarians, the early Pietists, the atomic materialists, and those who simply refused to accept the canons of order that the classicists were trying to foist on them and who openly glorified disorderly passion and pleasure. This very incomplete listing suffices to show the variety of thought in the seventeenth century; it also brings home the fact that the Cartesian and Newtonian rationalists were in the minority. Nonetheless, such was the drive of this determined group, supported by many men in governmental circles, that they managed to impose their form of expression on almost everyone, so that in the end, even those who mocked them did so in impeccable classical form.

Mathematical reason pervaded the arts, whose main theme now became the control of passion in man and of the physical nature in the material universe. Félibien's discussion of Poussin [7] is a good example of the classicist doctrine in the visual arts. If pushed to extremes, its effect was likely to be rather stifling. Fortunately, however, Velázquez, Van Dyck, Rembrandt, and the other painters of the first rank, either lived before the full impact of classicism became felt or did not follow its precepts too closely. Music followed a development all its own, with Italy holding the center of the stage throughout the seventeenth century. But even in music, by the time of Corelli (1653–1713) there had been a noticeable increase of the "geometric spirit" as far as form was concerned. In literature, Shakespeare, the Spaniards, and the Italians, who held sway in the first half of the century, gave way to the French classicists. To gain insight into the mind of a classicist of genius, one might read Racine's introductory remarks to his *Bérénice, Phèdre,* and *Britannicus,* and then examine the application of his precepts in these plays.

Turning to political thought, which is but a branch of intellectual history, we can detect the same phenomenon as elsewhere: the salvaging of certain elements from the past and their reinterpretation in an original manner. The crucial development here is the revival of the concept of natural law, and the key figure in this movement is Hugo Grotius [8]. Natural law is a set of norms that define the ideal, perfect state of the world, the world as it ought to be. Its ultimate author is God, and it can be derived from a part of the divine law. As a result of original sin, the dictates of natural law are not self-enforcing in the actual world, but they can be discovered by the use of reason. In the early seventeenth century the most comprehensive treatment of natural law was given by the Spanish Jesuit Suárez (1548–1617) in his *Tractatus de legibus ac Deo legislatore* (1613) (*Treatise on laws and on God, the lawgiver*). Grotius who held Suárez in high esteem, adopted his main concepts and applied them to international relations.

In the course of the sixteenth century and the first decades of the seventeenth, there was a growing tendency to derive the norms of international relations not from the law of nature but from the "law of nations" (*jus gentium*). The *jus gentium* was partly based on Roman law, but it mainly comprised the residual rules and practices that mankind shared in common beyond the purely local customs and peculiarities. It could be found by an inspection of the actual existing practices and was thus subject to change with the times. For this reason it was an unsatisfactory foundation for a set of norms, the temptation being to find the norms of one's conduct in one's convenience. This tendency to base the nascent international law on the *jus gentium* no doubt contributed to the deterioration of political mores, especially during the wars of religion. What Grotius did was to pull international law out from the quagmire of the law of nations and put it on the firm foundation of the law of nature. To judge by the immediate and widespread success of his *De jure belli ac pacis,* Grotius answered a deeply felt contemporary need. The treatise was read not only by philosophers and lawyers, but by the educated public in general. Gustavus Adolphus of Sweden, the very model of a man of action, is said to have kept a copy of it under his pillow while he campaigned in Germany. So complete was Grotius's triumph, that for a long time to come the very term "law of nations" changed its meaning: when Pufendorf arrived on the scene, the *jus gentium* had practically become an adjunct of the *jus naturae.*

The revival of the natural law in relations between states put a flicker of life into the "Christian Commonwealth" (*Res publica Christiana*), which had been moribund for some time. According to the old concept, all the Christian states formed one body politic; ideally, its members were bound to live in peace among themselves, their reciprocal relations being determined by customary law and by treaties. The ambassadors were "public servants," that is, servants of the Christian Commonwealth rather than of their particular sovereigns and employers; they were bound to disobey their masters' orders if they went contrary to the maintenance of the peace of Christendom; it was as public servants of the Christian Commonwealth that they enjoyed certain immunities. Such at least had been the prevalent theory, if not the practice, in the later Middle Ages. The emergent principle of sovereignty obscured this ideal, and in the sixteenth century the Christian Commonwealth existed mainly as an imaginary entity in opposition to the Turk. But in the seventeenth century there was a revival as well as a gradual transformation of the idea of the Christian Commonwealth. The reader will find curious echoes of it in Callières [15]. We cannot treat it in an offhand

manner, as a mere utopian dream, when we see it coloring the outlook and specific actions of such a past master of diplomacy as
William III, who made a clear distinction between "public interest"
or "public good" (of Europe or Christendom) and the individual
interest of his own countries (the Dutch Republic and Great
Britain): he invariably put the former before the latter. Since this
distinction appears mainly in William's secret business correspondence
with his most trusted collaborators, we would not be justified in
dismissing it as mere hypocrisy or propaganda, as might be the case
with a twentieth-century politician appearing on a television screen.
We must add, however, that after William III's death his ideal was
lost sight of among the statesmen.

In the course of the seventeenth century the Christian Commonwealth became secularized, and imperceptibly the concept of "Europe," which had existed side by side with it, took its place. The
exact stages of this transformation are not clear. But Europe was
not just a geographical area; it was above all a system of states which,
while they professed the Christian religion, were held together by
other than purely religious ties; for want of a better term, we can
call these ties cultural; they were also, to a considerable extent,
dynastic. One of the assumptions was that all legitimate governments
in this system had a right to exist. It was permissible to harm other
states, but to destroy a legitimate state was an unspeakable crime.
Certain treaty obligations and conventions (for instance, those
concerning postal relations, travel of individuals, dynastic intercourse)
remained in force between two parties at war with each other. The
system of Europe could thus survive a war between its members; in
fact, it reinforced the limitations that most governments consciously
imposed on warfare. Of course, this could be done successfully only
as long as nationalism did not appear on the scene—that is, until the
French Revolution. In practice, the system of Europe was maintained
by several intricate mechanisms of balance that operated in various
parts of Europe. A description of some of them can be found in
Pufendorf's chapter on the Spanish monarchy [16]. Strangely enough,
however, the concept of a "balance of Europe" as a whole was not
explicitly formulated until the early eighteenth century, and then
it was influenced by the spread of Newtonian ideas — at least, most
of the metaphors used by statesmen to describe it seem to have been
borrowed from Newtonian mechanics.

In the thinking about the nature of human society and of the state, the revival of the natural law concept produced many different, and sometimes conflicting, theories. Most of them regarded natural law as antecedent to the institution of the state and to human society itself. They put natural law beyond the reach of any sovereignty, no matter whether it was monarchic, aristocratic, or democratic in form. In the sixteenth and early seventeenth century, the Jesuits and the Calvinists had done much to keep alive this medieval view of the paramount authority of the law and to defend it from encroachments by the sovereign power of the state. In the course of the seventeenth century, the whole concept was gradually becoming secularized, though its proponents never lost sight of its theological foundation: natural law was paramount because it expressed God's will about the world. The most striking example of such a use of natural law is to be found in John Locke's *Treatises of Government* [12].

Locke assumed that the law of nature (that is, God, its author) willed the preservation and increase of human life. His political theory followed logically from this premise. If man, in his imperfect state, were simply left to his own devices, passion would have soon distorted the working of the law of nature; therefore society, and within society government, had to be set up, for the sole purpose of upholding the law of nature. Sovereignty was thus narrowly circumscribed: it was legitimate only in so far as it carried out the law of nature; if it did not, it became tyranny and brigandage and had to be treated as such. Without denying the government's primary responsibility before God, Locke also made it in some measure responsible before its subjects — at least, before its more enlightened subjects, who had a stake in the realm and who were capable of judging when the law of nature was flagrantly set at naught. Here the Lockian theory restated in modern terms the thesis of the medieval barons. In this, as well as in his denial of the indelible nature of the anointment to kingship, Locke differed from the partisans of the divine right of kings.

The theory of the divine right of kings was rather complex: it could accommodate a variety of modes of thought and was capable of several interpretations. The clearest and the most comprehensive exposition of it we can find in Bossuet's *Politics* [11]. Governments, according to Bossuet, were set up by Divine Providence to carry out God's will for the good of the governed. This good was achieved mainly through the maintenance of law — the divine law in the first place, then the natural law, the fundamental laws of each society, and even most of its positive laws. If the government had been responsible before the governed, this would have detracted from its full responsibility before God. Furthermore, such a government would be liable to fall under the influence of private interests and pressure groups, which would seek to run the state for their private benefit and not for the public good; such practices were bound to subvert the laws and reduce all to anarchy. Thus only an absolute government, freed from dependence on pressure groups and human institutions, could properly carry out the function for which it was designed. This did not mean that such an absolute government was irresponsible, for it was answerable directly to God for every failure to live up to its true purpose. Though not restricted by any human institution, the exercise of sovereignty was severely limited by its very purpose, by law, and by fear of God's chastisement. To assert that this last consideration had little practical meaning would be naive, for the vast majority of men in the seventeenth century were neither atheists nor agnostics.

Though Bossuet argued that a hereditary monarch was best cast for the role of absolute sovereign, he did not deny the validity of other forms of government. In fact, most writers on divine right, despite all the attention they paid to kingship, were really concerned with what made all governments legitimate. Thus it is not surprising to find similar lines of reasoning advanced in monarchies and in republics. A careful reading of De la Court's *Interest of Holland* [10] will bring out points of agreement between him and Bossuet; they disagreed on the best form of government, not on its basic nature or purpose.

Among the seventeenth-century political thinkers, Hobbes [9] occupied a solitary place. He managed to outrage both the neo-medieval constitutionalists of the school of Grotius and Locke and the believers in divine right. The former were scandalized by his rejection of the law of nature in the commonly accepted sense, the latter by his denial of legitimacy based on fundamental laws and on Providence. He advocated absolutism for the wrong reasons. Of the notable seventeenth-century thinkers only Pufendorf and Spinoza accepted some elements of Hobbesian thought. Pufendorf put a strong emphasis on the drive for individual self-preservation in the formation of society. Spinoza equated power and right, but in his case this followed logically from his pantheism. Beyond this, however, both Pufendorf and Spinoza parted company with Hobbes; they believed that man was a social being by nature and deduced the rest of their respective political theories from this premise. It was not until the nineteenth century that Hobbes was fully appreciated or found real followers.

The argument is sometimes advanced that, whatever was said about Hobbes, rulers like Louis XIV followed the Hobbesian principles, just as Frederick the Great followed many of Machiavelli's precepts, regardless of the treatise he wrote against Machiavelli. This view is justified only to the extent that Louis XIV and his fellow monarchs and statesmen acted on the belief that public safety was the supreme law. For the rest, there is no evidence to support this view; occasional abuses of power, of which all governments are capable, have nothing to do with the Hobbesian principles. On the contrary, the bulk of the evidence points to the contrary conclusion that seventeenth-century rulers followed, consciously or unconsciously, either one of the natural-law contract schools of thought or some variety of the divine-right school. But, most often, they made an amalgam of beliefs drawn from both of these and from other sources and followed it in accordance with their personal inclinations. In this they were not unlike all men of action who are not professional philosophers.

This brief overview of some of the main features of the seventeenth century shows that, despite the almost universal yearning and quest for order, the period was a complex one. No simple formula can adequately express its variety and its contradictions. Nor shall we ever understand the seventeenth century if, misled by its supposed modernity, we transfer into it the frame of reference of our own age.

SOURCES IN WESTERN CIVILIZATION

The Seventeenth Century

1

A Picaresque Novel on the Thirty Years War

LITTLE is known about the life of the German novelist Johann Jacob Christof von Grimmelshausen (1622?–76), partly because he himself was secretive about the circumstances of his early life and liked to hide his identity under a dozen pseudonyms, such as German Schleifheim von Sulsfort, which appears on the title page of his most famous novel, Der abenteuerliche Simplicissimus (The Adventurous Simplicissimus), published in 1669. Grimmelshausen seems to have been of rather obscure bourgeois origin, although he was ennobled at some time. Brought up as a Lutheran, he probably joined the Church of Rome in later life; all that is certain is that he disliked confessional barriers between different faiths. From very early youth Grimmelshausen served as a musketeer — apparently with success — in various armies during the Thirty Years War. His travels took him to many parts of Germany, Bohemia, the Swiss Cantons, the Netherlands, and France. In mid-1660's, the Bishop of Strasbourg, Egon von Fürstenberg, appointed him mayor of the township of Renchen, a dependency of his see.

The Adventurous Simplicissimus may or may not be an autobiographical work. The hero, who had lost his parents as an infant, was brought up by a peasant family and later by a hermit in the forest. The selections given below begin at the point of his guardian's death.

Grimmelshausen, Simplicissimus

I, 13] SIMPLICIUS LETS HIMSELF DRIFT, LIKE A PIECE OF REED ON A POND

A FEW days after my dear and worthy hermit's demise, I made my way to the parson mentioned above, reported my master's death to him, and asked his advice on how to act in this situation. Although he tried very hard to dissuade me from staying longer in the woods, and pointed out the obvious danger of doing so, I followed in my predecessor's footsteps bravely, and all summer long did as a pious anchorite should. But as time changes everything, the grief I felt for my hermit gradually lessened, and the severe cold of winter outside extinguished the ardor of my intentions inside. The more I began to waver, the lazier I became about my prayers, and instead of contemplating divine and heavenly things, I was overcome by a desire to look at the world. And since I wasn't much good anymore in the forest, I resolved to see the parson again and to find out if he would still advise me to leave the woods. To this end, I walked toward the village, and when I got there I saw it in flames; a troop of cavalry had just plundered and set it on fire, killed some of the peasants, run off many and captured a few, among them the parson. Oh, my God! How full of trials and tribulations is a man's life?! One misfortune hardly stops before another overtakes us.

The cavalrymen were about to leave, and the parson was led by a rope like a poor sinner and slave. Some were screaming. "Shoot the bastard!" Others wanted money from him. He raised his hands and begged them, for the sake of their souls, to spare him and treat him with Christian mercy — in vain, for one of them rode roughshod over him and hit him such a wallop over the head that blood

From Johann Jakob Christoffel von Grimmelshausen, Simplicius Simplicissimus, trans. by George Schulz-Behrend (New York, 1965), 26–34, 92–97, 123–127, 159–161. Reprinted by permission of the Liberal Arts Press Division of Bobbs-Merrill Company, Inc. Book I, chapter 17 and the first part of chapter 18 are from The Adventurous Simplicissimus, trans. by A. T. S. Goodrick (Lincoln, Neb., 1962), pp. 36–39. Reprinted by permission of the University of Nebraska Press.

trickled down; he fell, commended his soul to God, and lay there like a dead dog. The captured peasants didn't fare much better.

When it looked as if these horsemen had lost their minds in their tyrannical cruelty, an armed gang of peasants like an angry swarm of yellow jackets came charging out of the woods. They raised such a ghastly war whoop, attacked so furiously, and fired so savagely that my hair stood on end, for I had never attended this kind of free-for-all. Nobody's likely to make monkeys of our peasants from the Spessart — nor of the ones from Hesse, Sauerland, Vogelsberg, or the Black Forest! The horsemen made tracks, not only leaving the stolen cattle behind, but also throwing away the loot as they ran, giving up their prey lest they fall prey to the peasants. A few who were captured were given rough treatment.

This introductory entertainment almost spoiled my desire to see the world; I thought if this is the way things are, the wilderness is far more attractive. Still, I wanted to hear the parson's explanations, but he was rather faint from his injuries and the beating he had received. He admonished me that he couldn't help or advise me because in his present condition he would soon have to make a living as a beggar, and even if I wanted to stay in the woods, he wouldn't be able to give me any help, because, as I could see, his church and parsonage were at that very moment going up in smoke.

With these words I trotted sadly back toward the woods and my home. . . .

14] A STRANGE STORY OF FIVE PEASANTS

So that I might follow my decisions at once and be a genuine hermit, I dressed in the late hermit's hair shirt and put on his chain — not because I needed to mortify my rebellious flesh, but to resemble my predecessor in appearance as well as in manner of living and also to protect myself better against the cold of winter.

The day after the village had been plundered and burned, I was just sitting in my hut, frying yellow turnips and praying at the same time, when some forty or fifty musketeers surrounded me. Although they hardly believed their eyes when they saw me, these boys turned my place upside down looking for something that absolutely wasn't there, for I had only a couple of books, and they threw them helter-skelter because they were no good to them. After a while, when they had taken a second look at me and seen by the feathers what kind of bird they had caught, they decided there was no hope of booty. Then they wondered about my hard way of living and took pity on my tender youth, particularly the officer in charge. He did me the honor of requesting me to show them the way out of the woods, in which they had been lost for some time. I did not refuse for a moment. To get rid of these unfriendly guests as soon as possible, I led them by the nearest road to the village where the parson had been manhandled. Truth to tell, that was the only road I knew.

But before we got out of the woods we saw about ten peasants, some armed with guns, the others busy burying something. The soldiers approached them and shouted, "Halt!" The peasants answered with their guns. And when they saw how many soldiers there were, they rushed off this way and that so that the musketeers (who were tired) couldn't catch any of them. Then the soldiers wanted to uncover what the peasants had covered up — an easy job because the spades and picks were still there. They had hardly started when a voice came up from below and said, "You bloody rascals! You dirty crooks! You damn bastards! Do you think heaven will let you go unpunished for your unchristian cruelty? There are plenty of stout fellows who will retaliate for your bestiality, so that nobody will come to lick your ass!" The soldiers looked at each other and didn't know what to do next. Some thought they were hearing a ghost, but I thought I was dreaming. Their officer told them to go on digging. Soon they struck a barrel, opened it, and found inside a man whose nose and ears had been cut off. But he was still alive. As soon as this fellow had recovered enough to recognize some of the group, he told how the peasants had captured six soldiers who had been reconnoitering for feed. Only an hour ago, they had shot five of these, standing them one behind the other; since the bullet, having had to go through five bodies before him, had not killed him, the sixth in the line, they had cut off his ears and nose. But first they had forced him (I beg the reader's pardon) to lick their asses. When he saw himself so degraded by these dishonorable and dastardly knaves, he called them the vilest names he could think of, hoping to trick them into killing him, though they had vouchsafed his life, but in vain. After he had embittered them, they stuck him in this barrel and buried him alive, saying that since he tried so hard for death, for reasons of spite they did not want to humor him.

While this man was telling of his misery, another group of soldiers, infantry, came up out of the woods. They had captured five of the fugitive peasants and shot the others. Among the captives were four peasants to whom the mistreated cavalryman had been forced to do as he was told. Now, when both groups of soldiers discovered they were from the same army, the horseman had to tell once more what had happened to him and his comrades in arms.

You should have seen what happened to the peasants there! Some of the soldiers in their first fury wanted to fill them full of lead, but others said that these gay birds ought to be tortured a little; they ought to get a taste of what they did to our buddy. In the meantime, their ribs were being tickled with musket stocks. Finally a soldier stepped forward and said, "Gentlemen, since it is a crying shame to all soldiers that five peasants abused this rascal (he pointed to the cavalryman), it is no more than fair for us to erase this blot and let these bastards kiss our friend a hundred times." Another said, "This rat is not worthy of the honor. If he hadn't been such a numbskull he would have died a thousand times rather than act in a manner unbecoming to a soldier."

Finally they resolved that each of the peasants was to reciprocate on ten soldiers. Then they wanted to decide what else to do to the peasants. But the peasants were so obstinate that they could in no way be coerced. One soldier took the fifth peasant aside and promised to let him go where he pleased, if he denied God and all his saints. The peasant answered that he had never given a damn for the saints and his personal acquaintance with God had been slight. He swore he did not know God and wanted no part of his kingdom. The soldier fired a bullet at his head, but it ricocheted as if it had hit a steel wall. Then he pulled out his sword bayonet and shouted, "Is that the kind you are? I promised to let you go where you wanted, but since you don't want to go to heaven, I am now sending you to hell!" And he split his head apart down to the teeth. "This is the way to get revenge," said the soldier. "Send these villains to hell and keep 'em there!" . . .

15] SIMPLICIUS IS RAIDED, AND HAS A WONDROUS DREAM ABOUT PEASANTS AND HOW IT GOES IN TIME OF WAR

When I got back home, I found that all of my firewood, my household goods, and all of the frugal food I had saved and harvested in the garden all summer for the coming winter were completely gone. "What now?" I thought. At that moment, need taught me to pray. I called on all my modest wit to decide what would be best for me. But since my experience was limited and indifferent, I could not reach a good decision. The best I could do was to commend myself to God and to put my trust in him; otherwise I would surely have despaired and perished. Moreover, the predicaments of the injured parson and the five miserably wounded peasants which I had witnessed that day were before me all the time, and I thought not so much about food and survival as about the hatred that existed between soldiers and peasants. But in my simplicity I could not help thinking that since Adam's creation there must surely be not one but two kinds of people on earth — who cruelly chase each other like unreasoning animals. I was cold and troubled, and with such thoughts I fell asleep, on an empty stomach.

Then, as in a dream, I saw how all the trees standing around the place where I lived were suddenly changing and taking on an utterly different appearance. On top of each tree sat a cavalier; and instead of bearing leaves the branches were decorated with all sorts of men. Some of these fellows had long pikes, others muskets, pistols, halberds, small flags, and drums and fifes. The sight was a pleasure to look at, for everything was neatly divided by rank. The root was made up of lowly people like day-laborers, craftsmen, peasants, and such, who nevertheless gave the tree its strength and imparted vigor anew when it had been lost. In fact, to their own great disadvantage and even peril they made up for the deficiency caused by the fallen leaves. They were complaining about those sitting in the tree; and they had good cause, for the whole load rested on them and pressed them so hard that all their money was being squeezed out of their pockets and even out of the strongboxes which they had secured with seven locks. But if money was not forthcoming, certain commissioners curried them with combs (a process called military execution), and because of this there issued sighs from their hearts, tears from their eyes, blood from their nails, and marrow from their bones. Yet among them there were some jokers called funny birds who were little troubled by it all. They took everything easy, and in their misery they came up with all sorts of raillery so that they needed no consolation.

16] OMISSIONS AND COMMISSIONS OF MODERN
SOLDIERS, AND HOW HARD IT IS FOR A
COMMON SOLDIER TO GET A COMMISSION

The roots of these trees had sheer wretchedness to contend
with, but the men on the lowest branches had to endure even greater
trouble, hardship, and discomfort. And though the branch-dwellers
were jollier, they were also more defiant, tyrannical, and for the
most part ungodly; and they constituted at all times an unsupport-
able burden for the roots. About them there appeared these lines:

> Hunger, thirst, and poverty,
> Heat and cold and tyranny,
> Whence, whatever, where the ache,
> Mercenaries give and take.

These words were all the less equivocal because they described
the men's work perfectly; for their entire activity consisted of hard
drinking, suffering hunger and thirst, whoring and pederasty, rat-
tling dice and gambling, overeating and overdrinking, killing and
being killed, harassing and being harassed, hunting down and being
hunted down, frightening and being frightened, causing misery and
suffering it, beating and being beaten — in a few words, spoiling
and harming, and being despoiled and harmed in turn. And neither
winter nor summer, rain nor wind, mountain nor valley, fields nor
swamps, ditches, passes, seas, walls, water, fire, nor ramparts, danger
to their own bodies, souls, consciences, nay, not even loss of life,
heaven, or any other things of whatsoever name kept them from it.
On the contrary, they continued eagerly in their works until after a
while they gave up the ghost, died and croaked in battles, sieges,
storms, campaigns, and even in their quarters (where soldiers enjoy
paradise on earth, especially when they run into fat peasants) —
except only a few oldsters who (unless they had stashed away stolen
or extorted goods) made the very best panhandlers and beggars.
Right above these troubled people sat some old chicken thieves who
had squatted and suffered a few years on the lowest branches and
who had been lucky enough to escape death till now. These looked
a little more serious and respectable than the lowest bunch, for
they had climbed up one level. But above them there were some
still a little higher, and they also aspired to grandeur. Being the

lowest in the chain of command, they were called jacket-dusters: they beat the pikemen and musketeers and with their abuse and cursing dusted their backs and heads. Above these, the tree had a kind of break or separation, a smooth section without branches which was greased with the soap of envy so that no one (unless he was of the nobility) could climb up, no matter how smart or skillful he was. This section was polished more smoothly than a marble column or a steel mirror. Above this place sat those with flags or ensigns, some young, some older. The young ones had been given a boost by their cousins. The old ones had climbed up under their own power, either by means of a silver ladder called bribery, or else by means of a rope which luck had let them catch because there were no better men present just then. A little further up sat still higher ones, and they also had their afflictions, cares, and troubles. They did, however, enjoy the advantage of being able to line their purses most conveniently with a liner they were cutting out of the roots; and for this they were using a knife known as forced contributions. The situation became most pleasant, to the point where a commissioner happened along and emptied a tubful of money above the tree to refresh it. Then those on top caught almost all of the rain as it dropped, while practically nothing trickled down below. For this reason more of the lower squatters died of hunger than were killed by the enemy. The upper echelons were troubled by neither danger.

There was constant wrangling and climbing in this tree, for every one wanted to sit in the highest, happiest place. And yet, there were some lazy, devil-may-care louts who hardly tried for a better position and who sleepily did what they had to do. The lowest men were hoping for the fall of the uppermost so that they might sit in their seats. The struggle was fiercest and least rewarding in the slippery section, for whoever had a good sergeant did not want to lose him through promotion. So they found impoverished noblemen, ex-pages, poor cousins, and other starvelings, and made ensigns out of them, and these were taking the bread out of the mouths of meritorious old soldiers.

17] HOW IT HAPPENS THAT, WHEREAS IN
WAR THE NOBLES ARE EVER PUT BEFORE
THE COMMON MEN, YET MANY DO ATTAIN
FROM DESPISED RANK TO HIGH HONOURS

All this vexed a sergeant so much that he began loudly to complain: whereupon one Nobilis answered him: "Knowst thou not that
at all times our rulers have appointed to the highest offices in time
of war those of noble birth as being fittest therefor. For greybeards
defeat no foe: were it so, one could send a flock of goats for that
employ: We say:

'Choose out a bull that's young and strong to lead and keep the
    herd,
For though the veteran be good, the young must be preferred.
So let the herdsman trust to him, full young though he appears:
'Tis but a saw, and 'tis no law, that wisdom comes with years.'

Tell me," says he, "thou old cripple, is't not true that nobly born
officers be better respected by the soldiery than they that beforetime
have been but servants? And what discipline in war can ye find
where no respect is? Must not a general trust a gentleman more than
a peasant lad that had run away from his father at the plough-tail
and so done his own parents no good service? For a proper gentleman, rather than bring reproach upon his family by treason or
desertion or the like, will sooner die with honor. And so 'tis right
the gentles should have the first place. So doth Joannes de Platea
plainly lay it down that in furnishing of offices the preference
should ever be given to the nobility, and these properly set before
the commons. Such usage is to be found in all codes of laws, and is,
moreover, confirmed in Holy Writ: for 'happy is the land whose
king is of noble family,' saith Sirach in his tenth chapter: which is
a noble testimony to the preference belonging to gentle birth. And
even if one of your kidney be a good soldier enough that can smell
powder and play his part well in every venture, yet is he not therefore capable of command of others: which quality is natural to
gentlemen, or at least customary to them from their youth up. And
so saith Seneca, 'A hero's soul hath this property, that 'tis ever
alert in search of honor: and no lofty spirit hath pleasure in small
and unworthy things.' Moreover, the nobles have more means to

furnish their inferior officers with money and to procure recruits for their weak companies than a peasant. And so to follow the common proverb, it were not well to put the boor above the gentleman; yea, and the boors would soon become too high-minded if they be made lords straightway; for men say:

'Where will ye find a sharper sword, than peasant churl that's made a lord?'

Now had the peasants, by reason of long and respectable custom, possessed all offices in war and elsewhere, of a surety they would have let no gentleman into such. Yea, and besides, though ye soldiers of Fortune, as ye call yourselves, be often willingly helped to raise yourselves to higher ranks, yet ye are commonly so worn out that when they try you and would find you a better place, they must hesitate to promote you; for the heat of your youth is cooled down and your only thought is how ye can tend and care for your sick bodies which, by reason of much hardships, be crippled and of little use for war: yea, and a young dog is better for hunting than an old lion."

Then answered the old sergeant: "And what fool would be a soldier, if he might not hope by his good conduct to be promoted, and so rewarded for faithful service? Devil take such a war as that! For so 'tis all the same whether a man behave himself well or ill! Often did I hear our old colonel say he wanted no soldier in his regiment that had not the firm intention to become a general by his good conduct. And all the world must acknowledge that 'tis those nations which promote common soldiers, that are good soldiers too, that win victories, as may be seen in the case of the Turks and Persians; so says the verse

'Thy lamp is bright: yet feed it well with oil: and thou dost not, the flame sinks down and dies.
So by rewards repay the soldiers' toil, for service brave demands its pay likewise.'"

Then answered Nobilis: "If we see brave qualities and in an honest man, we shall not overlook them: for at this very time see how many there be who from the plough, from the needle, from shoemaking, and from shepherding have done well by themselves, and by such bravery have raised themselves up far above the poorer nobility to the ranks of counts and barons. Who was the Imperialist John de Werth?

Who was the Swede Stalhans? Who were the Hessians, Little Jakob and St. André? Of their kind there were many yet well known whom I, for brevity's sake, forbear to mention. So is it nothing new in the present time, nor will it be otherwise in the future, that honest men attain by war to great honors, as happened also among the ancients. Tamburlaine became a mighty king and the terror of the whole world, which was before but a swineherd: Agathocles, King of Sicily, was son of a potter; Emperor Valentinian's father was a ropemaker; Maurice the Cappadocian, a slave, the emperor after Tiberius II; Justin, that reigned before Justinian, was before he was emperor a swineherd; Hugh Capet, a butcher's son, was afterward King of France; Pizarro, likewise a swineherd, which afterwards was marquess in the West Indies, where he had to weigh out his gold in hundredweights."

The sergeant answered: "All this sounds fair enough for my purpose: yet well I see that the doors by which we might win to many dignities be shut against us by the nobility. For as soon as he is crept out of his shell, forthwith your nobleman is clapped into such a position as we cannot venture to set our thoughts upon, howbeit we have done more than many a noble who is now appointed a colonel. And just as among the peasants many noble talents perish for want of means to keep a lad at his studies, so many a brave soldier grows old under the weight of a musket, that more properly deserved a regiment and could have tendered great services to his general."

18] HOW SIMPLICISSIMUS TOOK HIS FIRST
STEP INTO THE WORLD AND THAT WITH
EVIL LUCK

I cared no longer to listen to this old ass, but grudged him not his complaints, for often he himself had beaten poor soldiers like dogs. I turned again to the trees whereof the whole land was full and saw how they swayed and smote against each other: and the fellows tumbled off them in batches. Now a crack; now a fall. One moment quick, the next dead. In a moment one lost an arm, another a leg, the third his head. And as I looked, methought all trees I saw were but one tree, at whose top sat the war-god Mars, and which covered with its branches all Europe. It seemed to me this tree could have overshadowed the whole world: but because it was blown about by envy and hate, by suspicion and unfairness, by pride and haughtiness and avarice, and other such fair virtues, as by bitter north winds, therefore it seemed thin and transparent: for which reason one had writ on its trunk these rhymes:

"The holmoak by the wind beset and brought to ruin,
Breaks its own branches down and proves its own undoing.
By civil war within and brothers' deadly feud
All's topsy-turvy turned and misery hath ensued."

By the mighty roaring of these cruel winds and the noise of the breaking of the tree itself I was awoke from my sleep, and found myself alone in my hut.

* * *

II, 17] HOW SIMPLICIUS RODE TO DANCE WITH THE WITCHES

Occasionally on my travels through the woods I met some peasants, but they always ran away from me. I don't know if the war had made them fearful, had perhaps robbed them of their homes, or whether the raiders had broadcast their encounter with me, so that the peasants who saw me thought the fiend himself was walking in their part of the woods.

Once when I had been lost in the forest for several days and was afraid my rations would run out, I was glad to hear two wood-cutters. I followed the sound of their axes, and when I saw them I took a handful of ducats out of the purse, sneaked up close to them, showed them this attractive gold, and said, "Gentlemen, if you will take care of me I'll give you this handful of gold." But the minute they saw me and my gold they took to their heels, leaving behind them axes, wedges, and hammers, as well as their lunch of cheese and bread. This I picked up, put it in my knapsack, and got lost in the woods again, almost despairing of ever getting back among people.

After much thinking I reached this conclusion: Who knows what will become of you? But you have money, and if you put it in a safe place with reliable people, you can live on it for a long time. Thus it occurred to me that I should hide it. From the donkey's ears that made people run I made two armbands, combined all my ducats, sewed them inside the armbands, and fastened them on above my elbow. When I had thus secured my treasure I again entered a peasant's house and took from their supplies what I needed and could lay my hands on; and though I was still quite simple-minded I had enough sense never to return to a place where I had once stolen the least bit. For this reason I was very lucky in my thefts and never got caught.

Once, toward the end of May, I again wanted to get some food in my usual (though forbidden) manner. I had made my way to a farmstead and gotten into the inner sanctum of the kitchen. When I heard people were still up, I opened wide a door leading out to the yard, to provide a way out in case of necessity. (N.B. I never went where they kept dogs.) I was waiting quietly for everyone to go to bed when I noticed a slit in a little serving window to the next room. I sidled up to it, to see if the people were going to bed. But my hope came to nothing, for instead of undressing they had just gotten dressed, and instead of a candle they had a bluish flame burning on a bench. They were greasing sticks, brooms, forks, chairs, and benches, and, one after the other, were riding out the window on them. I was greatly surprised and rather horrified. But since I was used to greater horrors and had neither heard nor read of ghosts, I did not worry too much.

When everyone was gone and it was quiet, I went into the room to look for whatever I could take along. I sat down astride a bench and had hardly touched the wood when I rode — no, whizzed — on this bench straight out the window. My gun and knapsack stayed behind as carfare! Sitting down, taking off, and landing took place in one instant, it seemed, and all at once I was in a big crowd of people who were all doing a strange dance, the like of which I had never seen. Holding each other by the hand, they had formed many circles, one within another, their backs toward the center, as the three graces are sometimes pictured. The innermost ring consisted of seven or eight persons; the second had twice as many; the third more than the first two, and so on, so that there were over two hundred people in the outer ring. Since one circle danced clockwise and the next counterclockwise, I could not distinguish exactly how many circles there were, or what occupied the center around which they all revolved. The way the heads all reeled past one another looked awfully funny.

And the music was as weird as the dance. I think everyone was singing the tune while dancing, making an extraordinary harmony. The bench that took me there set me down by the musicians who were standing outside the circles. Instead of clarinets, flutes, and whistles, they were busily playing on vipers, asps, and chicken snakes. Some were holding cats and blowing in their bungholes; when they fingered the tails, the sound was like a bagpipe. Others ran a bow across a horse's head as if it were a fiddle, and still others played on a cow's skeleton (like you sometimes find in a pasture) as on a harp. An old gaffer was holding a bitch, cranking her tail, and fingering her tits! Then there were devils using their noses for trumpets, and the echo resounded through the woods. When this dance came to an end, the whole hellish mob started racing, shouting, reeling, roaring, howling, raging, and raving as if everyone had gone stark mad. It is easy to imagine how frightened I was.

While this noise was going on, a chap came toward me, carrying on his hip a giant toad, big as a drum. Its entrails hung out the rear and were stuffed in at the front again. It looked so repulsive that it just about turned my stomach. "Lookee, Simplex," he said, "I know you are a good lute-player. Let's hear something!" I practically keeled over when I heard him address me by my name. I could not answer and felt as if I were in a deep dream. In my heart I prayed to God Almighty that he help me out of my dream and let me wake up. The chap with the toad looked me straight in the eye and flicked his nose in and out like a turkey; then he struck me such a blow on the chest that I couldn't breathe. I started shouting to God, "Jesus Christ!"

This strong word was no sooner out of my mouth than the whole army disappeared. In no time at all it was pitch dark, and I felt so bad I crossed myself at least a hundred times.

18] WHY IT IS UNLIKELY THAT SIMPLICIUS IS TELLING TALL TALES

Since there are people — some of them learned and influential — who don't believe that witches and ghosts exist, let alone fly through the air, there are bound to be those who will say at this point that Simplicius is pulling the wool over their eyes. Well, I don't want to argue with these people. Nowadays four-flushing is a very common practice, and I don't deny that I know how, for otherwise I would be something of a stick-in-the-mud.

But people who doubt that witches ride through the air should remember that Simon Magus was raised on high by an evil spirit and did not fall down until St. Peter had prayed. . . .

I have reported all this only because I want to let you know how witches and wizards have at times actually traveled to their conventions, and not because I want you to believe that *I* traveled that way. It's all the same to me whether you believe it or not; but whoever prefers to be skeptical, let him figure out a better way to get me from Hersfeld or Fulda — I don't know myself exactly where in the woods I was hanging out — to Magdeburg in such a short time.

19] SIMPLICIUS BECOMES A FOOL, JUST AS HE HAD BEEN BEFORE

But to resume my story: I assure the reader that I lay still on my stomach till daylight, for I hadn't the heart to sit up. I was in doubt whether I had dreamed what I have been telling. Though I was rather frightened, I was bold enough to fall asleep, for I thought at worst I might find myself in a wild forest; but even that wouldn't have been too bad, for since leaving home I had spent most of my time there and was quite used to it. About nine o'clock in the morning some foragers came and woke me up. Only then did I notice that I was in the middle of an open field.

The soldiers took me to a windmill and, when their feed had been ground there, to the camp outside of Magdeburg. I was assigned to a colonel of the infantry, who asked me where I came from and to whom I belonged. I told everything, down to the smallest detail; since I didn't know the Croatians' name, I described their clothing, gave examples of their speech, and told how I had escaped from them. I carefully neglected mentioning my ducats. The tale of my trip through the air and the witches' dance was considered foolishness and tall talk, especially since the rest of my story was also a little mixed up.

Meanwhile a mob of people collected about me, for one fool makes a thousand more, and among them was one who had been a prisoner of war in Hanau last year; he had joined the forces there, but afterward had gone back to the imperial troops. He recognized me and said immediately, "Ho-ho, this is the commander's calf at Hanau!" The colonel asked for particulars, but the chap knew only that I was good at lute-playing, that the Croatians had taken me away, and that the governor had hated to lose me because I was a good fool and jester. Now the colonel's wife sent to another colonel's wife, who could play the lute quite well, and therefore always carried one with her. She asked for this instrument, and when it was brought I was told to show what I could do. But it was my opinion I should be given something to eat first, because my empty stomach was no match for the bulging belly of the lute. This was done, and after I had eaten my fill and had swallowed a good stein of brown beer, I sounded both my own and the lute's voice, talked thirteen to the dozen, and without any trouble got everyone to believe I was what my calf's clothing seemed to indicate.

The colonel asked me where I wanted to go now, and when I answered that it was all the same to me, we soon agreed that I should stay with him and become his page. He wanted to know what had become of my donkey's ears. "Well," I said, "if you found out where they are I should still be wearing them." I kept mum because all my riches were contained in them.

*   *   *

30] HOW THE HUNTER PROSPERED WHEN HE BEGAN SOLDIERING. ANY YOUNG SOLDIER CAN LEARN A LOT FROM THIS CHAPTER

Because the commander at Soest needed a stable boy and I seemed to be the kind he liked, he was reluctant to see me become a soldier. He said he'd get me yet, for I wasn't old enough to pass for a man. Then he argued with my captain about it, sent for me, and said, "Listen, Hunterboy, you ought to be my servant!" I asked what I was to do in this position. He answered, "Help wait on the horses." "Sir," I replied, "we are far apart in this matter. I'd rather have a master in whose service the horses wait on me; but since I can't have that kind of a job, I'll stay a soldier." He said, "Your beard is too soft yet." "Oh no," I said, "I feel strong enough to outdo a man of eighty. It's not the beard that kills another man; otherwise billy goats would sell at a higher price." He said, "If your courage is as good as your tongue, I'll let it pass." I answered, "This you can find out in the next battle"; and so I let him know I wished to be a stable boy no longer.

Next I performed an autopsy on the dragoon's old pants. With their contents I bought a good horse and the best pistols I could find. Everything had to be spick-and-span, and because I liked the name "Hunterboy" I also had a new green suit made. I gave the old one to my stable boy, for I had outgrown it. So my boy and I rode side by side, and no longer could anyone consider me poor stuff. I was bold enough to decorate my hat with an outrageous plume, like an officer's, and soon I had plenty of enemies who were jealous of me. We exchanged angry words and finally came to blows. But as soon as I had shown a few of them what I had learned from the furrier in Paradise, and that I could repay every thrust in kind, they not only left me in peace but even sought my friendship.

I frequently volunteered to go raiding, either on foot or on horseback, for I was well mounted and faster on foot than many others. When we got involved with the enemy, it was neck or nothing with me, and I always wanted to be one of the first.

This activity soon made me well known and so famous among friend and foe that both sides reckoned with me, especially since the most dangerous tasks were given to me and I was put in charge of whole groups of raiders. About that time I started helping myself to everything, and whenever I got hold of something special I gave my officers such a big share of it that they helped me out and looked the other way when I raided off limits. General Götz had left three enemy garrisons in Westphalia, one each at Dorsten, Lippstadt, and Coesfeld. I annoyed them no end, for I was at them with small groups of raiders almost every day, now here, now there; and I took valuable loot. Because I came out on top everywhere, the people grew to think I could make myself invisible and was bulletproof, like iron or steel. Therefore, I was feared like the plague, and thirty of the enemy's men were not ashamed to run like rabbits when they knew me to be nearby with only fifteen men. It got to the point that I was sent to exact "contributions" from towns or to see that they paid what they owed. This benefited my purse and my name; officers and fellow soldiers loved their Hunterboy; the most prominent enemy raiders shook in their boots, and the peasants were kept on my side by love or fear. I punished my enemies and richly rewarded those who had done me the least favor; I spent almost half my plunder on rewards and information.

For this reason no enemy raiders proceeded, no convoy or expedition by the enemy took place that I didn't know of. I then guessed their intentions and made my plans accordingly. And since, with a little luck, I had for the most part anticipated well, everyone was surprised at my youthful success, and many officers and experienced soldiers, even on the enemy side, wanted to see me. Furthermore, I treated my prisoners with great consideration so that they often cost me more than I gained through them; and whenever I was able to show some courtesy to an enemy, especially to officers, I always did so, if it could be done without violating my duty and loyalty.

With this sort of behavior I would soon have been commissioned as an officer if my youth hadn't prevented it. For if one wanted to command a squadron at my age one had to be of ancient nobility; moreover, my captain could not promote me because at the moment there were no positions vacant in his company. He did not want to lose me, for in me he would have lost more than a milch cow. But he did make me a sergeant.

The honor of being preferred over older soldiers — though it was a slight thing — and the praise I received daily encouraged me to even greater achievements. I lay awake at night thinking of what I could do to make myself even greater, more renowned, and more admirable. I worried over lack of opportunity to show my skill with weapons, and often wished for the Trojan War or the Siege of Ostend, but, fool that I was, I did not consider that every grey goose gets caught at last. But when a rash young soldier has luck and pluck and money, that's how it goes. Pride and arrogance are sure to arise in him. Because of my arrogance I kept two hostlers instead of a stable boy. By giving them expensive clothes and horses, I incurred the envy of all the officers who begrudged me what they lacked the energy to go out and get.

31] HOW THE DEVIL STOLE THE PARSON'S BACON, AND HOW THE HUNTER GOT CAUGHT IN HIS OWN TRAP

I want to tell a story or two about the time before I joined the dragoons. These events are not of world-shaking importance, but they are entertaining; for I didn't undertake only big things — I didn't scorn the little ones either, if I could just make a name for myself and arouse admiration among the people.

My captain was ordered to proceed with some fifty men to the fortress of Recklingshausen, there to execute an assignment. Because we thought we might have to hide in the woods for a few days, each of us took along a week's rations. But when the convoy we were awaiting did not come in time, we ran out of food, and we couldn't steal it without giving away our presence and ruining the plans. We were starving and it hurt. Unfortunately in this place I had no helpers (as I had in most others) who might secretly bring me and my men vittles and information. So, unless we wanted to return empty-handed, we had to think of something. My comrade, a student who had only lately flunked out and joined the army, was longing for the good oatmeal his parents used to provide and which he had scornfully left behind. And while he was thinking about breakfast he remembered his studies. "Oh, brother," he said, "isn't it a shame I didn't study how to feed myself. . . . Hah! If I went to the parson over in the village he'd give me something to eat." I thought about this awhile and then spoke with the captain about using the student. Our situation was so bad and his trust in me so great that after some hesitation he consented.

I traded clothes with another soldier and then my student and I taking the long way around, trotted toward the village, which was only half an hour away as the crow flies. We reccognized the minister's house because it was close to the church, and because it looked somewhat citified and was built against a wall that enclosed the whole parsonage. I had already instructed my comrade what to say. He was still wearing his threadbare school clothes; I pretended to be a painter's journeyman. (I did not think I'd be called on to paint, because few peasants have painted houses.) The parson was polite, and when my pal addressed him in well-turned Latin phrases and told him (like a seasoned liar) that soldiers had robbed him and taken all his food and money, he was given a sandwich and a pot of beer. I pretended we did not belong together and said I would have a bite to eat at the inn and then come back and holler for him, so that we could travel some distance before nightfall. So I went toward the inn, more to see what could be picked up at night than to satisfy my hunger. On the way I had the good luck to spot a peasant sealing his oven; it was full of pumpernickel and they are baked for twenty-four hours! I thought, "Go right ahead sealing! One way or another we'll get at this good stuff."

I didn't stay long at the inn, because now I knew where to get bread, but I bought a few rolls to take to my captain; and when I got back to the parsonage the "student" had already finished eating and had told his host I was a painter on my way to Holland, where I wanted to continue studying art. The minister welcomed me cordially and asked me to accompany him inside the church where he had some art objects he wanted repaired. To avoid spoiling the plans, I had to go along, and when he opened the locked door that led to the churchyard — oh, marvelous sight! — I saw the heavens full of black stars — I mean hams, sausages, and sides of bacon hanging in a chimney that we passed. I looked at these hopefully, thinking that they were smiling back at me. . . .

*　　*　　*

III, 11] CONTAINING ALL SORTS OF THINGS OF SLIGHT IMPORTANCE BUT OF GREAT IMAGINATION

*　　*　　*

I started to live a little more respectably than before, for I had great hopes of soon becoming a junior officer. Gradually I began to associate with the officers and young noblemen who were waiting for exactly the same thing I imagined I would be getting before long. For this reason they were my worst enemies — except that to my face they acted like my best friends. The lieutenant colonel didn't particularly like me either, because he was under orders to advance me ahead of his relatives. My captain disliked me because I kept better horses, clothes, and weapons than he, and moreover, I no longer came across with gifts for the old miser. He would have preferred that they chop off my head instead of promising me a troop, for he had hoped to inherit my fine horses. And my lieutenant hated me because of *one* word that had slipped out recently.

It happened like this. On our last expedition he and I had been ordered to keep watch together at a difficult post. It had to be done lying down, though it was pitch dark, and when my turn came, he came crawling up to me on his belly like a snake and said, "Sentry, do you notice anything?" I answered, "Yes, sir, lieutenant." "What is it? What is it?" he asked. I answered, "I notice the lieutenant is scared."

From that time on he didn't like me, and I was ordered to go where the situation was most risky. In fact, he was looking high and low for opportunities to "get me" before I became an ensign — that is, while I could not defend myself against him. All the sergeants were my enemies, too, because I was preferred. Even the common soldiers started to waver in their love and friendship for me, because it appeared that I despised them since I kept company with the big wheels — who didn't like me any better. Worst of all, not one solitary person told me how everyone felt about me. I didn't notice anything because to my face each man played up to me, though he would rather have seen me dead. So I kept on living blindly in false security, and as time passed I became more and more conceited. Even though I knew that some people were disgusted when I outdid the nobles and the officers of rank with my showing-off, I did not stop doing it.

After I had become a corporal, I was bold enough to wear a leather collar worth sixty thalers, scarlet-red trousers, and sleeves of white satin embroidered all over with gold thread — all of which were worn at the time by the highest officers. Of course, everyone took notice. But I was a frightfully stupid fool to manage things this way, for if I had used the money I squandered on clothes for bribes in the right places, I would have gotten my command and not made so many enemies. But that wasn't all: I dressed up my best horse (the one Jumpup had gotten from the Hessian captain) with saddle, bridle, and arms, so that when I sat on him I might well have been mistaken for St. George. I hated it that I wasn't a nobleman and couldn't dress my man and the stable boy in my personal uniform.

I reasoned that everything had to have a beginning; once I had a coat of arms I could have liveried servants, and when I became an officer I would have a seal even though I wasn't a nobleman. I had not entertained this thought very long when an imperial count palatine gave me a coat of arms. It had three red masks of a white field, on the crest the bust of a young jester in calfskin with a pair of rabbit ears, and bells in front. I thought this matched my name perfectly, for I was called "Simplicius." So I properly became the first of my lineage, family, and coat of arms, and if someone had tried to make fun of this, I would have been quick to unsheath my sword or to pull a pair of pistols on him.

Although I did not care much for women yet, I went along with the nobles whenever they called on ladies, of whom there were many in town. I wanted to be seen and show off my precious wardrobe, my well-groomed hair, and the plumes on my hat. I must confess that I was preferred to all others because of my good figure, but I also heard that the spoiled females compared me to a handsome, well-carved wooden statue that has little to recommend it besides its beauty. Except for playing the lute I could not produce anything to please the ladies, for as yet I knew nothing of love. But when the men who were popular with ladies twitted me for my wooden manners — mostly in order to show off their own eloquence — I said that, for the time being, it was enough for me to enjoy a bright sword and a good musket. The ladies approved of this speech, and this so enraged the ladies' men that they secretly swore to kill me, though there was no one who had the heart to challenge me or provoke me to challenge him — for which a slap in the face or some insulting words would have sufficed, and I had laid myself wide open for that. From this behavior the ladies inferred that I must be a resolute youth; they said publicly that my appearance and resoluteness spoke louder than all the lisping compliments Cupid had ever invented, and that enraged the gentlemen even more.

2

A Scientific Society

FEDERICO CESI (1585–1630), son of the Duke of Acquasparta, a member of the high nobility of Rome, showed an early taste for mathematics and natural sciences. In 1603, at the age of eighteen, he organized, together with a few friends, a small scientific society that received the name of the Accademia dei Lincei (Academy of the Lynxes); Galileo later became its sixth member. This was the first learned society in Italy devoted primarily to mathematical and natural sciences rather than to literature and the classics. Cesi provided a natural history collection, a botanical garden, and a library for his Academy, as well as the precincts of the Cesi palace in Rome, where the Linceans held their meetings. Cesi's father deplored the squandering of the family fortune on such a venture and was violently opposed to the Academy. After Cesi's death and the condemnation of Galileo by the Roman Inquisition, the Lincean Academy gradually dissolved, although it was later revived as the Italian Academy of Sciences. But in the seventeenth century it served as a prototype to such scientific societies as the Royal Society in England and the French Academy of Sciences.

Given below are excerpts from an address delivered by Cesi to the Linceans on January 26, 1616. The text in the manuscript from which this speech was published is probably corrupt. In preparing a translation of these excerpts, the translator and editor have simplified Cesi's turgid style and eliminated many repetitions.

CESI

An Address to the Lincean Academy, 1616

IF there has arisen in any man the natural desire for knowledge, fed by the nobility and dignity of its aim, enhanced by the joy it offers, and encouraged by its usefulness and the perfection which it confers on men of every rank and profession, it will be known to him that learning is peculiar to man among all living creatures, and that for this purpose he is endowed with reason, for which there is no other or higher use than understanding. We shall say that very few men attain perfect knowledge and complete fulfilment of this innate desire. But is our natural inclination to satisfy at least a part of it, to obtain some special knowledge, therefore to remain unfulfilled? Shall the faculty of reason given us by God be hindered by the very resolve to make use of it? What are we to blame for this? Is it men, for their idleness in so important a pursuit, or for slackness in its execution? Or is it the fault of the object itself, for its difficulty renders it all but inaccessible because of the lack of methods and everything necessary? Let us admit at the outset that such a prospect, such a worthy intention, inspires in us such a terror of hard work as is sufficient to destroy it completely in most people, and to decrease it in all of us. . . . The delight and utility of learning come to be regarded as if from afar, as though cut off from us by the hardships of the long labor involved. . . .

But we do not flee from the effort required with as rapid a step as we pursue its reward. Nor do we understand that true and abundant reward is obtained through knowledge of the sciences, for the eye strays at once to money and possessions, the sources of pleasure and ease, reputation and power; these appear real and concrete rewards, while any others seem illusory and insubstantial, and it is a common opinion based on experience that the sciences, particularly those which contribute most to learning, bring in but small profit. Moreover many men fear that they will spend more time and money in acquiring knowledge than they can hope to recoup later by applying it, which they consider an uncertain and

From Atti della Reale Accademia dei Lincei, Anno CCLXXVII (1879–1880), Serie Terza, Memorie della Classe di Scienze Morali, Storiche e Filologiche, V. (Rome, 1880), pp. 249–261; presented by G. Govi. Trans. by Goeffrey W. Symcox.

dubious reward, indefinitely deferred. They recognise that chance plays its part and none will voluntarily submit to this, in view of the time and effort required. Consequently little of the desired reward can be hoped for from law and medicine, and none at all from philosophy and mathematics, which are the true realm of the inborn desire to learn, and men devote themselves more readily to matters from which they can expect more certain results. . . .

By its very nature studying requires Masters who can lecture, and books which set forth the material at greater length, revealing to us the efforts and speculations of others, and conveying them to our understanding in different words and various ways. They help us to hear the teaching of those far away and long past and place us at any time within the conversation of the greatest men of letters. Nor is this all; if we are to achieve anything on our own account we must study that great, true and all-encompassing book of the world. For this we must visit its different parts, and exercise ourselves in observing it and experimenting, so as to base upon these two good methods a profound and perceptive understanding, by first observing things as they are and as they differ, and then noting how we ourselves can vary and change them: we must discover how many parts (of the world) must be seen for this, what difficulties there are of access to certain places and times, undiscouraged by the fate of Pliny. . . .

That purity and openness of mind which, free of all passion and partiality, can of itself cleave to the desired truth, today seems so alien to the greater part of lettered men and students, though it is all the more necessary. Appeal is made to this or that ancient writer; this or that faction is upheld. And so while things thought out by others are taught, and only the fruits of others' intellect are enjoyed, because of the sterility and laziness of our own thinkers we are reduced to the condition of windbags rather than of philosophers.

This passionate devotion to Authority, once expressly forbidden by Aristotle and now scrupulously observed by the Aristotelians, prevents the necessary study of not only the book of the Universe but of any book that does not come from the favored sect and the revered Masters. . . .

We must further observe that the very degree once established to mark the completion of studies, and thereby to encourage this completion, now seems to crown any who finish the course, without regard to performance; it has come to mark the termination of everyone's studious efforts, either because he thinks there is nothing further for him to learn or because he sees so little value placed upon learning that it is useless to exert himself any further, which makes him [feel] greater than those who are content to go on studying. In this way the Doctorate normally closes the way to learning, for those who have it are not only incapable of teaching others but also know nothing on their own account, unless by knowledge we mean those high-sounding terms which are so often intoned in the schools.

Another harmful thing which causes further backwardness and neglect of the fine opportunities that we have, particularly in this century, for studying well, is the very vastness of the field of knowledge, by reason of the abundance of speculations and writings. No one considers that he can achieve much without help, merely filling his mind with a mass of undigested material, or investigating any subject in order to be able to make use of this knowledge. There are indexes, very full collections, dictionaries for all studies, anthologies summarizing the best authors. There are collections of axioms and handbooks for various subjects; there are libraries which present books already reviewed and arranged by author and subject; there is the method, or rather the art of synopsis which presents selections of materials by category, as we have tried to set before the reader in our *Mirror of Reason*. With the aid of these a more vivid memory, a sharper intelligence, aroused to mastery of the subject before it, may confidently go forward in discovery and composition. But these opportunities are sought so half-heartedly, and so little attention is paid to studies, and still less to aids, that it is no wonder if only a small number of even the few who study attain any worthwhile degree of knowledge.

I believe that this is caused firstly by the purpose of studies, which for most men is not knowledge but personal gain, honors, favors and advancement. While these cannot be obtained by continuing to study, men seek to complete their learning by chopping it up and narrowing their studies, so that they manage to master a small section of them, and by so doing they abuse the purpose of scientific inquiry and reason. Consequently most men who have studied follow the profession for which they are most fitted: medicine in public and private practice, so as to collect a daily living from house to house; or law, to secure an office at the courts of princes and legal practice, which brings no less profit.

The sciences that most satisfy the inborn desire for knowledge are the most neglected and abandoned, that is to say philosophy, mathematics, poetics, and philological erudition, which are the studies giving us the deepest understanding and refinement; there are few who on hearing only a mention of them will not immediately reject them and say they are not lucrative. . . .

A few will remain who wish to continue with their studies in order to become teachers, with the purpose either of filling some public lectureship, with a salary, or of being maintained by some prince. But since they aim not for knowledge but gain, it is no surprise that they never attain to any learning or that in them the natural desire for knowledge remains unfulfilled.

If they hold public lectureships they can acquire great renown and influence by ever advancing new arguments; they wish to appear, rather than to be, learned, to have a reputation rather than true knowledge. Because this depends, in the minds of the ignorant, upon the size and plaudits of the audience, they advance themselves by pandering to their hearers and by bringing forth only well-known and high-sounding doctrines without caring if they are true but only that they sound plausible and authoritative and are approved by the reigning school of thought. Then they defer to their students with an affected air of benevolence, laying aside all professorial dignity, vying with them in games, jokes, and fatuous entertainments; so that from being their superior the teacher becomes inferior to them, receives them at home, accompanies them to lectures, and indulges in polite formalities more suited to the court than to the university, and far from favorable to the furtherance of knowledge as all may judge.

A position supported by a prince, with due obsequiousness, wins the favor of the ruler and all his court, and also a reputation for learning, so that there is a great danger of falling from the honored station of a philosopher to the base condition of parasite, buffoon, or at least flatterer, as Aristippus shows us. . . .

It is certainly undeniable that public universities or academies, colleges, and seminaries, have had this aim [of furthering knowledge], at least in part, as have also the private academies, but they have not done enough in carrying out the purpose of their founders, which was the progress of science. For the most part they have fallen into the usual abuses and have debased their purpose, as was said above. Since these assemblies of scholars do not help the perfection of learning, nor do they provide the unity and correspondence necessary for education, finishing with the Doctorate; since their audiences testify that in their studies they learn no more than the elementary terms and rules, methods of study, how to open their books: so they must excuse the noise of rude applause, the ringing of bells, and whistling that normally accompany lectures which seem too long to the flagging appetites of the students, as usually happens every day. But it seems that once they have learned these basic principles they go no further with their studies, but succeed very well in obtaining the rewards and salaries to which the degree of Master opens the way. . . .

But even if all these studies were to proceed fruitfully and in good order, what of the philosophers and mathematicians? What aids and associations are there for them, when they are almost totally neglected and have nowhere to turn? In the public schools there perhaps remains an obscure corner, isolated and sheltered, without any danger of being disturbed, so that the lecturers customarily bring in friends and servants who know nothing of the subject, in order to appear worthy of their position by actually doing something and not to run the risk of being deprived of it for being useless and superfluous. Since therefore there is no regular institution, no philosophic army to further a cause so worthy, so great and so proper to man as the acquisition of knowledge, especially through the methods of its principal disciplines, the Academy or rather Association of the Lincei has been founded for this aim and purpose. With a balanced grouping of subjects, transactions, and preparations for this task, it will proceed in a well-ordered manner to making good all the above-mentioned deficiencies, removing all obstacles and fulfilling that good desire for knowledge. For continual encouragement the Academy will have before it the example of the sharp-eyed lynx as a reminder to acquire that perspicacity of the inner eye so necessary for observation, for minute and diligent scrutiny within and without of all objects as far as possible in this great theater of nature.

This Academy will cultivate especially these two great fields of philosophy and mathematics, and will adorn itself with philological and poetic learning, thus embracing those studies that are most neglected, most needful of attention and best fitted to gratify the natural desire for learning and to give understanding of nature. It will practise those studies which others customarily overlook or only touch on in passing, while those studies whose purpose is by no means pure knowledge, as is claimed for them, have a considerable following.

Strongly united for this purpose it will advance with all its forces in good order, omitting no aid or effort which may be necessary or helpful to its purpose.

It will in the first place be free of all the cares to which the body is heir, all its needs for sustenance and health being provided for not by hard studies directed to this sole purpose, as is the case with doctors and lawyers who customarily obtain their reward immediately after their studies, which cannot and should not be expected here, but by the establishment of special conditions, which these noble professions have lacked hitherto. . . .

This freedom will also be from business affairs, servants and clients, and from any kind of disturbance or trouble which can occur in such situations; in its place will reign that quiet which elevates the mind, strengthens it and makes it master of its profession.

Nor is this support to be limited to a term of years, or ended at a predetermined time or with a degree, but will extend to a whole lifetime, since it must always provide the conditions for study, by comparison with which life itself appears short, and which none can think of ending save by his death. Studies will therefore be assiduous and ever-increasing, without interruption or flagging. Nor will they be confined to the writings of this or that authority, but will be an exercise in universal speculation, always including practice, and will receive any knowledge which may come to us either through our own discoveries or through communication with others.

But above all each member will proceed in philosophic inquiry on his own in all honesty, without any passion to deflect him from the discovery of the truth, or to incline him more to one authority or sect rather than another, but impartially weighing the true evidence and causes, without being swayed by consideration of the authority which presents them.

The teaching which they personally present will be extensive; there will be well-stocked libraries, every facility for experimentation and for ordered examination of the contributions to learning of societies and authors; quick and accurate printing; the counsel and direction of older men and colleges who, making common cause with us, will produce better learning without any of the risks mentioned before, and in a spirit of friendly cooperation will continually emend, refine, and enrich our thoughts and awake new ones. . . .

It is far less to be feared that the desire for honors and rank should deter such men from their purpose and turn them elsewhere, because minds so well-balanced and dedicated to excellence will never entertain such passions; even when there is some other motive, for instance the normal desire for glory that justly rewards good actions, it will make them more enthusiastic in the pursuit of their studies. The main purpose of this Academy is not only to press forward in all branches of study to the attainment of the fullest understanding of the sciences referred to previously, and to master them so as to have the desired knowledge of things. It is also, after observation and experiment, after careful speculation, to record them in its own compositions and writings, bearing in mind that this work is not merely a complement or corroboration of the teachings of the authorities but a propagation of knowledge, a communication and perpetuation for the public good of their noble endeavors and the knowledge acquired by them, and that this productivity is owed to posterity in repayment of the debt of learning handed down by previous generations. . . .

Everyone may imagine how much honor and esteem is to be won by the publication of these private speculations; how much will be made known to princes, other men of letters, and all civilized society; what prizes it will bring in, not only in praises and honors, but also in dignities and fitting employments.

Furthermore learned men were little honored in the past, since it was seen how little order and zeal they put into their studies, and so few of them reached any high rank of learning, while those few that did were scattered and hidden away, without correspondence among themselves, or direction, or even evidence of their learning beside that false reputation which normally spreads among the ignorant crowd, which always favors the man who can put up a good show; it can easily be believed that it was the result of these shortcomings. Once they are removed and a community of scholars is set up with good correspondence, a council of lettered men uniting to advise and assist one another in the place where this Academy has its rooms, they will be regarded and esteemed otherwise, for here the greatest and most learned men, already highly renowned for their achievements, will incite the others to emulate them, so that all will continually burn with zeal for their studies. . . .

Thus when all hindrances which reduce or extinguish the inborn desire for knowledge have been removed and the conditions and aids for the fulfilment of this desire have been provided, it will appear more vividly to us, its dignity, utility and beauty being no longer obscured. . . .

We have examples of no small value to encourage us; we have good evidence of the power of such institutions, if we look backwards in time to the Chaldeans, Egyptians, Greeks, and Romans, whose associations of philosophers acquitted themselves well in all the branches of inquiry to which they devoted themselves. We particularly admire Pythagoras and Plato for their well-ordered schools, full of good learning. And what results were achieved! The origin of philosophy and mathematics, their voluminous writings, their hundreds and thousands of compositions. . . . We see a fine and harmonious chorus of poets under Augustus, that noble group of authors under Trajan; closer to our own times we have St. Thomas, St. Bonaventura, and their companions who, though of different Orders, still communed together on philosophic questions in a spirit of friendship and unity. A little later there is the noble Academy of Florence, under Lorenzo the Magnificent . . . and another under Leo X, from which we may note how valuable is every particle of unity and cooperation, and how princes will cherish good learning among their subjects when they see how fruitful it can be. . . .

Great good will accrue from this Academy to the public and to princes, for it is certain that from knowledge and excellence arise good customs, dexterous actions, and a love of peace; the propagation of peace and steadfast virtue will result from the extension of knowledge. Thus the people will have more reason to apply themselves to some trade, being skilful, intelligent, and judicious, while the prince will have more subjects loving justice and friends of peace, so that the laws will be broken less frequently and life will be more tranquil, without uproars and rebellions, seditions and plots.

Those who would normally halt when confronted by the need to study will without doubt forge ahead; many who would not normally study at all will apply themselves to it, spurred on by the example and exhortation of others in whom the active desire to learn makes up for its discomforts. . . .

The public will benefit from more books and compositions that I shall term useful and learned, and doubly so because many that would normally perish through neglect or accident or malice will thus be secured, and many that would not have come to birth for these reasons will then see the light of day, so that the labors of years will be passed on to others, years of observation, experiment, and meditation on all manner of subjects.

The public will similarly profit from the great and wonderful inventions that will come from such acute minds, which in the course of their researches, experiments, and speculations discover the properties of objects, and observe causes and effects. In this way marvellous instruments are developed, rare medicines, fires, machines, defences, weapons, means for controlling the flow of water; so many secrets for improving the arts, and for the maintenance of life, for comfort and health and even subsistence, as may be seen to have been achieved previously by the natural scientists, and as we shall particularly demonstrate in our *Panurge*. And from such methods still more may be expected in the future. . . .

By these achievements, discoveries, and practical actions, those who consider speculative science to be vain stand refuted, as do those who condemned philosophy as an idle pastime of no consequence, for which reason it has been foolishly neglected. These benefits will cause the world to love it and embrace it all the more fervently, so that it will produce its fruits in increasing abundance and will not remain sterile through the ignorance, neglect, or stupidity of its cultivators. . . .

The Academy will give not only to the public but also to the worthiest scholars in these noble subjects [i.e. philosophy and mathematics], and other deserving men of letters [a retreat] when, worn out with age, or engaged on some great and difficult project, or for some special study and experiment they need some remote haven of quiet where they can either rest, or complete their work and return into the world, as they wish.

Thus the Academy of the Lincei will be a congregation, a seminary, a retreat for professors, writers, and experimenters in philosophy and particularly in mathematics, though not without the refinement conferred by philology. It will be soundly based upon the mutual love of its members and on their general love of learning, to which they are wholly dedicated in honesty of purpose and through the good use of reciprocal aid and cooperation. They will be provided with whatever is necessary for their subsistence and their studies, free of every other care, ambition or interest, overcoming through the ardor of their desire, with the spur of glory and with the aid of methods and facilities any obstacle in their path;

without any distraction or discord achieving the mastery of these noble and neglected sciences, with the special purpose of making them known through their own efforts for the benefit of the public. Thus for men of letters and their studies the Academy will produce new honor, respect, comforts, and favors; ease of access to the public and honest use of this; wide and fruitful distribution by word of mouth, writings and actions at all times and places, of their discoveries, which today are so little known and expected. So that men's minds being stimulated and studies being facilitated, the numbers of learned men will continually increase and human perfection will be attained through the fulfilment of the natural desire for knowledge.

3

Investigations of Galileo

GALILEO GALILEI (1564–1642) was born in Pisa, where his father, a Florentine merchant, had settled. From 1592 to 1610 Galileo was Professor of Mathematics in the University of Padua in the Venetian Republic. In 1610 he was appointed Chief Mathematician and Philosopher to Grand Duke Cosimo II of Tuscany (1609–1621), and in the following year he became a member of the Accademia dei Lincei [2]. The three works, excerpts from which appear below (The Starry Messenger, the Letters on Sunspots, and the Letter to the Grand Duchess Christina), were written between 1610 and 1615; they are indicative of Galileo's trend of thought which found its final expression in the Dialogue Concerning the Two Chief World Systems. Ptolemaic and Copernican, published in 1632. In 1633, the Vatican authorities reacted in a manner typical of organization men faced by a grave crisis — in this instance the Thirty Years War: the Roman Inquisition condemned Galileo's views, forbade him to publish any more works, and placed him under perpetual arrest. However, there is no foundation for the story that Galileo was physically mistreated, either during his trial or during his subsequent arrest when he was placed under the supervision of his friend, the Archbishop of Siena. During the last five years of his life Galileo was totally blind. His chief scientific work, the Dialogues Concerning Two New Sciences, was printed in Holland in 1638.

GALILEO

a.

The Starry Messenger

GREAT indeed are the things which in this brief treatise I propose for observation and consideration by all students of nature. I say great, because of the excellence of the subject itself, the entirely unexpected and novel character of these things, and finally because of the instrument by means of which they have been revealed to our senses.

Surely it is a great thing to increase the numerous host of fixed stars previously visible to the unaided vision, adding countless more which have never before been seen, exposing these plainly to the eye in numbers ten times exceeding the old and familiar stars.

It is a very beautiful thing, and most gratifying to the sight, to behold the body of the moon, distant from us almost sixty earthly radii, as if it were no farther away than two such measures — so that its diameter appears almost thirty times larger, its surface nearly one hundred times, and its volume twenty-seven thousand times as large as when viewed with the naked eye. In this way one may learn with all the certainty of sense evidence that the moon is not robed in a smooth and polished surface but is in fact rough and uneven, covered everywhere, just like the earth's surface, with huge prominences, deep valleys, and chasms.

Again, it seems to me a matter of no small importance to have ended the dispute about the Milky Way by making its nature manifest to the very senses as well as to the intellect. Similarly it will be a pleasant and elegant thing to demonstrate that the nature of those stars which astronomers have previously called "nebulous" is far different from what has been believed hitherto. But what surpasses all wonders by far, and what particularly moves us to seek the attention of all astronomers and philosophers, is the discovery of four wandering stars not known or observed by any man before us. Like Venus and Mercury, which have their own periods about the sun, these have theirs about a certain star that is conspicuous among

From Discoveries and Opinions of Galileo, trans. by Stillman Drake (New York, 1957), pp. 27–32, 45–46, 49–51, 56–58, 89–91, 116–119, 140–143, 162–164, 175–184, 193–199, 209–210. Reprinted by permission of Doubleday & Company, Inc.

those already known, which they sometimes precede and sometimes follow, without ever departing from it beyond certain limits. All these facts were discovered and observed by me not many days ago with the aid of a spyglass which I devised, after first being illuminated by divine grace. Perhaps other things, still more remarkable, will in time be discovered by me or by other observers with the aid of such an instrument, the form and construction of which I shall first briefly explain, as well as the occasion of its having been devised. Afterwards I shall relate the story of the observations I have made.

About ten months ago a report reached my ears that a certain Fleming had constructed a spyglass by means of which visible objects, though very distant from the eye of the observer, were distinctly seen as if nearby. Of this truly remarkable effect several experiences were related, to which some persons gave credence while others denied them. A few days later the report was confirmed to me in a letter from a noble Frenchman at Paris, Jacques Badovere, which caused me to apply myself wholeheartedly to inquire into the means by which I might arrive at the invention of a similar instrument. This I did shortly afterwards, my basis being the theory of refraction. First I prepared a tube of lead, at the ends of which I fitted two glass lenses, both plane on one side while on the other side one was spherically convex and the other concave. Then placing my eye near the concave lens I perceived objects satisfactorily large and near, for they appeared three times closer and nine times larger than when seen with the naked eye alone. Next I constructed another one, more accurate, which represented objects as enlarged more than sixty times. Finally, sparing neither labor nor expense, I succeeded in constructing for myself so excellent an instrument that objects seen by means of it appeared nearly one thousand times larger and over thirty times closer than when regarded with our natural vision.

It would be superfluous to enumerate the number and importance of the advantages of such an instrument at sea as well as on land. But forsaking terrestrial observations, I turned to celestial ones, and first I saw the moon from as near at hand as if it were scarcely two terrestrial radii away. After that I observed often with wondering delight both the planets and the fixed stars, and since I saw these latter to be very crowded, I began to seek (and eventually found) a method by which I might measure their distances apart.

Here it is appropriate to convey certain cautions to all who intend to undertake observations of this sort, for in the first place it is necessary to prepare quite a perfect telescope, which will show all objects bright, distinct, and free from any haziness, while magnifying them at least four hundred times and thus showing them twenty times closer. Unless the instrument is of this kind it will be vain to attempt to observe all the things which I have seen in the heavens, and which will presently be set forth. . . .

Now let us review the observations made during the past two months, once more inviting the attention of all who are eager for true philosophy to the first steps of such important contemplations. Let us speak first of the surface of the moon which faces us. For greater clarity I distinguish two parts of this surface, a lighter and a darker; the lighter part seems to surround and to pervade the whole hemisphere, while the darker part discolors the moon's surface like a kind of cloud, and makes it appear covered with spots. Now those spots which are fairly dark and rather large are plain to everyone and have been seen throughout the ages; these I shall call the "large" or "ancient" spots, distinguishing them from others that are smaller in size but so numerous as to occur all over the lunar surface, and especially the lighter part. The latter spots had never been seen by anyone before me. From observations of these spots repeated many times I have been led to the opinion and conviction that the surface of the moon is not smooth, uniform, and precisely spherical as a great number of philosophers believe it (and the other heavenly bodies) to be, but is uneven, rough, and full of cavities and prominences, being not unlike the face of the earth, relieved by chains of mountains and deep valleys. The things I have seen by which I was enabled to draw this conclusion are as follows.

On the fourth or fifth day after the new moon, when the moon is seen with brilliant horns, the boundary which divides the dark part from the light does not extend uniformly in an oval line as would happen on a perfectly spherical solid, but traces out an uneven, rough, and very wavy line as shown in the figure below. Indeed, many luminous excrescences extend beyond the boundary into the darker portion, while on the other hand some dark patches invade the illuminated part. Moreover a great quantity of small blackish spots, entirely separated from the dark region, are scattered almost all over the area illuminated by the sun with the exception only of that part which is occupied by the large and ancient spots. Let us note, however, that the said small spots always agree in having their blackened parts directed toward the sun, while on the side opposite the sun they are crowned with bright contours, like shining summits. There is a similar sight on earth about sunrise, when we behold the valleys not yet flooded with light though the mountains surrounding them are already ablaze with glowing splendor on the side opposite the sun. And just as the shadows in the hollows on earth diminish in size as the sun rises higher, so these spots on the moon lose their blackness as the illuminated region grows larger and larger....

Let these few remarks suffice us here concerning this matter, which will be more fully treated in our *System of the world.* In that book, by a multitude of arguments and experiences, the solar reflection from the earth will be shown to be quite real — against those who argue that the earth must be excluded from the dancing whirl of stars for the specific reason that it is devoid of motion and of light. We shall prove the earth to be a wandering body surpassing the moon in splendor, and not the sink of all dull refuse of the universe; this we shall support by an infinitude of arguments drawn from nature.

Thus far we have spoken of our observations concerning the body of the moon. Let us now set forth briefly what has thus far been observed regarding the fixed stars. And first of all, the following fact deserves consideration: The stars, whether fixed or wandering,[1] appear not to be enlarged by the telescope in the same proportion as that in which it magnifies other objects, and even the moon itself. In the stars this enlargement seems to be so much less that a telescope which is sufficiently powerful to magnify other objects a hundred fold is scarcely able to enlarge the stars four or five times....

Third, I have observed the nature and the material of the Milky Way. With the aid of the telescope this has been scrutinized so directly and with such ocular certainty that all the disputes which have vexed philosophers through so many ages have been resolved, and we are at last freed from wordy debates about it. The galaxy is, in fact, nothing but a congeries of innumerable stars grouped together in clusters. Upon whatever part of it the telescope is directed, a vast crowd of stars is immediately presented to view. Many of them are rather large and quite bright, while the number of smaller ones is quite beyond calculation.

But it is not only in the Milky Way that whitish clouds are seen;

several patches of similar aspect shine with faint light here and there throughout the aether, and if the telescope is turned upon any of these it confronts us with a tight mass of stars. And what is even more remarkable, the stars which have been called "nebulous" by every astronomer up to this time turn out to be groups of very small stars arranged in a wonderful manner. Although each star separately escapes our sight on account of its smallness or the immense distance from us, the mingling of their rays gives rise to that gleam which was formerly believed to be some denser part of the aether that was capable of reflecting rays from stars or from the sun. . . .

We have now briefly recounted the observations made thus far with regard to the moon, the fixed stars, and the Milky Way. There remains the matter which in my opinion deserves to be considered the most important of all — the disclosure of four PLANETS never seen from the creation of the world up to our own time, together with the occasion of my having discovered and studied them, their arrangements, and the observations made of their movements and alterations during the past two months. I invite all astronomers to apply themselves to examine them and determine their periodic times, something which has so far been quite impossible to complete, owing to the shortness of the time. Once more, however, warning is given that it will be necessary to have a very accurate telescope such as we have described at the beginning of the discourse.

On the seventh day of January in this present year 1610, at the first hour of night, when I was viewing the heavenly bodies with a telescope, Jupiter presented itself to me; and because I had prepared a very excellent instrument for myself, I perceived (as I had not before, on account of the weakness of my previous instrument) that beside the planet there were three starlets, small indeed, but very bright. Though I believed them to be among the host of fixed stars, they aroused my curiosity somewhat by appearing to lie in an exact straight line parallel to the ecliptic, and by their being more splendid than others of their size. . . .

Such are the observations concerning the four Medicean planets recently first discovered by me, and although from these data their periods have not yet been reconstructed in numerical form, it is legitimate at least to put in evidence some facts worthy of note. Above all, since they sometimes follow and sometimes precede

Jupiter by the same intervals, and they remain within very limited distances either to east or west of Jupiter, accompanying that planet in both its retrograde and direct movements in a constant manner, no one can doubt that they complete their revolutions about Jupiter and at the same time effect all together a twelve-year period about the center of the universe. That they also revolve in unequal circles is manifestly deduced from the fact that at the greatest elongation from Jupiter it is never possible to see two of these planets in conjunction, whereas in the vicinity of Jupiter they are found united two, three, and sometimes all four together. It is also observed that the revolutions are swifter in those planets which describe smaller circles about Jupiter, since the stars closest to Jupiter are usually seen to the east when on the previous day they appeared to the west, and vice versa, while the planet which traces the largest orbit appears upon accurate observation of its returns to have a semimonthly period.

Here we have a fine and elegant argument for quieting the doubts of those who, while accepting with tranquil mind the revolutions of the planets about the sun in the Copernican system, are mightily disturbed to have the moon alone revolve about the earth and accompany it in an annual rotation about the sun. Some have believed that this structure of the universe should be rejected as impossible. But now we have not just one planet rotating about another while both run through a great orbit around the sun; our own eyes show us four stars which wander around Jupiter as does the moon around the earth, while all together trace out a grand revolution about the sun in the space of twelve years.

And finally we should not omit the reason for which the Medicean stars appear sometimes to be twice as large as at other times, though their orbits about Jupiter are very restricted. We certainly cannot seek the cause in terrestrial vapors, as Jupiter and its neighboring fixed stars are not seen to change size in the least while this increase and diminution are taking place. It is quite unthinkable that the cause of variation should be their change of distance from the earth at perigee and apogee, since a small circular rotation could by no means produce this effect, and an oval motion (which in this case would have to be nearly straight) seems unthinkable and quite inconsistent with the appearances. But I shall gladly explain what occurs to me on this matter, offering it freely to the judgment and criticism of thoughtful men. It is known that the interposition of terrestrial vapors makes the sun and moon appear large, while the fixed stars and planets are made to appear smaller. Thus the two great luminaries are seen larger when close to the horizon, while the stars appear smaller and for the most part hardly visible. Hence the stars appear very feeble by day and in twilight, though the moon does not, as we have said. Now from what has been said above, and even more from what we shall say at greater length in our *System,* it follows that not only the earth but also the moon is surrounded by an envelope of vapors, and we may apply precisely the same judgment to the rest of the planets. Hence it does not appear entirely impossible to assume that around Jupiter also there exists an envelope denser than the rest of the aether, about which the Medicean planets revolve as does the moon about the elemental sphere. Through the interposition of this envelope they appear larger when they are in perigee by the removal, or at least the attenuation, of this envelope.

Time prevents my proceeding further, but the gentle reader may expect more soon.

b.

Letters to Mark Welser Concerning Sunspots and Their Phenomena

FIRST LETTER: MAY 4, 1612

MOST WORTHY SIR:
Tardy in replying to the courteous letter Your Excellency wrote me three months ago, I have been forced to silence by various circumstances. In particular a long indisposition — or I should say a series of long indispositions preventing all exercises and occupations on my part — has made it impossible for me to write. And so it does to a large extent yet, though not so completely that I cannot reply to at least some letters from my friends and patrons, of which I find not a few awaiting answers.

I have remained silent also until I might hope to give some satisfaction to your inquiry about the solar spots, concerning which you have sent me some brief essays by the mysterious "Apelles."[2] The difficulty of this matter, combined with my inability to make many continued observations, has kept (and still keeps) my judgment in suspense. And I, indeed, must be more cautious and circumspect than most other people in pronouncing upon anything new. As Your Excellency well knows, certain recent discoveries that depart from common and popular opinions have been noisily denied and impugned, obliging me to hide in silence every new idea of mine until I have more than proved it. Even the most trivial error is charged to me as a capital fault by the enemies of innovation, making it seem better to remain with the herd in error than to stand alone in reasoning correctly. I might add that I am quite content to be last and to come forth with a correct idea, rather than to get ahead of other people and later be compelled to retract what might be said sooner, indeed, but with less consideration.

These considerations have made me slow to respond to Your Excellency's request and still make me hesitate to do more than advance a rather negative case by appearing to know rather what sunspots are not than what they really are, it being much harder for me to discover the truth than to refute what is false. But in order to satisfy Your Excellency's wishes in part at least, I shall consider those things which seem to me worthy of notice in the three letters of this man Apelles, as you require, and in particular what he has to say with regard to determining the essence, the location, and the motion of these spots.

First of all, I have no doubt whatever that they are real objects and not mere appearances or illusions of the eye or of the lenses of the telescope, as Your Excellency's friend well establishes in his first letter. I have observed them for about eighteen months, having shown them to various friends of mine, and at this time last year I had many prelates and other gentlemen at Rome observe them there. It is also true that the spots do not remain stationary upon the body of the sun, but appear to move in relation to it with regular motions, as your author has noted in that same letter. Yet to me it appears that this motion is in the opposite direction from what Apelles says — that is, they move from west to east, slanting from south to north, and not from east to west and north to south. This may be clearly perceived in the observations he himself describes, which

compare in this regard with my own observations and with what
I have seen of those made by other people.

*　　*　　*

SECOND LETTER: AUGUST 14, 1612
*　　*　　*

I have . . . been much impressed by the courtesy of nature, which
thousands of years ago arranged a means by which we might come
to notice these spots, and through them to discover things of greater
consequence. For without any instruments, from any little hole
through which sunlight passes, there emerges an image of the sun
with its spots, and at a distance this becomes stamped upon any
surface opposite the hole. It is true that these spots are not nearly
as sharp as those seen through the telescope, but the majority of
them may nevertheless be seen. If in church some day Your Excellency sees the light of the sun falling upon the pavement at a distance from some broken windowpane, you may catch this light
upon a flat white sheet of paper, and there you will perceive the
spots. I might add that nature has been so kind that for our instruction she has sometimes marked the sun with a spot so large
and dark as to be seen merely by the naked eye, though the false
and inveterate idea that the heavenly bodies are devoid of all mutation or alteration has made people believe that such a spot was
the planet Mercury coming between us and the sun, to the disgrace
of past astronomers. Such a spot, no doubt, was that which is mentioned in the *Annals of French History* by Pithoeus, printed at Paris
in 1588, on page 62, where (in the *Life of Charlemagne*) one
reads that for eight days together the people of France saw a black
spot in the solar disk, whose ingress and exit from the sun's face could
not be observed because of clouds. This was believed to be Mercury,
then in conjunction with the sun; but this is too gross an error,
seeing that Mercury's movement is so fast that it cannot remain
conjoined with the sun for even seven hours when it passes between
us and the sun. Therefore this phenomenon was definitely one of
those very large and very dark spots, of which another may be encountered in the future; and perhaps by applying ourselves to diligent observation we may see one very soon. Had this discovery
been made several years ago, it would have saved Kepler the trouble

of interpreting the above passage by altering the text and emending the reported times. But I shall not bother about this at present, being certain that Kepler, as a true philosopher and not recalcitrant about manifest events, will no sooner hear of these observations and discourses of mine than he will lend his assent to them.

Now, in order that we may harvest some fruit from the unexpected marvels that have remained hidden until this age of ours, it will be well if in the future we once again lend ear to those wise philosophers whose opinions of the celestial substance differed from Aristotle's. He himself would not have departed so far from their view if his knowledge had included our present sensory evidence, since he not only admitted manifest experience among the ways of forming conclusions about physical problems, but even gave it first place. So when he argued the immutability of the heavens from the fact that no alteration had been seen in them during all the ages, it may be believed that had his eyes shown him what is now evident to us, he would have adopted the very opinion to which we are led by these remarkable discoveries. I should even think that in making the celestial material alterable, I contradict the doctrine of Aristotle much less than do those people who still want to keep the sky inalterable; for I am sure that he never took its inalterability to be as certain as the fact that all human reasoning must be placed second to direct experience. Hence they will philosophize better who give assent to propositions that depend upon manifest observations, than they who persist in opinions repugnant to the senses and supported only by probable reasons. And as if to remove all doubt from our minds, a host of observations come to teach us that comets are generated in the celestial regions. If their evidence is quickly come and gone, still greater things stubbornly remain for our instruction: behold how new flames of longer duration are sent in the form of bright novae, produced and then dissolved in the most remote parts of the sky — though of course even this is not enough to persuade people who cannot be reached by the force of geometric demonstrations. But finally, in that part of the sky which deserves to be considered the most pure and serene of all — I mean in the very face of the sun — these innumerable multitudes of dense, obscure, and foggy materials are discovered to be produced and dissolved continually in brief periods. Here is a parade of productions and destructions that does not end in a moment, but will endure through all future ages, allowing the human mind time to observe at pleasure and to learn those doctrines which will finally prove the true location of the spots.

Yet in this respect also we must recognize divine Providence, in that the means to such knowledge are very easy and may be speedily apprehended. Anyone is capable of procuring drawings made in distant places, and comparing them with those he has made himself on the same days. I have already received some made in Brussels by Sig. Daniello Antonini which fit to a hair those made by me, and others sent to me from Rome by Sig. Lodovico Cigoli, the famous painter and architect. This argument alone should be enough to persuade anybody that such spots are a long way beyond the moon.

And here I shall stop troubling Your Excellency further. Do me the favor of sending the drawings to Apelles at your convenience, accompanied by my highest regard to him. I kiss Your Excellency's hand reverently, and pray God for your happiness.

From Florence, August 14, 1612.

Your Illustrious Excellency's very devoted servitor,

GALILEO GALILEI L[INCEAN]

THIRD LETTER: DECEMBER 1, 1612

* * *

I believe that there are not a few Peripatetics on this side of the Alps who go about philosophizing without any desire to learn the truth and the causes of things, for they deny these new discoveries or jest about them, saying that they are illusions. It is about time for us to jest right back at these men and say that they likewise have become invisible and inaudible. They go about defending the inalterability of the sky, a view which perhaps Aristotle himself would abandon in our age. Their view of sunspots resembles that of Apelles, save that where he puts a single star for each spot, these fellows make the spots a congeries of many minute stars which gather together in greater or smaller numbers to form spots of irregular and varying shapes. Now though it is true in general that when many objects unite, each in itself being too small or too distant to be visible, they may form an aggregate which becomes perceptible to our sight. Still, one may not conclude as these men do from such a generalization; one must come down to the particular things observed in stars and in spots. A captain who has but a small number of soldiers to defend a fortress must not dash with his whole force to some point under attack, leaving all other positions open and undefended. When trying to defend the inalterability of the heavens, we must not forget the perils to which other positions just as essential to the Peripatetic philosophy may be exposed. To maintain the integrity and solidity of that philosophy, its other propositions must be supported by saying that some stars are fixed and others wandering; those are called "fixed" which are all in one single sphere and which move with its motion while remaining fixed with respect to each other, and "wandering" stars are those of which each has its own special motion. These propositions being true, the "solar stars" cannot be said to be fixed, for if they did not change with respect to one another it would be impossible to see the continual mutations that are observed in the spots, and the same patterns would always return. Hence anyone who wished to maintain that the spots were a congeries of minute stars would have to introduce into the sky innumerable movements, tumultuous, uneven, and without any regularity. But this does not harmonize with any plausible philosophy. And to what purpose would it be done? To keep the heavens free from even the tiniest alteration of material. Well, if alteration were annihilation, the Peripatetics would have some reason for concern; but since it is nothing but mutation, there is no reason for such bitter hostility to it. It seems to me unreasonable to call "corruption" in an egg that which produces a chicken. Besides, if "corruption" and "generation" are discovered in the moon, why deny them to the sky? If the earth's small mutations do not threaten its existence (if, indeed, they are ornaments rather than imperfections in it), why deprive the other planets of them? Why fear so much for the dissolution of the sky as a result of alterations no more inimical than these?

These men are forced into their strange fancies by attempting to measure the whole universe by means of their tiny scale. Our special hatred of death need not render fragility odious. Why should we want to become less mutable? We should thereby suffer the fate caused by the Medusa's head, being converted to marble and losing our senses and qualities which could not exist in us without corporeal alterations. But I shall not go on; I reserve to another time the examination of the Peripatetic arguments, merely remarking that it appears to me not entirely philosophical to cling to conclusions once they have been discovered to be manifestly false. These men are persuaded that if Aristotle were back on earth in our age, he would do the same — as if it were a sign of more perfect judgment and a more noble consequence of deep learning to defend what is false than to learn the truth! People like this, it seems to me, give us reason to suspect that they have not so much plumbed the profundity of the Peripatetic arguments as they have conserved the imperious authority of Aristotle. It would be enough for them, and would save them a great deal of trouble, if they were to avoid these really dangerous arguments; for it is easier to consult indexes and look up texts than to investigate conclusions and form new and conclusive proofs. Besides, it seems to me that we abase our own status too much and do this not without some offense to Nature (and I might add to divine Providence), when we attempt to learn from Aristotle that which he neither knew nor could find out, rather than consult our own senses and reason. For she, in order to aid our understanding of her great works, has given us two thousand more years of observations, and sight twenty times as acute as that which she gave Aristotle. . . .

c.

Letter to Christina of Lorraine, Grand Duchess of Tuscany, 1615

GALILEO GALILEI

TO

THE MOST SERENE

GRAND DUCHESS MOTHER:

SOME YEARS ago, as Your Serene Highness well knows, I discovered in the heavens many things that had not been seen before our own age. The novelty of these things, as well as some consequences which followed from them in contradiction to the physical notions commonly held among academic philosophers, stirred up against me no small number of professors — as if I had placed these things in the sky with my own hands in order to upset nature and overturn the sciences. They seemed to forget that the increase of known truths stimulates the investigation, establishment, and growth of the arts; not their diminution or destruction.

Showing a greater fondness for their own opinions than for truth, they sought to deny and disprove the new things which, if they had cared to look for themselves, their own senses would have demonstrated to them. To this end they hurled various charges and published numerous writings filled with vain arguments, and they made the grave mistake of sprinkling these with passages taken from places in the Bible which they had failed to understand properly, and which were ill suited to their purposes.

These men would perhaps not have fallen into such error had they but paid attention to a most useful doctrine of St. Augustine's, relative to our making positive statements about things which are obscure and hard to understand by means of reason alone. Speaking of a certain physical conclusion about the heavenly bodies, he wrote: "Now keeping always our respect for moderation in grave piety, we ought not to believe anything inadvisedly on a dubious point, lest in favor to our error we conceive a prejudice against something that truth hereafter may reveal to be not contrary in any way to the sacred books of either the Old or the New Testament."[3]

Well, the passage of time has revealed to everyone the truths that I previously set forth; and, together with the truth of the facts, there has come to light the great difference in attitude between those who simply and dispassionately refused to admit the discoveries to be true, and those who combined with their incredulity some reckless passion of their own. Men who were well grounded in astronomical and physical science were persuaded as soon as they received my first message. There were others who denied them or remained in doubt only because of their novel and unexpected character, and because they had not yet had the opportunity to see for themselves. These men have by degrees come to be satisfied. But some, besides allegiance to their original error, possess I know not what fanciful interest in remaining hostile not so much toward the things in question as toward their discoverer. No longer being able to deny them, these men now take refuge in obstinate silence, but being more than ever exasperated by that which has pacified and quieted other men, they divert their thoughts to other fancies and seek new ways to damage me.

I should pay no more attention to them than to those who previously contradicted me — at whom I always laugh, being assured of the eventual outcome — were it not that in their new calumnies and persecutions I perceive that they do not stop at proving themselves more learned than I am (a claim which I scarcely contest), but go as far as to cast against me imputations of crimes which must be, and are, more abhorrent to me than death itself. I cannot remain satisfied merely to know that the injustice of this is recognized by those who are acquainted with these men and with me, as perhaps it is not known to others.

Persisting in their original resolve to destroy me and everything mine by any means they can think of, these men are aware of my views in astronomy and philosophy. They know that as to the arrangement of the parts of the universe, I hold the sun to be situated motionless in the center of the revolution of the celestial orbs while the earth rotates on its axis and revolves about the sun. They know also that I support this position not only by refuting the arguments of Ptolemy and Aristotle, but by producing many counter-arguments; in particular, some which relate to physical effects whose causes can perhaps be assigned in no other way. In addition there are astronomical arguments derived from many things in my new celestial discoveries that plainly confute the Ptolemaic system while admirably agreeing with and confirming the contrary hypothesis. Possibly because they are disturbed by the known truth of other propositions of mine which differ from those commonly held, and therefore mistrusting their defense so long as they confine themselves to the field of philosophy, these men have resolved to fabricate a shield for their fallacies out of the mantle of pretended religion and the authority of the Bible. These they apply, with little judgment, to the refutation of arguments that they do not understand and have not even listened to.

First they have endeavored to spread the opinion that such propositions in general are contrary to the Bible and are consequently damnable and heretical. They know that it is human nature to take up causes whereby a man may oppress his neighbor, no matter how unjustly, rather than those from which a man may receive some just encouragement. Hence they have had no trouble in finding men who would preach the damnability and heresy of the new doctrine from their very pulpits with unwonted confidence, thus doing impious and inconsiderate injury not only to that doctrine and its followers but to all mathematics and mathematicians in general. Next, becoming bolder, and hoping (though vainly) that this seed which first took root in their hypocritical minds would send out branches and ascend to heaven, they began scattering rumors among the people that before long this doctrine would be condemned by the supreme authority. They know, too, that official condemnation would not only suppress the two propositions which I have mentioned, but would render damnable all other astronomical and physical statements and observations that have any necessary relation or connection with these.

In order to facilitate their designs, they seek so far as possible (at least among the common people) to make this opinion seem new and to belong to me alone. They pretend not to know that its author, or rather its restorer and confirmer, was Nicholas Copernicus; and that he was not only a Catholic, but a priest and a canon. He was in fact so esteemed by the church that when the Lateran Council under Leo X took up the correction of the church calender, Copernicus was called to Rome from the most remote parts of Germany to undertake its reform. At that time the calendar was defective because the true measures of the year and the lunar month were not exactly known. The Bishop of Culm, then superintendent of this matter, assigned Copernicus to seek more light and greater certainty concerning the celestial motions by means of constant study and labor. With Herculean toil he set his admirable mind to this task, and he made such great progress in this science and brought our knowledge of the heavenly motions to such precision that he became celebrated as an astronomer. Since that time not only has the calendar been regulated by his teachings, but tables of all the motions of the planets have been calculated as well.

Having reduced his system into six books, he published these at the instance of the Cardinal of Capua and the Bishop of Culm. And since he had assumed his laborious enterprise by order of the supreme pontiff, he dedicated this book *On the celestial revolutions* to Pope Paul III. When printed, the book was accepted by the holy Church, and it has been read and studied by everyone without the faintest hint of any objection ever being conceived against its doctrines. Yet now that manifest experiences and necessary proofs have shown them to be well grounded, persons exist who would strip the author of his reward without so much as looking at his book, and add the shame of having him pronounced a heretic. All this they would do merely to satisfy their personal displeasure conceived without any cause against another man, who has no interest in Copernicus beyond approving his teachings.

Now as to the false aspersions which they so unjustly seek to cast upon me, I have thought it necessary to justify myself in the eyes of all men, whose judgment in matters of religion and of reputation I must hold in great esteem. I shall therefore discourse of the particulars which these men produce to make this opinion detested and to have it condemned not merely as false but as heretical. To this end they make a shield of their hypocritical zeal for religion. They go about invoking the Bible, which they would have minister to their deceitful purposes. Contrary to the sense of the Bible and the intention of the holy Fathers, if I am not mistaken, they would extend such authorities until even in purely physical matters — where faith is not involved — they would have us altogether abandon reason and the evidence of our senses in favor of some biblical passage, though under the surface meaning of its words this passage may contain a different sense.

I hope to show that I proceed with much greater piety than they do, when I argue not against condemning this book, but against condemning it in the way they suggest — that is, without understanding it, weighing it, or so much as reading it. For Copernicus never discusses matters of religion or faith, nor does he use arguments that depend in any way upon the authority of sacred writings which he might have interpreted erroneously. He stands always upon physical conclusions pertaining to the celestial motions, and deals with them by astronomical and geometrical demonstrations founded primarily upon sense experiences and very exact observations. He did not ignore the Bible, but he knew very well that if his doctrine were proved, then it could not contradict the Scriptures when they were rightly understood. . . .

Such are the people who labor to persuade us that an author like Copernicus may be condemned without being read, and who produce various authorities from the Bible, from theologians, and from Church Councils to make us believe that this is not only lawful but commendable. Since I hold these to be of supreme authority, I consider it rank temerity for anyone to contradict them — when employed according to the usage of the holy Church. Yet I do not believe it is wrong to speak out when there is reason to suspect that other men wish, for some personal motive, to produce and employ such authorities for purposes quite different from the sacred intention of the holy Church.

Therefore I declare (and my sincerity will make itself manifest) not only that I mean to submit myself freely and renounce any errors into which I may fall in this discourse through ignorance of matters pertaining to religion, but that I do not desire in these matters to engage in disputes with anyone, even on points that are disputable. My goal is this alone; that if, among errors that may abound in these considerations of a subject remote from my profession, there is anything that may be serviceable to the holy Church in making a decision concerning the Copernican system, it may be taken and utilized as seems best to the superiors. And if not, let my book be torn and burnt, as I neither intend nor pretend to gain from it any fruit that is not pious and Catholic. And though many of the things I shall reprove have been heard by my own ears, I shall freely grant to those who have spoken them that they never said them, if that is what they wish, and I shall confess myself to have been mistaken. Hence let whatever I reply be addressed not to them, but to whoever may have held such opinions.

The reason produced for condemning the opinion that the earth moves and the sun stands still is that in many places in the Bible one may read that the sun moves and the earth stands still. Since the Bible cannot err, it follows as a necessary consequence that anyone takes an erroneous and heretical position who maintains that the sun is inherently motionless and the earth moveable.

With regard to this argument, I think in the first place that it is very pious to say and prudent to affirm that the holy Bible can never speak untruth — whenever its true meaning is understood. But I believe nobody will deny that it is often very abstruse, and may say things which are quite different from what its bare words signify. Hence in expounding the Bible if one were always to confine oneself to the unadorned grammatical meaning, one might fall into error. Not only contradictions and propositions far from true might thus be made to appear in the Bible, but even grave heresies and follies. Thus it would be necessary to assign to God feet, hands, and eyes, as well as corporeal and human affections, such as anger, repentance, hatred, and sometimes even the forgetting of things past and ignorance of those to come. These propositions uttered by the Holy Ghost were set down in that manner by the sacred scribes in order to accommodate them to the capacities of the common people, who are rude and unlearned. For the sake of those who deserve to be separated from the herd, it is necessary that wise expositors should produce the true senses of such passages, together with the special reasons for which they were set down in these words. This doctrine is so widespread and so definite with all theologians that it would be superfluous to adduce evidence for it.

Hence I think that I may reasonably conclude that whenever the Bible has occasion to speak of any physical conclusion (especially those which are abstruse and hard to understand), the rule has been observed of avoiding confusion in the minds of the common people which would render them contumacious toward the higher mysteries. Now the Bible, merely to condescend to popular capacity, has not hesitated to obscure some very important pronouncements, attributing to God himself some qualities extremely remote from (and even contrary to) His essence. Who, then, would positively declare that this principle has been set aside, and the Bible has confined itself rigorously to the bare and restricted sense of its words, when speaking but casually of the earth, of water, of the sun, or of any other created thing? Especially in view of the fact that these things in no way concern the primary purpose of the sacred writings, which is the service of God and the salvation of souls — matters infinitely beyond the comprehension of the common people.

This being granted, I think that in discussions of physical problems we ought to begin not from the authority of scriptural passages, but from sense-experiences and necessary demonstrations; for the holy Bible and the phenomena of nature proceed alike from the divine Word, the former as the dictate of the Holy Ghost and the latter as the observant executrix of God's commands. It is necessary for the Bible, in order to be accommodated to the understanding of every man, to speak many things which appear to differ from the absolute truth so far as the bare meaning of the words is concerned. But Nature, on the other hand, is inexorable and immutable; she never transgresses the laws imposed upon her, or cares a whit whether her abstruse reasons and methods of operation are understandable to men. For that reason it appears that nothing physical which sense-experience sets before our eyes, or which necessary demonstrations prove to us, ought to be called in question (much less condemned) upon the testimony of biblical passages which may have some different meaning beneath their words. For the Bible is not chained in every expression to conditions as strict as those which govern all physical effects; nor is God any less excellently revealed in Nature's actions than in the sacred statements of the Bible. Perhaps this is what Tertullian meant by these words:

"We conclude that God is known first through Nature, and then again, more particularly, by doctrine; by Nature in His works, and by doctrine in His revealed word."[4]

From this I do not mean to infer that we need not have an extraordinary esteem for the passages of holy Scripture. On the contrary, having arrived at any certainties in physics, we ought to utilize these as the most appropriate aids in the true exposition of the Bible and in the investigation of those meanings which are necessarily contained therein, for these must be concordant with demonstrated truths. I should judge that the authority of the Bible was designed to persuade men of those articles and propositions which, surpassing all human reasoning could not be made credible by science, or by any other means than through the very mouth of the Holy Spirit.

Yet even in those propositions which are not matters of faith, this authority ought to be preferred over that of all human writings which are supported only by bare assertions or probable arguments, and not set forth in a demonstrative way. This I hold to be necessary and proper to the same extent that divine wisdom surpases all human judgment and conjecture.

But I do not feel obliged to believe that that same God who has endowed us with senses, reason, and intellect has intended to forgo their use and by some other means to give us knowledge which we can attain by them. He would not require us to deny sense and reason in physical matters which are set before our eyes and minds by direct experience or necessary demonstrations. This must be especially true in those sciences of which but the faintest trace (and that consisting of conclusions) is to be found in the Bible. Of astronomy, for instance, so little is found that none of the planets except Venus are so much as mentioned, and this only once or twice under the name of "Lucifer." If the sacred scribes had had any intention of teaching people certain arrangements and motions of the heavenly bodies, or had they wished us to derive such knowledge from the Bible, then in my opinion they would not have spoken of these matters so sparingly in comparison with the infinite number of admirable conclusions which are demonstrated in that science.

Far from pretending to teach us the constitution and motions of the heavens and the stars, with their shapes, magnitudes, and distances, the authors of the Bible intentionally forbore to speak of these things, though all were quite well known to them. Such is the opinion of the holiest and most learned Fathers. . . .

* * *

Let us grant then that theology is conversant with the loftiest divine contemplation, and occupies the regal throne among sciences by dignity. But acquiring the highest authority in this way, if she does not descend to the lower and humbler speculations of the subordinate sciences and has no regard for them because they are not concerned with blessedness, then her professors should not arrogate to themselves the authority to decide on controversies in professions which they have neither studied nor practiced. Why, this would be as if an absolute despot, being neither a physican nor an architect but knowing himself free to command, should undertake to administer medicines and erect buildings according to his whim — at grave peril of his poor patients' lives, and the speedy collapse of his edifices.

Again, to command that the very professors of astronomy themselves see to the refutation of their own observations and proofs as mere fallacies and sophisms is to enjoin something that lies beyond any possibility of accomplishment. For this would amount to commanding that they must not see what they see and must not understand what they know, and that in searching they must find the opposite of what they actually encounter. Before this could be done they would have to be taught how to make one mental faculty command another, and the inferior powers the superior, so that the imagination and the will be forced to believe the opposite of what the intellect understands. I am referring at all times to merely physical propositions, and not to supernatural things which are matters of faith.

I entreat those wise and prudent Fathers to consider with great care the difference that exists between doctrines subject to proof and those subject to opinion. Considering the force exerted by logical deductions, they may ascertain that it is not in the power of the professors of demonstrative sciences to change their opinions at will and apply themselves first to one side and then to the other. There is a great difference between commanding a mathematician or a philosopher and influencing a lawyer or a merchant, for demonstrated conclusions about things in nature or in the heavens cannot be changed with the same facility as opinions about what is or is not lawful in a contract, bargain, or bill of exchange. This difference was well understood by the learned and holy Fathers . . .

I conceive that I may deduce this doctrine: That in the books of the sages of this world there are contained some physical truths which are soundly demonstrated, and others that are merely stated; as to the former, it is the office of wise divines to show that they do not contradict the holy Scriptures. And as to the propositions which are stated but not rigorously demonstrated, anything contrary to the Bible involved by them must be held undoubtedly false and should be proved so by every possible means. . . .

If in order to banish the opinion in question from the world it were sufficient to stop the mouth of a single man — as perhaps those men persuade themselves who, measuring the minds of others by their own, think it impossible that this doctrine should be able to continue to find adherents — then that would be very easily done. But things stand otherwise. To carry out such a decision it would be necessary not only to prohibit the book of Copernicus and the writings of other authors who follow the same opinion, but to ban the whole science of astronomy. Furthermore, it would be necessary to forbid men to look at the heavens, in order that they might not see Mars and Venus sometimes quite near the earth and sometimes very distant, the variation being so great that Venus is forty times and Mars sixty times as large at one time as another. And it would be necessary to prevent Venus being seen round at one time and forked at another, with very thin horns; as well as many other sensory observations which can never be reconciled with the Ptolemaic system in any way, but are very strong arguments for the Copernican. And to ban Copernicus now that his doctrine is daily reinforced by many new observations and by the learned applying themselves to the reading of his book, after this opinion has been allowed and tolerated for those many years during which it was less followed and less confirmed, would seem in my judgment to be a contravention of truth, and an attempt to hide and suppress her the more as she revealed herself the more clearly and plainly. Not to abolish and censure his whole book, but only to condemn as erroneous this particular proposition, would (if I am not mistaken) be a still greater detriment to the minds of men, since it would afford

them occasion to see a proposition proved that it was heresy to believe. And to prohibit the whole science would be but to censure a
hundred passages of holy Scripture which teach us that the glory
and greatness of Almighty God are marvelously discerned in all his
works and divinely read in the open book of heaven. For let no
one believe that reading the lofty concepts written in that book leads
to nothing further than the mere seeing of the splendor of the sun
and the stars and their rising and setting, which is as far as the eyes
of brutes and the vulgar can penetrate. Within its pages are couched
mysteries so profound and concepts so sublime that the vigils, labors,
and studies of hundreds upon hundreds of the most acute minds
have still not pierced them, even after continual investigations for
thousands of years. The eyes of an idiot perceive little by beholding
the external appearance of a human body, as compared with the
wonderful contrivances which a careful and practiced anatomist or
philosopher discovers in that same body when he seeks out the use
of all those muscles, tendons, nerves, and bones; or when examining
the functions of the heart and the other principal organs, he seeks
the seat of the vital faculties, notes and observes the admirable
structure of the sense organs, and (without ever ceasing in his
amazement and delight) contemplates the receptacles of the imagination, the memory, and the understanding. Likewise, that which
presents itself to mere sight is as nothing in comparison with the
high marvels that the ingenuity of learned men discover in the
heavens by long and accurate observation. And that concludes what
I have to say on this matter.

Next let us answer those who assert that those physical propositions of which the Bible speaks always in one way, and which the
Fathers all harmoniously accept in the same sense, must be taken
according to the literal sense of the words without glosses or interpretations, and held as most certain and true. The motion of the
sun and stability of the earth, they say, is of this sort; hence it is
a matter of faith to believe in them, and the contrary view is
erroneous.

To this I wish first to remark that among physical propositions
there are some with regard to which all human science and reason
cannot supply more than a plausible opinion and a probable conjecture in place of a sure and demonstrated knowledge; for example,
whether the stars are animate. Then there are other propositions of
which we have (or may confidently expect) positive assurances

through experiments, long observation, and rigorous demonstration; for example, whether or not the earth and the heavens move, and whether or not the heavens are spherical. As to the first sort of propositions, I have no doubt that where human reasoning cannot reach — and where consequently we can have no science but only opinion and faith — it is necessary in piety to comply absolutely with the strict sense of Scripture. But as to the other kind, I should think, as said before, that first we are to make certain of the fact, which will reveal to us the true senses of the Bible, and these will most certainly be found to agree with the proved fact (even though at first the words sounded otherwise), for two truths can never contradict each other. I take this to be an orthodox and indisputable doctrine, and I find it specifically in St. Augustine when he speaks of the shape of heaven and what we may believe concerning that. Astronomers seem to declare what is contrary to Scripture, for they hold the heavens to be spherical, while the Scripture calls it "stretched out like a curtain." St. Augustine opines that we are not to be concerned lest the Bible contradict astronomers; we are to believe its authority if what they say is false and is founded only on the conjectures of frail humanity. But if what they say is proved by unquestionable arguments, this holy Father does not say that the astronomers are to be ordered to dissolve their proofs and declare their own conclusions to be false. Rather, he says it must be demonstrated that what is meant in the Bible by "curtain" is not contrary to their proofs. . . .

He then proceeds to admonish us that we must be no less careful and observant in reconciling a passage of the Bible with any demonstrated physical proposition than with some other biblical passage which might appear contrary to the first. The circumspection of this saint indeed deserves admiration and imitation, when even in obscure conclusions (of which we surely can have no knowledge through human proofs) he shows great reserve in determining what is to be believed. . . .

The intention of the holy Fathers appears to be (if I am not mistaken) that in questions of nature which are not matters of faith it is first to be considered whether anything is demonstrated beyond doubt or known by sense-experience, or whether such knowledge or proof is possible; if it is, then, being the gift of God, it ought to be applied to find out the true senses of holy Scripture in those passages which superficially might seem to declare differently. These senses would unquestionably be discovered by wise theologians, together with the reasons for which the Holy Ghost sometimes wished to veil itself under words of different meaning, whether for our exercise, or for some purpose unknown to me. . . .

Your Highness may thus see how irregularly those persons proceed who in physical disputes arrange scriptural passages (and often those ill-understood by them) in the front rank of their arguments. If these men really believe themselves to have the true sense of a given passage, it necessarily follows that they believe they have in hand the absolute truth of the conclusion they intend to debate. Hence they must know that they enjoy a great advantage over their opponents, whose lot it is to defend the false position; and he who maintains the truth will have many sense-experiences and rigorous proofs on his side, whereas his antagonist cannot make use of anything but illusory appearances, quibbles, and fallacies. Now if these men know they have such advantages over the enemy even when they stay within proper bounds and produce no weapons other than those proper to philosophy, why do they, in the thick of battle, betake themselves to a dreadful weapon which cannot be turned aside, and seek to vanquish the opponent by merely exhibiting it? If I may speak frankly, I believe they have themselves been vanquished, and, feeling unable to stand up against the assaults of the adversary, they seek ways of holding him off. To that end they would forbid him the use of reason, divine gift of Providence, and would abuse the just authority of holy Scripture — which, in the general opinion of theologians, can never oppose manifest experiences and necessary demonstrations when rightly understood and applied. If I am correct, it will stand them in no stead to go running to the Bible to cover up their inability to understand (let alone resolve) their opponents' arguments, for the opinion which they fight has never been condemned by the holy Church. If they wish to proceed in sincerity, they should by silence confess themselves unable to deal with such matters. Let them freely admit that although they may argue that a position is false, it is not in their power to censure a position as erroneous — or in the power of anyone except the Supreme Pontiff, or the Church Councils. Reflecting upon this, and knowing that a proposition cannot be both true and heretical, let them employ themselves in the business which is proper to them; namely, demonstrating its falsity. And when that is revealed, either there will no longer be any necessity to prohibit it (since it will have no followers), or else it may safely be prohibited without the risk of any scandal.

*   *   *

d. Objections Against Galileo

SOME of the main objections against Galileo were best stated by the learned Cardinal Robert Bellarmine (1542–1621). The following is a letter that Bellarmine wrote on April 12, 1615, to Father Antonio Foscarini, a Carmelite priest, who had published a book shortly before in the defense of the Copernican-Galilean system.

I HAVE gladly read the letter in Italian and the essay in Latin that Your Reverence has sent me, and I thank you for both, confessing that they are filled with ingenuity and learning. But since you ask my opinion, I shall give it to you briefly, as you have little time for reading and I for writing.

"First. I say that it appears to me that Your Reverence and Sig. Galileo did prudently to content yourselves with speaking hypothetically and not positively, as I have always believed Copernicus did. For to say that assuming the earth moves and the sun stands still saves all the appearances better than eccentrics and epicycles is to speak well. This has no danger in it, and it suffices for mathematicians. But to wish to affirm that the sun is really fixed in the center of the heavens and merely turns upon itself without traveling from east to west, and that the earth is situated in the third sphere and revolves very swiftly around the sun, is a very dangerous thing, not only by irritating all the theologians and scholastic philosophers, but also by injuring our holy faith and making the sacred Scripture false. For Your Reverence has indeed demonstrated many ways of expounding the Bible, but you have not applied them specifically, and doubtless you would have had a great deal of difficulty if you had tried to explain all the passages that you yourself have cited.

"Second. I say that, as you know, the Council [of Trent] would prohibit expounding the Bible contrary to the common agreement of the holy Fathers. And if Your Reverence would read not only all

their works but the commentaries of modern writers on Genesis,
Psalms, Ecclesiastes, and Joshua, you would find that all agree in
expounding literally that the sun is in the heavens and travels swiftly
around the earth, while the earth is far from the heavens and remains motionless in the center of the world. Now consider whether,
in all prudence, the Church could support the giving to Scripture of
a sense contrary to the holy Fathers and all the Greek and Latin
expositors. Nor may it be replied that this is not a matter of faith,
since if it is not so with regard to the subject matter, it is with regard to those who have spoken. Thus that man would be just as
much a heretic who denied that Abraham had two sons and Jacob
twelve, as one who denied the virgin birth of Christ, for both are
declared by the Holy Ghost through the mouths of the prophets
and apostles.

"Third. I say that if there were a true demonstration that the sun
was in the center of the universe and the earth in the third sphere,
and that the sun did not go around the earth but the earth went
around the sun, then it would be necessary to use careful consideration in explaining the Scriptures that seemed contrary, and we
should rather have to say that we do not understand them than to
say that something is false which had been proven. But I do not
think there is any such demonstration, since none has been shown
to me. To demonstrate that the appearances are saved by assuming
the sun at the center and the earth in the heavens is not the same
thing as to demonstrate that in fact the sun is in the center and the
earth in the heavens. I believe that the first demonstration may exist,
but I have very grave doubts about the second; and in case of doubt
one may not abandon the Holy Scriptures as expounded by the holy
Fathers. I add that the words *The sun also riseth, and the sun goeth
down, and hasteneth to the place where he ariseth*[5] were written by
Solomon, who not only spoke by divine inspiration, but was a man
wise above all others, and learned in the human sciences and in the
knowledge of all created things, which wisdom he had from God;
so it is not very likely that he would affirm something that was
contrary to demonstrated truth, or truth that might be demonstrated.
And if you tell me that Solomon spoke according to the appearances,
and that it seems to us that the sun goes round when the
earth turns, as it seems to one aboard ship that the beach moves
away, I shall answer thus. Anyone who departs from the beach,
though to him it appears that the beach moves away, yet knows

that this is an error and corrects it, seeing clearly that the ship moves and not the beach; but as to the sun and earth, no sage has needed to correct the error, since he clearly experiences that the earth stands still and that his eye is not deceived when it judges the sun to move, just as he is likewise not deceived when it judges that the moon and the stars move. And that is enough for the present.

NOTES

1. That is, planets. Among these bodies Galileo counted his newly discovered satellites of Jupiter. The term "satellites" was introduced somewhat later by Kepler.

2. Pseudonym of Father Christopher Scheiner, a Jesuit and a professor at the University of Ingolstadt.

3. *De Genesi ad literam,* end of bk. ii.

4. *Adversus Marcionem,* ii, 18.

5. Ecclesiastes 1:5.

4

Cartesianism

RENÉ DESCARTES (1595–1650), a minor French nobleman, was sent at the age of eight to the Jesuit school at La Flèche, where he received a classic education and a grounding in the scholastic method and mathematics. After studying law at the University of Poitiers in 1612–1616, he decided to see the world and went to the Netherlands to join the army of Maurice of Nassau, who was especially interested in the application of mathematics to military science. During the early stages of the Thirty Years War, Descartes served in the army of Maximilian of Bavaria; it was here that he experienced, on November 10, 1619, his moment of truth described in the Discourse on Method. In 1622 Descartes returned to France, where he sold his estate in Poitou in order to be free to devote himself to intellectual work; he then went traveling in the Swiss Cantons and in Italy until 1625. After 1629 he lived mainly in Holland, a virtual recluse. It was only in 1637 that he first appeared in print, when his Discourse on the Method and Essays was published anonymously at Leyden. The Treatise on the Passions of the Soul was written in 1645–1646; before its publication in 1649, it was read in manuscript and commented on by Descartes' friends, among whom were Princess Elizabeth of the Palatinate and Queen Christina of Sweden. In October 1649 Descartes arrived at the court of Queen Christina in Stockholm, where he had to give daily lessons of philosophy to his royal pupil at five o'clock in the morning; within four months his health failed and he died.

In the excerpts below Descartes means by "the Schools" institutions of scholastic learning. The term "passion" is used in its etymological meaning: "an affection by an external agency."

Descartes, Discourse on the Method of Rightly Conducting the Reason and Seeking for Truth in the Sciences

PART I

GOOD SENSE is of all things in the world the most equally distributed, for everybody thinks himself so abundantly provided with it, that even those most difficult to please in all other matters do not commonly desire more of it than they already possess. It is unlikely that this is an error on their part; it seems rather to be evidence in support of the view that the power of forming a good judgment and of distinguishing the true from the false, which is properly speaking what is called Good sense or Reason, is by nature equal in all men. Hence too it will show that the diversity of our opinions does not proceed from some men being more rational than others, but solely from the fact that our thoughts pass through diverse channels and the same objects are not considered by all. For to be possessed of good mental powers is not sufficient; the principal matter is to apply them well. The greatest minds are capable of the greatest vices as well as of the greatest virtues, and those who proceed very slowly may, provided they always follow the straight road, really advance much faster than those who, though they run, forsake it.

For myself I have never ventured to presume that my mind was in any way more perfect than that of the ordinary man; I have even longed to possess thought as quick, or an imagination as accurate and distinct, or a memory as comprehensive or ready, as some others. And besides these I do not know any other qualities that make for the perfection of the human mind. For as to reason or sense, inasmuch as it is the only thing that constitutes us men and distinguishes us from the brutes, I would fain believe that it is to be found com-

From The Philosophical Works of Descartes, trans. by Elizabeth S. Haldane and G. R. T. Ross, 2nd ed., 2 vols. (Cambridge, 1931) I, pp. 81–94, 100–106, 118–122, 331–333, 335–336, 340–341, 344, 349–350, 355, 366, 398–399, 425–427. Reprinted by permission of the Cambridge University Press.

plcte in cach individual, and in this I follow the common opinion of
the philosophers, who say that the question of more or less occurs
only in the sphere of the *accidents* and does not affect the *forms* or
natures of the *individuals* in the same *species*.

But I shall not hesitate to say that I have had great good fortune
from my youth up, in lighting upon and pursuing certain paths
which have conducted me to considerations and maxims from which
I have formed a Method, by whose assistance it appears to me I
have the means of gradually increasing my knowledge and of little
by little raising it to the highest possible point which the mediocrity
of my talents and the brief duration of my life can permit me to
reach. For I have already reaped from it fruits of such a nature that,
even though I always try in the judgments I make on myself to lean
to the side of self-depreciation rather than to that of arrogance, and
though, looking with the eye of a philosopher on the diverse actions
and enterprises of all mankind, I find scarcely any which do not
seem to me vain and useless, I do not cease to receive satisfaction in
the progress which I seem to have already made in the search after
truth, and to form such hopes for the future as to venture to believe that, if amongst the occupations of men, simply as men, there
is some one in particular that is excellent and important, that is the
one which I have selected.

It must always be recollected, however, that possibly I deceive
myself, and that what I take to be gold and diamonds is perhaps no
more than copper and glass. I know how subject we are to delusion
in whatever touches ourselves, and also how much the judgments of
our friends ought to be suspected when they are in our favor. But in
this Discourse I shall be very happy to show the paths I have followed, and to set forth my life as in a picture, so that everyone
may judge of it for himself; and thus in learning from the common
talk what are the opinions which are held of it, a new means of
obtaining self-instruction will be reached, which I shall add to those
which I have been in the habit of using.

Thus my design is not here to teach the Method which everyone
should follow in order to promote the good conduct of his Reason,
but only to show in what manner I have endeavored to conduct
my own. Those who set about giving precepts must esteem themselves more skilful than those to whom they advance them, and if
they fall short in the smallest matter they must of course take the
blame for it. But regarding this Treatise simply as a history, or, if

you prefer it, a fable in which, amongst certain things which may be imitated, there are possibly others also which it would not be right to follow, I hope that it will be of use to some without being hurtful to any, and that all will thank me for my frankness.

I have been nourished on letters since my childhood, and since I was given to believe that by their means a clear and certain knowledge could be obtained of all that is useful in life, I had an extreme desire to acquire instruction. But so soon as I had achieved the entire course of study at the close of which one is usually received into the ranks of the learned, I entirely changed my opinion. For I found myself embarrassed with so many doubts and errors that it seemed to me that the effort to instruct myself had no effect other than the increasing discovery of my own ignorance. And yet I was studying at one of the most celebrated Schools in Europe, where I thought that there must be men of learning if they were to be found anywhere in the world. I learned there all that others learned; and not being satisfied with the sciences that we were taught, I even read through all the books which fell into my hands, treating of what is considered most curious and rare. Along with this I knew the judgments that others had formed of me, and I did not feel that I was esteemed inferior to my fellow-students, although there were amongst them some destined to fill the places of our masters. And finally our century seemed to me as flourishing, and as fertile in great minds, as any which had preceded. And this made me take the liberty of judging all others by myself and of coming to the conclusion that there was no learning in the world such as I was formerly led to believe it to be.

I did not omit, however, always to hold in esteem those exercises which are the occupation of the Schools. I knew that the Languages which one learns there are essential for the understanding of all ancient literature; that fables with their charm stimulate the mind and histories of memorable deeds exalt it; and that, when read with discretion, these books assist in forming a sound judgment. I was aware that the reading of all good books is indeed like a conversation with the noblest men of past centuries who were the authors of them, nay a carefully studied conversation, in which they reveal to us none but the best of their thoughts. I deemed Eloquence to have a power and beauty beyond compare; that Poesy has most ravishing delicacy and sweetness; that in Mathematics there are the subtlest discoveries and inventions which may accomplish much, both in satisfying the curious, and in furthering all the arts, and in diminishing man's labor; that those writings that deal with Morals contain much that is instructive, and many exhortations to virtue which are most useful; that Theology points out the way to Heaven; that Philosophy teaches us to speak with an appearance of truth on all things, and causes us to be admired by the less learned; that Jurisprudence, Medicine and all other sciences bring honor and riches to those who cultivate them; and finally that it is good to have examined all things, even those most full of superstition and falsehood, in order that we may know their just value, and avoid being deceived by them.

But I considered that I had already given sufficient time to language and likewise even to the reading of the literature of the ancients, both their histories and their fables. For to converse with those of other centuries is almost the same thing as to travel. It is good to know something of the customs of different peoples in order to judge more sanely of our own, and not to think that everything of a fashion not ours is absurd and contrary to reason, as do those who have seen nothing. But when one employs too much time in travelling, one becomes a stranger in one's own country, and when one is too curious about things which were practised in past centuries, one is usually very ignorant about those which are practised in our own time. Besides, fables make one imagine many events possible which in reality are not so, and even the most accurate of histories, if they do not exactly misrepresent or exaggerate the value of things in order to render them more worthy of being read, at least omit in them all the circumstances which are basest and least notable; and from this fact it follows that what is retained is not portrayed as it really is, and that those who regulate their conduct by examples which they derive from such a source, are liable to fall into the extravagances of the knights-errant of Romance, and form projects beyond their power of performance.

I esteemed Eloquence most highly and I was enamoured of Poesy, but I thought that both were gifts of the mind rather than fruits of study. Those who have the strongest power of reasoning, and who most skilfully arrange their thoughts in order to render them clear and intelligible, have the best power of persuasion even if they can but speak the language of Lower Brittany and have never learned Rhetoric. And those who have the most delightful original ideas and who know how to express them with the maximum of style and suavity, would not fail to be the best poets even if the art of Poetry were unknown to them.

Most of all was I delighted with Mathematics because of the certainty of its demonstrations and the evidence of its reasoning; but I did not yet understand its true use, and, believing that it was of service only in the mechanical arts, I was astonished that, seeing how firm and solid was its basis, no loftier edifice had been reared thereupon. On the other hand I compared the works of the ancient pagans which deal with Morals to palaces most superb and magnificent, which are yet built on sand and mud alone. They praise the virtues most highly and show them to be more worthy of being prized than anything else in the world, but they do not sufficiently teach us to become acquainted with them, and often that which is called by a fine name is nothing but insensibility, or pride, or despair, or parricide.

I honored our Theology and aspired as much as anyone to reach to heaven, but having learned to regard it as a most highly assured fact that the road is not less open to the most ignorant than to the most learned, and that the revealed truths which conduct thither are quite above our intelligence, I should not have dared to submit them to the feebleness of my reasonings; and I thought that, in order to undertake to examine them and succeed in so doing, it was necessary to have some extraordinary assistance from above and to be more than a mere man.

I shall not say anything about Philosophy, but that, seeing that it has been cultivated for many centuries by the best minds that have ever lived, and that nevertheless no single thing is to be found in it which is not subject of dispute, and in consequence which is not dubious, I had not enough presumption to hope to fare better there than other men had done. And also, considering how many conflicting opinions there may be regarding the self-same matter, all supported by learned people, while there can never be more than one which is true, I esteemed as well-nigh false all that only went as far as being probable.

Then as to the other sciences, inasmuch as they derive their principles from Philosophy, I judged that one could have built nothing solid on foundations so far from firm. And neither the honor nor the promised gain was sufficient to persuade me to cultivate them, for, thanks be to God, I did not find myself in a condition which obliged me to make a merchandise of science for the improvement of my fortune; and, although I did not pretend to scorn all glory like the Cynics, I yet had very small esteem for what I could not hope to acquire, excepting through fictitious titles. And, finally, as to false doctrines, I thought that I already knew well enough what they were worth to be subject to deception neither by the promises of an alchemist, the predictions of an astrologer, the impostures of a magician, the artifices or the empty boasting of any of those who make a profession of knowing that of which they are ignorant.

This is why, as soon as age permitted me to emerge from the control of my tutors, I entirely quitted the study of letters. And resolving to seek no other science than that which could be found in myself, or at least in the great book of the world, I employed the rest of my youth in travel, in seeing courts and armies, in intercourse with men of diverse temperaments and conditions, in collecting varied experiences, in proving myself in the various predicaments in which I was placed by fortune, and under all circumstances bringing my mind to bear on the things which came before it, so that I might derive some profit from my experience. For it seemed to me that I might meet with much more truth in the reasonings that each man makes on the matters that specially concern him, and the issue of which would very soon punish him if he made a wrong judgment, than in the case of those made by a man of letters in his study touching speculations which lead to no result, and which bring about no other consequences to himself excepting that he will be all the more vain the more they are removed from common sense, since in this case it proves him to have employed so much the more ingenuity and skill in trying to make them seem probable. And I always had an excessive desire to learn to distinguish the true from the false, in order to see clearly in my actions and to walk with confidence in this life.

It is true that while I only considered the manners of other men I found in them nothing to give me settled convictions; and I remarked in them almost as much diversity as I had formerly seen in the opinions of philosophers. So much was this the case that the greatest profit which I derived from their study was that, in seeing many things which, although they seem to us very extravagant and ridiculous, were yet commonly received and approved by other great nations, I learned to believe nothing too certainly of which I had only been convinced by example and custom. Thus little by little I was delivered from many errors which might have obscured our natural vision and rendered us less capable of listening to Reason. But after I had employed several years in thus studying the book of the world and trying to acquire some experience, I one day formed the resolution of also making myself an object of study and of employing all the strength of my mind in choosing the road I should follow. This succeeded much better, it appeared to me, than if I had never departed either from my country or my books.

PART II

I was then in Germany, to which country I had been attracted by the wars which are not yet at an end. And as I was returning from the coronation of the Emperor to join the army, the setting in of winter detained me in a quarter where, since I found no society to divert me, while fortunately I had also no cares or passions to trouble me, I remained the whole day shut up alone in a stove-heated room, where I had complete leisure to occupy myself with my own thoughts. One of the first of the considerations that occurred to me was that there is very often less perfection in works composed of several portions, and carried out by the hands of various masters, than in those on which one individual alone has worked. Thus we see that buildings planned and carried out by one architect alone are usually more beautiful and better proportioned than those which many have tried to put in order and improve, making use of old walls which were built with other ends in view. In the same way also, those ancient cities which, originally mere villages, have become in the process of time great towns, are usually badly constructed in comparison with those which are regularly laid out on a plain by a surveyor who is free to follow his own ideas. Even though, considering their buildings each one apart, there is often as much or more display of skill in the one case than in the other, the former have large buildings and small buildings indiscriminately placed together, thus rendering the streets crooked and irregular, so that it might be said that it was chance rather than the will of men guided by reason that led to such an arrangement. And if we consider that this happens despite the fact that from all time there have been certain officials who have had the special duty of looking after the buildings of private individuals in order that they may be public ornaments, we shall understand how difficult it is to bring about much that is satisfactory in operating only upon the works of others. Thus I imagined that those people who were once half-savage, and who have become civilized only by slow degrees, merely forming their laws as the disagreeable necessities of their crimes and quarrels constrained them, could not succeed in establishing so good a system of government as those who, from the time they first came together as communities, carried into effect the constitution laid down by some prudent legislator. Thus it is quite certain that the constitution of the true Religion whose ordinances are of God alone is incomparably better regulated than any other. And, to come down to human affairs, I believe that if Sparta was very flourishing in former times, this was not because of the excellence of each and every one of its laws, seeing that many were very strange and even contrary to good morals, but because, being drawn up by one individual, they all tended towards the same end. And similarly I thought that the sciences found in books — in those at least whose reasonings are only probable and which have no demonstrations, composed as they are of the gradually accumulated opinions of many different individuals — do not approach so near to the truth as the simple reasoning which a man of common sense can quite naturally carry out respecting the things which come immediately before him. Again I thought that since we have all been children before being men, and since it has for long fallen to us to be governed by our appetites and by our teachers (who often enough contradicted one another, and none of whom perhaps counselled us always for the best), it is almost impossible that our judgments should be so excellent or solid as they should have been had we had complete use of our reason since our birth, and had we been guided by its means alone.

It is true that we do not find that all the houses in a town are rased to the ground for the sole reason that the town is to be rebuilt in another fashion, with streets made more beautiful; but at the same time we see that many people cause their own houses to be knocked down in order to rebuild them, and that sometimes they are forced so to do where there is danger of the houses falling of themselves, and when the foundations are not secure. From such examples I argued to myself that there was no plausibility in the claim of any private individual to reform a state by altering everything, and by overturning it throughout, in order to set it right again. Nor is it likewise probable that the whole body of the

Sciences, or the order of teaching established by the Schools, should be reformed. But as regards all the opinions which up to this time I had embraced, I thought I could not do better than endeavor once for all to sweep them completely away, so that they might later on be replaced, either by others which were better, or by the same, when I had made them conform to the uniformity of a rational scheme. And I firmly believed that by this means I should succeed in directing my life much better than if I had only built on old foundations, and relied on principles of which I allowed myself to be in youth persuaded without having inquired into their truth. For although in so doing I recognised various difficulties, these were at the same time not unsurmountable, nor comparable to those which are found in reformation of the most insignificant kind in matters which concern the public. In the case of great bodies it is too difficult a task to raise them again when they are once thrown down, or even to keep them in their places when once thoroughly shaken; and their fall cannot be otherwise than very violent. Then as to any imperfections that they may possess (and the very diversity that is found between them is sufficient to tell us that these in many cases exist) custom has doubtless greatly mitigated them, while it has also helped us to avoid, or insensibly corrected a number against which mere foresight would have found it difficult to guard. And finally the imperfections are almost always more supportable than would be the process of removing them, just as the great roads which wind about amongst the mountains become, because of being frequented, little by little so well-beaten and easy that it is much better to follow them than to try to go more directly by climbing over rocks and descending to the foot of precipices.

This is the reason why I cannot in any way approve of those turbulent and unrestful spirits who, being called neither by birth nor fortune to the management of public affairs, never fail to have always in their minds some new reforms. And if I thought that in this treatise there was contained the smallest justification for this folly, I should be very sorry to allow it to be published. My design has never extended beyond trying to reform my own opinion and to build on a foundation which is entirely my own. If my work has given me a certain satisfaction, so that I here present to you a draft of it, I do not so do because I wish to advise anybody to imitate it. Those to whom God has been most beneficent in the bestowal of His graces will perhaps form designs which are more elevated; but

I fear much that this particular one will seem too venturesome for many. The simple resolve to strip oneself of all opinions and beliefs formerly received is not to be regarded as an example that each man should follow. . . .

Among the different branches of Philosophy, I had in my younger days to a certain extent studied Logic; and in those of Mathematics, Geometrical Analysis and Algebra — three arts or sciences which seemed as though they ought to contribute something to the design I had in view. But in examining them I observed in respect to Logic that the syllogisms and the greater part of the other teaching served better in explaining to others those things that one knows . . . than in learning what is new. . . . And as to the Analysis of the ancients and the Algebra of the moderns, besides the fact that they embrace only matters the most abstract, such as appear to have no actual use, the former is always so restricted to the consideration of symbols that it cannot exercise the Understanding without greatly fatiguing the Imagination; and in the latter one is so subjected to certain rules and formulas that the result is the construction of an art which is confused and obscure, and which embarrasses the mind, instead of a science which contributes to its cultivation. This made me feel that some other Method must be found, which, comprising the advantages of the three, is yet exempt from their faults. And as a multiplicity of laws often furnishes excuses for evil-doing, and as a State is hence much better ruled when, having but very few laws, these are most strictly observed; so, instead of the great number of precepts of which Logic is composed, I believed that I should find the four which I shall state quite sufficient, provided that I adhered to a firm and constant resolve never on any single occasion to fail in their observance.

The first of these was to accept nothing as true which I did not clearly recognise to be so: that is to say, carefully to avoid precipitation and prejudice in judgments, and to accept in them nothing more than what was presented to my mind so clearly and distinctly that I could have no occasion to doubt it.

The second was to divide up each of the difficulties which I examined into as many parts as possible, and as seemed requisite in order that it might be resolved in the best manner possible.

The third was to carry on my reflections in due order, commencing with objects that were the most simple and easy to understand, in order to rise little by little, or by degrees, to knowledge of the most complex, assuming an order, even if a fictitious one, among those which do not follow a natural sequence relatively to one another.

The last was in all cases to make enumerations so complete and reviews so general that I should be certain of having omitted nothing.

Those long chains of reasoning, simple and easy as they are, of which geometricians make use in order to arrive at the most difficult demonstrations, had caused me to imagine that all those things which fall under the cognizance of man might very likely be mutually related in the same fashion; and that, provided only that we abstain from receiving anything as true which is not so, and always retain the order which is necessary in order to deduce the one conclusion from the other, there can be nothing so remote that we cannot reach to it, nor so recondite that we cannot discover it. And I had not much trouble in discovering which objects it was necessary to begin with, for I already knew that it was with the most simple and those most easy to apprehend. Considering also that of all those who have hitherto sought for the truth in the Sciences, it has been the mathematicians alone who have been able to succeed in making any demonstrations, that is to say producing reasons which are evident and certain, I did not doubt that it had been by means of a similar kind that they carried on their investigations. I did not at the same time hope for any practical result in so doing, except that my mind would become accustomed to the nourishment of truth and would not content itself with false reasoning. But for all that I had no intention of trying to master all those particular sciences that receive in common the name of Mathematics; but observing that, although their objects are different, they do not fail to agree in this, that they take nothing under consideration but the various relationships or proportions which are present in these objects, I thought that it would be better if I only examined these proportions in their general aspect, and without viewing them otherwise than in the objects which would serve most to facilitate a knowledge of them. Not that I should in any way restrict them to these objects, for I might later on all the more easily apply them to all other objects to which they were applicable. Then, having carefully noted that in order to comprehend the proportions I should sometimes require to consider each one in particular, and sometimes merely keep them in mind, or take them in groups, I thought that, in order the better to consider them in detail, I should picture them in the form of lines, because I could find no method more simple nor more capable of being distinctly represented to my imagination and senses. I considered, however, that in order to keep them in my memory or to embrace several at once, it would be essential that I should explain them by means of certain formulas, the shorter the better. And for this purpose it was requisite that I should borrow all that is best in Geometrical Analysis and Algebra, and correct the errors of the one by the other. . . .

But what pleased me most in this Method was that I was certain by its means of exercising my reason in all things, if not perfectly, at least as well as was in my power. And besides this, I felt in making use of it that my mind gradually accustomed itself to conceive of its objects more accurately and distinctly; and not having restricted this Method to any particular matter, I promised myself to apply it as usefully to the difficulties of other sciences as I had done to those of Algebra. Not that on this account I dared undertake to examine just at once all those that might present themselves; for that would itself have been contrary to the order which the Method prescribes. But having noticed that the knowledge of these difficulties must be dependent on principles derived from Philosophy in which I yet found nothing to be certain, I thought that it was requisite above all to try to establish certainty in it. I considered also that since this endeavor is the most important in all the world, and that in which precipitation and prejudice were most to be feared, I should not try to grapple with it till I had attained to a much riper age than that of three and twenty, which was the age I had reached.

* * *

PART IV

I do not know that I ought to tell you of the first meditations there made by me [i.e. in Holland, where Descartes settled in 1629], for they are so metaphysical and so unusual that they may perhaps not be acceptable to everyone. And yet at the same time, in order that one may judge whether the foundations which I have laid are sufficiently secure, I find myself constrained in some measure to refer to them. For a long time I had remarked that it is sometimes requisite in common life to follow opinions which one knows to be most uncertain, exactly as though they were indisputable, as has been said above. But because in this case I wished to give myself entirely to the search after Truth, I thought that it was necessary for me to take an apparently opposite course, and to reject as absolutely false everything as to which I could imagine the least ground of doubt, in order to see if afterwards there remained anything in my belief that was entirely certain. Thus, because our senses sometimes deceive us, I wished to suppose that nothing is just as they cause us to imagine it to be; and because there are men who deceive themselves in their reasoning and fall into paralogisms, even concerning the simplest matters of geometry, and judging that I was as subject to error as was any other, I rejected as false all the reasons formerly accepted by me as demonstrations. And since all the same thoughts and conceptions which we have while awake may also come to us in sleep, without any of them being at that time true, I resolved to assume that everything that ever entered into my mind was no more true than the illusions of my dreams. But immediately afterwards I noticed that whilst I thus wished to think all things false, it was absolutely essential that the 'I' who thought this should be somewhat, and remarking that this truth '*I think, therefore I am*' was so certain and so assured that all the most extravagant suppositions brought forward by the sceptics were incapable of shaking it, I came to the conclusion that I could receive it without scruple as the first principle of the Philosophy for which I was seeking.

And then, examining attentively that which I was, I saw that I could conceive that I had no body, and that there was no world nor place where I might be; but yet that I could not for all that conceive that I was not. On the contrary, I saw from the very fact that I thought of doubting the truth of other things, it very evidently and certainly followed that I was; on the other hand if I had only ceased from thinking, even if all the rest of what I had ever imagined had really existed, I should have no reason for thinking that I had existed. From that I knew that I was a substance the whole essence or nature of which is to think, and that for its existence there is no need of any place, nor does it depend on any material thing; so that this 'me,' that is to say, the soul by which I am what I am, is entirely distinct from body, and is even more easy to know than is the latter; and even if body were not, the soul would not cease to be what it is.

After this I considered generally what in a proposition is requisite in order to be true and certain; for since I had just discovered one which I knew to be such, I thought that I ought also to know in what this certainty consisted. And having remarked that there was nothing at all in the statement '*I think, therefore I am*' which assures me of having thereby made a true assertion, excepting that I see very clearly that to think it is necessary to be, I came to the conclusion that I might assume, as a general rule, that the things which we conceive very clearly and distinctly are all true — remembering, however, that there is some difficulty in ascertaining which are those that we distinctly conceive.

Following upon this, and reflecting on the fact that I doubted, and that consequently my existence was not quite perfect (for I saw clearly that it was a greater perfection to know than to doubt), I resolved to inquire whence I had learnt to think of anything more perfect than I myself was; and I recognised very clearly that this conception must proceed from some nature which was really more perfect. As to the thoughts which I had of many other things outside of me, like the heavens, the earth, light, heat, and a thousand others, I had not so much difficulty in knowing whence they came, because, remarking nothing in them which seemed to render them superior to me, I could believe that, if they were true, they were dependencies upon my nature, in so far as it possessed some perfection; and if they were not true, that I held them from nought, that is to say, that they were in me because I had something lacking in my nature. But this could not apply to the idea of a Being more perfect than my own, for to hold it from nought would be manifestly impossible; and because it is no less contradictory to say of the more perfect that it is what results from and depends on the less perfect, than to say that there is something which proceeds from nothing, it was equally impossible that I should hold it from myself. In this way it could but follow that it had been placed in me by a Nature which was really more perfect than mine could be, and which even had within itself all the perfections of which I could form any idea — that is to say, to put it in a word, which was God. To which I added that since I knew some perfections which I did not possess, I was not the only being in existence (I shall here use freely, if you will allow, the terms of the School); but that there was necessarily some other more perfect Being on which I depended, or from which I acquired all that I had. For if I had existed alone and independent of any others, so that I should have had from myself all that perfection of being in which I participated to however small an extent, I should have been able for the same reason to have had all the remainder which I knew that I lacked; and thus I myself should have been infinite, eternal, immutable, omniscient, all-powerful, and, finally, I should have all the perfections which I could discern in God. For, in pursuance of the reasonings which I have just carried on, in order to know the nature of God as far as my nature is capable of knowing it, I had only to consider in reference to all these things of which I found some idea in myself, whether it was a perfection to possess them or not. And I was assured that none of those which indicated some imperfection were in Him, but that all else was present; and I saw that doubt, inconstancy, sadness, and such things, could not be in Him considering that I myself should have been glad to be without them. In addition to this, I had ideas of many things which are sensible and corporeal, for, although I might suppose that I was dreaming, and that all that I saw or imagined was false, I could not at the same time deny that the ideas were really in my thoughts. But because I had already recognised very clearly in myself that the nature of the intelligence is distinct from that of the body, and observing that all composition gives evidence of dependency, and that dependency is manifestly an imperfection, I came to the conclusion that it could not be a perfection in God to be composed of these two natures, and that consequently He was not so composed. I judged, however, that if there were any bodies in the world, or even any intelligences or other natures which were not wholly perfect, their existence must depend on His power in such a way that they could not subsist without Him for a single moment.

After that I desired to seek for other truths, and having put before myself the object of the geometricians, which I conceived to be a continuous body, or a space indefinitely extended in length, breadth, height or depth, which was divisible into various parts, and which might have various figures and sizes, and might be moved or transposed in all sorts of ways (for all this the geometricians suppose to be in the object of their contemplation), I went through some of their simplest demonstrations, and having noticed that this great certainty which everyone attributes to these demonstrations is founded solely on the fact that they are conceived of with clearness, in accordance with the rule which I have just laid down, I also noticed that there was nothing at all in them to assure me of the existence of their object. For, to take an example, I saw very well that if we suppose a triangle to be given, the three angles must certainly be equal to two right angles; but for all that I saw no reason to be assured that there was any such triangle in existence, while on the contrary, on reverting to the examination of the idea which I had of a Perfect Being, I found that in this case existence was implied in it in the same manner in which the equality of its three angles to two right angles is implied in the idea of a triangle; or in the idea of a sphere, that all the points on its surface are equidistant from its centre, or even more evidently still. Consequently it is at least as certain that God, who is a Being so perfect, is, or exists, as any demonstration of geometry can possibly be. . . .

. . . That which I have just taken as a rule, that is to say, that all the things that we very clearly and very distinctly conceive of are true, is certain only because God is or exists, and that He is a Perfect Being, and that all that is in us issues from Him. From this it follows that our ideas or notions, which to the extent of their being clear or distinct are ideas of real things issuing from God, cannot but to that extent be true. So that though we often enough have ideas which have an element of falsity, this can only be the case in regard to those which have in them somewhat that is confused or obscure, because in so far as they have this character they participate in negation — that is, they exist in us as confused only because we are not quite perfect. And it is evident that there is no less repugnance in the idea that error or imperfection, inasmuch as it is imperfection, proceeds from God, than there is in the idea of truth or perfection proceeding from nought. But if we did not know that all that is in us of reality and truth proceeds from a perfect and infinite Being, however clear and distinct were our ideas, we should not have any reason to assure ourselves that they had the perfection of being true.

But after the knowledge of God and of the soul has thus rendered us certain of this rule, it is very easy to understand that the dreams which we imagine in our sleep should not make us in any way doubt the truth of the thoughts which we have when awake. For even if in sleep we had some very distinct idea such as a geometrician might have who discovered some new demonstration, the fact of being asleep would not militate against its truth. And as to the most ordinary error in our dreams, which consists in their representing to us various objects in the same way as do our external senses, it does not matter that this should give us occasion to suspect the truth of such ideas, because we may be likewise often enough deceived in them without our sleeping at all, just as when those who have the jaundice see everything as yellow, or when stars or other bodies which are very remote appear much smaller than they really are. For, finally, whether we are awake or asleep, we should never allow ourselves to be persuaded excepting by the evidence of our Reason. And it must be remarked that I speak of our Reason and not of our imagination nor of our senses; just as though we see the sun very clearly, we should not for that reason judge that it is of the size of which it appears to be; likewise we could quite well distinctly imagine the head of a lion on the body of a goat, without necessarily concluding that a chimera exists. For Reason does not insist that whatever we see or imagine thus is a truth, but it tells us clearly that all our ideas or notions must have some foundation of truth. For otherwise it could not be possible that God, who is all perfection and truth, should have placed them within us.

*   *   *

PART VI

It is three years since I arrived at the end of the Treatise which contained all these things; and I was commencing to revise it in order to place it in the hands of a printer, when I learned that certain persons, to whose opinions I defer, and whose authority cannot have less weight with my actions than my own reason has over my thoughts, had disapproved of a physical theory published a little while before by another person [i.e. Galileo]. I will not say that I agreed with this opinion, but only that before their censure I observed in it nothing which I could possibly imagine to be prejudicial either to Religion or the State, or consequently which could have prevented me from giving expression to it in writing, if my reason had persuaded me to do so: and this made me fear that among my own opinions one might be found which should be misunderstood, notwithstanding the great care which I have always taken not to accept any new beliefs unless I had very certain proof of their truth, and not to give expression to what could tend to the disadvantage of any person. This sufficed to cause me to alter the resolution which I had made to publish. For, although the reasons for my former resolution were very strong, my inclination, which always made me hate the profession of writing books, caused me immediately to find plenty of other reasons for excusing myself from doing so. And these reasons, on the one side and on the other, are of such a nature that not only have I here some interest in giving expression to them, but possibly the public may also have some interest in knowing them.

I have never made much of those things which proceed from my own mind, and so long as I culled no other fruits from the Method which I use, beyond that of satisfying myself respecting certain difficulties which pertain to the speculative sciences, or trying to regulate my conduct by the reasons which it has taught me, I never believed myself to be obliged to write anything about it. For as regards that which concerns conduct, everyone is so confident of his own common sense, that there might be found as many reformers as heads, if it were permitted that others than those whom God has established as the sovereigns of his people, or at least to whom He has given sufficient grace and zeal to be prophets, should be allowed to make any changes in that. And, although my speculations give me the greatest pleasure, I believed that others also had speculations which possibly pleased them even more. But so soon as I had acquired some general notions concerning Physics, and as, beginning to make use of them in various special difficulties, I observed to what point they might lead us, and how much they differ from the principles of which we have made use up to the present time, I believed that I could not keep them concealed without greatly sinning against the law which obliges us to procure, as much as in us lies, the general good of all mankind. For they caused me to see that it is possible to attain knowledge which is very useful in life, and that, instead of that speculative philosophy which is taught in the Schools, we may find a practical philosophy by means of which, knowing the force and the action of fire, water, air, the stars, heavens and all other bodies that environ us, as distinctly as we know the different crafts of our artisans, we can in the same way employ them in all those uses to which they are adapted, and thus render ourselves the masters and possessors of nature. This is not merely to be desired with a view to the invention of an infinity of arts and crafts which enable us to enjoy without any trouble the fruits of the earth and all the good things which are to be found there, but also principally because it brings about the preservation of health, which is without doubt the chief blessing and the foundation of all other blessings in this life. For the mind depends so much on the temperament and disposition of the bodily organs that, if it is possible to find a means of rendering men wiser and cleverer than they have hitherto been, I believe that it is in medicine that it must be sought. It is true that the medicine which is now in vogue contains little of which the utility is remarkable; but, without having any intention of decrying it, I am sure that there is no one, even among those who make its study a profession, who does not confess that all that men know is almost nothing in comparison with what remains to be known; and that we could be free of an infinitude of maladies both of body and mind, and even also possibly of the infirmities of age, if we had sufficient knowledge of their causes, and of all the remedies with which nature has provided us. But, having the intention of devoting all my life to the investigation of a knowledge which is so essential, and having discovered a path which appears to me to be of such a nature that we must by its means infallibly reach our end if we pursue it, unless, indeed, we are prevented by the shortness of life or by lack of experience, I judged that there was no better provision against these two impediments than faithfully to communicate to the public the little which I should myself have discovered, and to beg all well-inclined persons to proceed further by contributing, each one according to his own inclination and ability, to the experiments which must be made, and then to communicate to the public all the things which they might discover, in order that the last should commence where the preceding had left off; and thus, by joining together the lives and labors of many, we should collectively proceed much further than any one in particular could succeed in doing.

I remarked also respecting experiments, that they become so much the more necessary the more one is advanced in knowledge, for to begin with it is better to make use simply of those which present themselves spontaneously to our senses, and of which we could not be ignorant provided that we reflected ever so little, rather than to seek out those which are more rare and recondite; the reason of this is that those which are more rare often mislead us so long as we do not know the causes of the more common, and the fact that the circumstances on which they depend are almost always so particular and so minute that it is very difficult to observe them. But in this the order which I have followed is as follows: I have first tried to discover generally the principles or first causes of everything that is or that can be in the world, without considering anything that might accomplish this end but God Himself who has created the world, or deriving them from any source excepting from certain germs of truths which are naturally existent in our souls. After that I considered which were the primary and most ordinary effects which might be deduced from these causes, and it seems to me that in this way I discovered the heavens, the stars, an earth, and even on the earth, water, air, fire, the minerals and some other such things, which are the most common and simple of any that exist, and consequently the easiest to know. Then, when I wished to descend to those which were more particular, so many objects of various kinds presented themselves to me, that I did not think it was possible for the human mind to distinguish the forms or species of bodies which are on the earth from an infinitude of others which might have been so if it had been the will of God to place them there, or consequently to apply them to our use, if it were not that we arrive at the causes by the effects, and avail ourselves of many particular experiments. In subsequently passing over in my mind all the objects which have ever been presented to my senses, I can truly venture to say that I have not there observed anything which I could not easily explain by the principles which I had discovered. But I must also confess that the power of nature is so ample and so vast, and these principles are so simple and general, that I observed hardly any particular effect as to which I could not at once recognise that it might be deduced from the principles in many different ways; and my greatest difficulty is usually to discover in which of these ways the effect does depend upon them. As to that, I do not know any other plan but again to try to find experiments of such a nature that their result is not the same if it has to be explained by one of the methods, as it would be if explained by the other. For the rest, I have now reached a position in which I discern, as it seems to me, sufficiently clearly what course must be adopted in order to make the majority of the experiments which may conduce to carry out this end. But I also perceive that they are of such a nature, and of so great a number, that neither my hands nor my income, though the latter were a thousand times larger than it is, could suffice for the whole; so that just in proportion as henceforth I shall have the power of carrying out more of them or less, shall I make more or less progress in arriving at a knowledge of nature. This is what I had promised myself to make known by the Treatise which I had written, and to demonstrate in it so clearly the advantage which the public might receive from it, that I should induce all those who have the good of mankind at heart — that is to say, all those who are really virtuous in fact, and not only by a false semblance or by opinion — both to communicate to me those experiments that they have already carried out, and to help me in the investigation of those that still remain to be accomplished.

* * *

b.
The Passions of the Soul

ARTICLE I. THAT WHAT IN RESPECT OF A SUBJECT IS PASSION, IS IN SOME OTHER REGARD ALWAYS ACTION

THERE IS nothing in which the defective nature of the sciences which we have received from the ancients appears more clearly than in what they have written on the passions; for, although this is a matter which has at all times been the object of much investigation, and though it would not appear to be one of the most difficult, inasmuch as since every one has experience of the passions within himself, there is no necessity to borrow one's observations from elsewhere in order to discover their nature; yet that which the ancients have taught regarding them is both so slight, and for the most part so far from credible, that I am unable to entertain any hope of approximating to the truth excepting by shunning the paths which they have followed. This is why I shall be here obliged to write just as though I were treating of a matter which no one had ever touched on before me; and, to begin with, I consider that all that which occurs or that happens anew, is by the philosophers, generally speaking, termed a passion, in as far as the subject to which it occurs is concerned, and an action in respect of him who causes it to occur. Thus although the agent and the recipient [patient] are frequently very different, the action and the passion are always one and the same thing, although having different names, because of the two diverse subjects to which it may be related.

ARTICLE 2. THAT IN ORDER TO UNDERSTAND THE PASSIONS OF THE SOUL ITS FUNCTIONS MUST BE DISTINGUISHED FROM THOSE OF BODY

Next I note also that we do not observe the existence of any subject which more immediately acts upon our soul than the body to which it is joined, and that we must consequently consider that what in the soul is a passion is in the body commonly speaking an action; so that there is no better means of arriving at a knowledge of our passions than to examine the difference which exists between soul and body in order to know to which of the two we must attribute each one of the functions which are within us.

ARTICLE 3. WHAT RULE WE MUST FOLLOW TO BRING ABOUT THIS RESULT

As to this we shall not find much difficulty if we realise that all that we experience as being in us, and that to observation may exist in wholly inanimate bodies, must be attributed to our body alone; and, on the other hand, that all that which is in us and which we cannot in any way conceive as possibly pertaining to a body, must be attributed to our soul.

ARTICLE 4. THAT THE HEAT AND MOVEMENT OF THE MEMBERS PROCEED FROM THE BODY, THE THOUGHTS FROM THE SOUL

Thus because we have no conception of the body as thinking in any way, we have reason to believe that every kind of thought which exists in us belongs to the soul; and because we do not doubt there being inanimate bodies which can move in as many as or in more diverse modes than can ours, and which have as much heat or more (experience demonstrates this to us in flame, which of itself has much more heat and movement than any of our members), we must believe that all the heat and all the movements which are in us pertain only to body, inasmuch as they do not depend on thought at all.

ARTICLE 5. THAT IT IS AN ERROR TO BELIEVE THAT THE SOUL SUPPLIES THE MOVEMENT AND HEAT TO BODY

By this means we shall avoid a very considerable error into which many have fallen; so much so that I am of opinion that this is the primary cause which has prevented our being able hitherto satisfactorily to explain the passions and the other properties of the soul. It arises from the fact that from observing that all dead bodies are devoid of heat and consequently of movement, it has been thought that it was the absence of soul which caused these movements and this heat to cease; and thus, without any reason, it was thought that our natural heat and all the movements of our body depend on the soul: while in fact we ought on the contrary to believe that the soul quits us on death only because this heat ceases, and the organs which serve to move the body disintegrate.

ARTICLE 6. THE DIFFERENCE THAT EXISTS BETWEEN A LIVING BODY AND A DEAD BODY

In order, then, that we may avoid this error, let us consider that death never comes to pass by reason of the soul, but only because some one of the principal parts of the body decays; and we may judge that the body of a living man differs from that of a dead man just as does a watch or other automaton (i.e. a machine that moves of itself), when it is wound up and contains in itself the corporeal principle of those movements for which it is designed along with all that is requisite for its action, from the same watch or other machine when it is broken and when the principle of its movement ceases to act.

* * *

ARTICLE 10. HOW THE ANIMAL SPIRITS ARE PRODUCED IN THE BRAIN

But what is here most worthy of remark is that all the most animated and subtle portions of the blood which the heat has rarefied in the heart, enter ceaselessly in large quantities into the cavities of the brain. And the reason which causes them to go there rather than elsewhere, is that all the blood which issues from the heart by the great artery takes its course in a straight line towards that place, and not being able to enter it in its entirety, because there are only very narrow passages there, those of its parts which are the most agitated and the most subtle alone pass through, while the rest spreads abroad in all the other portions of the body. But these very subtle parts of the blood form the animal spirits; and for this end they have no need to experience any other change in the brain, unless it be that they are separated from the other less subtle portions of the blood; for what I here name spirits are nothing but material bodies and their one peculiarity is that they are bodies of extreme minuteness and that they move very quickly like the particles of the flame which issues from a torch. Thus it is that they never remain at rest in any spot, and just as some of them enter into the cavities of the brain, others issue forth by the pores which are in its substance, which pores conduct them into the nerves, and from there into the muscles, by means of which they move the body in all the different ways in which it can be moved.

*   *   *

ARTICLE 17. WHAT THE FUNCTIONS OF THE SOUL ARE

After having thus considered all the functions which pertain to the body alone, it is easy to recognise that there is nothing in us which we ought to attribute to our soul excepting our thoughts, which are mainly of two sorts, the one being the actions of the soul, and the other its passions. Those which I call its actions are all our desires, because we find by experience that they proceed directly from our soul, and appear to depend on it alone: while, on the other hand, we may usually term one's passions all those kinds of perception or forms of knowledge which are found in us, because it is often not our soul which makes them what they are, and because it always receives them from the things which are represented by them.

ARTICLE 18. OF THE WILL

Our desires, again, are of two sorts, of which the one consists of the actions of the soul which terminate in the soul itself, as when we desire to love God, or generally speaking, apply our thoughts to some object which is not material; and the other of the actions which terminate in our body, as when from the simple fact that we have the desire to take a walk, it follows that our legs move and that we walk.

ARTICLE 19. OF THE PERCEPTIONS

Our perceptions are also of two sorts, and the one have the soul as a cause and the other the body. Those which have the soul as a cause are the perceptions of our desires, and of all the imaginations or other thoughts which depend on them. For it is certain that we cannot desire anything without perceiving by the same means that we desire it; and, although in regard to our soul it is an action to desire something, we may say that it is also one of its passions to perceive that it desires. Yet because this perception and this will are really one and the same thing, the more noble always supplies the denomination, and thus we are not in the habit of calling it a passion, but only an action.

*   *   *

ARTICLE 27. THE DEFINITION OF THE
PASSIONS OF THE SOUL

After having considered in what the passions of the soul differ from all its other thoughts, it seems to me that we may define them generally as the perceptions, feelings, or emotions of the soul which we relate specially to it, and which are caused, maintained, and fortified by some movement of the spirits.

*   *   *

ARTICLE 40. THE PRINCIPAL EFFECT OF THE PASSIONS

For it is requisite to notice that the principal effect of all the passions in men is that they incite and dispose their soul to desire those things for which they prepare their body, so that the feeling of fear incites it to desire to fly, that of courage to desire to fight, and so on.

ARTICLE 41. THE POWER OF THE SOUL IN REGARD TO THE BODY

But the will is so free in its nature, that it can never be constrained; and of the two sorts of thoughts which I have distinguished in the soul (of which the first are its actions, i.e. its desires, the others its passions, taking this word in its most general significance, which comprises all kinds of perceptions), the former are absolutely in its power, and can only be indirectly changed by the body, while on the other hand the latter depend absolutely on the actions which govern and direct them, and they can only indirectly be altered by the soul, excepting when it is itself their cause. And the whole action of the soul consists in this, that solely because it desires something, it causes the little gland to which it is closely united to move in the way requisite to produce the effect which relates to this desire.

*   *   *

ARTICLE 49. THAT THE STRENGTH OF THE SOUL DOES NOT SUFFICE WITHOUT THE KNOWLEDGE OF THE TRUTH

It is true that there are very few men so weak and irresolute that they desire nothing except what their passion dictates to them. The most part have determinate judgments, in pursuance of which they regulate a part of their actions; and although often their judgments are false or even founded on certain passions by which the will formerly allowed itself to be vanquished or led astray, yet, because it continues to follow them when the passion which has caused them is absent, they may be considered as its proper arms, and we may reflect that souls are stronger or weaker by reason of the fact that they are able to follow these judgments more or less closely, and resist the present passions which are contrary to them. Yet there is a great difference between the resolutions which proceed from a false opinion, and those which are founded only on the knowledge of the truth, inasmuch as if we follow the latter we are assured that we shall never regret nor repent it, whereas we do so always when we have followed the first-mentioned, and hence discovered our error in doing so.

ARTICLE 50. THAT THERE IS NO SOUL SO FEEBLE THAT IT CANNOT, IF WELL DIRECTED, ACQUIRE AN ABSOLUTE POWER OVER ITS PASSIONS

*   *   *

ARTICLE 79. THE DEFINITION OF LOVE AND HATE

Love is an emotion of the soul caused by the movement of the spirits which incites it to join itself willingly to objects which appear to it to be agreeable. And hatred is an emotion caused by the spirits which incite the soul to desire to be separated from the objects which present themselves to it as hurtful. I say that these emotions are caused by the spirits in order to distinguish love and hate, which are passions and depend on the body, both from the judgments which also induce the soul by its free will to unite itself with the things which it esteems to be good, and to separate itself from those it holds to be evil, and from the emotions which these judgments excite of themselves in the soul.

ARTICLE 80. WHAT IT IS TO JOIN OR SEPARATE ONESELF BY ONE'S FREE WILL

For the rest, by the word will I do not here intend to talk of desire, which is a passion apart, and one which relates to the future, but of the consent by which we consider ourselves from this time forward as united with what we love, so that we imagine a whole of which we conceive ourselves as only constituting one part, while the thing loved constitutes another part. In the case of hatred, on the other hand, we consider ourselves only as a whole, entirely separated from the matter for which we possess an aversion.

* * *

ARTICLE 147. OF THE INTERIOR EMOTIONS OF THE SOUL

I shall only add here a consideration which, it seems to me, we shall find of much service in preventing us from suffering any inconvenience from the passions; and that is that our good and our harm depend mainly on the interior emotions which are only excited in the soul by the soul itself, in which respect they differ from its passions, which always depend on some movement of the spirits. And, although these emotions of the soul are frequently united to the passions which are similar to them, they may likewise often be met with along with others, and even take their origin from those which are contrary to them. . . .

ARTICLE 148. THAT THE EXERCISE OF VIRTUE IS A SOVEREIGN REMEDY AGAINST THE PASSIONS

And, inasmuch as these inward emotions touch us most nearly, and in consequence have much more power over us than the passions from which they differ, and which are met with in conjunction with them, it is certain that, provided our soul is always possessed of something to content itself with inwardly, none of the troubles that come from elsewhere have any power to harm it, but rather serve to increase its joy, inasmuch as, seeing that it cannot be harmed by them, it is made sensible of its perfection. And in order that our soul may thus have something with which to be content, it has no need but to follow exactly after virtue. For whoever has lived in such a way that his conscience cannot reproach him for ever having failed to perform those things which he has judged to be the best (which is what I here call following after virtue) receives from this a satisfaction which is so powerful in rendering him happy that the most violent efforts of the passions never have sufficient power to disturb the tranquillity of his soul.

*   *   *

ARTICLE 211. A GENERAL REMEDY AGAINST THE PASSIONS

And now that we are acquainted with them all, we have much less reason to fear them than we formerly had. For we see that they are all good in their nature and that we have nothing to avoid but their evil uses or their excesses, against which the remedies which I explained might suffice, if each one of us took sufficient heed to practise them. But because I have placed amongst these remedies the forethought and diligence whereby we can correct our natural faults in exercising ourselves in separating within us the movements of the blood and spirits from the thoughts to which they are usually united, I confess that there are few people who are sufficiently prepared in this way to meet all the accidents of life, and that these movements excited in the blood by the objects of the passions follow so promptly from these single impressions that are made in the brain and from the disposition of the organs, although the soul contributes in no wise to them, that there is no human wisdom capable of resisting them when sufficient preparation is not made for doing so. . . . But what we can always do on such occasions, and what I think I can here put forward as the most general remedy and that most easy to practise against all excesses of the passions, is that, when we feel our blood to be thus agitated, we should be warned of the fact, and recollect that all that presents itself before the imagination tends to delude the soul and causes the reasons which serve to urge it to accomplish the object of its passion to appear much stronger than they are, and those which serve to dissuade it to be much weaker. And when the passions urge us only towards things the execution of which necessitates some delay, we ought to abstain from pronouncing any judgment on the spot, and to divert ourselves by other thoughts until time and rest shall have entirely calmed the emotion which is in the blood. And finally, when it incites us to actions regarding which it is requisite that an immediate resolution should be taken, the will must make it its main business to consider and follow up the reasons which are contrary to those set up by the passions, although they appear to be less strong; just as when we are suddenly attacked by some enemy, the occasion does not permit of our taking time to deliberate. But it seems to me that what those who are accustomed to reflect on their actions can always do when they feel themselves to be seized with fear, is to try to turn their thoughts away from the consideration of danger by representing to themselves the reasons which prove that there is much more certainty and honour in resistance than in flight. And on the other hand, when they feel that the desire of vengeance and anger incites them to run thoughtlessly towards those who attack them, they will recollect that it is imprudence to lose their lives when they can without dishonour save themselves, and that, if the match is very unequal, it is better to beat an honourable retreat or ask quarter, than to expose oneself doggedly to certain death.

ARTICLE 212. THAT IT IS ON THEM ALONE THAT ALL THE GOOD AND EVIL OF THIS LIFE DEPENDS

For the rest, the soul may have pleasures of its own, but as to those which are common to it and the body, they depend entirely on the passions, so that the men whom they can most move are capable of partaking most of enjoyment in this life. It is true that such men may also find most bitterness when they do not know how to employ them well, or fortune is contrary to them. But the principal use of prudence or self-control is that it teaches us to be masters of our passions, and to so control and guide them that the evils which they cause are quite bearable, and that we even derive joy from them all.

5

Skepticism

RENÉ RAPIN (1621–87), a French theologian and literary figure, joined the Society of Jesus at the age of eighteen and gave himself up to the study and teaching of the humanities. He was a prolific writer on poetics, history, the antiquities, philosophy, theology, Jansenism, and horticulture, as well as a practicing poet. Rapin occupies an important place in the development of the skeptical school of thought, which endeavored to undermine all the philosophical systems ever devised by man. Like many of his fellow-skeptics of the seventeenth century, he sought to vindicate the ultimate value of faith by demonstrating the uncertainty of all human knowledge. He thus takes up a peculiar position between the combatants in the war between the Ancients and the Moderns.

In 1676, Rapin brought out his Reflections upon Ancient and Modern Philosophy. excerpts from which are given here. It should be noted that in the original French book, Part IV of Rapin's work is entitled "Reflections on Physics" (evidently in the Aristotelian sense), which the English translator of the time rendered as "Reflexions on Natural Philosophy."

Rapin, Reflections upon Ancient and Modern Philosophy

I] REFLEXIONS ON PHILOSOPHY IN GENERAL

7] ARISTOTLE is a wit so far above others that few know him, for by an unparalleled reach of understanding he soars above the highest. He is an eagle that mounts so high that men easily lose sight of him, and there is so much force in his thoughts, so great elevation in his sentiments, that he cannot be followed. He it was who first collected the several parts of Philosophy, that he might unite them into one body and reduce them to a complete system. No man had ever so great a discernment of truth and falsehood as that philosopher; for he not only dived into reason that he might discover it, under what cloud soever it hid itself, but upon discovery thereof, had the art to make it perceptible to others in all its force, and intelligible in its full extent: so happy and penetrating was his genius. By that quality of mind he became so exact an observer of the works of Nature that Plato called him the Genius of Nature, as if Nature had made use of his spirit as an instrument to discover her secrets. In all his sentiments there sparkles a sage and judicious character, which always satisfies the mind, so regular and solid he is. And there is hardly ever anything said reasonably in Philosophy that bears not some signature and impression of the spirit of Aristotle. So that all the judgments that have been made on his doctrine in succeeding ages have only differed according to the greatness and mediocrity of light and knowledge that have swayed them, for in a word, none have given greater weight to human reason, nor carried it farther than Aristotle. His method is more solid than that of all others because his principles are better founded on reason and his reason more grounded on experience. But when he speaks, one cannot tell whether it be to hide his

From René Rapin, S.J., *Réflexions sur la philosophie ancienne et moderne, et sur l'usage qu'on en doit faire pour la religion* (Paris, 1676), pp. 15–19, 52–66, 162–166; *Reflections upon Ancient and Modern Philosophy*, translated by "A.L." (London, 1686), pp. 15–19, 52–65, 159–162. The spelling has been modernized, and the English text has been modified to comply with the canons of The Free Press Style manual.

doubts or to make himself reverenced that he is obscure. It seems he writes only that he may not be understood and that his works are not so much to instruct his own age as to give exercise to the following; therefore it is that Diogenes Laertius compares him to that fish that troubles the water for fear of being taken. But there is some justice due to Aristotle as to that reproach that is cast upon him. His obscurity is not so much the defect of his understanding as of his subject matter. In the manner how he fathoms things, it is not very easy to pierce the darkest clouds of Nature, to unfold her most hidden secrets, to dig into nothing but abysses, to walk only on precipices, not to pursue truth but by ways unknown to all other heads, and to be intelligible to all men. That is the reason that the discourses of Aristotle have always more politeness and force than perspicuity: because he confines himself to a short and concise style, the constraint whereof will not allow but a perplexed elocution; and that is also the reason that he writes in a manner more apt to amaze than persuade his readers. One must have heard him, says Psellus, to be able to comprehend his doctrine. He masked sometimes with an affected obscurity what Pythagoras disguised under symbols and Plato under allegories. But in fine, there is so great a depth of judgment to be found in all that Aristotle said, when one can penetrate into it, that he is not to be found fault with if he have not always the art to make himself be understood. It is in vain therefore, that a brood of stinted spirits have let fly against the reputation of that great man, under the conduct of Telesius, Patricius, Bacon, Campanella, and some others, to discredit his doctrine in these last ages; who by censuring Aristotle have pretended to be wiser than all the ages and nations that have esteemed him.

*   *   *

18] In fine, seeing the love of learning, and especially of Philosophy, became confined to Europe, the different nations thereof applied themselves variously to it, according to the diversity of their geniuses and inclinations. The Spaniards, according to the character of their wits, cut out for dialectic and reflexions, became subtle in their reasonings, formalists and metaphysicians. The Italians took a more agreeable air; they grew for the most part curious in lovely ideas. The works of Triphus, one of the learned of the last ages, inspired into them love for the philosophy of Aristotle, and the books of

Cardinal Bessarion and Marcilius Ficinus gave them an inclination for the philosophy of Plato, to which they accommodated themselves better than other nations by the quality of their fine genius, naturally quick but lazy. The French, who found themselves capable of all sciences, embraced all, and by that character of capacity and curiosity copied what they found good amongst other nations and succeeded in everything. The English, by that depth of wit which is common to their nation, loved the methods that were profound, abstruse, and far-sought and by a headstrong application to labor set themselves to the observations of Nature more than other nations, as appears by the works that they have published. The Germans, by the necessity which the climate imposed upon them to keep themselves by the fire, and by the conveniency of their stoves, addicted themselves to chemistry, as did other northern people. Thus the southern countries contributed to make Philosophy profound and subtle, and the northern to render it laborious and mechanical. And of all the modern philosophers, those that have made greatest noise are Galileus, an Italian; Bacon, Hobbes, and Boyle, English; Gassendus and Descartes, French; and Vanhelmont, Dutchman. Galileus seems to be the most ingenious of all, and he I think may be called the father of Modern Philosophy. His method resembles much that of the Platonists; his style is pleasant; and by his manner of writing he conceals many defects. Though he hath copied many things from the primitive philosophers, yet all seems to be his own; he is taken for the original in several places where he is but the transcriber. Bacon has a ranging wit that dives not deep into anything; his too great reach hinders him from being exact, and the most part of his sentiments are rather overtures for meditation than maxims to be followed. His opinions are somewhat subtle and sparkling, and if they be rightly considered, they resemble more sparks of fire than an entire and natural light. Hobbes is obscure without delight, singular in his notions, learned, but not very solid, and inconstant in his doctrine; for he is sometimes Epicurean, sometimes Peripatetic. Boyle is exact in his observations; no man in Europe hath enriched Philosophy with so many experiments as he. He reasons upon his experiments with indifferent good consequence, which after all are not always unquestionable because his principles are not always certain: he is, in a word, an able philosopher and great naturalist. Gassendus, who desired only to pass for the restorer of the Philosophy of Democritus and Epicurus, speaks little of his own head;

there is nothing almost in him but the beauty of style, that may give him the credit of an admirable author. To refute his natural philosophy there needs no more but the arguments of Aristotle against Democritus and his disciples. Descartes is one of the most extraordinary geniuses that hath appeared in these last times, one of a fertile wit and profound meditation: the concatenation of his doctrine reaches his point, the order of it is well devised according to his principles, and his system, though made up of the Ancient and Modern, is well digested. The truth is, he teaches men too much to doubt, and that is no good model for spirits naturally incredulous: but, in fine, he is more original than others. Vanhelmont, through the knowledge that he had of Nature after his way, performed such prodigious things by his remedies, that he was put into the Inquisition, upon suspicion that what he did was above the power of Nature. In a word, Galileus is the most agreeable of the moderns, Bacon the most subtle, Gassendus the most learned, Hobbes the most plodding and thoughtful, Boyle the most curious, Descartes the most ingenious, and Vanhelmont the greatest naturalist, but too much wedded to Paracelsus. . . .

19] Upon the retail of all these notions of Ancient and Modern Philosophy, and upon the different character of both, this comparison may be made: the Ancient Philosophy is more founded on authority, and the Modern on experience; the Ancient is simple and natural, the Modern artificial and elaborate; the former is more modest and grave, the latter more imperious and pedantic. The Ancient is peaceable and calm; for it was so far from disputing, that it would have the minds of youth prepared by the Mathematics, that they might be accustomed to submit to demonstration without hesitation. The Modern is of a strain of disputing of everything and of training up youth to noise and the tumult of the school. The Ancient inquires only into truth out of a sincere desire to find it; the Modern takes pleasure to dispute it, even when it is discovered. The one advances more securely in its method, because it hath always the Metaphysics for a guide: the other is unsure in its steps when it is once deprived of that conduct. Constancy, fidelity, sound judgment, and steadfastness, was that which men called Philosophy in the days of Plato. And the dislike of business, peevishness, the renouncing of pleasures when the use of them is lost through the extinction of passions, I know not what authority that is derived from the graybeard, counterfeit audacity, phlegmatic sullenness, moderation, and all that wisdom which springs from the weakness of age and constitution, is the Philosophy of a great many nowadays. The Ancient is universally more learned, it aims at all: and the Modern confines itself to the sole consideration of Nature, resting satisfied to be a mere naturalist. In fine, the Ancient is more addicted to study, more laborious and indefatigable in what it undertakes, for the primitive philosophers spent their lives in study; the Modern is less constant in its application, more superficial in its pains, and more precipitate in its studies. And this precipitation accustoms it by little and little to ground too easily reasonings not very exact upon certain rumors, testimonies of little credit, and experiments not well agreed upon. It pronounces so boldly upon doubts and uncertainties to satisfy in some manner the eagerness, that it sometimes has to vent its imaginations and to give vogue to novelties. To make a decision between both, I am of the opinion of that intelligent philosopher of these last ages who, all things being well considered, was of the mind to stick to the Ancients, and leave the Moderns to themselves, for the plain common sense of the primitive philosophers is preferable to all the art and quaintness of the new. But let us conclude without prejudice that as from what cloud soever the day breaks out, it should be accounted pleasant; so from what part soever truth comes, it ought to be esteemed. Let us no more distinguish ancient reason from new, because on what side soever we behold it, and what color soever we give it, it is always the same. And let us make this reflexion, that if there be some opinions better received by the public than others, it is but sometimes because their cabals have been more powerful or their stars more favorable.

20] There are therefore two extremities to be avoided in the course that is to be held between the Ancient and Modern philosophers. The first is of those who, out of a good opinion that they have of themselves, find nothing comparable to their own age. The zeal that they have to free themselves from the tyranny, which the authority of the Ancients have usurped over men's minds, is a false zeal; that is the way to impose new laws on reason under pretext of giving it liberty. And all these fair precepts that men give us to shake off the prejudices of education, custom, authority, and to cure ourselves of popular anticipations, are but snares laid for our credulity: they speak to us of liberty only to impose upon us a new yoke. It is only to give to the Moderns what men would take from the Ancients, and to destroy the credit of Aristotle to set up the reputation of Descartes; but is it just to despise those whom all antiquity have respected? Tradition alone and the universal consent of all people might oblige us to do justice to those great men who have been the founders of sciences. For the world is a great assembly wherein every age has its vote, and to know who is preferable in the judgment we pass on men, we must look on those who have deserved from the public the most universal approbation. None but superficial minds can be pleased with novelties. . . . Let us but cast our eyes on the ages past, and that will teach us modesty. These great men, besides the extraordinary genius they had for sciences, spent their lives in continual pains, with a docility of spirit without example. . . . Plato was the disciple of Socrates, Archytas, and Eurytus above forty years. Aristotle studied under Plato more than twenty years. And shall we, forsooth, after two years slight study, under very ordinary masters, pretend to compare with these great men?!

21] The other extremity to be avoided is the pertinacious adhering to the Ancients, sometimes without reason; men make an idol of their authority by a blind prejudicated persuasion of their merit. Such was the headstrongness of George of Trabisond, who made a book to prove the conformity of Aristotle with the Holy Scriptures, and of Marcilius Ficinus, who pretends that Plato knew the mystery of the Trinity — for which Medina, a Spanish divine, condemns him of boldness injurious to the purity of our religion, which contains nothing but what is supernatural. . . . There is therefore a mean to be observed between the Ancients and Moderns; these are to be respected without vilifying of those. So let us endeavor to discover new truths and not neglect the ancient. Let us not overthrow things established to establish things that are uncertain; let us preserve our liberty and not lose the use of our reason by a blind adoration of the sentiments either of the Ancients or Moderns; let us do justice to both and value merit wherever it be, without minding whether it be old or new.

22] But though a man may have his mind sufficiently armed against the prejudices that arise from the authority of the Ancients and the inclination that he may have to the Modern, yet has he hardly ever the power to strip himself wholly of the natural love which he has for his own opinions. That is one of the great infirmities of the mind of man, because self-love believes nothing to be so much its own as its opinion: men look upon that as a creature of their own and renounce all other interests to maintain this. . . .

*   *   *

IV] REFLEXIONS ON NATURAL PHILOSOPHY

1] I very well conceive that man may frame to himself principles of Logic and Moral Philosophy, because reasoning and manners, which are the object of these two sciences, are the work of man; but I cannot conceive how he dares form principles of Natural Philosophy, whereof Nature is the object, and that the Work of God. In effect what means have we to know the design of the Creator who many times have not understanding enough to know the designs of the creature? Did God advise with you, when he suspended in the air the foundations of the earth, to frame a universe? And which of the philosophers hath sounded that eternal wisdom, which was before all things, that he might discover the depth of his thoughts? St. Augustine says that the world is a great theatre where the art of him that made it shines forth on all hands; but is it not rather a great riddle that the philosophers have essayed to explain without being able to succeed in it? It is true that there have been minds sufficiently qualified to know the effects of Nature by examining their causes, but never was there any as yet capable of seeing into the intentions of the Creator and of discovering the hidden secrets of his art by knowing the principles of this great work. For if the smallest creatures that are within the reach of our senses, and that we have so long studied, have something that is incomprehensible, if the smallest herbs of the fields have qualities unknown to man, shall we be so vain as to pretend to know the virtue of those great machines that compose the world and to ascend to the source of all the wonders that we admire therein? Let us not deceive ourselves: Nature hath her mysteries; she attains her ends by ways that we are ignorant of; and since men have applied themselves to the knowledge of her secrets, there hath been so little of certainty discovered that one would think nothing should more bring down the pride of man than the study of Natural Philosophy. It is an abstruse and profound science, wherein there is little agreed upon amongst men. Those that have spoken of it best have as yet said nothing to the purpose; therefore let us not beat our brains to

imagine new systems. That matter hath already passed through so
many heads that if there had been any better than what we know,
it would have been found out; indeed, after so much thinking on
the matter, it is even wisdom to mind it no more and to content
ourselves, by an humble acknowledgment of our own ignorance, to
admire the depth of the knowledge of God. It is true, there is
nothing so capable fully to satisfy the mind of man as the consideration of Nature and natural beings; no other science tickles so
much our curiosity. Happy is he that can know anything thereof;
but Nature shows herself to us only by her outside. The knowledge
that we have of her is but superficial, and God Almighty, to punish
our pride, takes pleasure to abandon us to our curiosity, as to a
chastisement; because by inspiring into us a desire to know all
things, He reduces us to the pass of being ignorant of all, and even
of ourselves.

2] But by how much that science is vain through the obscurity and
uncertainty of the matters it treats of, by so much it is frivolous
through the diversity of opinions that are to be found in the sentiments of the greatest men who studied it; for all the Ancient Philosophy hath hardly as yet been able to establish any principle that
is agreed upon. . . .

[Rapin continues with a destructive criticism of Natural Philosophers, Ancient and Modern.]

6

The Newtonian System

SIR ISAAC NEWTON (1642–1727), though a man of humble origin, was educated at Cambridge, where he graduated in 1665 and was elected fellow of Trinity College in 1667. It was at Cambridge in the 1660's that Newton conceived his major discoveries: the binomial theorem, the differential calculus, investigation of the forces of gravity in connection with the orbit of the moon, and his first experiments in optics. Though twice elected to Parliament, Newton shunned direct involvement in politics, except when James II tried to meddle in university appointments at Cambridge. In 1701 he was appointed Master of the Mint; resigning his positions at Cambridge, he settled in London. From 1703 until his death Newton was President of the Royal Society, of which he had been a member since 1672. In 1705 Queen Anne conferred knighthood on Newton.

In 1687 Newton published his Philosophiae Naturalis Principia Mathematica, which was first translated into English in 1729 by Motte; its cosmology reigned virtually unchallenged until the twentieth century. Some of the positions adumbrated in the Principia are further developed in the Opticks, on which Newton worked on and off from 1675 until it was published in 1704. Selections from these two works are given here. Newton also wrote a number of theological treatises, some of which have not been published to this day.

a. Newton, The Principia

PREFACE TO THE FIRST EDITION

SINCE the Ancients (as we are told by Pappus) esteemed the science of mechanics of greatest importance in the investigation of natural things, and the moderns, rejecting substantial forms and occult qualities, have endeavored to subject the phenomena of nature to the laws of mathematics, I have in this treatise cultivated mathematics as far as it relates to philosophy. The ancients considered mechanics in a twofold respect; as rational, which proceeds accurately by demonstration, and practical. To practical mechanics all the manual arts belong, from which mechanics took its name. But as artificers do not work with perfect accuracy, it comes to pass that mechanics is so distinguished from geometry that what is perfectly accurate is called geometrical; what is less so, is called mechanical. However, the errors are not in the art, but in the artificers. He that works with less accuracy is an imperfect mechanic; and if any could work with perfect accuracy, he would be the most perfect mechanic of all, for the description of right lines and circles, upon which geometry is founded, belongs to mechanics. Geometry does not teach us to draw these lines, but requires them to be drawn, for it requires that the learner should first be taught to describe these accurately before he enters upon geometry, then it shows how by these operations problems may be solved. To describe right lines and circles are problems, but not geometrical problems. The solution of these problems is required from mechanics, and by geometry the use of them, when so solved, is shown; and it is the glory of geometry that from those few principles, brought from without, it is able to produce so many things. Therefore geometry is founded in mechanical practice, and is nothing but that part of universal mechanics which accurately proposes and demonstrates the art of

From Sir Isaac Newton, Mathematical Principles of Natural Philosophy and his System of the World, trans. by Andrew Motte, rev. by Florian Cajori, 2 vols. (Berkeley and Los Angeles, 1962), I, pp. xvii–xviii; II, pp. 397–400, 543–547. Reprinted by permission of the University of California Press. Opticks: Isaaci Newtoni Opera quae exstant omnia, ed. by Samuel Horsley, 5 vols. (London, 1779–1785), IV, pp. 237–238. 258–264. No alterations have been made in spelling; punctuation has been modernized.

measuring. But since the manual arts are chiefly employed in the moving of bodies, it happens that geometry is commonly referred to their magnitude, and mechanics to their motion. In this sense rational mechanics will be the science of motions resulting from any forces whatsoever, and of the forces required to produce any motions, accurately proposed and demonstrated. This part of mechanics, as far as it extended to the five powers which relate to manual arts, was cultivated by the ancients, who considered gravity (it not being a manual power) no otherwise than in moving weights by those powers. But I consider philosophy rather than arts and write not concerning manual but natural powers, and consider chiefly those things which relate to gravity, levity, elastic force, the resistance of fluids, and the like forces, whether attractive or impulsive; and therefore I offer this work as the mathematical principles of philosophy, for the whole burden of philosophy seems to consist in this — from the phenomena of motions to investigate the forces of nature, and then from these forces to demonstrate the other phenomena; and to this end the general propositions in the first and second Books are directed. In the third Book I give an example of this in the explication of the System of the World; for by the propositions mathematically demonstrated in the former Books, in the third I derive from the celestial phenomena the forces of gravity with which bodies tend to the sun and the several planets. Then from these forces, by other propositions which are also mathematical, I deduce the motions of the planets, the comets, the moon, and the sea. I wish we could derive the rest of the phenomena of Nature by the same kind of reasoning from mechanical principles, for I am induced by many reasons to suspect that they may all depend upon certain forces by which the particles of bodies, by some causes hitherto unknown, are either mutually impelled towards one another, and cohere in regular figures, or are repelled and recede from one another. These forces being unknown, philosophers have hitherto attempted the search of Nature in vain; but I hope the principles here laid down will afford some light either to this or some truer method of philosophy. . . .

III] SYSTEM OF THE WORLD

IN the preceding books I have laid down the principles of philosophy; principles not philosophical but mathematical: such, namely, as we may build our reasonings upon in philosophical inquiries. These principles are the laws and conditions of certain motions, and powers or forces, which chiefly have respect to philosophy; but, lest they should have appeared of themselves dry and barren, I have illustrated them here and there with some philosophical scholiums, giving an account of such things as are of more general nature, and which philosophy seems chiefly to be founded on; such as the density and the resistance of bodies, spaces void of all bodies, and the motion of light and sounds. It remains that, from the same principles, I now demonstrate the frame of the System of the World. Upon this subject I had, indeed, composed the third Book in a popular method, that it might be read by many; but afterwards, considering that such as had not sufficiently entered into the principles could not easily discern the strength of the consequences, nor lay aside the prejudices to which they had been many years accustomed, therefore, to prevent the disputes which might be raised upon such accounts, I chose to reduce the substance of this Book into the form of Propositions (in the mathematical way), which should be read by those only who had first made themselves masters of the principles established in the preceding Books: not that I would advise anyone to the previous study of every Proposition of those Books; for they abound with such as might cost too much time, even to readers of good mathematical learning. It is enough if one carefully reads the Definitions, the Laws of Motion, and the first three sections of the first Book. He may then pass on to this Book, and consult such of the remaining Propositions of the first two Books, as the references in this, and his occasions, shall require.

RULES OF REASONING IN PHILOSOPHY

I. We are to admit no more causes of natural things than such as are both true and sufficient to explain their appearances.

To this purpose the philosophers say that Nature does nothing in vain, and more is in vain when less will serve; for Nature is pleased with simplicity, and affects not the pomp of superfluous causes.

II. Therefore to the same natural effects we must, as far as possible, assign the same causes.

As to respiration in a man and in a beast; the descent of stones in *Europe* and in *America;* the light of our culinary fire and of the sun; the reflection of light in the earth, and in the planets.

III. The qualities of bodies, which admit neither intensification nor remission of degrees, and which are found to belong to all bodies within the reach of our experiments, are to be esteemed the universal qualities of all bodies whatsoever.

For since the qualities of bodies are only known to us by experiments, we are to hold for universal all such as universally agree with experiments; and such as are not liable to diminution can never be quite taken away. We are certainly not to relinquish the evidence of experiments for the sake of dreams and vain fictions of our own devising; nor are we to recede from the analogy of Nature, which is wont to be simple, and always consonant to itself. We no other way know the extension of bodies than by our senses, nor do these reach it in all bodies; but because we perceive extension in all that are sensible, therefore we ascribe it universally to all others also. That abundance of bodies are hard, we learn by experience; and because the hardness of the whole arises from the hardness of the parts, we therefore justly infer the hardness of the undivided particles not only of the bodies we feel but of all others. That all bodies are impenetrable, we gather not from reason, but from sensation. The bodies which we handle we find impenetrable, and thence conclude impenetrability to be an universal property of all bodies whatsoever. That all bodies are movable, and endowed with certain powers (which we call the inertia) of persevering in their motion, or in their rest, we only infer from the like properties observed in the bodies which we have seen. The extension, hardness, impenetrability, mobility, and inertia of the whole, result from the extension, hardness, impenetrability, mobility, and inertia of the parts; and hence we conclude the least particles of all bodies to be also all extended, and hard and impenetrable, and movable, and endowed with their proper inertia. And this is the foundation of all philosophy. Moreover, that the divided but contiguous particles of bodies may be separated from one another, is matter of observation; and, in the particles that remain undivided, our minds are able to distinguish yet lesser parts, as is mathematically demonstrated. But whether the parts so distinguished, and not yet divided, may, by the powers of Nature, be actually divided and separated from one another, we cannot certainly determine. Yet, had we the proof of but one experiment that any undivided particle, in breaking a hard and solid body, suffered a division, we might by virtue of this rule conclude that the undivided as well as the divided particles may be divided and actually separated to infinity.

Lastly, if it universally appears, by experiments and astronomical observations, that all bodies about the earth gravitate towards the earth, and that in proportion to the quantity of matter which they severally contain; that the moon likewise, according to the quantity of its matter, gravitates towards the earth; that, on the other hand, our sea gravitates towards the moon; and all the planets one towards another; and the comets in like manner towards the sun; we must, in consequence of this rule, universally allow that all bodies whatsoever are endowed with a principle of mutual gravitation. For the argument from the appearances concludes with more force for the universal gravitation of all bodies than for their impenetrability; of which, among those in the celestial regions, we have no experiments, nor any manner of observation. Not that I affirm gravity to be essential to bodies: by their *vis insita* I mean nothing but their inertia. This is immutable. Their gravity is diminished as they recede from the earth.

IV. In experimental philosophy we are to look upon propositions inferred by general induction from phenomena as accurately or very nearly true, notwithstanding any contrary hypotheses that may be imagined, till such time as other phenomena occur, by which they may either be made more accurate, or liable to exceptions.

This rule we must follow, that the argument of induction may not be evaded by hypotheses.

*   *   *

GENERAL SCHOLIUM[1]

*   *   *

Bodies projected in our air suffer no resistance but from the air. Withdraw the air, as is done in Mr. *Boyle's* vacuum, and the resistance ceases; for in this void a bit of fine down and a piece of solid gold descend with equal velocity. And the same argument must apply to the celestial spaces above the earth's atmosphere; in these spaces, where there is no air to resist their motions, all bodies will move with the greatest freedom; and the planets and comets will constantly pursue their revolutions in orbits given in kind and position, according to the laws above explained; but though these bodies may, indeed, continue in their orbits by the mere laws of gravity, yet they could by no means have at first derived the regular position of the orbits themselves from those laws.

The six primary planets are revolved about the sun in circles concentric with the sun, and with motions directed towards the same parts, and almost in the same plane. Ten moons are revolved about the earth, Jupiter, and Saturn, in circles concentric with them, with the same direction of motion, and nearly in the planes of the orbits of those planets; but it is not to be conceived that mere mechanical causes could give birth to so many regular motions, since the comets range over all parts of the heavens in very eccentric orbits; for by that kind of motion they pass easily through the orbs of the planets, and with great rapidity; and in their aphelions,[2] where they move the slowest, and are detained the longest, they recede to the greatest distances from each other, and hence suffer the least disturbance from their mutual attractions. This most beautiful system of the sun, planets, and comets, could only proceed from the counsel and dominion of an intelligent and powerful Being. And if the fixed stars are the centres of other like systems, these, being formed by the like wise counsel, must be all subject to the dominion of One; especially since the light of the fixed stars is of the same nature with the light of the sun, and from every system light passes into all the other systems: and lest the systems of the fixed stars should, by their gravity, fall on each other, he hath placed those systems at immense distances from one another.

This Being governs all things, not as the soul of the world, but as Lord over all; and on account of his dominion he is wont to be called *Lord God* παντοκράτωρ, or *Universal Ruler;* for *God* is a relative word, and has a respect to servants; and *Deity* is the dominion of God not over his own body, as those imagine who fancy God to be the soul of the world, but over servants. The Supreme God is a Being eternal, infinite, absolutely perfect; but a being, however perfect, without dominion, cannot be said to be Lord God; for we say, my God, your God, the God of *Israel,* the God of Gods, and Lord of Lords; but we do not say, my Eternal, your Eternal, the Eternal of *Israel,* the Eternal of Gods; we do not say, my Infinite, or my Perfect: these are titles which have no respect to servants. The word God usually signifies *Lord;* but every lord is not a God. It is the dominion of a spiritual being which constitutes a God: a true, supreme, or imaginary dominion makes a true, supreme, or imaginary God. And from his true dominion it follows that the true God is a living, intelligent, and powerful Being; and, from his other perfections, that he is supreme, or most perfect. He is eternal and infinite, omnipotent and omniscient; that is, his duration reaches from eternity to eternity; his presence from infinity to infinity; he governs all things, and knows all things that are or can be done. He is not eternity and infinity, but eternal and infinite; he is not duration or space, but he endures and is present. He endures forever, and is everywhere present; and, by existing always and everywhere, he constitutes duration and space. Since every particle of space is *always,* and every indivisible moment of duration is *everywhere,* certainly the Maker and Lord of all things cannot be *never* and *nowhere.* Every soul that has perception is, though in different times and in different organs of sense and motion, still the same indivisible person. There are given successive parts in duration, coexistent parts in space, but neither the one nor the other in the person of a man, of his thinking principle; and much less can they be found in the thinking substance of God. Every man, so far as he is a thing that has perception, is one and the same man during his whole life, in all and each of his organs of sense. God is the same God, always and everywhere. He is omnipresent not *virtually* only, but also *substantially;* for virtue cannot subsist without substance. In him are all things contained and moved; yet neither affects the other: God suffers nothing from the motion of bodies; bodies find no resistance from the omnipresence of God. It is allowed by all that the Supreme God exists necessarily; and by the same necessity he exists *always* and *everywhere.* Whence also he is all similar, all eye, all ear, all brain, all arm, all power to perceive, to understand, and to act; but in a manner not at all human, in a manner not at all corporeal, in a manner utterly unknown to us. As a blind man has no idea of colors, so have we no idea of the manner by which the all-wise God perceives and understands all things. He is utterly void of all body and bodily figure, and can therefore neither be seen, nor heard, nor touched; nor ought he to be worshiped under the representation of any corporeal thing. We have ideas of his attributes, but what the real substance of anything is we know not. In bodies, we see only their figures and colors, we hear only the sounds, we touch only their outward surfaces, we smell only the smells, and taste the savors; but their inward substances are not to be known either by our senses, or by any reflex act of our minds: much less, then, have we any idea of the substance of God. We know him only by his most wise and excellent contrivances of things, and final causes; we admire him for his perfections; but we reverence and adore him on account of his dominion: for we adore him as his servants; and a god without dominion, providence, and final causes, is nothing else but Fate and Nature. Blind metaphysical necessity, which is certainly the same always and everywhere, could produce no variety of things. All that diversity of natural things which we find suited to different times and places could arise from nothing but the ideas and will of a Being necessarily existing. But, by way of allegory, God is said to see, to speak, to laugh, to love, to hate, to desire, to give, to receive, to rejoice, to be angry, to fight, to frame, to work, to build; for all our notions of God are taken from the ways of mankind by a certain similitude, which, though not perfect, has some likeness, however. and thus much concerning God; to discourse of whom from the appearances of things, does certainly belong to Natural Philosophy.

Hitherto we have explained the phenomena of the heavens and of our sea by the power of gravity, but have not yet assigned the cause of this power. This is certain, that it must proceed from a cause that penetrates to the very centres of the sun and planets, without suffering the least diminution of its force; that operates not according to the quantity of the surfaces of the particles upon which it acts (as mechanical causes used to do), but according to the quantity of the solid matter which they contain, and propagates its virtue on all sides to immense distances, decreasing always as the inverse square of the distances. Gravitation towards the sun is made up out of the gravitations towards the several particles of which the body of the sun is composed; and in receding from the sun decreases accurately as the inverse square of the distances as far as the orbit of Saturn, as evidently appears from the quiescence of the aphelion of the planets; nay, and even to the remotest aphelion of the comets, if those aphelions are also quiescent. But hitherto I have not been able to discover the cause of those properties of gravity from phenomena, and I frame no hypothesis; for whatever is not deduced from the phenomena is to be called an hypothesis; and hypotheses, whether metaphysical or physical, whether of occult qualities or mechanical, have no place in experimental philosophy. In this philosophy particular propositions are inferred from the phenomena, and afterwards rendered general by induction. Thus it was that the impenetrability, the mobility, and the impulsive force of bodies, and the laws of motion and of gravitation, were discovered. And to us it is enough that gravity does really exist, and act according to the laws which we have explained, and abundantly serves to account for all the motions of the celestial bodies, and of our sea.

And now we might add something concerning a certain most subtle spirit which pervades and lies hid in all gross bodies; by the force and action of which spirit the particles of bodies attract one another at near distances, and cohere, if contiguous; and electric bodies operate to greater distances, as well repelling as attracting the neighboring corpuscles; and light is emitted, reflected, refracted, inflected, and heats bodies; and all sensation is excited, and the members of animal bodies move to the command of the will, namely, by the vibrations of this spirit, mutually propagated along the solid filaments of the nerves, from the outward organs of sense to the brain, and from the brain into the muscles. But these are things that cannot be explained in few words, nor are we furnished with that sufficiency of experiments which is required to an accurate determination and demonstration of the laws by which this electric and elastic spirit operates.

[End of the *Principia*]

b.

Opticks

III. 1] . . . The main business of natural philosophy is to argue from phaenomena without feigning hypotheses, and to deduce causes from effects, till we come to the very First Cause, which certainly is not mechanical; and not only to unfold the mechanism of the world, but chiefly to resolve these and such like questions: What is there in places almost empty of Matter, and whence it is that the sun and planets gravitate towards one another, without dense matter between them? Whence is it that Nature doth nothing in vain; and whence arises all that order and beauty which we see in the world? To what end are comets, and whence is it that planets move all one and the same way in orbs concentrick, while comets move all manner of ways in orbs very excentrick; and what hinders the fixed stars from falling upon one another? How came the bodies of animals to be contrived with so much Art, and for what ends were their several Parts? Was the eye contrived without skill in Opticks, and the ear without knowledge of sounds? How do the motions of the body follow from the will, and whence is the instinct in animals? Is not the sensory[3] of animals that place to which the sensitive substance is present, and into which the sensible species of things are carried through the nerves and brain, that there they may be perceived by their immediate presence to that substance? And these things being rightly dispatched does it not appear from phaenomena that there is a Being incorporeal, living, intelligent, omnipresent, who, in infinite space, as it were in his Sensory, sees the things themselves intimately, and throughly perceives them, and comprehends them wholly by their immediate presence to himself: of which things the images only, carried through the organs of sense into our little sensoriums, are there seen and beheld by that which in us perceives and thinks. And though every true step made in this philosophy brings us not immediately to the knowledge of the First Cause, yet it brings us nearer to it, and on that account is to be highly valued.

* * *

And thus Nature will be very conformable to herself and very simple, performing all the great motions of the heavenly bodies by the attraction of gravity which intercedes those bodies, and almost all the small ones of their particles by some other Attractive and Repelling powers which intercede the particles. The *vis inertiae* is a passive principle, by which bodies persist in their motion or rest, receive motion in proportion to the force impressing it, and resist as much as they are resisted. By this principle alone there never could have been any motion in the world. Some other principle was necessary for putting bodies into motion; and now they are in motion, some other principle is necessary for conserving the motion. For from the various composition of two motions, it is very certain that there is not always the same Quantity of motion in the world. For if two globes joined by a slender rod revolve about their common center of gravity with a uniform motion, while the center moves on uniformly in a right line drawn in the plane of their circular motion, the sum of the motions of the two globes, as often as the globes are in the right line described by their common center of gravity, will be bigger than the sum of their motions when they are in a line perpendicular to that right line. By this instance it appears that motion may be got or lost. But by reason of the tenacity of fluids, and attrition of their parts, and the weakness of elasticity in solids, motion is much more apt to be lost than got, and is always upon the decay. . . . Seeing therefore the variety of motion which we find in the world is always decreasing, there is a necessity of conserving and recruiting it by active principles, such as are the cause of gravity, by which planets and comets keep their motions in their orbs, and bodies acquire great motion in falling; and the cause of fermentation, by which the heart and blood of animals are kept in perpetual motion and heat; the inward parts of the earth are constantly warmed, and in some places grow very hot; bodies burn and shine, mountains take fire, the caverns of the earth are blown up, and the sun continues violently hot and lucid, and warms all things by his light. For we meet with very little motion in the world, besides what is owing to these active principles. And if it were not for these principles, the bodies of the earth, planets, comets, sun, and all things in them would grow cold and freeze, and become inactive masses; and all putrefaction, generation, vegetation, and life would cease, and the planets and comets would not remain in their orbs.

And these things being considered, it seems probable to me, that God in the beginning formed matter in solid, massy, hard, impenetrable, moveable particles, of such sizes and figures, and with such other properties, and in such proportion to space, as most conduced to the end for which he formed them; and that these primitive particles, being solids, are incomparably harder than any porous bodies compounded of them; even so very hard, as never to wear or break in pieces; no ordinary power being able to divide what God himself made One in the first creation. While the particles continue entire, they may compose bodies of one and the same nature and texture in all ages: but should they wear away, or break in pieces, the nature of things depending on them would be changed. Water and earth, composed of old worn particles and fragments of particles, would not be of the same nature and texture now with water and earth composed of entire particles in the beginning. And therefore, that nature may be lasting, the changes of corporeal things are to be placed only in the various separations and new associations and motions of these permanent particles; compound bodies being apt to break not in the midst of solid particles, but where those particles are laid together and only touch in a few points.

It seems to me farther, that these particles have not only a *Vis inertiae,* accompanied with such Passive laws of motion as naturally result from that force, but also that they are moved by certain Active principles, such as that of gravity, and that which causes fermentation and the cohesion of bodies. These principles I consider not as Occult qualities, supposed to result from the specifick forms of things, but as general laws of Nature, by which the things themselves are formed; their truth appearing to us by phaenomena, though their causes be not yet discovered. For these are manifest qualities, and their causes only are occult. And the *Aristotelians* gave the name of Occult qualities not to manifest qualities, but to such qualities only as they supposed to lie hid in bodies, and to the unknown causes of manifest effects: such as would be the causes of gravity, and of Magnetick and Electrick attractions, and of fermentations, if we should suppose that these forces or actions arose from qualities unknown to us, and uncapable of being discovered and made manifest. Such Occult qualities put a stop to the improvement of Natural Philosophy, and therefore of late years have been rejected. To tell us that every species of things is endowed with an occult specifick quality by which it acts and produces manifest effects, is to tell us nothing. But to derive two or three general principles of motion from phaenomena, and afterwards to tell us how the properties and actions of all corporeal things follow from those manifest principles, would be a very great step in philosophy, though the causes of those principles were not yet discovered. And therefore I scruple not to propose the principles of motion above mentioned, they being of very general extent, and leave their causes to be found out.

Now, by the help of these principles, all material things seem to have been composed of the hard and solid particles above-mentioned, variously associated in the first creation by the counsel of an intelligent Agent. For it became Him who created them to set them in order. And if he did so, it is unphilosophical to seek for any other origin of the world, or to pretend that it might arise out of a Chaos by the mere laws of Nature; though being once formed, it may continue by those laws for many ages. For while comets move in very excentrick orbs in all manner of positions, blind Fate could never make all the planets move one and the same way in orbs concentrick, some inconsiderable irregularities excepted, which may have risen from the mutual actions of comets and planets upon one another, and which will be apt to increase, till this system wants a reformation. Such a wonderful uniformity in the planetary system must be allowed the effect of choice. And so must the uniformity in the bodies of animals, they having generally a right and a left side shaped alike, and on either side of their bodies two legs behind, and either two arms or two legs, or two wings before upon their shoulders, and between their shoulders a neck running down into a back-bone, and a head upon it; and in the head two ears, two eyes, a nose, a mouth, and a tongue, alike situated. Also the first contrivance of those very artificial parts of animals, the eyes, ears, brain, muscles, heart, lungs, midriff, glands, larynx, hands, wings, swimming bladders, natural spectacles, and other organs of sense and motion; and the instinct of brutes and insects, can be the effect of nothing else than the wisdom and skill of a powerful ever-living Agent, who, being in all places, is more able by his will to move the bodies within his boundless uniform sensorium, and thereby to form and reform the parts of the universe, than we are by our will to move the parts of our own bodies.

And yet we are not to consider the world as the body of God, or the several parts thereof as the parts of God. He is an uniform Being, void of organs, members, or parts, and they are his creatures subordinate to him and subservient to his will; and he is no more the soul of them, than the soul of a man is the soul of the species of things carried through the organs of sense into the place of its sensation, where it perceives them by means of its immediate presence, without the intervention of any third thing. The organs of sense are not for enabling the soul to perceive the species of things in its sensorium, but only for conveying them thither; and God has no need of such organs, he being every where present to the things themselves. And since space is divisible *in infinitum,* and Matter is not necessary in all places, it may be also allowed that God is able to create particles of matter of several sizes and figures, and in several proportions to space, and perhaps of different densities and forces, and thereby to vary the laws of Nature, and make worlds of several sorts in several parts of the universe. At least, I see nothing of contradiction in all this.

As in Mathematicks, so in Natural Philosophy, the investigation of difficult things by the method of analysis ought ever to precede the method of composition. This analysis consists in making experiments and observations, and in drawing general conclusions from them by induction, and admitting of no objections against the conclusions, but such as are taken from experiments, or other certain truths. For hypotheses are not to be regarded in Experimental Philosophy. And although the arguing from experiments and observations by induction be no demonstration of general conclusions, yet it is the best way of arguing which the nature of things admits of, and may be looked upon as so much the stronger by how much the induction is more general. And if no exception occur from phaenomena, the conclusion may be pronounced generally. But if at any time afterwards any exception shall occur from experiments, it may then begin to be pronounced with such exceptions as occur. By this way of analysis we proceed from compounds to ingredients, and from motions to the forces producing them; and, in general, from effects to their causes, and from particular causes to more general ones, till the argument end in the most general. This is the method of Analysis. And the Synthesis consists in assuming the causes discovered and established as principles, and by them explaining the phaenomena proceeding from them, and proving the explanations.

. . . And if Natural Philosophy in all its parts, by pursuing this method, shall at length be perfected, the bounds of Moral Philosophy will also be enlarged. For so far as we can know by Natural Philosophy what is the First cause, what power he has over us, and what benefits we receive from him, so far our duty towards him, as well as that towards one another, will appear to us by the light of Nature. And no doubt, if the worship of false gods had not blinded the heathen, their Moral Philosophy would have gone farther than to the four Cardinal Virtues; and instead of teaching the transmigration of souls, and to worship the sun and moon, and dead heroes, they would have taught us to worship our true Author and Bene-

factor, as their ancestors did under the government of Noah and his
sons before they corrupted themselves.

[End of the *Opticks*.]

NOTES

1. Explanatory comment.
2. Point of the orbit farthest from the sun.
3. Sensory, or sensorium: the seat of sensation.

7

Classicism in the Visual Arts

ANDRÉ FÉLIBIEN, sieur des Avaux et de Javercy (1619–1695) went to Rome in 1647 as a secretary to the French ambassador; it was there that he developed an abiding interest in the plastic arts, both ancient and modern, and began to write on painting, sculpture, and architecture. After his return to France, he enjoyed the protection first of Nicolas Fouquet, Superintendent of Finances and himself a connoisseur of the arts, and later of Colbert; the latter, though lacking in personal appreciation of art, understood its value as an asset to the French monarchy. Félibien was made "historiographer of the buildings," then Secretary to the Academy of Architecture (1671), and later curator of the "Cabinet of Antiquities" (1673). Between 1666 and 1688 he published five volumes of Discussions on the Lives and Works of the Most Illustrious Painters, Ancient and Modern, in the form of dialogues between himself and an imaginary friend, Pymander. In the passage quoted here, Félibien summarizes his remarks on Nicolas Poussin (1594–1665), who had established the "classical style" of painting in France on a firm foundation. Like Félibien, Poussin was strongly influenced by his experience in Rome, where he spent most of his life.

Félibien, Discussion of Poussin's Paintings

"I DON'T ASK," said Pymander, "that you try to remember any more paintings; you have named quite enough. But continue, if you don't mind, with your analysis of the great qualities of this illustrious painter. For although I believe that I am well acquainted with him from what I have seen of his work and from what I have just heard you say, I confess that I had not suspected that he held

From André Félibien, Entretiens sur les Vies et sur les Ouvrages des plus excellens Peintres, anciens et modernes, IV (Paris, 1685), pp. 400–410. English translation in Ideas and Institutions in European History, 800–1715, Ed. by T. C. Mendenhall, B. D. Henning, and A. S. Foord (New York, 1948). Reprinted by permission of Holt, Rinehart and Winston, Inc.

such a considerable place among the most celebrated painters; and I am delighted that France has produced a man so distinguished that the Italians themselves, as you said so often, have recognized him as the Raphael of France."

"It is true," I replied, "that France and Italy have never had more expert painters. They greatly resemble each other in the grandeur of their conceptions, in their choice of noble and lofty subjects, in the good taste of their drawing, the beautiful and natural disposition of their figures, in their strong and vivid expression of all the feelings of the soul. Both are more interested in form than in color, and have preferred that which interests and satisfies the reason and the spirit to that which satisfies only the eyes. Also, the more one considers their work, the more one loves and admires them.

"Please do not imagine that the comparison I make between these two men is a means I use to praise Poussin all the more. I do not intend to establish his worth by comparing his works to those of great painters, either those of the past, those of his own period, or those who have worked since, no matter in what country. Each one has had particular talents; and if some of them have possessed great talent, I do not believe that for such a reason one should lessen the esteem in which Poussin is held. I have at other times talked to you of the different qualities which gave Titian and Correggio their reputations: the excellence and singular beauty of their work did not prevent people from considering Raphael as their master since he possessed qualities so great that they made him unequalled.

"But if one wished to make some distinction between Raphael and Poussin one could say that Raphael received from Heaven his knowledge and the skill of his brush, whereas Poussin's wonderful understanding and everything that was marvellous in his art derived from the force of his genius and from the extent of his studies.

"In order to evaluate correctly our foremost French painter, it is necessary to consider him alone, without comparing him to others; and taking into account his particular talents, one would have difficulty finding among those I have mentioned any who could be compared to him.

"It seems to me that I have acquainted you adequately with the force of his inventive genius and his good taste in choosing only great and illustrious subjects. The paintings which I have described to you must have convinced you of his knowledge of composition. You have been able to see the science behind the art of drawing figures, giving the proper proportions to people according to sex, age, and different conditions. It was he who first made apparent the admirable art of handling subjects in the most noble way, and who, like a torch, shed light on what others had done only in disorder and confusion.

"He studied continuously everything pertaining to his profession and never started a picture without first having thought over carefully the positions of the figures, all of which he drew with great care. One could even tell from his first ideas and simple sketches that he made of them that his work would be as good as could be expected of him. He put out on the table little models which he covered with clothes to judge the effect and the arrangement of all the figures together; and tried so hard to make things true to life that I have seen him considering stones, lumps of earth, and even pieces of wood, in order to secure a better imitation of terraces and tree trunks. He painted carefully and in a very special manner. The colors arranged on his palette were always the right ones so that he never made an unnecessary stroke of the brush and never mixed his colors. It is true that his hand shook, so that he could not work as easily as other painters, but the force of his genius and his good judgment made up for the weakness of his hand.

"No matter what he was working on, he never acted with undue energy. He took things easily, never seeming more tired at the end of his work than at the beginning, because the fire that warmed his imagination was always of the same strength. The light which illuminated his thoughts was of uniform quality, always pure and unclouded. Even though he was forced to show vehemence and sometimes anger and indignation in his pictures, even though he was obliged to depict sorrow, he never got too upset, but always acted with the same prudence and wisdom. When he wanted poetic subjects he painted them in a flowery and elegant manner; and if, in the Bacchanals, he had to please and amuse the humorous actions and ways in which one sees them, he nevertheless has done so with more gravity and modesty than many other painters who have taken too many liberties.

"It is true that one can see in his work, as if it were a special skill, the care which he has taken to paint with love and charm this kind of subject, embellishing them more than the historical subjects he painted, in which are found pure and well adorned but unlabored truths, and in which he often dispensed with some of the opulence the subjects should have had, the lack being compensated for by the beauty of the figures. . . .

"One never sees depicted in his paintings any motions which do not seem suitable to the people who make them. That disagreeable foreshortening, that unreality of uneasy and often ridiculous poses and action, for which certain painters seek, and for which they have such a strong preference because they say this gives more life to their figures, are never found in Poussin's pictures. Everything in his work seems natural, easy, suitable and agreeable; each person does gracefully and well what he should be doing.

"He succeeded just as well in expressing all the passions of the soul. I have pointed out to you that no matter what sort they are, he never exaggerates them; he knows exactly to what degree they should be recorded. And what is more, he knows perfectly how to discern the people capable of strong emotions, and in what manner to depict them.

"One can find nothing too studied, nor too carelessly treated, in his pictures. The buildings, the clothes, all the arrangements generally, are suitable to his subject. Light and shadow are diffused as nature shows them. He does not try to make his figures seem nobler nor to make them seem stronger or weaker than they should be. He understands perfectly the relationship between colors, and even though he uses clear and bright colors equally in the foreground and background, he disperses them, weakens them, and arranges them so that none of them nullifies another. And they always give a good effect. I have talked so often to you of his skill in painting all sorts of landscapes and making them pleasing and natural, that one can say that, excepting Titian, one cannot find a painter who has done any comparable to his. He painted all kinds of trees perfectly, expressing their differences and their motion. He arranged terraces in a natural but well chosen way, made water look clear, embellishing it with reflections of adjacent objects, decorated the fields and hills with cities and well constructed buildings, making the farthest objects look smaller with wonderful skill; and, which gives his work that special quality, depicting the atmosphere of different days by arrangements of clouds and vapors rising in the air, knowing exactly the difference between those of morning and evening. . . .

"That is the way in which he painted perfectly all kinds of subjects, even the most extraordinary aspects of Nature, no matter how difficult they might be to represent, adding to his landscapes suitable stories or actions. . . .

"Should not all these things which I have been telling you be considered favorable to Poussin without our being also obliged to wait for the judgment of some acknowledged authority?"

"Indeed," said Pymander, "I believe that what is approved by the public should also be approved by the more erudite men. The great esteem in which everyone holds Poussin's paintings constitutes a kind of popular judgment in which I see no difference of opinion between the ignorant and the more educated.". . . .

8

Natural Law

HUIG DE GROOT, better known as Hugo Grotius (1583–1645), a Dutch
lawyer, diplomat, and magistrate, was the author of many treatises and
state papers. After the fall of his mentor, the Grand Pensionary
Oldenbarnevelt, Grotius was condemned to life imprisonment in the
fortress of Loevestein. Nevertheless, in 1621, he contrived to escape in
a wooden box that was normally used to carry his books to and from
prison; he spent most of the rest of his life in Paris. In 1622 Grotius
began to write his most famous work, De Jure Belli ac Pacis Libri Tres
(Three Books on the Law of War and Peace), which first appeared in
1625. In subsequent editions Grotius revised and expanded his work,
without changing its fundamental frame of reference; the last, and
definitive, edition appeared in Amsterdam in 1646. The excerpts below
are taken from the Prolegomena, or Foreword, to Grotius's magnum
opus.

Grotius, On the Law of War and Peace

PROLEGOMENA

1] THE municipal law of Rome and of other states has been
treated by many, who have undertaken to elucidate it by means
of commentaries or to reduce it to a convenient digest. That body
of law, however, which is concerned with the mutual relations
among states or rulers of states, whether derived from nature, or established by divine ordinances, or having its origin in custom and tacit

From Hugo Grotius, De Jure Belli ac Pacis Libri Tres, trans. by Francis
W. Kelsey and others (Oxford: The Clarendon Press, 1925): Publication sponsored by the Carnegie Endowment for International Peace,
Division of International Law, No. 3, ed. by James Brown Scott, II, pp.
9–21, 23–24, 26–30. Reprinted by permission of the Carnegie Endowment for International Peace.

agreement, few have touched upon. Up to the present time no one has treated it in a comprehensive and systematic manner; yet the welfare of mankind demands that this task be accomplished. . . .

3] Such a work is all the more necessary because in our day, as in former times, there is no lack of men who view this branch of law with contempt as having no reality outside of an empty name. On the lips of men quite generally is the saying of Euphemus, which Thucydides quotes, that in the case of a king or imperial city nothing is unjust which is expedient. Of like implication is the statement that for those whom fortune favors might makes right, and that the administration of a state cannot be carried on without injustice.

Furthermore, the controversies which arise between peoples or kings generally have Mars as their arbiter. That war is irreconcilable with all law is a view held not alone by the ignorant populace; expressions are often let slip by well-informed and thoughtful men which lend countenance to such a view. Nothing is more common than the assertion of antagonism between law and arms. Thus Ennius says:

> Not on grounds of right is battle joined,
> But rather with the sword do men
> Seek to enforce their claims.

Horace, too, describes the savage temper of Achilles in this wise:

> Laws, he declares, were not for him ordained,
> By dint of arms he claims all for himself. . . .

5] Since our discussion concerning law will have been undertaken in vain if there is no law, in order to open the way for a favourable reception of our work and at the same time to fortify it against attacks, this very serious error must be briefly refuted. In order that we may not be obliged to deal with a crowd of opponents, let us assign to them a pleader. And whom should we choose in preference to Carneades?[1] For he had attained to so perfect a mastery of the peculiar tenet of his Academy that he was able to devote the power of his eloquence to the service of falsehood not less readily than to that of truth.

Carneades, then, having undertaken to hold a brief against justice, in particular against that phase of justice with which we are concerned, was able to muster no argument stronger than this, that, for reasons of expediency, men imposed upon themselves laws, which

vary according to customs, and among the same peoples often
undergo changes at times change; moreover that there is no law of
nature, because all creatures, men as well as animals, are impelled
by nature toward ends advantageous to themselves; that, consequently, there is no justice, or, if such there be, it is supreme folly,
since one does violence to his own interests if he consults the advantage of others.

6] What the philosopher here says, and the poet reaffirms in verse,

> And just from unjust Nature cannot know,

must not for one moment be admitted. Man is, to be sure, an animal,
but an animal of a superior kind, much farther removed from all
other animals than the different kinds of animals are from one
another; evidence on this point may be found in the many traits
peculiar to the human species. But among the traits characteristic
of man is an impelling desire for society, that is, for the social life
— not of any and every sort, but peaceful, and organized according
to the measure of his intelligence, with those who are of his own
kind; this social trend the Stoics called 'sociableness'. Stated as a
universal truth, therefore, the assertion that every animal is impelled
by nature to seek only its own good cannot be conceded.

7] Some of the other animals, in fact, do in a way restrain the
appetency for that which is good for themselves alone, to the advantage, now of their offspring, now of other animals of the same
species. This aspect of their behaviour has its origin, we believe, in
some extrinsic intelligent principle, because with regard to other
actions, which involve no more difficulty than those referred to, a
like degree of intelligence is not manifest in them. The same thing
must be said of children. . . .

8] This maintenance of the social order, which we have roughly
sketched, and which is consonant with human intelligence, is the
source of law properly so called. To this sphere of law belong the
abstaining from that which is another's, the restoration to another
of anything of his which we may have, together with any gain which
we may have received from it; the obligation to fulfil promises, the
making good of a loss incurred through our fault, and the inflicting
of penalties upon men according to their deserts.

9] From this signification of the word law there has flowed another
and more extended meaning. Since over other animals man has the
advantage of possessing not only a strong bent towards social life,

of which we have spoken, but also a power of discrimination which enables him to decide what things are agreeable or harmful (as to both things present and things to come), and what can lead to either alternative: in such things it is meet for the nature of man, within the limitations of human intelligence, to follow the direction of a well-tempered judgment, being neither led astray by fear or the allurement of immediate pleasure, nor carried away by rash impulse. Whatever is clearly at variance with such judgement is understood to be contrary also to the law of nature, that is, to the nature of man. ...

11] What we have been saying would have a degree of validity even if we should concede that which cannot be conceded without the utmost wickedness, that there is no God, or that the affairs of men are of no concern to Him. The very opposite of this view has been implanted in us partly by reason, partly by unbroken tradition, and confirmed by many proofs as well as by miracles attested by all ages. Hence it follows that we must without exception render obedience to God as our Creator, to Whom we owe all that we are and have. ...

12] Herein, then, is another source of law besides the source in nature, that is, the free will of God, to which beyond all cavil our reason tells us we must render obedience. But the law of nature of which we have spoken, comprising alike that which relates to the social life of man that which is so called in a larger sense, proceeding as it does from the essential traits implanted in man, can nevertheless rightly be attributed to God, because of His having willed that such traits exist in us. In this sense, too, Chrysippus and the Stoics used to say that the origin of law should be sought in no other source than Jupiter himself; and from the name Jupiter the Latin word for law (*ius*) was probably derived.

13] There is an additional consideration in that, by means of the laws which He has given, God has made those fundamental traits more manifest, even to those who possess feebler reasoning powers; and He has forbidden us to yield to impulses drawing us in opposite directions — affecting now our own interest, now the interest of others — in an effort to control more effectively our more violent impulses and to restrain them within proper limits. ...

15] Again, since it is a rule of the law of nature to abide by pacts (for it was necessary that among men there be some method of obligating themselves one to another, and no other natural method can be imagined), out of this source the bodies of municipal law have arisen. For those who had associated themselves with some group, or had subjected themselves to a man or to men, had either expressly promised, or from the nature of the transaction must be understood impliedly to have promised, that they would conform to that which should have been determined, in the one case by the majority, in the other by those upon whom authority had been conferred.

16] . . . For the very nature of man, which even if we had no lack of anything would lead us into the mutual relations of society, is the mother of the law of nature. But the mother of municipal law is that obligation which arises from mutual consent; and since this obligation derives its force from the law of nature, nature may be considered, so to say, the great-grand-mother of municipal law.

The law of nature nevertheless has the reinforcement of expediency; for the Author of nature willed that as individuals we should be weak, and should lack many things needed in order to live properly, to the end that we might be the more constrained to cultivate the social life. But expediency afforded an opportunity also for municipal law, since that kind of association of which we have spoken, and subjection to authority, have their roots in expediency. From this it follows that those who prescribe laws for others in so doing are accustomed to have, or ought to have, some advantage in view.

17] But just as the laws of each state have in view the advantage of that state, so by mutual consent it has become possible that certain laws should originate as between all states, or a great many states; and it is apparent that the laws thus originating had in view the advantage, not of particular states, but of the great society of states. And this is what is called the law of nations, whenever we distinguish that term from the law of nature. . . .

18] Wrongly, moreover, does Carneades ridicule justice as folly. For since, by his own admission, the national who in his own country obeys its laws is not foolish, even though, out of regard for that law, he may be obliged to forgo certain things advantageous for himself, so that nation is not foolish which does not press its own advantage to the point of disregarding the laws common to nations. The reason in either case is the same. For just as the national, who violates the law of his country in order to obtain an immediate advantage, breaks down that by which the advantages of himself and his posterity are for all future time assured, so the state which transgresses the laws of nature and of nations cuts away also the bulwarks which safeguard its own future peace. Even if no advantage were to be contemplated from the keeping of the law, it would be a mark of wisdom, not of folly, to allow ourselves to be drawn towards that to which we feel that our nature leads. . . .

20] Nevertheless law, even though without a sanction, is not entirely void of effect. For justice brings peace of conscience, while injustice causes torments and anguish, such as Plato describes, in the breast of tyrants. Justice in approved, and injustice condemned, by the common agreement of good men. But, most important of all, in God injustice finds an enemy, justice a protector. He reserves His judgments for the life after this, yet in such a way that He often causes their effects to become manifest even in this life, as history teaches by numerous examples.

21] Many hold, in fact, that the standard of justice which they insist upon in the case of individuals within the state is inapplicable to a nation or the ruler of a nation. The reason for the error lies in this, first of all, that in respect to law they have in view nothing except the advantage which accrues from it, such advantage being apparent in the case of citizens who, taken singly, are powerless to protect themselves. But great states, since they seem to contain in themselves all things required for the adequate protection of life, seem not to have need of that virtue which looks toward the outside, and is called justice. . . .

23] If no association of men can be maintained without law, as Aristotle showed by his remarkable illustration drawn from brigands, surely also that association which binds together the human race, or binds many nations together, has need of law; this was perceived by him who said that shameful deeds ought not to be committed even for the sake of one's country. Aristotle takes sharply to task those who, while unwilling to allow any one to exercise authority over themselves except in accordance with law, yet are quite indifferent as to whether foreigners are treated according to law or not. . . .

25] Least of all should that be admitted which some people imagine, that in war all laws are in abeyance. On the contrary war ought not to be undertaken except for the enforcement of rights; when once undertaken, it should be carried on only within the bounds of law and good faith. Demosthenes well said that war is directed against those who cannot be held in check by judicial processes. For judgements are efficacious against those who feel that they are too weak to resist; against those who are equally strong, or think that they are, wars are undertaken. But in order that wars may be justified, they must be carried on with not less scrupulousness than judicial processes are wont to be.

26] Let the laws be silent, then, in the midst of arms, but only the laws of the State, those that the courts are concerned with, that are adapted only to a state of peace; not those other laws, which are of perpetual validity and suited to all times. It was exceedingly well said by Dio of Prusa, that between enemies written laws, that is, laws of particular states, are not in force, but that unwritten laws are in force, that is, those which nature prescribes, or the agreement of nations has established. This is set forth by that ancient formula of the Romans, 'I think that those things ought to be sought by means of a war that is blameless and righteous.' . . .

28] Fully convinced, by the considerations which I have advanced, that there is a common law among nations, which is valid alike for war and in war, I have had many and weighty reasons for undertaking to write upon this subject. Throughout the Christian world I observed a lack of restraint in relation to war, such as even barbarous races should be ashamed of; I observed that men rush to arms for slight causes, or no cause at all, and that when arms have once been taken up there is no longer any respect for law, divine or human; it is as if, in accordance with a general decree, frenzy had openly been let loose for the committing of all crimes.

29] Confronted with such utter ruthlessness many men, who are the very furthest from being bad men, have come to the point of forbidding all use of arms to the Christian, whose rule of conduct above everything else comprises the duty of loving all men. To this opinion sometimes John Ferus [Johann Wild] and my fellow-countryman Erasmus seem to incline, men who have the utmost devotion to peace in both Church and State; but their purpose, as I take it, is, when things have gone in one direction, to force them in the opposite direction, as we are accustomed to do, that they may come back to a true middle ground. But the very effort of pressing too hard in the opposite direction is often so far from being helpful that it does harm, because in such arguments the detection of what is extreme is easy, and results in weakening the influence of other statements which are well within the bounds of truth. For both extremes therefore a remedy must be found, that men may not believe either that nothing is allowable, or that everything is.

30] At the same time through devotion to study in private life I have wished — as the only course now open to me, undeservedly forced out from my native land, which had been graced by so many of my labours — to contribute somewhat to the philosophy of the law, which previously, in public service, I practised with the utmost degree of probity of which I was capable. Many heretofore have purposed to give to this subject a well-ordered presentation; no one has succeeded. And in fact such a result cannot be accomplished unless — a point which until now has not been sufficiently kept in view — those elements which come from positive law are properly separated from those which arise from nature. For the principles of the law of nature, since they are always the same, can easily be brought into a systematic form; but the elements of positive law, since they often undergo change and are different in different places, are outside the domain of systematic treatment, just as other notions of particular things are.

31] If now those who have consecrated themselves to true justice should undertake to treat the parts of the natural and unchangeable philosophy of law, after having removed all that has its origin in the free will of man; if one, for example, should treat legislation, another taxation, another the administration of justice, another the determination of motives, another the proving of facts, then by assembling all these parts a body of jurisprudence could be made up.

32] What procedure we think should be followed we have shown by deed rather than by words in this work, which treats by far the noblest part of jurisprudence.

*   *   *

40] In order to prove the existence of this law of nature, I have, furthermore, availed myself of the testimony of philosophers, historians, poets, finally also of orators. Not that confidence is to be reposed in them without discrimination; for they were accustomed to serve the interests of their sect, their subject, or their cause. But when many at different times, and in different places, affirm the same thing as certain, that ought to be referred to a universal cause; and this cause, in the lines of inquiry which we are following, must be either a correct conclusion drawn from the principles of nature, or common consent. The former points to the law of nature; the latter, to the law of nations.

The distinction between these kinds of law is not to be drawn from the testimonies themselves (for writers everywhere confuse the terms law of nature and law of nations), but from the character of the matter. For whatever cannot be deduced from certain principles by a sure process of reasoning, and yet is clearly observed everywhere, must have its origin in the free will of man.

41] These two kinds of law, therefore, I have always particularly sought to distinguish from each other and from municipal law. Furthermore, in the law of nations I have distinguished between that which is truly and in all respects law, and that which produces merely a kind of outward effect simulating that primitive law, as, for example, the prohibition to resist by force, or even the duty of defence in any place by public force, in order to secure some advantage, or for the avoidance of serious disadvantages. How necessary it is, in many cases, to observe this distinction, will become apparent in the course of our work.

With not less pains we have separated those things which are strictly and properly legal, out of which the obligation of restitution arises from those things which are called legal because any other classification of them conflicts with some other stated rule of right reason. In regard to this distinction of law we have already said something above.

42] Among the philosophers Aristotle deservedly holds the foremost place, whether you take into account his order of treatment, or the subtlety of his distinctions, or the weight of his reasons. Would that this pre-eminence had not, for some centuries back, been turned into a tyranny, so that Truth, to whom Aristotle devoted faithful service, was by no instrumentality more repressed than by Aristotle's name!

For my part, both here and elsewhere I avail myself of the liberty of the early Christians, who had sworn allegiance to the sect of no one of the philosophers, not because they were in agreement with those who said that nothing can be known — than which nothing is more foolish — but because they thought that there was no philosophic sect whose vision had compassed all truth, and none which had not perceived some aspect of truth. Thus they believed that to gather up into a whole the truth which was scattered among the different philosophers and dispersed among the sects, was in reality to establish a body of teaching truly Christian.

* * *

45] . . . Our purpose is to make much account of Aristotle, but reserving in regard to him the same liberty which he, in his devotion to truth, allowed himself with respect to his teachers.

46] History in relation to our subject is useful in two ways: it supplies both illustrations and judgements. The illustrations have greater weight in proportion as they are taken from better times and better peoples; thus we have preferred ancient examples, Greek and Roman, to the rest. And judgements are not to be slighted, especially when they are in agreement with one another; for by such statements the existence of the law of nature, as we have said, is in a measure proved, and by no other means, in fact, is it possible to establish the law of nations.

47] The views of poets and of orators do not have so great weight; and we make frequent use of them not so much for the purpose of gaining acceptance by that means for our argument, as of adding, from their words, some embellishment to that which we wished to say.

48] I frequently appeal to the authority of the books which men inspired by God have either written or approved, nevertheless with a distinction between the Old Testament and the New. There are some who urge that the Old Testament sets forth the law of nature. Without doubt they are in error, for many of its rules come from the free will of God. And yet this is never in conflict with the true law of nature; and up to this point the Old Testament can be used as a source of the law of nature, provided we carefully distinguish between the law of God, which God sometimes executes through men, and the law of men in their relations with one another. . . .

50] The New Testament I use in order to explain — and this cannot be learned from any other source — what is permissible to Christians. This, however — contrary to the practice of most men — I have distinguished from the law of nature, considering it as certain that in that most holy law a greater degree of moral perfection is enjoined upon us than the law of nature, alone and by itself, would require. And nevertheless I have not omitted to note the things that are recommended to us rather than enjoined, that we may know that, while the turning aside from what has been enjoined is wrong and involves the risk of punishment, a striving for the highest excellence implies a noble purpose and will not fail of its reward.

51] The authentic synodical canons are collections embodying the general principles of divine law as applied to cases which come up; they either show what the divine law enjoins, or urge us to that which God would fain persuade. And this truly is the mission of the Christian Church, to transmit those things which were transmitted to it by God, and in the way in which they were transmitted.

Furthermore customs which were current, or were considered praiseworthy, among the early Christians and those who rose to the measure of so great a name, deservedly have the force of canons. . . .

52] The Schoolmen, who succeeded these writers, often show how strong they are in natural ability. But their lot was cast in an unhappy age, which was ignorant of the liberal arts; wherefore it is less to be wondered at if among many things worthy of praise there are also some things which we should receive with indulgence. Nevertheless when the Schoolmen agree on a point of morals, it rarely happens that they are wrong, since they are especially keen in seeing what may be open to criticism in the statements of others. And yet in the very ardour of their defence of themselves against opposing views, they furnish a praiseworthy example of moderation; they contend with one another by means of arguments — not, in accordance with the practice which has lately begun to disgrace the calling of letters, with personal abuse, base offspring of a spirit lacking self-mastery.

["Those who profess knowledge of the Roman law" are treated in paragraphs 53–55.]

55] . . . The French have tried rather to introduce history into their study of laws. Among them Bodin and Hotman have gained a great name, the former by an extensive treatise, the latter by separate questions; their statements and lines of reasoning will frequently supply us with material in searching out the truth.

56] In my work as a whole I have, above all else, aimed at three things: to make the reasons for my conclusions as evident as possible; to set forth in a definite order the matters which needed to be treated; and to distinguish clearly between things which seemed to be the same and were not.

57] I have refrained from discussing topics which belong to another subject, such as those that teach what may be advantageous in practice. For such topics have their own special field, that of politics, which Aristotle rightly treats by itself, without introducing extraneous matter into it. Bodin, on the contrary, mixed up politics with the body of law with which we are concerned. In some places nevertheless I have made mention of that which is expedient, but only in passing, and in order to distinguish it more clearly from what is lawful.

58] If any one thinks that I have had in view any controversies of own times, either those that have arisen or those which can be foreseen as likely to arise, he will do me an injustice. With all truthfulness I aver that, just as mathematicians treat their figures as abstracted from bodies, so in treating law I have withdrawn my mind from every particular fact. ...

61] ... And now if anything has here been said by me inconsistent with piety, with good morals, with Holy Writ, with the concord of the Christian Church, or with any aspect of truth, let it be as if unsaid.

[End of the *Prolegomena*]

NOTES

1. Greek philosopher of the second century B.C.; a skeptic, opposed both to the Stoics and to the Epicureans.

9

The Leviathan State

THOMAS HOBBES (1588–1679), the son of an Anglican clergyman, graduated from Oxford in 1608 and became tutor in the Cavendish family, with whom he maintained close relations to the of of his days, and in whose house he died. As a young man, he also served as an amanuensis to Francis Bacon. He accompanied members of the Cavendish family on several prolonged sojourns on the Continent, where he became a close friend of Gassendi. Like Bacon and Descartes, Hobbes developed a dislike for "the Schools," although he liked classical literature, especially Thucydides; like Descartes, he became enamored of the method of geometry. However, unlike Descartes and Spinoza after him, he founded his system on a kind of atomic materialism, trying to explain everything, apart from the origin of the world, by molecular motion.

In 1640, in view of the impending political troubles in England, Hobbes thought it prudent to remove himself to France, where he remained for eleven years. At the English court in exile he served as tutor in mathematics to the future Charles II. But, in 1651, he made his submission to the Parliamentary regime and returned to England. Hobbes's two chief political works, De Cive (1642) and Leviathan (1651), were written in France. Both of them, especially the latter, greatly scandalized the constitutionalists, whether of parliamentary or of royalist hue, for reasons that the selections from the Leviathan printed below make obvious. Charles II, however, retained a liking for Hobbes; after the Restoration he granted him a pension and protected him from his enemies.

Hobbes, Leviathan

THE INTRODUCTION

NATURE, the art whereby God hath made and governs the world, is by the *art* of man, as in many other things, so in this also imitated, that it can make an artificial animal. For seeing life is but a motion of limbs, the beginning whereof is in some principal part within; why may we not say, that all *automata* (engines that move themselves by springs and wheels as doth a watch) have an artificial life? For what is the *heart,* but a *spring;* and the *nerves,* but so many *strings;* and the *joints,* but so many *wheels,* giving motion to the whole body, such as was intended by the artificer? *Art* goes yet further, imitating that rational and most excellent work of nature, *man.* For by art is created that great LEVIATHAN called a COMMONWEALTH, or STATE, in Latin CIVITAS, which is but an artificial man; though of greater stature and strength than the natural, for whose protection and defence it was intended; and in which the *sovereignty* is an artificial *soul,* as giving life and motion to the whole body; the *magistrates,* and other *officers* of judicature and execution, artificial *joints; reward* and *punishment,* by which fastened to the seat of the sovereignty every joint and member is moved to perform his duty, are the *nerves,* that do the same in the body natural; the *wealth* and *riches* of all the particular members, are the *strength; salus populi,* the *people's safety,* its *business; counsellors,* by whom all things needful for it to know are suggested unto it, are the *memory; equity,* and *laws,* an artificial *reason* and *will; concord, health; sedition, sickness;* and *civil war, death.* Lastly, the *pacts* and *covenants,* by which the parts of this body politic were at first made, set together, and united, resemble that *fiat,* or the *let us make man,* pronounced by God in the creation.

To describe the nature of this artificial man, I will consider.

First, the *matter* thereof, and the *artificer;* both which is *man.*

From Thomas Hobbes, Leviathan, ed. with an introd. by John Plamenatz. (Cleveland and New York, 1963), pp. 59–62, 114–116, 118, 129–131, 136–137, 139–145, 173–179, 196–197, 204–205, 209–214, 310–311, 318, 334, 336–338, 340–341, 374–375, 377, 391. Reprinted with permission of the World Publishing Company. No alterations have been made in spelling or punctuation.

Secondly, *how,* and by what *covenants* it is made; what are the *rights* and just *power* or *authority* of a *sovereign;* and what it is that *preserveth* or *dissolveth* it.

Thirdly, what is a *Christian commonwealth.*

Lastly, what is the *kingdom of darkness.*

Concerning the first, there is a saying much usurped of late, that *wisdom* is acquired, not by reading of *books,* but of *men.* Consequently whereunto, those persons, that for the most part can give no other proof of being wise, take great delight to show what they think they have read in men, by uncharitable censures of one another behind their backs. But there is another saying not of late understood, by which they might learn truly to read one another, if they would take the pains; that is, *nosce teipsum, read thyself:* which was not meant, as it is now used, to countenance, either the barbarous state of men in power, towards their inferiors; or to encourage men of low degree, to a saucy behaviour towards their betters; but to teach us, that for the similitude of the thoughts and passions of one man, to the thoughts and passions of another, whosoever looketh into himself, and considereth what he doth, when he does *think, opine, reason, hope, fear,* &c. and upon what grounds; he shall thereby read and know, what are the thoughts and passions of all other men upon the like occasions. I say the similitude of *passions,* which are the same in all men, *desire, fear, hope,* &c.; not the similitude of the *objects* of the passions, which are the things *desired, feared, hoped,* &c.: for these the constitution individual, and particular education, do so vary, and they are so easy to be kept from our knowledge, that the characters of man's heart, blotted and confounded as they are with dissembling, lying, counterfeiting, and erroneous doctrines, are legible only to him that searcheth hearts. And though by men's actions we do discover their design sometimes; yet to do it without comparing them with our own, and distinguishing all circumstances, by which the case may come to be altered, is to decypher without a key, and be for the most part deceived, by too much trust, or by too much diffidence; as he that reads, is himself a good or evil man.

But let one man read another by his actions never so perfectly, it serves him only with his acquaintance, which are but few. He that is to govern a whole nation, must read in himself, not this or that particular man; but mankind: which though it be hard to do, harder than to learn any language or science; yet when I shall have set down my own reading orderly, and perspicuously, the pains left another, will be only to consider, if he also find not the same in himself. For this kind of doctrine admitteth no other demonstration.

I, OF MAN I] OF SENSE

CONCERNING the thoughts of man, I will consider them first singly, and afterwards in train, or dependence upon one another. Singly, they are every one a *representation* or *appearance,* of some quality, or other accident of a body without us, which is commonly called an *object.* Which object worketh on the eyes, ears, and other parts of a man's body; and by diversity of working, produceth diversity of appearances.

The original of them all, is that which we call SENSE, for there is no conception in a man's mind, which hath not at first, totally, or by parts, been begotten upon the organs of sense. The rest are derived from that original.

To know the natural cause of sense, is not very necessary to the business now in hand; and I have elsewhere written of the same at large. Nevertheless, to fill each part of my present method, I will briefly deliver the same in this place.

The cause of sense, is the external body, or object, which presseth the organ proper to each sense, either immediately, as in the taste and touch; or mediately, as in seeing, hearing, and smelling; which pressure, by the mediation of the nerves, and other strings and membranes of the body, continued inwards to the brain and heart, causeth there a resistance, or counter-pressure, or endeavour of the heart to deliver itself, which endeavour, because *outward,* seemeth to be some matter without. And this *seeming,* or *fancy,* is that which men call *sense;* and consisteth, as to the eye, in a *light,* or *colour figured;* to the ear, in a *sound;* to the nostril, in an *odour;* to the tongue and palate, in a *savour;* and to the rest of the body, in *heat, cold, hardness, softness,* and such other qualities as we discern by *feeling.* All which qualities, called *sensible,* are in the object, that causeth them, but so many several motions of the matter, by which it presseth our organs diversely. Neither in us that are pressed, are they any thing else, but divers motions; for motion produceth nothing but motion. But their appearance to us is fancy, the same waking, that dreaming. And as pressing, rubbing, or striking the eye, makes us fancy a light; and pressing the ear, produceth a din; so do the bodies also we see, or hear, produce the same by their strong, though unobserved action. For if those colours and sounds were in the bodies, or objects that cause them, they could not be severed from them, as by glasses, and in echoes by reflection, we see they are; where we know the thing we see is in one place, the appearance in another. And though at some certain distance, the real and very object seem invested with the fancy it begets in us; yet still the object is one thing, the image or fancy is another. So that sense, in all cases, is nothing else but original fancy, caused, as I have said, by the pressure, that is, by the motion, of external things upon our eyes, ears, and other organs thereunto ordained. . . .

*   *   *

10] OF POWER, WORTH, DIGNITY, HONOUR, AND WORTHINESS

THE POWER *of a man,* to take it universally, is his present means; to obtain some future apparent good; and is either *original* or *instrumental.*

Natural power, is the eminence of the faculties of body, or mind: as extraordinary strength, form, prudence, arts, eloquence, liberality, nobility. *Instrumental* are those powers, which acquired by these, or by fortune, are means and instruments to acquire more: as riches, reputation, friends, and the secret working of God, which men call good luck. For the nature of power, is in this point, like to fame, increasing as it proceeds; or like the motion of heavy bodies, which the further they go, make still the more haste.

The greatest of human powers, is that which is compounded of the powers of most men, united by consent, in one person, natural, or civil, that has the use of all their powers depending on his will; such as is the power of a common-wealth: or depending on the wills of each particular; such as is the power of a faction or of divers factions leagued. Therefore to have servants, is power; to have friends, is power: for they are strengths united.

Also riches joined with liberality, is power; because it procureth friends, and servants: without liberality, not so; because in this case they defend not; but expose men to envy, as a prey.

Reputation of power, is power; because it draweth with it the adherence of those that need protection.

So is reputation of love of a man's country, called popularity, for the same reason.

Also, what quality soever maketh a man beloved, or feared of many; or the reputation of such quality, is power; because it is a means to have the assistance, and service of many.

Good success is power; because it maketh reputation of wisdom, or good fortune; which makes men either fear him, or rely on him.

Affability of men already in power, is increase of power; because it gaineth love.

Reputation of prudence in the conduct of peace or war, is power; because to prudent men, we commit the government of ourselves, more willingly than to others.

Nobility is power, not in all places, but only in those commonwealths, where it has privileges: for in such privileges, consisteth their power.

Eloquence is power, because it is seeming prudence.

Form is power; because being a promise of good, it recommendeth men to the favour of women and strangers.

The sciences, are small power; because not eminent; and therefore, not acknowledged in any man; nor are at all, but in a few, and in them, but of a few things. For science is of that nature, as none can understand it to be, but such as in a good measure have attained it.

Arts of public use, as fortification, making of engines, and other instruments of war; because they confer to defence, and victory, are power: and though the true mother of them, be science, namely the mathematics; yet, because they are brought into the light, by the hand of the artificer, they be esteemed, the midwife passing with the vulgar for the mother, as his issue.

The *value*, or WORTH of a man, is as of all other things, his price; that is to say, so much as would be given for the use of his power: and therefore is not absolute; but a thing dependant on the need and judgment of another. An able conductor of soldiers, is of great price in time of war present, or imminent; but in peace not so. A learned and uncorrupt judge, is much worth in time of peace; but not so much in war. And as in other things, so in men, not the seller, but the buyer determines the price. For let a man, as most men do, rate themselves at the highest value they can; yet their true value is no more than it is esteemed by others.

The manifestation of the value we set on one another, is that which is commonly called honouring, and dishonouring. To value a man at a high rate, is to *honour* him; at a low rate, is to *dishonour* him. But high, and low, in this case, is to be understood by comparison to the rate that each man setteth on himself.

The public worth of a man, which is the value set on him by the commonwealth, is that which men commonly call DIGNITY. And this value of him by the commonwealth, is understood, by offices of command, judicature, public employment; or by names and titles, introduced for distinction of such value.

To pray to another, for aid of any kind, is to HONOUR; because a sign we have an opinion he has power to help; and the more difficult the aid is, the more is the honour.

To obey, is to honour, because no man obeys them, whom they think have no power to help, or hurt them. And consequently to disobey, is to *dishonour*. . . .

Honourable is whatsoever possession, action, or quality, is an argument and sign of power.

And therefore to be honoured, loved, or feared of many, is honourable; as arguments of power. To be honoured of few or none, *dishonourable*.

Dominion, and victory is honourable; because acquired by power; and servitude, for need, or fear, is dishonourable.

Good fortune, if lasting, honourable; as a sign of the favour of God. Ill fortune, and losses, dishonourable. Riches, are honourable for they are power. Poverty, dishonourable. Magnanimity, liberality, hope, courage, confidence, are honourable; for they proceed from the conscience of power. Pusillanimity, parsimony, fear, diffidence, are dishonourable.

Timely resolution, or determination of what a man is to do, is honourable; as being the contempt of small difficulties, and dangers. And irresolution, dishonourable; as a sign of too much valuing of little impediments, and little advantages: for when a man has weighed things as long as the time permits, and resolves not, the difference of weight is but little; and therefore if he resolve not, he overvalues little things, which is pusillanimity.

All actions, and speeches, that proceed, or seem to proceed, from much experience, science, discretion, or wit, are honourable; for all

these are powers. Actions, or words that proceed from error, ignorance, or folly, dishonourable. . . .

* * *

12] OF RELIGION

SEEING there are no signs, nor fruit of *religion,* but in man
only; there is no cause to doubt, but that the seed of *religion,* is also
in man; and consisteth in some peculiar quality, or at least in some
eminent degree thereof, not to be found in any other living creatures.

And first, it is peculiar to the nature of man, to be inquisitive
into the causes of the events they see, some more, some less; but
all men so much, as to be curious in the search of the causes of their
own good and evil fortune.

Secondly, upon the sight of anything that hath a beginning, to
think also it had a cause, which determined the same to begin, then
when it did, rather than sooner or later.

Thirdly, whereas there is no other felicity of beasts, but the enjoying of their quotidian food, ease, and lusts; as having little or no
foresight of the time to come, for want of observation, and memory
of the order, consequence, and dependence of the things they see;
man observeth how one event hath been produced by another; and
remembereth in them antecedence and consequence; and when he
cannot assure himself of the true causes of things, (for the causes
of good and evil fortune for the most part are invisible), he supposes causes of them, either such as his own fancy suggesteth; or
trusteth the authority of other men, such as he thinks to be his
friends, and wiser than himself.

The two first, make anxiety. . . .

This perpetual fear, always accompanying mankind in the ignorance of causes, as it were in the dark, must needs have for object
something. And therefore when there is nothing to be seen, there
is nothing to accuse, either of their good, or evil fortune, but some
power, or agent *invisible:* in which sense perhaps it was, that some
of the old poets said, that the gods were at first created by human
fear; which spoken of the gods, that is to say, of the many gods of
the Gentiles, is very true. But the acknowledging of one God,
eternal, infinite, and omnipotent, may more easily be derived, from
the desire men have to know the causes of natural bodies, and their

several virtues, and operations; than from the fear of what was to befall them in time to come. For he that from any effect he seeth come to pass, should reason to the next and immediate cause thereof, and from thence the cause of that cause, and plunge himself profoundly in the pursuit of causes; shall at last come to this, that there must be, as even the heathen philosophers confessed, one first mover; that is, a first, and an eternal cause of all things; which is that which men mean by the name of God: and all this without thought of their fortune; the solicitude whereof, both inclines to fear, and hinders them from the search of the causes of other things; and thereby gives occasion of feigning of as many gods, as there be men that feign them.

. . . Therefore, men that by their own meditation, arrive to the acknowledgment of one infinite, omnipotent, and eternal God, chose rather to confess he is incomprehensible, and above their understanding, than to define his nature by *spirit incorporeal,* and then confess their definition to be unintelligible: or if they give him such a title, it is not *dogmatically,* with intention to make the divine nature understood; but *piously,* to honour him with attributes, or significations, as remote as they can from the grossness of bodies visible. . . .

And therefore the first founders, and legislators of commonwealths among the Gentiles, whose ends were only to keep the people in obedience, and peace, have in all places taken care; first, to imprint in their minds a belief, that those precepts which they gave concerning religion, might not be thought to proceed from their own device, but from the dictates of some god, or other spirit; or else that they themselves were of a higher nature than mere mortals, that their laws might the more easily be received. . . . Secondly, they have had a care, to make it believed, that the same things were displeasing to the gods, which were forbidden by the laws. Thirdly, to prescribe ceremonies, supplications, sacrifices, and festivals, by which they were to believe, the anger of the gods might be appeased; and that ill success in war, great contagions of sickness, earthquakes, and each man's private misery, came from the anger of the gods, and their anger from the neglect of their worship, or the forgetting, or mistaking some point of the ceremonies required. . . .

And by these, and such other institutions, they obtained in order to their end, which was the peace of the commonwealth, that the common people in their misfortunes, laying the fault on neglect, or error in their ceremonies, or on their own disobedience to the laws, were the less apt to mutiny against their governors; and being entertained with the pomp, and pastime of festivals, and public games, made in honour of the gods, needed nothing else but bread to keep them from discontent, murmuring, and commotion against the state. And therefore the Romans, that had conquered the greatest part of the then known world, made no scruple of tolerating any religion whatsoever in the city of Rome itself; unless it had something in it, that could not consist with their civil government; nor do we read, that any religion was there forbidden, but that of the Jews; who, being the peculiar kingdom of God, thought it unlawful to acknowledge subjection to any mortal king or state whatsoever. And thus you see how the religion of the Gentiles was a part of their policy.

But where God himself, by supernatural revelation, planted religion; there he also made to himself a peculiar kingdom: and gave laws, not only of behaviour towards himself, but also towards one another; and thereby in the kingdom of God, the policy, and laws civil, are a part of religion; and therefore the distinction of temporal, and spiritual domination, hath there no place. It is true, that God is king of all the earth: yet may he be king of a peculiar, and chosen nation. For there is no more incongruity therein, than that he that hath the general command of the whole army, should have withal a peculiar regiment, or company of his own. God is king of all the earth by his power: but of his chosen people, he is king by covenant. . . .

And whereas in the planting of Christian religion, the oracles ceased in all parts of the Roman empire, and the number of Christians increased wonderfully every day, and in every place, by the preaching of the Apostles, and Evangelists; a great part of that success, may reasonably be attributed, to the contempt, into which the priests of the Gentiles of that time, had brought themselves, by their uncleanness, avarice, and juggling between princes. Also the religion of the church of Rome, was partly, for the same cause abolished in England, and many other parts of Christendom; insomuch, as the failing of virtue in the pastors, maketh faith fail in the people: and partly from bringing of the philosophy, and doctrine of Aristotle into religion, by the Schoolmen; from whence there arose so many contradictions, and absurdities, as brought the clergy into a reputation both of ignorance, and of fraudulent intention; and inclined people to revolt from them, either against the will of their

own princes, as in France and Holland; or with their will, as in
England....

13] OF THE NATURAL CONDITION OF
MANKIND AS CONCERNING THEIR FELICITY,
AND MISERY

NATURE hath made men so equal, in the faculties of the body,
and mind; as that though there be found one man sometimes
manifestly stronger in body, or of quicker mind than another; yet
when all is reckoned together, the difference between man, and man,
is not so considerable, as that one man can thereupon claim to himself any benefit, to which another may not pretend, as well as he.
For as to the strength of body, the weakest has strength enough to
kill the strongest, either by secret machination, or by confederacy
with others, that are in the same danger with himself.

And as to the faculties of the mind, setting aside the arts grounded
upon words, and especially that skill of proceeding upon general,
and infallible rules, called science; which very few have, and but in
few things; as being not a native faculty, born with us; nor attained,
as prudence, while we look after somewhat else, I find yet a greater
equality amongst men, than that of strength. For prudence, is but
experience; which equal time, equally bestows on all men, in those
things they equally apply themselves unto. That which may perhaps
make such equality incredible, is but a vain conceit of one's own
wisdom, which almost all men think they have in a greater degree,
than the vulgar; that is, than all men but themselves, and a few
others, whom by fame, or for concurring with themselves, they
approve. For such is the nature of men, that howsoever they may
acknowledge many others to be more witty, or more eloquent, or
more learned; yet they will hardly believe there be many so wise as
themselves; for they see their own wit at hand, and other men's at a
distance. But this proveth rather that men are in that point equal,
than unequal. For there is not ordinarily a greater sign of the equal
distribution of any thing, than that every man is contented with his
share.

From this equality of ability, ariseth equality of hope in the attaining of our ends. And therefore if any two men desire the same thing,
which nevertheless they cannot both enjoy, they become enemies;
and in the way to their end, which is principally their own con-

servation, and sometimes their delectation only, endeavour to destroy, or subdue one another. And from hence it comes to pass, that where an invader hath no more to fear, than another man's single power; if one plant, sow, build, or possess a convenient seat, others may probably be expected to come prepared with forces united, to dispossess, and deprive him, not only of the fruit of his labour, but also of his life, or liberty. And the invader again is in the like danger of another.

And from this diffidence of one another, there is no way for any man to secure himself, so reasonable, as anticipation; that is, by force, or wiles, to master the persons of all men he can, so long, till he see no other power great enough to endanger him: and this is no more than his own conservation requireth, and is generally allowed. Also because there be some, that taking pleasure in contemplating their own power in the acts of conquest, which they pursue farther than their security requires; if others, that otherwise would be glad to be at ease within modest bounds, should not by invasion increase their power, they would not be able, long time, by standing only on their defence, to subsist. And by consequence, such augmentation of dominion over men being necessary to a man's conservation, it ought to be allowed him.

Again, men have no pleasure, but on the contrary a great deal of grief, in keeping company, where there is no power able to over-awe them all. For every man looketh that his companion should value him, at the same rate he sets upon himself: and upon all signs of contempt, or undervaluing, naturally endeavours, as far as he dares (which amongst them that have no common power to keep them in quiet, is far enough to make them destroy each other), to extort a greater value from his contemners, by damage; and from others, by the example.

So that in the nature of man, we find three principal causes of quarrel. First, competition; secondly, diffidence; thirdly, glory.

The first, maketh men invade for gain; the second, for safety; and the third, for reputation. The first use violence, to make themselves masters of other men's persons, wives, children, and cattle; the second, to defend them; the third, for trifles, as a word, a smile, a different opinion, and any other sign of undervalue, either direct in their persons, or by reflection in their kindred, their friends, their nation, their profession, or their name.

Hereby it is manifest, that during the time men live without a common power to keep them all in awe, they are in that condition which is called war; and such a war, as is of every man, against every man. For WAR, consisteth not in battle only, or the act of fighting; but in a tract of time, wherein the will to contend by battle is sufficiently known: and therefore the notion of *time,* is to be considered in the nature of war; as it is in the nature of weather. For as the nature of foul weather, lieth not in a shower or two of rain; but in an inclination thereto of many days together: so the nature of war, consisteth not in actual fighting; but in the known disposition thereto, during all the time there is no assurance to the contrary. All other time is PEACE.

Whatsoever therefore is consequent to a time of war, where every man is enemy to every man; the same is consequent to the time, wherein men live without other security, than what their own strength, and their own invention shall furnish them withal. In such condition, there is no place for industry; because the fruit thereof is uncertain: and consequently no culture of the earth; no navigation, nor use of the commodities that may be imported by sea; no commodious building; no instruments of moving, and removing, such things as require much force; no knowledge of the face of the earth; no account of time; no arts; no letters; no society; and which is worst of all, continual fear, and danger of violent death; and the life of man, solitary, poor, nasty, brutish, and short.

It may seem strange to some man, that has not well weighed these things; that nature should thus dissociate, and render men apt to invade, and destroy one another: and he may therefore, not trusting to this inference, made from the passions, desire perhaps to have the same confirmed by experience. Let him therefore consider with himself, when taking a journey, he arms himself, and seeks to go well accompanied; when going to sleep, he locks his doors; when even in his house he locks his chests; and this when he knows there be laws, and public officers, armed, to revenge all injuries shall be done him; what opinion he has of his fellow-subjects, when he rides armed; of his fellow citizens, when he locks his doors; and of his children, and servants, when he locks his chests. Does he not there as much accuse mankind by his actions, as I do by my words? But neither of us accuse man's nature in it. The desires, and other passions of man, are in themselves no sin. No more are the actions, that proceed from these passions, till they know a law that forbids them:

which till laws be made they cannot know: nor can any law be made, till they have agreed upon the person that shall make it.

It may peradventure be thought, there was never such a time, nor condition of war as this; and I believe it was never generally so, over all the world: but there are many places, where they live so now. For the savage people in many places of America, except the government of small families, the concord whereof dependeth on natural lust, have no government at all; and live at this day in that brutish manner, as I said before. Howsoever, it may be perceived what manner of life there would be, where there were no common power to fear, by the manner of life, which men that have formerly lived under a peaceful government, use to degenerate into, in a civil war.

But though there had never been any time, wherein particular men were in a condition of war one against another; yet in all times, kings, and persons of sovereign authority, because of their independency, are in continual jealousies, and in the state and posture of gladiators; having their weapons pointing, and their eyes fixed on one another; that is, their forts, garrisons, and guns upon the frontiers of their kingdoms; and continual spies upon their neighbours; which is a posture of war. But because they uphold thereby, the industry of their subjects; there does not follow from it, that misery, which accompanies the liberty of particular men.

To this war of every man, against every man, this also is consequent; that nothing can be unjust. The notions of right and wrong, justice and injustice have there no place. Where there is no common power, there is no law: where no law, no injustice. Force, and fraud, are in war, the two cardinal virtues. Justice, and injustice are none of the faculties neither of the body, nor mind. If they were, they might be in a man that were alone in the world, as well as his senses, and passions. They are qualities, that relate to men in society, not in solitude. It is consequent also to the same condition, that there be no propriety, no dominion, no *mine* and *thine* distinct; but only that to be every man's, that he can get; and for so long, as he can keep it. And thus much for the ill condition, which man by mere nature is actually placed in; though with a possibility to come out of it, consisting partly in the passions, partly in his reason.

The passions that incline men to peace, are fear of death; desire of such things as are necessary to commodious living; and a hope by their industry to obtain them. And reason suggesteth convenient articles of peace, upon which men may be drawn to agreement. These articles, are they, which otherwise are called the Laws of Nature. . . .

*   *   *

II, OF COMMONWEALTH 17] OF THE CAUSES, GENERATION, AND DEFINITION OF A COMMONWEALTH

THE final cause, end, or design of men, who naturally love liberty, and dominion over others, in the introduction of that restraint upon themselves, in which we see them live in commonwealths, is the foresight of their own preservation, and of a more contented life thereby; that is to say, of getting themselves out from that miserable condition of war, which is necessarily consequent, as hath been shown in chapter 13, to the natural passions of men, when there is no visible power to keep them in awe, and tie them by fear of punishment to the performance of their covenants, and observation of those laws of nature set down in the fourteenth and fifteenth chapters.

For the laws of nature, as *justice, equity, modesty, mercy,* and, in sum, *doing to others, as we would be done to,* of themselves, without the terror of some power, to cause them to be observed, are contrary to our natural passions, that carry us to partiality, pride, revenge, and the like. And covenants, without the swords, are but words, and of no strength to secure a man at all. Therefore notwithstanding the laws of nature, which every one hath then kept, when he has the will to keep them, when he can do it safely, if there be no power erected, or not great enough for our security; every man will, and may lawfully rely on his own strength and art, for caution against all other men. And in all places, where men have lived by small families, to rob and spoil one another, has been a trade, and so far from being reputed against the law of nature, that the greater spoils they gained, the greater was their honour; and men observed no other laws therein, but the laws of honour; that is, to abstain from cruelty, leaving to men their lives, and instruments of husbandry. And as small families did then; so now do cities and kingdoms which are but greater families, for their own security, enlarge their dominions, upon all pretences of danger, and fear of invision, or assistance that may be given to invaders, and endeavour as much as they can, to subdue, or weaken their neighbours, by open force, and secret arts, for want of other caution, justly; and are remembered for it in after ages with honour.

Nor is it the joining together of a small number of men, that gives them this security; because in small numbers, small additions on the one side or the other, make the advantage of strength so great, as is sufficient to carry the victory; and therefore gives encouragement to an invasion. The multitude sufficient to confide in for our security, is not determined by any certain number, but by comparison with the enemy we fear; and is then sufficient, when the odds of the enemy is not of so visible and conspicuous moment, to determine the event of war, as to move him to attempt.

And be there never so great a multitude; yet if their actions be directed according to their particular judgments, and particular appetites, they can expect thereby no defence, nor protection, neither against a common enemy, nor against the injuries of one another. For being distracted in opinions concerning the best use and application of their strength, they do not help but hinder one another; and reduce their strength by mutual opposition to nothing: whereby they are easily, not only subdued by a very few that agree together; but also when there is no common enemy, they make war upon each other, for their particular interests. For if we could suppose a great multitude of men to consent in the observation of justice, and other laws of nature, without a common power to keep them all in awe; we might as well suppose all mankind to do the same; and then there neither would be, nor need to be any civil government, or commonwealth at all; because there would be peace without subjection.

Nor is it enough for the security, which men desire should last all the time of their life, that they be governed, and directed by one judgment, for a limited time; as in one battle, or one war. For though they obtain a victory by their unanimous endeavour against a foreign enemy; yet afterwards when either they have no common enemy, or he that by one part is held for an enemy, is by another part held for a friend, they must needs by the difference of their interests dissolve, and fall again into a war amongst themselves. . . .

The only way to erect such a common power, as may be able to defend them from the invasion of foreigners, and the injuries of one another, and thereby to secure them in such sort, as that by their own industry, and by the fruits of the earth, they may nourish themselves and live contentedly; is, to confer all their power and strength upon one man, or upon one assembly of men, that may reduce all their wills, by plurality of voices, unto one will: which is as much as to say, to appoint one man, or assembly of men, to bear their person; and every one to own, and acknowledge himself to be author of whatsoever he that so beareth their person, shall act, or cause to be acted, in those things which concern the common peace and safety; and therein to submit their wills, every one to his will, and their judgments, to his judgment. This is more than consent, or concord; it is a real unity of them all, in one and the same person, made by covenant of every man with every man, in such manner, as if every man should say to every man, *I authorize and give up my right of governing myself, to this man, or to this assembly of men, on this condition, that thou give up thy right to him, and authorize all his actions in like manner.* This done, the multitude so united in one person, is called a COMMONWEALTH, in Latin CIVITAS. This is the generation of the great LEVIATHAN, or rather, to speak more reverently, of that *mortal god,* to which we owe under the *immortal God,* our peace and defence. For by this authority, given him by every particular man in the commonwealth, he hath the use of so much power and strength conferred on him, that by terror thereof, he is enabled to perform the wills of them all, to peace at home, and mutual aid against their enemies abroad. And in him consisteth the essence of the commonwealth; which, to define it, is *one person, of whose acts a great multitude, by mutual covenants one with another, have made themselves every one the author, to the end he may use the strength and means of them all, as he shall think expedient, for their peace and common defence.*

And he that carrieth this person, is called SOVEREIGN, and said to have *sovereign power;* and every one besides, his SUBJECT.

The attaining to this sovereign power, is by two ways. One, by natural force; as when a man maketh his children, to submit themselves, and their children to his government; as being able to destroy them if they refuse; or by war subdueth his enemies to his will, giving them their lives on that condition. The other, is when men agree amongst themselves, to submit to some man, or assembly of men, voluntarily, on confidence to be protected by him against all others. This latter, may be called a political commonwealth, or commonwealth by *institution;* and the former, a commonwealth by *acquisition.* And first, I shall speak of a commonwealth by institution.

18] OF THE RIGHTS OF SOVEREIGNS BY INSTITUTION

A *commonwealth* is said to be *instituted,* when a *multitude* of men do agree, and *covenant, every one, with every one,* that to whatsoever *man,* or *assembly of men,* shall be given by the major part, the *right* to *present* the person of them all, that is to say, to be their *representative;* every one, as well he that *voted for it,* as he that *voted against it,* shall *authorize* all the actions and judgments, of that man, or assembly of men, in the same manner, as if they were his own, to the end, to live peaceably amongst themselves, and be protected against other men.

From this institution of a commonwealth are derived all the *rights,* and *faculties* of him, or them, on whom sovereign power is conferred by the consent of the people assembled.

First, because they covenant, it is to be understood, they are not obliged by former covenant to anything repugnant hereunto. And consequently they that have already instituted a commonwealth, being thereby bound by covenant, to own the actions, and judgments of one, cannot lawfully make a new covenant, amongst themselves, to be obedient to any other, in any thing whatsoever, without his permission. And therefore, they that are subjects to a monarch, cannot without his leave cast off monarchy, and return to the confusion of a disunited multitude; nor transfer their person from him that beareth it, to another man, or other assembly of men. . . . If he that attempteth to depose his sovereign, be killed, or punished by him for such attempt, he is author of his own punishment, as being by the institution, author of all his sovereign shall do: and because it is unjustice for a man to do anything, for which he may be punished by his own authority, he is also upon that title, unjust. And whereas some men have pretended for their disobedience to their sovereign, a new covenant, made, not with men, but with God; this also is unjust: for there is no covenant with God, but by mediation of somebody that representeth God's person; which none doth but God's lieutenant, who hath the sovereignty under God. But this pretence of covenant with God, is so evident a lie, even in the pretenders' own consciences, that it is not only an act of an unjust, but also of a vile, and unmanly disposition.

Secondly, because the right of bearing the person of them all, is given to him they make sovereign, by covenant only of one to another, and not of him to any of them; there can happen no breach of covenant on the part of the sovereign; and consequently none of his subjects, by any pretence of forfeiture, can be freed from his subjection. . . .

*   *   *

20] OF DOMINION PATERNAL, AND DESPOTICAL

A commonwealth *by acquisition,* is that, where the sovereign power is acquired by force; and it is acquired by force, when men singly, or many together by plurality of voices, for fear of death, or bonds, do authorize all the actions of that man, or assembly, that hath their lives and liberty in his power.

And this kind of dominion, or sovereignty, differeth from sovereignty by institution, only in this, that men who choose their sovereign, do it for fear of one another, and not of him whom they institute: but in this case, they subject themselves, to him they are afraid of. In both cases they do it for fear: which is to be noted by them, that hold all such covenants, as proceed from fear of death or violence, void: which if it were true, no man, in any kind of commonwealth, could be obliged to obedience. It is true, that in a commonwealth once instituted, or acquired, promises proceeding from fear of death or violence, are no convenants, nor obliging when the thing promised is contrary to the laws; but the reason is not, because it was made upon fear, but because he that promiseth, hath no right in the thing promised. Also, when he may lawfully perform, and doth not, it is not the invalidity of the covenant, that absolveth him, but the sentence of the sovereign. Otherwise, whensoever a man lawfully promiseth, he unlawfully breaketh: but when the sovereign, who is the actor, acquitteth him, then he is acquitted by him that extorted the promise, as by the author of such absolution.

But the rights, and consequences of sovereignty, are the same in both. His power cannot, without his consent, be transferred to another: he cannot forfeit it: he cannot be accused by any of his subjects, of injury; he cannot be punished by them: he is judge of what is necessary for peace; and judge of doctrines: he is sole legislator; and supreme judge of controversies; and of the times and occasions of war, and peace: to him it belongeth to choose magistrates, counsellors, commanders, and all other officers, and ministers; and to determine of rewards, and punishments, honour, and order. . . .

* * *

21] OF THE LIBERTY OF SUBJECTS

Liberty, or freedom, signifieth, properly, the absence of opposition; by opposition, I mean external impediments of motion; and may be applied no less to irrational, and inanimate creatures, than to rational. . . . But when the impediment of motion, is in the constitution of the thing itself, we use not to say; it wants the liberty; but the power to move; as when a stone lieth still, or a man is fastened to his bed by sickness.

And according to this proper, and generally received meaning of the word, a FREEMAN, *is he, that in those things, which by his strength and wit he is able to do, is not hindered to do what he has a will to.* . . .

Fear and liberty are consistent; as when a man throweth his goods into the sea for *fear* the ship should sink, he doth it nevertheless very willingly, and may refuse to do it if he will: it is therefore the action of one that was *free:* so a man sometimes pays his debt, only for *fear* of imprisonment, which because nobody hindered him from detaining, was the action of a man at *liberty.* And generally all actions which men do in commonwealths, for *fear* of the law, are actions, which the doers had *liberty* to omit.

Liberty, and *necessity* are consistent: as in the water, that hath not only *liberty,* but a *necessity* of descending by the channel: so likewise in the actions which men voluntarily do: which, because they proceed from their will, proceed from *liberty;* and yet, because every act of man's will, and every desire, and inclination proceedeth from some cause, and that from another cause, in a continual chain, whose first link is in the hand of God the first of all causes, proceed from *necessity.* So that to him that could see the connexion of those causes, the *necessity* of all men's voluntary actions, would appear manifest. And therefore God, that seeth, and disposeth all things, seeth also that the *liberty* of man in doing what he will, is accompanied with the *necessity* of doing that which God will, and no more, or less. . . .

. . . Seeing sovereignty by institution, is by covenant of every one to every one; and sovereignty by acquisition, by covenants of the vanquished to the victor, or child to the parent; it is manifest, that every subject has liberty in all those things, the right whereof cannot by covenant be transferred. I have shewn before in the 14th chapter, that covenants, not to defend a man's own body, are void. Therefore,

If the sovereign command a man, though justly condemned, to kill, wound, or maim himself; or not to resist those that assault him; or to abstain from the use of food, air, medicine, or any other thing, without which he cannot live; yet hath that man the liberty to disobey.

If a man be interrogated by the sovereign, or his authority, concerning a crime done by himself, he is not bound, without assurance of pardon, to confess it; because no man, as I have shown in the same chapter, can be obliged by covenant to accuse himself.

Again, the consent of a subject to sovereign power, is contained in these words, *I authorize, or take upon me, all his actions;* in which is no restriction at all, of his own former natural liberty: for by allowing him to *kill me,* I am not bound to kill myself when he commands me. It is one thing to say, *kill me, or my fellow, if you please;* another thing to say, *I will kill myself, or my fellow.* . . .

To resist the sword of the commonwealth, in defence of another man, guilty, or innocent, no man hath liberty; because such liberty, takes away from the sovereign, the means of protecting us: and is therefore destructive of the very essence of government. But in case a great many men together, have already resisted the sovereign power unjustly, or committed some capital crime, for which every one of them expecteth death, whether have they not the liberty then to join together, and assist, and defend one another? Certainly they have: for they but defend their lives, which the guilty man may as well do, as the innocent. There was indeed injustice in the first breach of their duty; their bearing of arms subsequent to it, though it be to maintain what they have done, is no new unjust act. And if it be only to defend their persons, it is not unjust at all. But the offer of pardon taketh from them, to whom it is offered, the plea of self-defence, and maketh their perseverance in assisting, or defending the rest, unlawful.

As for other liberties, they depend on the silence of the law. In cases where the sovereign has prescribed no rule, there the subject hath the liberty to do, or forbear, according to his own discretion. And therefore such liberty is in some places more, and in some less; and in some times more, in other times less, according as they that have the sovereignty shall think most convenient. . . .

The obligation of subjects to the sovereign, is understood to last as long, and no longer, than the power lasteth, by which he is able to protect them. For the right men have by nature to protect themselves, when none else can protect them, can by no covenant be relinquished. The sovereignty is the soul of the commonwealth; which once departed from the body, the members do not more receive their motion from it. The end of the obedience is protection; which, wheresoever a man seeth it, either in his own, or in another's sword, nature applieth his obedience to it, and his endeavour to maintain it. And though sovereignty, in the intention of them that make it, be immortal; yet it is in its own nature, not only subject to violent death, by foreign war; but also through the ignorance, and passions of men, it hath in it, from the very institution, many seeds of a natural mortality, by intestine discord. . . .

If a monarch shall relinquish the sovereignty, both for himself, and his heirs; his subjects return to the absolute liberty of nature; because, though nature may declare who are his sons, and who are the nearest of his kin; yet it dependeth on his will, as hath been said in the precedent chapter, who shall be his heir. If therefore he will have no heir, there is no sovereignty, nor subjection. The case is the same, if he die without known kindred, and without declaration of his heir. For then there can no heir be known, and consequently no subjection be due.

If the sovereign banish his subject; during the banishment, he is not subject. But he that is sent on a message, or hath leave to travel, is still subject; but it is, by contract between sovereigns, not by virtue of the covenant of subjection. For whosoever entereth into another's dominion, is subject to all the laws thereof; unless he have a privilege by the amity of the sovereigns, or by special licence.

If a monarch subdued by war, render himself subject to the victor, his subjects are delivered from their former obligation, and become obliged to the victor. But if he be held prisoner, or have not the liberty of his own body; he is not understood to have given away the right of sovereignty: and therefore his subjects are obliged to yield obedience to the magistrates formerly placed, governing not in their own name, but in his. For, his right remaining, the question is only of the administration; that is to say, of the magistrates and officers; which, if he have not means to name, he is supposed to approve those, which he himself had formerly appointed.

*   *   *

31] OF THE KINGDOM OF GOD BY NATURE

. . . There wants only, for the entire knowledge of civil duty, to know what are those laws of God. For without that, a man knows not, when he is commanded any thing by the civil power, whether it be contrary to the law of God, or not: and so, either by too much civil obedience, offends the Divine Majesty; or through fear of offending God, transgresses the commandments of the commonwealth. To avoid both these rocks, it is necessary to know what are the laws divine. And seeing the knowledge of all law, dependeth on the knowledge of the sovereign power, I shall say something in that which followeth, of the KINGDOM OF GOD.

God is king, let the earth rejoice, saith the psalmist. (xcvii, 1) . . . Whether men will or not, they must be subject always to the divine power. By denying the existence, or providence of God, men may shake off their ease, but not their yoke. But to call this power God, which extendeth itself not only to man, but also to beasts, and plants, and bodies inanimate, by the name of kingdom, is but a metaphorical use of the word. For he only is properly said to reign, that governs his subjects by his word, and by promise of rewards to those that obey it, and by threatening them with punishment that obey it not. Subjects therefore in the kingdom of God, are not bodies inanimate, nor creatures irrational; because they understand no precept as his: nor atheists, nor they that believe not that God has any care of the actions of mankind; because they acknowledge no word for his, nor have hope of his rewards or fear of his threatenings. They therefore that believe there is a God that governeth the world, and hath given precepts, and propounded rewards, and punishments to mankind, are God's subjects; all the rest, are to be understood as enemies.

To rule by words, requires that such words be manifestly made known; for else they are no laws: for to the nature of laws belongeth a sufficient, and clear promulgation, such as may take away the excuse of ignorance; which in the laws of men is but of one only kind, and that is, proclamation, or promulgation by the voice of man. But God declareth his laws three ways; by the dictates of *natural reason,* by *revelation,* and by the *voice* of some *man,* to whom by the operation of miracles, he procureth credit with the rest. From hence there ariseth a triple word of God, *rational, sensible,* and *prophetic:* to which correspondeth a triple hearing; *right reason, sense supernatural,* and *faith.* As for sense supernatural, which consisteth in revelation or inspiration, there have not been any universal laws so given, because God speaketh not in that manner but to particular persons, and to divers men divers things.

From the difference between the other two kinds of God's word, *rational,* and *prophetic,* there may be attributed to God, a twofold kingdom, *natural,* and *prophetic:* natural, wherein he governeth as many of mankind as acknowledge his providence, by the natural dictates of right reason; and prophetic, wherein having chosen but one peculiar nation, the Jews, for his subjects, he governed them, and none but them, not only by natural reason, but by positive laws, which he gave them by the mouths of his holy prophets. . . .

But seeing a commonwealth is but one person, it ought also to exhibit to God but one worship; which then it doth, when it commandeth it to be exhibited by private men, publicly. And this is public worship; the property whereof, is to be *uniform:* for those actions that are done differently, by different men, cannot be said to be a public worship. And therefore, where many sorts of worship be allowed, proceeding from the different religions of private men, it cannot be said there is any public worship, nor that the commonwealth is of any religion at all. . . .

III, OF A CHRISTIAN COMMONWEALTH

* * * 41] OF THE OFFICE OF OUR BLESSED SAVIOUR

We find in Holy Scripture three parts of the office of the Messiah: the first of a *Redeemer* or *Saviour;* the second of a *pastor, counsellor,* or *teacher,* that is, of prophet sent from God to convert such as God hath elected to salvation: the third of a *king,* an *eternal king,* but under his Father, as Moses high-priests were in their several times. . . .

If then Christ, whilst he was on earth, had no kingdom in this world, to what end was his first coming? It was to restore unto God, by a new covenant, the kingdom, which being his by the old covenant, had been cut off by the rebellion of the Israelites in the election of Saul. Which to do, he was to preach unto them, that he was the *Messiah,* that is, the king promised to them by the prophets; and to offer himself in sacrifice for the sins of them that should by faith submit themselves thereto; and in case the nation generally should refuse him, to call to his obedience such as should believe in him amongst the Gentiles. So that there are two parts of our Saviour's office during his abode upon the earth: one to proclaim himself the Christ; and another by teaching, and by working of miracles, to persuade and prepare men to live so, as to be worthy of the immortality believers were to enjoy, at such time as he should come in majesty to take possession of his Father's kingdom. And therefore it is, that the time of his preaching is often by himself called the *regeneration;* which is not properly a kingdom, and thereby a warrant to deny obedience to the magistrates that then were; for he commanded to obey those that sat then in Moses' chair, and to pay tribute to Caesar; but only an earnest of the kingdom of God that was to come, to those to whom God has given the grace to be his disciples, and to believe in him; for which cause the godly are said to be already in the *kingdom of grace,* as naturalized in that heavenly kingdom. . . .

As for the third part of his office, which was to be *king,* I have already shown that his kingdom was not to begin till the resurrection. But then he shall be king, not only as God, in which sense he is king already, and ever shall be, of all the earth, in virtue of his omnipotence; but also peculiarly of his own elect, by virtue of the pact they make with him in their baptism.

42] OF POWER ECCLESIASTICAL

* * *

Thus we see how the power ecclesiastical was left by our Saviour to the apostles; and how they were, to the end they might the better exercise that power, endued with the Holy Spirit, which is therefore called sometimes in the New Testament *paracletus,* which signifieth an *assister,* or one called to for help, though it be commonly translated a *comforter.* Let us now consider the power itself, what it was, and over whom.

Cardinal Bellarmine, in his third general controversy, hath handled a great many questions concerning the ecclesiastical power of the pope of Rome; and begins with this, whether it ought to be monarchial, aristocratical, or democratical: all which sorts of power are sovereign and coercive. If now it should appear, that there is no coercive power left them by our Saviour, but only a power to proclaim the kingdom of Christ, and to persuade men to submit themselves thereunto; and by precepts and good counsel, to teach them that have submitted, what they are to do, that they may be received into the kingdom of God when it comes; and that the apostles, and other ministers of the Gospel, are our schoolmasters, and not our commanders, and their precepts not laws, but wholesome counsels: then were all that dispute in vain.

I have shown already, in the last chapter, that the kingdom of Christ is not of this world: therefore neither can his ministers, unless they be kings, require obedience in his name. For if the supreme king have not his regal power in this world; by what authority can obedience be required to his officers? . . .

And first, we are to remember, that the right of judging what documents are fit for peace, and to be taught the subjects, is in all commonwealths inseparably annexed, as hath been already proved, to the sovereign power civil, whether it be in one man, or in one assembly of men. For it is evident to the meanest capacity, that men's actions are derived from the opinions they have of the good or evil, which from those actions redound unto themselves; and consequently, men that are once possessed of an opinion, that their obedience to the sovereign power will be more hurtful to them than their disobedience, will disobey the laws, and thereby overthrow the commonwealth, and introduce confusion and civil war; for the avoiding whereof, all civil government was ordained. And therefore in all commonwealths of the heathen, the sovereigns have had the name of pastors of the people, because there was no subject that could lawfully teach the people, but by their permission and authority.

This right of the heathen kings cannot be thought taken from them by their conversion to the faith of Christ; who never ordained that kings, for believing in him, should be deposed, that is, subjected to any but himself, or, which is all one, be deprived of the power necessary for the conservation of peace amongst their subjects, and for their defence against foreign enemies. And therefore Christian kings are still the supreme pastors of their people, and have power to ordain what pastors they please, to teach the Church, that is, to teach the people committed to their charge.

Again, let the right of choosing them be, as before the conversion of kings, in the Church; for so it was in the time of the apostles themselves, as hath been shown already in this chapter; even so also the right will be in the civil sovereign, Christian. For in that he is a Christian, he allows the teaching; and in that he is the sovereign, which is so much as to say, the Church by representation, the teachers he elects are elected by the Church. And when an assembly of Christians choose their pastor in a Christian commonwealth, it is the sovereign that electeth him, because it is done by his authority. . . .

From this consolidation of the right politic and ecclesiastic in Christian sovereigns, it is evident, they have all manner of power over their subjects, that can be given to man, for the government of men's external actions, both in policy and religion; and may make such laws as themselves shall judge fittest, for the government of their own subjects, both as they are the commonwealth, and as they are the Church; for both State and Church are the same men.

If they please, therefore, they may, as many Christian kings now do, commit the government of their subjects in matters of religion to the Pope; but then the Pope is in that point subordinate to them, and exerciseth that charge in another's dominion *jure civili,* in the right of the civil sovereign; not *jure divino,* in God's right; and may therefore be discharged of that office, when the sovereign, for the good of his subjects, shall think it necessary. They may also, if they please, commit the care of religion to one supreme pastor, or to an assembly of pastors; and give them what power over the Church, or one over another, they think most convenient. . . .

43] OF WHAT IS NECESSARY FOR MAN'S RECEPTION INTO THE KINGDOM OF HEAVEN

. . . And when the civil sovereign is an infidel, every one of his own subjects that resisteth him, sinneth against the laws of God, (for such are the laws of nature), and rejecteth the counsel of the apostles, that admonisheth all Christians to obey their princes, and all children and servants to obey their parents and masters in all things. And for their *faith,* it is internal, and invisible; they have the license that Naaman had, and need not put themselves into danger for it. But if they do, they ought to expect their reward in heaven, and not complain of their lawful sovereign; much less make war upon him. For he that is not glad of any just occasion of martyrdom, has not the faith he professeth, but pretends it only, to set some colour upon his own contumacy. . . .

* * *

10

Republicanism

THOUGH Pieter De la Court (1618–1685) never held any office in the Dutch state, he belonged to that segment of the wealthy bourgeoisie which provided the Dutch Republic with its patrician class ("the Regents"). A son of a rich cloth merchant and manufacturer, he studied the classics, law, and theology. His ventures in the family business, as well as his judicious marriages, netted him a fortune of over a million guilders; his less successful enterprises included an attempt to grow pineapples in Holland. But above all De la Court was known as a political controversialist, expressing the views of the extreme anti-Orangist wing of the States Party. Het Interest van Holland, first published in 1662, and later revised in 1666–1667, aroused a storm of protest in the Orangist camp, and was not wholly approved of in the more moderate circles of the States Party. Some of the contemporaries in France and in England attributed this tract to John De Witt. Though De Witt had read De la Court's work in manuscript and made some emendations, it cannot be said to represent the thought of the Grand Pensionary. The reader should be warned that De la Court speaks of "Holland" in the narrow sense, meaning the Province of Holland; he treats the other provinces of the Dutch Republic as virtually foreign states.

De la Court, The Interest of Holland

**I, 1] WHEREIN ARE LAID DOWN THE
GENERAL POLITICAL MAXIMS WHICH
TEND TO THE PROSPERITY OF ALL
COUNTRIES . . .**

THAT we may not abruptly speak of the true interest and political maxims of Holland and West Friesland, nor yet surprise the reader with unknown matters, I judge it necessary to begin with a general discourse of the universal and true political maxims of all countries: that the reader being enlightened by such reasoning, may the better comprehend the true political maxims of Holland and West Friesland. And seeing that almost all the people in Europe, as the Spaniards, Italians, French, etc., do express the same by the word interest, I shall often have occasion to use the same likewise here for brevity sake, in the same sense that they do: *viz.,* seeing the true interest of all countries consists in the joint welfare of the governors and governed; and the same is known to depend on a good government, that being the true foundation whereon all the prosperity of any country is built; we are therefore to know, that a good government is not that where the well or ill-being of the subjects depends on the virtues or vices of the rulers; but (which is worthy of observation) where the well or ill-being of the rulers necessarily follows or depends on the well or ill-being of the subjects. For seeing we must believe that in all societies or assemblies of men, self is always preferred; so all sovereigns or supreme powers will in the first place seek their own advantage in all things, though to the prejudice of the subject. But seeing on the other hand true interest cannot be compassed by a government, unless the generality of the people partake thereof; therefore the public welfare which very aptly agrees with our Latin and Dutch proverb that . . . we are only sensible of public afflictions, in so far

From The True Interest and Political Maxims of the Republick of Holland and West-Friesland. Written by John De Witt and other Great Men in Holland. (London, 1702), pp. 1–9, 292–94, 314–15, 366–73, 375–76, 378–79, 388–96, 487–89. The spelling has been modernized in these excerpts.

as they touch our private affairs; for nobody halts of another man's sore.

Whereby it clearly follows, that all wise men, whether monarchs, princes, sovereign lords, or rulers of republics are always inclined to strengthen their country, kingdom, or city, that they may defend themselves against the power of any stronger neighbor. The ruler's welfare therefore does so far necessarily depend on the welfare of the subject; else they would soon be conquered by stronger neighboring princes, and be turned out of their government. Those monarchs and supreme powers who by bad education, and great prosperity, follow their pleasures, suffer their government to fall into the hands of favorites and courtiers, and do commonly neglect this first duty; the said favorites in the meantime finding themselves vested with such sovereign power, do for the most part rule to the benefit of themselves, and to the prejudice, not only of such voluptuous and unwary chief magistrates, but also of their subjects; and by consequence to the weakening of the political state; so that we have often seen revolutions of such monarchies by the ill government of favorites. But such princes as are wise, and do not entrust their power in other men's hands, will not omit to strengthen their dominions against their neighbors as much as possible. But when monarchies, or republics are able enough to do this, and have nothing to fear from their neighboring states or potentates, then they do usually, according to the opportunity put into their hands by the form of their government, take courses quite contrary to the welfare of the subject.

For then it follows as truly from the said general maxims of all rulers, that the next duty of monarchs, and supreme magistrates, is to take special care that their subjects may not be like generous and mettlesome horses which, when they cannot be commanded by the rider, but are too headstrong, wanton, and powerful for their master, they reduce, and keep so tame and manageable, as not to refuse the bit and bridle, I mean taxes and obedience. For which end it is highly necessary to prevent the greatness and power of their cities, that they may not out of their own wealth be able to raise and maintain an army in the field, not only to repel all foreign power, but also to make head against their own lord, or expel him. And as little, yea much less, may prudent sovereign lords or monarchs permit that their cities, by their strong fortifications, and training their inhabitants to arms, should have an opportunity easily, if they pleased, to discharge and turn off their sovereign. But if herein a sovereign had neglected his duty, there's no way left for him, but to wait an opportunity to command such populous cities and strongholds by citadels, and to render them weak and defenseless. And though Aristotle says that it very well suits an oligarchical state to have their cities under command of a castle, yet this is only true of a great and populous city, that hath a prince over it, and not of a city that governs itself, or hath a share in the supreme government; for in such a republic, the governor of that citadel would certainly be able to make himself master of that city, and to subjugate or overtop his rulers. And we see that this reason is so strong and clear, and confirmed by experience that the history of all former ages, as well as the age we live in, teach us, that the rulers of republics, whatever they are, have wisely forborne erecting citadels, and do still continue to do so. So that it appears that the said maxim tending to the overthrow of great and populous cities, may be attributed to monarchs and princes at all times, but never to republics, unless when they have inconsiderately subdued great cities; and though not willing to demolish them, yet are willing to keep them distinct from the sovereign government. But if the inconsiderate reader be so far prepossessed in favor of monarchy and against common freedom, that he neither can nor will submit himself to this way of reasoning, nor to the venerable and ancient lessons of old and renowned philosophers, then let him know, that the Christian and Invincible Monarch Justinian has for ever established the said monarchical maxim by form of law in the *Corpus Juris,* now become the common law-book of all civilized people, and especially of Christians. For the said Emperor having by his Captain General of the East, Belisarius, reconquered from the Goths that part of Africa which he had formerly lost, and brought it under his subjection, gave him no order that the inhabitants of great cities should be better disciplined and provided with arms, or strengthened by good walls, that they might jointly with ease defend themselves and their great populous cities against the assaults of those barbarous people. But on the contrary, he commands the said Captain General Belisarius (and consequently, according to the Roman laws, all his other governors of provinces) to make such provision, that no city or stronghold lying on the frontiers be so great as it could not be well kept; but in such cases so to order them to be built, that they may be well defended with few soldiers, and particularly such as were in pay and depended only on the Emperor of Rome.

And though weak, voluptuous, dull and sluggish monarchs neglect all these things, yet will not the courtiers who govern in their stead neglect to seek themselves, and to fill their coffers whether in war or peace: and thus the subjects' estates being exhausted by rapine, those great and flourishing cities become poor and weak. And to the end that the subject should not be able to hinder or prevent such rapine, or revenge themselves, those favorites omit no opportunities to divest those populous cities of all fortifications, provision, ammunition of war, and to hinder the exercising of the commonalty in the use of arms. Since it appears from the said maxims, that the public is not regarded but for the sake of private interest; and consequently that is the best government where the chief rulers may best obtain their own welfare by that of the people: it follows then to be the duty of the governors of republics to seek for great cities, and to make them as populous and strong as possible, that so all rulers and magistrates, and likewise all others that serve the public either in country or city, may thereby gain the more power, honor, and benefit, and more safely possess it, whether in peace or war. And this is the reason why commonly we see that all republics thrive and flourish far more in arts, manufacture, traffic, populousness and strength, than the dominions and cities of monarchs: for where there is liberty, there will be riches and people.

To bring all this home, and make it suit with our state, we ought to consider that Holland may easily be defended against her neighbors; and that the flourishing of manufactures, fishing, navigation, and traffic, whereby that province subsists, and (its natural necessities or wants being well considered) depends perpetually on them; else would be uninhabited: I say, the flourishing of those things will infallibly produce great, strong, populous and wealthy cities, which by reason of their convenient situation, may be impregnably fortified. All which to a monarch, or one supreme head, is altogether intolerable. And therefore, I conclude, that the inhabitants of Holland, whether rulers or subjects, can receive no greater mischief in their polity, than to be governed by a monarch, or supreme lord: and that on the other side, God can give no greater temporal blessing to a country in our condition, than to introduce and preserve a free commonwealth government.

But seeing this conclusion opposeth the general and long-continued prejudices of all ignorant persons, and consequently of most of the inhabitants of these United Provinces, and that some of my readers might distaste this treatise upon what I have already said, unless somewhat were spoken to obviate their mistakes, I shall therefore offer them these reasons.

Although by what hath been already said, it appears that the inhabitants of a republic are infinitely more happy than the subjects of a land governed by one supreme head; yet the contrary is always thought in a country where a prince is already reigning, or in republics, where one supreme head is ready to be accepted.

For not only officers, courtiers, idle gentry, and soldiery, but also all those that would be such, knowing, that under the worst government they use to fare best, because they hope that with impunity they may plunder and rifle the citizens and country people, and so by the corruption of the government enrich themselves, or attain to grandeur, they cry up monarchical government for their private interest to the very heavens; although God did at first mercifully institute no other but a commonwealth government, and afterwards in his wrath appointed one sovereign over them. Yet for all this, those blood-suckers of the state, and indeed of mankind, dare to speak of republics with the utmost contempt, make a mountain of every molehill, discourse of the defects of them at large, and conceal all that is good in them, because they know none will punish them for what they say: wherefore all the rabble (according to the old Latin verse) being void of knowledge and judgment, and therefore inclining to the weather or safer side, and mightily valuing the vain and empty pomp of kings and princes, say *amen* to it; especially when kept in ignorance, and irritated against the lawful government by preachers, who aim at dominion, or would introduce an independent and arbitrary power of Church-government; and such (God amend it) are found in Holland, and the other United Provinces, insomuch, that all virtuous and intelligent people have been necessitated to keep silence, and to beware of disclosing the vices of their princes, or of such as would willingly be their governors, or of courtiers and rude military men and such ambitious and ungovernable preachers as despise God, and their Native Country.

*   *   *

II, 10] INFERENCES DRAWN FROM
WHAT HAS BEEN SAID OF ALLIANCES

*   *   *

It is, and always will be dangerous for Holland, to make alliances with France, Spain, or England, because 'tis probable that they who are more esteemed only because they are kings, and possess larger territories than we, will always oblige us to perform our engagements first, and expound all ambiguous points to their own advantage. But so long as we are in the least fear of France, that is, so long as Spain can keep the Netherlands, we may best enter into alliance with that kingdom of common defense, against those that might wrong, or make war against the one or the other. But when France is like to be master of the Netherlands, and become our neighbor, it is not only necessary for Holland to prevent that potent, and always bold and insolent neighbor, and to take great care not to make any league, by which France may in any measure increase in power; but all the potentates and states of Europe ought to combine together to hinder the growth of that kingdom, which hath already overgrown all its neighbors.

Likewise, so long as we must dread England in the highest degree, it is perfectly useless to make the least alliance with that kingdom, save such as is grounded upon a common fear of a greater power, as now France is; seeing all written alliances, without common necessity, are interpreted in favor of the greatest, as happens in all doubtful cases: besides that England will thus find more cause with appearance of right to make war against us. For if that be found true, which mean persons conclude, that all that are in partnership have a master; and that all such partnerships begin *In the Name of God,* but use to end in that of the Devil: 'tis much more true of kings and princes, who have outgrown all justice, and consequently as true, that so long as England intends to have the quiet or disquiet of Holland at their own disposal, she would be the worst and most tyrannical ally for us that were to be found in the whole world, unless the dread of a more powerful neighbor should curb that pernicious inclination.

To sum up all: So long as Holland can stand on its own legs, it is utterly unadvisable to make any alliance with those who are more potent; and especially it is not good to perform any thing first, or be beforehand with those unconstant monarchs and princes, in hope that they will perform with us afterwards, according to the old saying: "They that eat cherries with great men must pay for them themselves", and besides suffer them to choose the fairest, and expect at last to be pelted with the stones, instead of thanks for the favor received.

And consequently it is certain, that all the advantage in articles of an alliance consists in this, that Holland do always covenant that the other allies shall first perform their engagements. All other sort of alliances are very prejudicial to us; for by the proper constitution, or ancient custom of our government, the deputies of the Provinces upon all occasion will, where they can expect any private benefit, suffer themselves to be moved by foreign ambassadors to draw in Holland to their party, when they can see no detriment to accrue thereby to their particular Provinces.

* * *

12] THAT HOLLAND DURING ITS FREE GOVERNMENT CANNOT BE RUINED BY ANY INTESTINE POWER

'Tis evident that no domestic power can subvert the republic of Holland, nor destroy the welfare of the inhabitants, except by a general conspiracy, sedition, insurrection, and civil war of the people and cities of Holland against one another, because they are so wonderfully linked together by a common good, that those home-bred tumults and wars are not to be supposed able to be raised except by inhabitants of such eminent strength as is able to force the Magistracy of the country to the execution of such destructive counsels. And seeing now in Holland and West Friesland there is no Captain-General or Stadtholder, nor any illustrious person except the prince of Orange; therefore we will consider, whether if the said prince who is in no office of the Generality, continuing in these Provinces, might be able to cause or effect such ruinous and destructive divisions in Holland.

And indeed as I have a prospect, that if he should happen to get into any administration, he might occasion such divisions and breaches: yet on the other side, I cannot see how without employment, either from the Generality, or this Province, he should obtain so great an interest in the government of these countries, as to be able to cause a civil war, and make himself master of them, either with the old or a new title; for he being no general, nor having any military dependents, and out of all command, though he might by seditious preachers cause a few of the rabble to rise against their lawful rulers; yet this would not be like to happen at one time, and in so many places together, as to make an alteration in the Provincial Government. And that free government remaining entire, the new magistrates obtruded on the people upon this rising, would be turned out, and the seditious every time signally punished. And this would also tend to the great prejudice of the honor of the Prince of Orange; besides that by this means he would lose all hopes and appearances of ever being employed in the Country's service; and on the other side might fear that he and his posterity should forever be excluded from all government and service in these United Netherlands by a perpetual law.

And if the Prince of Orange be not able to cause such seditions and divisions, I suppose it could less be done by any College of the Generality: for I would fain know in which of the cities of Holland would the States General, or the Council of State, without a military head, be now able to alter the present free government by force or faction? Assuredly not in any one city. And from the lesser Colleges of the Generality such mischiefs are less to be feared.

*　*　*

III, 1] WHEREIN ENQUIRY IS MADE IN WHAT THE INTEREST OF THE FREE RULERS OF HOLLAND, AS TO ALL THE PARTICULARS BY WHICH THE PEOPLE MAY LIVE HAPPILY, CONSISTS

Having hitherto shown that the welfare of the inhabitants of Holland is grounded upon the preservation and improvement of fisheries, manufactures, traffic and shipping, and that the same cannot be acquired nor kept but by liberty, or to speak plainer a toleration of all religions, though differing from the Reformed, and by a free burger-right for all strangers that will cohabit with us, with licence to follow all their trades and occupations whatever, without trouble or molestation from their fellow inhabitants, in respect of any societies, companies, halls, guilds, or corporations: and by such moderation about convoy monies and tolls, that no ships or goods coming in, or going out, may be charged with, or eased and freed from all taxes, otherwise than as it may be subservient to the improvement of our fisheries, manufactures, traffic and navigation. Moreover, having shown that all the things beforementioned are not sufficient to preserve and keep up the said fisheries, manufactures, traffic and navigation, unless the courts of justice, and laws be constituted and executed more than hitherto in favor of the inhabitants, and of traffic. And lastly that in foreign countries, colonies of Hollanders ought to be established and protected.

And in the second book having likewise shown, how necessary it is that the sea be cleared of all free-booters and pirates, and that peace be sought with all men. And moreover, having shown that Holland is to beware of entering into any prejudicial alliances with its neighbors, and potentates, but rather to strengthen their own frontiers, and inland cities, and exercise their inhabitants well in arms, and to keep the sword in their own hands, against all domestic and foreign power, which would be as great a strengthening and security to them, yea, and more than any other country. Therefore I judge it now useful deliberately to examine whether a land having such interests ought to be governed by a republican or monarchical form of government: for it is certain that all public power to improve, or impair the interest of a land, and to preserve and enlarge, or diminish and ruin a state, must be, and is in the hands of the lawful rulers of a country, whether they be monarchs, princes, statesmen, or the common burgers. . . .

By the word republic and republican rulers, I mean, not only such a state wherein a certain sovereign assembly hath the right and authority for coming to all resolutions, making of orders and laws, or to break them, as also of requiring or prohibiting obedience to them. But I understand thereby such a state wherein an assembly, though possibly without any right, yet hath the power to cause all their resolutions, orders, and laws, to be obeyed and put in execution. . . .

For though it be true, that the republican form of government is so acceptable to the merchants and all wise and virtuous men that many will object, that the bare name, shadow, and appearance of freedom hath been able to encourage the traffic and navigation of Holland; yet to me it seems to be no less true that we ought to expect many more good fruits from the thing itself than from the appearance of it: and besides, it cannot be denied, but that the name and the shadow must, and shall always give way to, and vanish before the power, effect, and thing itself. So that he that will narrowly inquire into the good or bad fruits which are to be expected of such or such a kind of government would do very ill if he should not let his thoughts and observations, in this particular, run more on the power which can operate without right, than upon right which without power is insignificant, and when violence or force comes, must always cease.

And that this may more clearly appear, the reader may please to consider, that by the word (lawful government) is meant, and must be meant, the right of compelling obedience to that government; and that this is grounded upon ancient possession, or upon laws, customs, or oaths, or upon all together, which are of themselves weak, unless they be backed by persons authorized, that are willing and ready at the command of the lawful rulers to punish such rebellious or perjured subjects. Whereas on the other side, a greater or stronger adherence of people to a governor, or some leading men, and without the least right, may have so great a power, that they shall destroy all good orders and customs; and such are wont to cast all the ancient and virtuous lawful rulers out of their right and possession. . . .

And if the said maxim, that he that is master of the places of strength and soldiery is also master, or may make himself so, of the state, be infallibly true; then it is a more material truth that he who besides the command of the soldiery, possesseth the favor of most of the inhabitants, or the rude rabble, can make himself master of the State when he assembles the said soldiery for that end. So that if any one may do this by a deputed power, we must consider him, though a servant or minister to the State, as having in all respects the power of the Republic in his hands; and therefore the thing itself being duly considered, he is already sovereign monarch of that State, and is so to be understood, that the name and the right of that free Republican Government will likewise soon vanish, and consequently after that not any of the fruits of free government or anything like it ought to be expected. But on the contrary, all that used to proceed from a Monarchical Government, must be supposed to happen; and therefore such a government ought no more to be called a Republic, but a Monarchy in practice and in fact. . . .

It is very well worth observation, that in republics the rulers, magistrates, and other public ministers have very little reward and salary for their service; who, while they are in the condition of citizens, neither may nor can enrich themselves with the revenues of the land, and therefore are necessitated by other ways than that of magistracy, and public employments, to maintain themselves and their families, as by merchandizing, etc. Thus it is still, or was lately in the republics of Venice, Genoa, Ragusa, Lucca, Milan, Florence, etc. At least it is well known that in Holland very many rulers and magistrates maintain themselves by the fisheries, manufactures, traffic and navigation.

Or, if some of the rulers and servants of the Republic of Holland do possess such estates as to be able to live at ease on their lands and revenues, yet it is evident that the Reformed Religion, permitting no cloisters or spiritual revenues, and the public worship being performed by ministers for a very small reward or salary, and by the elders and deacons *gratis,* there is no relief to be had thence for distressed, impoverished relations and families. So that many rulers being sensible, that according to the proverb "Many swine cause but thin wash," either they themselves, or at least their posterity in the third or fourth generation, must in this naturally poor, though for merchandize well situated country, rise again by traffic. And hence it is that all the rulers of Holland are derived of parents that have lived by the fisheries, manufactures, traffic or navigation, and so their children after them; and that the said rulers do still daily to maintain their families find it proper to marry their children to rich merchants, or their children. So that such rulers, whether considered in themselves by their consanguinity or affinity, are in all respects interested in the welfare or illfare of the fisheries, manufactures, traffic, and navigation of this country. . . .

As to the administration or service of the Church, by the Preacher, Elder and Deacon in Holland; it must be confessed that those services there are of so little profit and credit that the Rulers and Magistrates, or their friends, are very seldom inclined to perform those functions: so that the freedom and toleration of the assemblies of different worship in Holland, cannot be expected (from such a supreme head) by Rulers or Magistrates, because the dissenters, under pretence of assembling for the service of God, would endeavor to make insurrections, and thereby depose the Rulers to domineer over the state, and the established religion. Against which it may be said, that the honest dissenting inhabitants, who fare well in this country, or possess any considerable estates, ought not to be presumed to fall into such seditious thoughts, so destructive to themselves and the country, so long as they are not embittered by persecution; but on the contrary will be obliged by such liberty, easy and moderate government, to show their gratitude to so good a magistracy. Wherefore the rascally people, or those of mean estates, and ambitious and seditious inhabitants, would be deprived of all adherents, whom otherwise under the cloak of Religion they might the more easily gain to carry on their ill designs.

And moreover it is well known to all prudent men, that such persons as seek after sovereignty, do usually favor seditious preachers, and zealous devotees, that by the help of those tumultuous spirits they may arrive at that dignity; and yet no sooner do they acquire that sovereign power, but presently they are sensible how unfit those stubborn and imprudent devotees and seditious preachers are to be made use of in Magistracy or Government; insomuch that they then use to desert them, and in lieu of preferring and enriching them, use to punish them for their sedition. . . .

And therefore we may presume that our wise free rulers will ever continue to indulge and permit the religious assemblies of dissenters, hereby to invite over continually more dissenting people into Holland; and will plant and improve the Reformed Religion, not by compulsion, but moderation and soft means among their good dissenting inhabitants; and that they will always preserve, and maintain in like manner, our present public worship, without ever admitting of an Episcopal or any other coercive spiritual authority.

An open or free burgership, with a right for all foreign inhabitants to follow their employments, being added to liberty of conscience in matters religious; it will certainly cause very great and populous cities, and incredible many conveniences and divertisements for all the inhabitants: so that all civil magistrates ought for that reason, were there no other, to endeavor it; and the more the better, if we observe that in such lands and cities, offices do exceedingly multiply, and are made profitable, and that then the rulers would have the power to prefer many, if not all their friends to make them to live in credit and ease.

Moreover, in such lands and cities there will be found naturally among the inhabitants diversities in religion, nations, tongues, and occupations: so that there would be no occasions ministered to the few aristocratical rulers who govern our republic, and cities, of dividing the people by artificial, and often impious designs, in order to govern them: for by these natural divisions, and the diversity of the peoples' occupations, they may as peaceably and safely govern them, as in the open country; for in the great cities of Holland, and other cities filled with foreign inhabitants, as Amsterdam, Leyden, Haarlem, etc., there have been nothing near so many seditions against the rulers, as in other countries, and much less and worse peopled cities, unless when they have been stirred up to mutiny or sedition by a sovereign head. For in such a case, I confess that no countries or cities, great or small, are or can be at rest, and without uproars of the subjects against their rulers and magistrates any longer than such a head pleaseth to leave such lands and cities in peace.

Finally, it is to be observed, that the rulers of such populous open countries and cities, are also much better able to defend themselves against all foreign power, whether by an army formed of their own inhabitants or by strengthening their respective cities by good fortifications, and repelling all enemies from their walls. And seeing on the other side the rulers of Holland will not be advantaged by a burgership that excludes all foreigners, we may therefore believe that they will easily approve of it.

As to societies or companies erected by patents, halls and guilds, upon manufactures, trades, fisheries, commerce, and navigation; it is certain that the rulers, governors, and masters of guilds, having power at their pleasure, or at certain times and places, to call assemblies, and by a general interest having an united number of dependents, members and their followers, whether of mariners, soldiers, clothiers, and brethren of the guild or workmen, may have fair opportunities by sedition to displace a few aristocratical rulers, and put themselves into their places, as hath been seen in all Netherlandish cities, where heretofore such halls and guilds have been erected, *viz.*, Ghent, Bruges, Ypres, Louvain, Antwerp, Dordt, Liege, etc., wherein there were many tumults proceeding from that cause.

And though hitherto there hath arisen no seditious commotion of note from the patent companies, yet it is certain that they tend only to the advantage of some very few persons, and to the detriment of all other inhabitants of that way of dealing; and having laid the foundation of one government within another, they may in time expect from thence, especially under a free government, more commotions, unless the civil rulers do be so prudent and happy as to appoint their deputies in all the said assemblies, who will not seek their own welfare in the government by faction or combination, but by a praiseworthy desire after the welfare of their native country, to seek the common good. . . .

Concerning the rates of convoy-money or customs upon goods exported or imported; let them be laid on with such prudence and moderation, that they may be calculated purely for the benefit of our manufactures, fisheries, traffic, and navigation. I have already shown how much the rulers of Holland are concerned in the flourishing of those particulars. Wherefore on the other side it is evident, that during a free government a very good account of all monies received ought to be given, and that the same ought to be employed for the clearing of the seas. It is self-evident that the rulers cannot enrich themselves with the money issuing thence; and therefore the said rulers of the Holland cities will not henceforth be inclined to charge goods with such high and prejudicial rates, but rather in process of time to favor the merchants in that particular; and that the seas be cleared by such monies as are the public revenue of the land, raised of all the inhabitants as such, and to defend the merchant from oppression by sea.

Moreover, from what is said before it may be fairly inferred, that such interested free rulers should incline to enact good orders and laws, and so to frame justice, that there may be quicker dispatch made, and better justice done, and that knavish bankrupts be punished and the honest merchants protected in their right: for the civil rulers by increasing the number of subordinate judges and counsellors, may be able to bestow on their best friends more honorable and profitable employments, and by that means the better settle themselves in the government and magistracy. Whereas by the contrary, such judges will rather be prejudiced than advantaged by bribes, and the favor or disfavor of the rulers, because possibly they would not give so much money on that score as others would.

As to colonies, it is evident that the rulers of republics do not pay out of their own purses the expense of erecting and protecting them from outward violence; but it is paid out of the Public Treasury, and in the meanwhile they would reap this benefit for their indigent relations to send them to such colonies, when they are not able to prefer them all in Holland: and the like might be done with many other inhabitants that are ambitious of government, or public employment; and the said colonies would in no other regard be hurtful to the republican rulers. So that since those colonies would be so generally profitable for the land and inhabitants of Holland, as is heretofore described, we are then 'rationally to expect that they will be erected by our rulers.

As to the clearing of the seas against enemies and piccaroons, it is certain that during a free Republican Government, the treasure requisite for building and setting forth ships, proceeds not out of the rulers' purses; and that they and their friends that trade at sea, being as liable as other inhabitants to lose their goods by such enemies, and that this may be prevented without putting them to any charge, we may likewise expect the same of them. And that the sea may with honor and safety for the State be cleared by the free rulers, cannot be denied. For though the Admiral of a Fleet going to sea without a sufficient strength, should lose the said Fleet to the enemies of the State, and thereby might exceedingly mischieve our Republic, yet would it not totally bereave us of our liberty, nor should it be dissolved by such a treachery; but on the contrary, our Republic has ever been able to be recruited, and has oft-times been reinforced by our land forces, when they have been entrusted to Captain-Generals; and even when they have thought fit to use their strength to conquer the cities of Holland, and to seize their deputies when they were assembled by summons. And therefore since the free rulers will not incline to carry on an offensive war, and consequently to send a chargeable army into the field to take cities from our neighbors; it is not credible that the said convoy-monies paid for clearing the seas will be taken from the Admiralties to make therewith any needless and yet chargeable conquests by land and in the meanwhile to abandon our inhabitants, or their goods to the depredations of the sea robbers.

Lastly, it is certain that the rulers of Holland, and all their trafficking subjects would fare much better in times of peace than in war, because then they would be reverenced and obeyed by them without any opposition. And besides, our City Magistrates cannot receive any considerable profit by war, either by land or sea, but must bear all new burdens and taxes thereby arising, as well as the other inhabitants, and cannot be freed from the same, as the late Heads of our Republic were. It is evident the soldiery, and their officers, who are for monarchical government and an illustrious general *ad vitam*, would not use their due and strenuous endeavors to perform the commands and counsels of the Republic, or those that are in authority for the state: so that the rulers of the Republic of Holland, in case of an unsuccessful war, would soon see their respect from the subject diminished, and be every way aspersed by the sottish ill-natured rabble, who always judge of things by the success, and ever hate, and are ready to impeach the aristocratical rulers of their republic; with whom some lavish, ambitious and debauched people, whether rulers or subjects, might join themselves to stir up sedition, and under pretence of being of the Prince's or Captain-General's faction, turn this Republic into a Monarchy, in hope of attaining the most eminent and profitable employments under the monarch.

And above all, the present free governors would be liable to that hazard in case they should make use of such a field general in their wars by land, whose ancestors have had the same trust reposed in them; for then, whether in good or bad successes, those few citizens that rule in Holland during life and serve in the magistracy but a year or two, would soon find that none amongst them would dare to tie the bell about the cat's neck, to discharge such a Captain-General with so many dependents and adherents, when they have no further need of his service, or to punish him when he deserved it, whether by disobedience, correspondency with the enemy, or any attempt against the free government, even though an open endeavor to gain the sovereignty; so that thereby alone our Republic would be really changed into a Monarchy.

And moreover, suppose we should choose a meaner person to be our Captain-General, and give to him the command of the whole troops of this State, and that but for a short time, yet it is evident that the rulers of Holland would put themselves in greater danger of being overmastered by that Captain-General, as by innumerable examples which happened here and in other countries may be perceived; unless men could make the dull Hollanders to believe that God hath induced them with two miraculous privileges above all other people in the world; the first is, that they shall never choose any Captain-General but out of such excellent and blessed families, that though they could, yet differing from all other men, they would not rather choose to be lords than servants; and that therefore that ambition that is natural to all men, even to their very graves, should find no place in him during his whole life. And the second is, that the Hollanders having at first, whether voluntarily or inadvertently, and after that by succession or constraint, placed over themselves a Monarch *in fieri,* that then God from heaven will snatch away such a monarch suddenly, and by an unexpected judgment deliver a people from slavery, who are so unworthy of liberty, as indeed hath sometimes happened.

*   *   *

8] THE CONCLUSION OF THE WHOLE BOOK, WITH A DECLARATION OF THE AUTHOR'S DESIGN, AND A CAUTION BOTH TO THE ILL AND WELL AFFECTED READERS

. . . My intent was, both in general and in particular, to show briefly wherein the interest of Holland consists, *viz.,* that as in all countries of the world, the highest perfection of a political society, and in a land by accident laboring under taxes, and naturally indigent, as Holland is, there is an absolute necessity that the commonalty be left in as great a natural liberty for seeking the welfare of their souls and bodies, and for the improvement of their estates, as possible. For as the inhabitants of the most plentiful country upon Earth, by want only of that natural liberty, and finding themselves every way encumbered and perplexed, do really inhabit a Bridewell or House of Correction, fit for none but miserable condemned slaves, and consequently a hell upon earth. Whereas a power of using their natural rights and properties for their own safety, provided it tends not to the destruction of the society, will be to the commonalty, though in a barren and indigent country, an earthly paradise: for the liberty of a man's own mind, especially about matters wherein all his welfare consists, is to such a one as acceptable as an empire or kingdom.

I have likewise shown, that such a liberty and prosperity of the subject does very well consist in Holland with the present uncontrolled power of the free government, and with none other.

So that all good patriots, and true lovers of our Native Country, who peruse this book, are earnestly entreated to consider deliberately whether the two most weighty points beforementioned are not strongly and sufficiently demonstrated.

But whether, when, and how the particulars here treated of, may all at once or at several times be set about, or perused, was not my intention in the least to direct. For the higher powers, whom it only concerns in a republic to conclude of these matters, and all politicians know that such things as may be borne with less inconvenience than removed or changed ought to continue, and remain in being. And when such wise and good patriots will make any alteration, they must go by degrees, and as far as they conveniently may; yet they must rather stand still, or remain as they are, than run their heads against a wall.

And indeed reformation in political affairs depends on so many, and such various circumstances, namely customs, times, places, rulers, subjects, allies, neighboring and foreign countries, that such a reformation is either proper, or improper to be undertaken according as the several circumstances are well weighed, such especially in a free Republic, which is governed and managed by prudent Assemblies of the States, venerable City Councils, and reputable Colleges; in which it would be a great presumption and self-conceit, yea, indeed, a crime for a private person to dare to conclude anything, and in so doing to arrogate it to himself, or to put a hand to that work which properly and of right belongs only to the States of Holland, and those that are thereunto authorized.

*   *   *

11

Divine Right of Kings

JACQUES-BÉNIGNE BOSSUET (1627–1704) came from a family long connected with parlementary officialdom. In his youth he steeped himself in patristic studies. But it was chiefly as a brilliant preacher that he attracted the attention of the court of Louis XIV in the 1660's. In 1669 he was made bishop of Condom, and became a member of the French Academy in 1671. In 1670 the King appointed him preceptor to the Dauphin, and two years later Bossuet resigned his see in order to devote himself to the task of educating this rather dull-witted youth. After 1681, when Bossuet became Bishop of Meaux, he devoted himself mainly to church affairs and was rarely seen at Versailles, though he retained the King's friendship and esteem.

There was hardly a theological controversy of his day, hardly any discussion of a moral issue, hardly any Catholic catechetic effort in France to which Bossuet did not contribute in his voluminous writings, usually defending with vigor what he considered to be a middle-of-the-road position. For the Dauphin he wrote the Discourse on Universal History and the Politics drawn from the very Words of the Holy Scriptures. Bossuet completed Books I–VI of the Politics in 1679; in 1692 he gave the manuscript to Fénelon and Duc de Beauvilliers, who were then charged with the upbringing of the Duke of Burgundy, the Dauphin's eldest son. Bossuet returned to his treatise in 1700, and worked intermittently until his death on Books VII–X and on revision of the entire text, which was first published in 1709. In quoting the Scriptures, Bossuet usually relies on the Vulgate; however, he sometimes turns to the Greek and Hebrew originals, of which he gives free, not to say cavalier, translations of his own.

Bossuet, Politics Drawn from the Scriptures

BK. I] THE PRINCIPLES OF HUMAN SOCIETY:

Article IV. On Law.

Proposition II: In which the original principles of all the laws are established.

ALL LAW has its foundation in the first of all laws, which is the law of nature; that is to say, in right reason and natural equity. Matters human and divine, public and private, must be governed by law; and law has its origin in nature, as St. Paul says in the following: "when the Gentiles, which have not the law, do by nature the things contained in the law, these, having not the law, are a law unto themselves: Which show the works of the law written in their hearts, their conscience also bearing witness, and their thoughts the meanwhile accusing or else excusing one another." (Rom. II, 14–15)

The law should establish customs sacred and profane, public and private usages; in brief, the just observance among the people of ordinances human and divine, with due rewards and punishments. . . .

Proposition III: That there is order in the laws.

The first principle of law is to acknowledge the Deity, from whom we receive all blessings and our very existence. "Fear God, and keep his commandments: for this is the whole duty of man." (Ecc. XII, 13) And the other is "Whatsoever ye would that men should do unto you, do ye even so to them." (Matt. VII, 12)

Proposition VI: That the law is holy and inviolable.

For a complete understanding of the law, it should be observed that all who have well discussed it, have considered it in origin a

From J. B. Bossuet, Politique tirée des propres Paroles de l'Écriture Sainte, in Œuvres complètes, ed. by F. Lachat, 31 vols. (Paris, 1862–66), XXIII, pp. 496–501, 515–517, 523–529, 532–533, 537–563, 578–580, 583–607, 642–646; XXIV, pp. 8–10, 14–16, 22–32, 42–47, 64, 69–70, 73–80, 84–106, 110–116. Trans. by Geoffrey W. Symcox.

solemn pact or covenant by which men agree together, under the authority of their princes, on the conditions necessary for founding their society.

This is not to say that the law is dependent for its authority upon the consent or acquiescence of the people; but only that the prince, who, moreover, by his very nature, has no interest besides the public good, is aided by the counsel of the wisest men of the nation, and supported by the experience of past centuries. . . .

It should be observed that God did not need the consent of men to give His law validity, for He is their Creator and can constrain them to do whatever He pleases; yet nevertheless, to make the agreement more solemn and enduring, He embodies their acceptance of the law in a free and particular covenant.

Proposition VII: That the law is presumed to be of divine origin.

The covenant we have just discussed has a dual purpose: it unites the nation to God, and the people among themselves.

The people could not be joined by an inviolable bond of association, were the treaty not originally agreed in the presence of a higher power, like the power of God, who is the natural guardian of human society, and the implacable avenger of every breach of the law.

But when men bind themselves to God, swearing to observe both before Him and their fellows the articles of the law which He ordains, then the agreement is inviolable, being endorsed by a power to which all is subject.

For this reason all nations have sought to ascribe their laws to a divine origin, and those that have it not, have tried to counterfeit it. . . .

Proposition VIII: That there are fundamental principles which cannot be changed; and that it is even dangerous to alter needlessly those which may be changed.

It is written principally with reference to these fundamental laws that in breaking them "all the foundations of the earth are out of course," (Ps. LXXXII, 5) from which nothing can ensue but the fall of empires.

In general, laws are not truly such unless they be in some way inviolable. To reveal their immutability and enduring firmness, Moses commanded that "thou shalt write upon the stones all the words of this law very plainly." (Deut. XXVII, 8) Joshua fulfilled this commandment. (Jos. VIII, 32)

The other civilised nations concur in this principle. "Let there go a royal commandment from the King, and let it be written among the laws of the Persians, and the Medes, that it be not altered," spoke the wise men to Ahasuerus, who were always about him. And these wise men knew the laws and customs of the ancients. (Esther I, 13, 19) This reverence for the laws and ancient customs strengthens societies and makes states last for ever.

This regard for the laws is lost if they are seen to change frequently. It is then that nations seem to stagger as though stirred and heavy with wine, as the prophet says. (Isaiah XIX, 14) Confusion overtakes them and their ruin is inevitable, "because they have transgressed the laws, changed the ordinance, broken the everlasting covenant." (Isaiah XXIV, 5) Their condition is that of the restless invalid, not knowing which way to turn [for relief]. . . .

* * *

BK. II] ON AUTHORITY—SHOWING THAT
HEREDITY ROYAL IS THE MOST FITTING
FORM OF GOVERNMENT:

Article I. By whom authority has been exercised since the beginning of the world.

Proposition I: That God is the true King.

A great king acknowledged it thus when he spoke in the presence of all his people: "Blessed by Thou, Lord God of Israel, our father forever and ever. Thine, O Lord, is the greatness, and the power, and the glory, and the victory, and the majesty: for all that is in the heaven and in the earth is thine; thine is the kingdom, O Lord, and thou art exalted as head above all. Both riches and honour come of thee, and thou reignest over all; and in thy hand is power and might, and in thine hand it is to make great, and to give strength unto all." (I Chron. XXIX, 10–12)

The kingdom of God is eternal, and therefore He is called the King of all the ages.

The kingdom of God is absolute. "For who shall say, What hast thou done? or who shall withstand thy judgment?" (Wisdom XII, 12)

This absolute dominion of God has as its origin and first title the Creation. He brought forth all from nothing, and so all is in His hands. . . .

Proposition II: That God has visibly wielded His authority over men.

Thus He acted at the beginning of the world. He was at that time the sole ruler of men, and governed them visibly . . .

It was He who established the kings. He caused Saul and David to be anointed by Samuel: He confirmed the kingship in the house of David, and commanded him to make his son Solomon his successor.

That is why the throne of the kings of Israel was called the throne of God. . . .

Proposition VII: That monarchy is the most common, the most ancient and also the most natural form of government.

The children of Israel spontaneously adopted the kingship, as being the form of government universally accepted. "Now make us a king to judge us like all the nations." (I Sam. VIII, 5)

That this displeased God was because hitherto He had ruled the people Himself, and was their true king. Which is why He said to Samuel, "they have not rejected thee, but they have rejected me, that I should not reign over them." (*ibid.,* 7)

Moreover this form of government was so much the most natural, that it was the earliest found in every nation. . . .

Thus we have seen that it takes its foundation and pattern from paternal control, that is from nature itself.

Men are all born subjects: and paternal authority, which accustoms them to obedience, at the same time teaches them to have but one head.

Proposition VIII: That monarchical government is the best form.

If it is the most natural, it is therefore the most enduring, and in consequence the strongest form of government.

It is also the best defense against division, which is the deadliest disease of states, and the most certain cause of their downfall, as is seen from the words already noted: "Every kingdom divided against itself is brought to desolation; and every city or house divided against itself shall not stand." (Matt. XII, 25)

We see that in this sentence our Lord indicated the natural sequence of authority, and that he seems to wish to designate to kingdoms and cities the same type of unity which nature has established within families.

In fact it is natural that when families unite to form a body politic, they should establish it as it were spontaneously in their own image.

The purpose of founding states is unity, and there is no greater unity than being under one ruler. There is also no greater strength, for all [the wills] concur. . . .

Proposition IX: That of all forms of monarchy, the hereditary form is best, above all when it is by male primogeniture.

It is this form which God established among His people. . . .

The kingship was thus vested by right of succession in the house of David and Solomon: "and the throne of David shall be established for ever" (II Sam. VII, 16) . . .

Proposition X: That hereditary monarchy has three principal advantages.

Three arguments prove this form of government best.

The first is that it is the most natural, and self-regenerating. Nothing is more lasting than a state which maintains and prolongs itself by the same causes which preserve the universe, and perpetuate the human species. . . .

Nations grow accustomed to it of themselves. "I considered all the living which walk under the sun, with the second child that shall stand up in his stead" (that is, the king's son). (Ecc. IV, 15)

There are no disputes, no factions in a state which makes its kings as nature makes them: the dead, as we say, invests the living, and the king never dies.

That form of government is best which is furthest from anarchy. For an institution as essential as government among men, the simplest principles should be followed, and an order which subsists of itself.

The second reason favoring this form of government, is that it is the type which best identifies the interest of the ruling powers with the preservation of the state. The prince who labors for his state, labors for his sons; and his love for his kingdom becomes part of his nature by being mingled with his love for his family.

It is natural and good to show the prince no successor but his son; that is his own image, or that which is closest to him. Then he can see his kingdom pass into other hands without jealousy, just as David heard with joy the acclamation of his people: "God make the name of Solomon better than thy name, and make his throne greater than thy throne." (I Kings 1, 47) . . .

The third reason has its origins in the honor of the houses in which the kingship is hereditary. . . .

The peoples grow attached to their royal houses. Their natural envy for those set above them changes to love and respect; even the greatest subjects willingly obey a house which has always reigned, and to which they know no other house can ever be compared.

There is no surer way of extinguishing faction, and maintaining in their obedience equals divided by ambition and jealousy.

Proposition XII: That the form of government already found in the country should be maintained.

"Let every soul be subject unto the higher powers. For there is no power but of God: the powers that be are ordained of God. Whosoever therefore resisteth the power, resisteth the ordinance of God." (Rom. XIII, 1–2)

There is no form of government nor human institution without imperfections; so that it is necessary to continue in that state to which time has accustomed the people. Which is why God takes under His protection all legitimate governments, in whatever form they were established; he who seeks to procure their ruin is not only the enemy of the people, but also the enemy of God.

* * *

Conclusion

. . . Thus we have shown that by the action of Divine Providence the constitution of this realm was from the first in that form most acceptable to God's will, as set forth in the Holy Scriptures.

We have not forgotten, however, that other forms of government were known in antiquity, concerning which God did not instruct mankind: so that each nation should follow the form of government established in its country, as a divine institution, for

God is a peaceful God, who wishes for composure in human affairs.

But since we are writing in a monarchical state, and for a prince whose concern is the succession of so great a kingdom, we shall now turn to the prescriptions which we find in Holy Scripture regarding the form of government under which we live: although from the conclusions that we reach concerning that form, it will be easy to lay down principles for the others.

BK. III] IN WHICH WE BEGIN TO EXPLAIN THE NATURE AND PROPERTIES OF ROYAL AUTHORITY:

Article I. In which its essential characteristics are noted

Sole Proposition: That there are four essential characteristics of royal authority.

First, royal authority is sacred.
Second, it is paternal.
Third, it is absolute.
Fourth, it is subject to reason.
This is to be proved in order in the following articles.

Article II. Royal authority is holy.

Proposition IV: That kings should respect their powers and only employ them for the general good.

Since their power comes from above, as has been stated, they should not believe that they are masters of it and may use it just as they please; they should exercise it with fear and restraint, as a thing conferred on them by God, for which they are answerable to Him. "Hear therefore, O ye Kings, and understand; learn, ye that be judges of the ends of the earth. Give ear, ye that rule the people, and glory in the multitude of nations. For power is given you of the Lord, and sovereignty from the Highest, who shall try your works and search out your counsels. Because, being ministers of His kingdom, ye have not judged aright, nor kept the law, nor walked after the counsel of God. Horribly and speedily shall He come upon you: for a sharp judgment shall be to them that are in high places. For mercy will soon pardon the meanest; but the mighty shall be mightily tormented. For He which is Lord over all shall fear no man's person, neither shall He stand in awe of any man's greatness: for He hath made the small and great, and careth for all alike. But a sore trial shall come upon the mighty. Unto you therefore, O kings, do I speak, that ye may learn wisdom, and not fall away." (Wis. VI, 1–9)

Kings should therefore tremble to exercise the power which God has given to them, and remember how terrible a sacrilege it is to abuse the power which comes from God.

We have seen kings seated on the throne of the Lord, holding in their hand the sword which He has committed to their charge. What blasphemy and presumption it is for an unjust ruler to occupy the throne of God and give judgments contrary to His law, to wield the sword which He has placed in their hands to oppress and destroy His children!

They should therefore have regard for their power, for it is not theirs, but God's, to be used righteously and in fear. St. Gregory Nazianzene spoke thus to the Emperors: "Respect your purple; confess the great mystery of God shown forth by your persons; the heavens He rules alone, the earth He shares with you. Be therefore gods to your subjects." That is to say, govern them as God himself governs, nobly, impartially, benevolently; in a word, divinely.

Article III. Royal authority is paternal, and its true quality is goodness

Proposition   I: That goodness is a royal quality, and the true accompaniment of greatness. . . .

Proposition   II: That the prince is born not for his own sake, but for his people. . . .

Proposition   III: That the prince should provide for the needs of his people. . . .

Proposition   IV: That of his subjects, those for whom the prince should have the greatest care are the weak. . . .

Proposition   V: That the true function of a prince is to provide for the needs of his people, just as the tyrant thinks only of himself. . . .

Proposition   VI: That a prince who fails to ensure the welfare of his people will be as harshly punished as the tyrant who oppresses them. . . .

Proposition VII: That the goodness of the prince should not be withdrawn because of the ingratitude of the people. . . .

Proposition VIII: That the prince should not be swayed by resentment or by mood. . . .

Proposition IX: That a good prince is sparing of men's blood. . . .

Proposition X: That a good prince abhors acts of violence. . . .

Proposition XI: That good princes will risk their life for the safety of their subjects and preserve it for love of them. . . .

Proposition XII: That government should be gentle. . . .

Proposition XIII: That princes are made to be loved. . . .

Proposition XIV: That a prince who is hated for his violence hangs always on the brink of ruin. . . .

Proposition XV: That a prince should refrain from harsh or wounding words.

*   *   *

BK. IV] THE CHARACTER OF KINGSHIP, CONTINUED:

Article I. Royal authority is absolute

Many pretend to confound absolute with arbitrary government, in order to render the name odious and intolerable. But no two forms are more different, as will be seen when we come to consider justice.

Proposition I: That the prince is accountable to none for his actions.

. . . Without this absolute authority he can neither do good nor suppress evil; his power should be such that none can hope to escape him; and the sole defense of the individual against the public power should be innocence.

This doctrine is in accord with the words of St. Paul: "Wilt thou then not be afraid of the power? do that which is good." (Rom. XIII, 3)

Proposition II: That there is no higher judgment than that of the prince.

The highest judgments are ascribed to God himself. When Jehoshaphat established the judges over the people, he said: "Ye judge not for man, but for the Lord, who is with you in the judgment." (II Chron. XIX, 6)

It is what causes the writer of Ecclesiasticus to say: "Go not to law with a judge." (VIII, 17) This is even more true of the sovereign judge who is the King. And the reason that he gives is "that he judges according to justice." This is not to say that he himself always judges, but that judgment is ascribed to him, and none has the right to judge or review after him.

Princes should therefore be obeyed as justice itself, or there will be no order or direction in affairs.

Kings are gods, and partake in some measure of the independence of God: "I have said, Ye are gods; and all of you are children of the most High." (Ps. LXXXII, 6)

God alone can call in question their persons and their judgments. "God standeth in the congregation of the mighty; he judgeth among the gods." (*ibid.*, 1)

It is for this reason that St. Gregory, bishop of Tours, said to King Chilperic in council: "We speak to you; but you are not bound to hear us if you do not please to. If you will not, who is to upbraid you, unless it be He who has said that He is justice itself?" (Greg. Tur. *Hist.* lib. VI)

From this we conclude that he who refuses obedience to the prince is not to be referred to another judgment, but condemned to death without appeal, as an enemy of the public peace and of human society. "And the man that will do presumptuously and will not hearken unto the priest that standeth to minister there before the Lord thy God, or unto the judge, even that man shall die; and thou shalt put away the evil from Israel." (Deut. XVII, 12) And again: "He who will not hearken unto thy words in all that thou commandest him, he shall be put to death." (Joshua I, 18) It was the people itself who spoke thus to Joshua.

The prince can correct himself, when he knows that he has erred; but against his authority there can be no redress save in that authority itself.

And this is why great attention must be given to all that he commands. "Take heed what ye do; all your judgments will fall upon you; let the fear of the Lord be upon you; take heed and do it." (cf. II Chron. XIX, 6–7)

Thus did Jehoshaphat instruct the judges on whom he conferred his authority; how much must he himself have considered these things when he sat in judgment!

Proposition III: That the prince is not subject to coercion.

Coercion is defined as the exercise of power to procure obedience to what is commanded lawfully. Only the prince can command lawfully, and to him alone belongs the power of coercion.

For this reason St. Paul commits the sword to him alone. "But if thou do evil, be afraid; for he beareth not the sword in vain." (Rom. XIII, 4)

Within the state the prince alone bears arms; if not, all falls into confusion, and the state dissolves into anarchy.

He who becomes a sovereign prince takes into his hands both the right of final judgment, and all the forces of the state. "That our king may judge us, and go out before us, and fight our battles." (I Sam. VIII, 20) So said the children of Israel when they asked for a king. Samuel declared to them in answer that the power of their prince should be absolute, beyond restraint by any other power. "This will be the manner of the king that shall reign over you: he will take your sons and appoint them for himself; and he will take your fields, and your vineyards, and your olive yards, even the best of them, and give them to his servants," etc. (*ibid.,* 11, 14)

Had they the lawful right to do all this? It was not pleasing to God, for He does not give such power. But with respect to human justice, they would have the right to do this with impunity. Which is why David said: "Against thee, thee only, have I sinned; O Lord, have mercy upon me." (Ps. LI) For, as St. Jerome observes in connection with this text, he was king and had only God to fear. . . .

Proposition IV: That kings are not therefore above the law.

"When thou shalt set him king over thee, he shall not multiply horses and carriages to himself, neither shall he multiply wives to himself, that would enfeeble his courage; neither shall he greatly multiply to himself silver and gold. And it shall be, when he sitteth upon the throne of his kingdom that he shall write himself a copy of this law in a book out of that which is before the priests the Levites: and it shall be with him, and he shall read therein all the days of his life: that he may learn to fear the Lord his God, to keep all the words of this law and these statutes, to do them: that his heart be not lifted up above his brethren, and that he turn not aside from the law of God, to the right hand or to the left: to the end that he may have a long reign, he, and his children." (cf. Deut. XVII, 15–20)

It is to be noted that this law concerned not only religion, but also the law of the land, to which the prince was subject as much or even more than any other, by the rectitude of his will.

This is what princes find difficult to comprehend. "What prince can you show me," asked St. Ambrose, "who believes that that which is not right is forbidden to him, who holds himself answerable to his own laws; who believes that power should not permit itself what justice denies? For power does not absolve from the duty of acting justly: rather, it is only in following the dictates of justice that power remains guiltless. The king is not above the laws: if he sin, he destroys the laws by his example." He adds: "He who judges others, can he avoid his own judgment, and do what he condemns?" (Ambr. 1, 11, Apol. David altera III, 8)

From this stems that good principle of a Roman emperor: "It is a maxim worthy of the dignity of a prince, to own himself subject to the laws."

Kings are therefore, as others, subject to the equity of the laws, both because they are bound to act justly, and because they owe it to the people to set an example of fairness. But they are not liable to the penalties of the law: or, in the language of theology, princes are subject to the laws in their directive, but not in their coercive function.

* * *

Article II. Concerning weakness, vacillation and false firmness

Proposition IV: That the fear of God is the true counterpoise of power, the prince fearing Him all the more because he fears Him alone.

To set public order and the power of the state on a firm foundation, we have seen that the prince must be endowed with a power independent of all other earthly powers. But this is no reason for him to forget himself or act irresponsibly, for the less the account to be rendered to men, the greater is that to be rendered to God.

Those wicked ones who have nothing to fear from men, are still more unfortunate, for they are set apart like Cain for God's vengeance. "And the Lord set a mark upon Cain, lest any finding him should kill him." (Gen. IV, 15) This did not mean that he had forgiven that fratricide, but that a divine hand was needed to punish him as he deserved.

He deals as strictly with kings. Impunity before men reserves them for still more terrible punishment from God. We have seen that the eminence of their position calls down upon them increased torment. "For mercy will soon pardon the meanest: but mighty men shall be mightily tormented." (Wis. VI, 6)

Mark well how God smites them in this life. . . .

These punishments are terrifying. But His rigour and implacability on this earth are but a shadow compared to the punishments in the next world. "It is a fearful thing to fall into the hands of the living God." (Heb. X, 31)

He lives for ever; His wrath is unappeasable and burns eternally; His power is invincible; He forgets not, He tires not; nothing escapes Him.

BK. V] FOURTH AND LAST CHARACTERISTIC OF ROYAL AUTHORITY:

Article I. That royal authority is subject to reason

Proposition I: That government is the work of reason and intelligence.

"Be wise now therefore, O ye kings: be instructed, ye judges of the earth." (Ps. II, 10)

All men are endowed with understanding; but you, on whom a whole great nation principally depends, who must be the mind and soul of the state, who must be the first cause of all its movement: the less you are obliged to explain your reasons to others, the more reason and intelligence you yourself must possess.

The opposite of rational action is action motivated by passion or mood. To act through emotion, as Saul did with David, to be impelled by jealousy or obsessed with dark melancholy, results in every sort of irregularity, inconsistency, partiality, irrationality, injustice and rashness.

To manage a horse or to drive a flock requires reason: how much more necessary then is reason to lead men or a rational flock?

"The Lord took David from following the ewes great with young and he brought him to feed Jacob his people, and Israel his inheritance: so he fed them according to the integrity of his heart; and guided them by a skillful and intelligent hand." (Ps. LXXVIII, 70–72)

All the affairs of men are directed by intelligence and counsel. "Through wisdom is an house builded; and by understanding it is established. And by knowledge the chambers shall be filled with all precious and pleasant riches. A wise man is strong; yea, a man of knowledge increases in strength. For by wise counsel thou shalt make thy war: and in multitude of counsellors there is safety." (Prov. XXIV, 3–6)

Wisdom herself says: "By me kings reign, and law-givers decree justice." (*ibid.*, VIII, 15)

Wisdom is so born to command that she gives the government even to those born in slavery. . . .

Proposition   II: That true firmness is the fruit of intelligence. . . .

Proposition   III: That the wisdom of the prince produces the happiness of his people. . . .

Proposition   IV: That wisdom more than strength is the salvation of states. . . .

Proposition   V: That the wise are feared and respected. . . .

Proposition   VI: That wisdom comes from God. . . .

Proposition   VII: That wisdom must be studied. . . .

Proposition   VIII: That the prince should study useful things, and cause them to be studied; what his studies should include. . . .

Proposition   IX: That the prince should know the law. . . .

Proposition   X: That the prince should be versed in matters of state. . . .

Proposition   XI: That the prince should know how to choose times and occasions. . . .

Proposition   XII: That the prince should know men. . . .

Proposition   XIII: That the prince should know himself. . . .

Proposition   XIV: That the prince should know what happens inside and outside his realm. . . .

Proposition XV: That the prince should know how to speak. . . .

Proposition XVI: That the prince should know how to keep silence; that secrecy is the essence of good counsel. . . .

Proposition XVII: That the prince should have foresight. . . .

Proposition XVIII: That the prince should be able to instruct his ministers.

*　　*　　*

Article IV. Consequences of the previous maxim: concerning majesty and its adjuncts

Proposition I: Definition of majesty. . . .

*　　*　　*

I do not call majesty that ceremonial which surrounds kings, or that external show which dazzles the vulgar. That is the pomp of majesty, but not its true self.

Majesty is the reflection of the greatness of God in a prince.

God is infinite, God is all. The prince, in his quality of prince, is not considered as an individual; he is a public personage, all the state is comprised in him; the will of all the people is included in his own. Just as all virtue and excellence are united in God, so the strength of every individual is comprehended in the person of the prince. What greatness this is, for one man to contain so much!

The power of God can be felt in a moment from one end of the world to the other: the royal power acts simultaneously throughout the kingdom. It holds the whole kingdom in position just as God holds the whole world.

Were God to withdraw his hand, the entire world would return to nothing: if authority fail in the kingdom, all lapses into anarchy.

Consider the prince in his council-chamber. From thence flow the commands which coordinate the efforts of magistrates and captains, of citizens and soldiers, of provinces and armies, by land and by sea. It is the image of God, who directs all nature from his throne in the highest heaven.

"What is done solely at the emperor's bidding?" asks St. Augustine. "He has only to move his lips, the least of all movements, and the whole empire stirs. It is he who does all things by his command, in the image of God. He spoke, and it was done; he commanded, and all was created." (Aug., In Psalm CXLVIII, n.2)

We marvel at his works: nature is a subject for the curious to debate. "God hath set the world in their heart, so that no man can find out the work that God maketh from the beginning to the end." (Ecc. III, 11) We can unfold a tiny part, but the depths are impenetrable. And so too is the mystery of kingship.

The intentions of a prince are only known by their execution. The counsels of God are revealed in the same way: until then none penetrates them except those to whom God imparts knowledge.

If the power of God extends everywhere, so also does His magnificence. Nowhere in the universe is there a lack of striking signs of His goodness. You see order, justice and peace throughout the realm: these are the natural fruits of royal authority.

Nothing is more majestic than all-embracing goodness: and there is no greater debasement of majesty than misery brought upon subjects by the prince.

Let the wicked seek to hide themselves; the light of God pursues them everywhere, His arm will strike them down, whether in the highest heavens or in the lowest depths. . . .

Thus God enables the prince to discover the most deep-laid plots. His eyes and hands are everywhere. We have seen how the birds of the air bring him news of what occurs. And he even receives from God, in the course of handling affairs, a degree of penetration akin to the power of devination. Conspiracies once unravelled, his long arms seek out his enemies at the ends of the earth and uncover them in the deepest abysses. Against such power as his there is no sure refuge.

Finally, gather together all that we have said of the grandeur and magnificence of royal authority. You have seen a great nation united under one man: You have seen his sacred power, paternal and absolute: you have seen that secret reason which directs the body politic, enclosed in one head: you have seen the reflection of God in the prince, and you will come to understand the majesty of kingship.

God is the essence of holiness, goodness, power, reason. In these consists the divine majesty. In their reflection consists the majesty of the prince.

So great is this majesty that its source cannot be found to reside in the prince: it is borrowed from God, who entrusts it to the prince for the good of his people, to which end it is well that it be restrained by a higher power.

An undefinable element of divinity is possessed by the prince, and inspires fear in his subjects. The king himself would do well to remember this. "I have said, Ye are gods; and all of you are children of the most High. But ye shall die like men, and fall like one of the princes." (Ps. LXXXIII, 6–7) I have said: you are gods; this signifies that you possess in your authority, you bear on your forehead, the stamp of the divine. You are all children of the most High: it is He who has established your power for the good of mankind. But, O gods of flesh and blood, of mud and dust, you will die like other men, you will fall like the greatest. Greatness divides men for a little while; a common fall levels them all in the end.

O kings, be bold therefore in the exercise of your power; for it is divine and beneficial to the human race; but wield it with humility. It is conferred on you from without. It leaves you in the end weak and mortal, it leaves you still sinners: and it lays upon you a heavier charge to render to God.

Proposition II. That magnanimity, magnificence and all the great virtues are part of majesty.

Grandeur demands the greatest accompaniments: with the highest grandeur are associated the highest virtues.

The prince should think of great things: "Let the prince think princely thoughts."

Base thoughts are unbecoming to majesty. When Saul was chosen king, God "gave him another heart, and he was turned into another man." (I Sam. X, 6, 9)

Be silent, base thoughts: yield to thoughts worthy of royalty.

Thoughts worthy of royalty are those which concern the general good; great men are not born to serve themselves alone: great powers which are in the sight of all the world, are created for the good of all.

The prince is by his office the man furthest removed from small interests, closest to the public good: his true interest is that of the state. He can therefore never take too high a view; he can never be too far above petty thoughts and narrow views. . . .

BK. VI] THE DUTIES OF SUBJECTS TO THE
PRINCE, BASED UPON THE PREVIOUS
ARGUMENT:

Article II. On the obedience due to the ruler

Proposition I: That subjects owe their ruler complete obedience.

If the prince is not scrupulously obeyed, public order is overthrown, and there is no further unity, and in consequence no further
cooperation or peace within the state.

This is why we have seen that whosoever disobeys public authority
is judged worthy of death. "And the man that will do presumptuously, and will not hearken unto the priest or unto the judge, even
that man shall die: and thou shalt put away the evil from Israel."
(Deut. XVII, 12)

God has established these powers in order to prevent disorder, and
we hear St. Paul say in His name: "Let every soul be subject unto
the higher powers. For there is no power but of God: the powers
that be are ordained of God. Whosoever therefore resisteth the power,
resisteth the ordinance of God." (Rom. XIII, 1–2)

"Put them in mind to be subject to principalities and powers, to
obey them scrupulously, to be ready for every good work." (Titus
III, 1)

God has made kings and princes his viceroys on earth, in order
to make their authority sacred and inviolable. This leads St. Paul
to observe once again that they are "the ministers of God," (Rom.
XIII, 4) in accordance with what is written in the Wisdom of
Solomon, "that the princes are the ministers of his kingdom."

From this St. Paul concludes that "ye must needs be subject, not
only for wrath, but also for conscience' sake." (Rom. XIII, 5)

St. Peter also says: "Submit yourselves to every ordinance of man
for the Lord's sake: whether it be to the king, as supreme; or unto
governors, as unto them that are sent by him. . . . For this is the
will of the Lord." (I Peter II, 13–15)

And as we have already seen, the words of the two apostles refer
to this when they say: "Servants, be obedient to your masters with
all fear, not only to the good and gentle, but also to the forward."
(*Ibid,* 18) "Not with eye-service, as men-pleasers; but as the servants

of Christ, doing the will of God from the heart." (Ephesians VI, 5)

All the proofs that we have seen of the sacred character of royal power confirm the truth of what we say here: and nothing is better founded on the word of God than the obedience which is due by reason of religion and conscience to legitimate authority.

Finally when Jesus said to the Jews: "Render unto Caesar that which is Caesar's (Matt XXII, 21), he did not call in question the basis of the power of the Caesars: it was suffcient that he found them established in authority, and he intended that the divine order and the foundation of public peace should be respected in the form of their authority.

Proposition II: That there is only one exception to the obedience due to the prince, which is when his commands run contrary to God's.

Respect for authority requires this. "Submit yourselves . . . to the king, as supreme; or unto governors, as unto them that are sent by him." (I Peter II, 13–14) And again: "There are divers degrees, the one above the other: the powerful man is subject to one more powerful, and the king gives commandments to all his subjects." (cf. Eccles. V, 8)

Obedience is due to each according to his rank, and the governor must never be obeyed if his orders are detrimental to the princes'.

Above all empires is the empire of God. It is the only empire which can truly be called absolutely sovereign, and from which all others derive: from Him all power stems.

Since then obedience must be paid to the governor, if there is nothing in his commands which seems contrary to the king's; so the king's orders must be obeyed, if there is nothing in them which seems to conflict with the commandments of God. For the same reason, just as one must not obey the governor against the orders of the king, even less must one obey the king against the commandments of God.

It was for this reason that the Apostles replied to the magistrates: "We ought to obey God rather than men." (Acts V, 29)

Proposition V: That open impiety, and even persecution do not free subjects from the obligation of obedience to their rulers.

The royal dignity is holy and sacred even in pagan princes; we have seen that Cyrus is called by Isaiah "the anointed of the Lord." (Isaiah XV, 1)

Such were the pride and impiety of Nebuchadnezzar that he strove to be the equal of God, and sought to put to death those who refused to perform sacrilegious rites in his honor; yet Daniel said to him: "Thou, O king, art a king of kings; for the God of heaven hath given thee a kingdom, power, and strength, and glory." (Daniel II, 37)

This is why God's people prayed for the lives of Nebuchadnezzar and of Belshazzar, (Baruch I, 11) and of Ahasuerus. (I Isdra VI, 10)

Ahab and Jesebel executed all the prophets of the Lord: Elijah lamented this before the Lord, but remained obedient. (I Kings XIX, 10, 14)

At this very time the prophets wrought amazing miracles to preserve the king and the kingdom. (*Ibid.*, XX)

Elisha did the same under Jehoram, the son of Ahab, who was as impious as his father. (II Kings III, VI, VII)

Nothing has ever equalled the impiety of Manasseh, who sinned and caused Judah to sin before the Lord, whose worship he sought to abolish, persecuting the faithful servants of God and making Jerusalem run with their blood. (II Kings XXI, 2–3, 16). And yet Isaiah and the holy prophets who reproached him for his crimes never aroused the least rebellion against him.

This doctrine has been maintained in the Christian religion.

It was during the reign of Tiberius, not only a pagan but also an evil man, that our Lord said to the Jews: "Render unto Caesar that which is Caesar's." (Matt. XXII, 21)

St. Paul appealed to Caesar, thereby recognising his power.

He ordered prayers to be said for the Emperors, (I Tim. II, 1–2) although the emperor reigning at that time was Nero, the most impious and wicked of men.

His reason for ordering the prayer was the need for public peace, which requires that all live together in concord, even under wicked and persecuting princes.

He and St. Peter enjoined the faithful to obey the powers that be. We have noted their words, and have also seen which were the powers under whose forms the Apostles bade the faithful respect the authority of God.

Because of this apostolic injunction the first Christians, though persecuted for three hundred years, never raised the least opposition within the Empire. We learn their sentiments from Tertullian and see them continued throughout the history of the Church.

They continued to pray for the emperors even in the midst of the torments to which they were unjustly condemned. "Be of good courage, O worthy judges," said Tertullian, "and tear from the Christians a soul which bursts forth with praise of the Emperor." (Apolog., no. 30)

Constantius the son of Constantine the Great, although protector of the Arians and persecutor of the orthodox, found the Church unshakably loyal.

His successor Julian the Apostate, who restored the pagan cults proscribed by his predecessors, found the Christians no less faithful and zealous in his service in spite of this, so well were they able to separate the prince's impiety from the sacred dignity of his sovereign majesty.

Many heretical emperors followed: Valens, Justin, Zeno, Basiliscus, Anastasius, Heraclius, Constantius. Even though they deposed orthodox bishops and even Popes, and deluged the Church with bloodshed and massacre, they never saw their authority questioned or undermined by the Catholics.

Finally, for seven hundred years there was not a single example of disobedience to the emperor for religious pretexts. In the eighth century the whole empire remained faithful to Leo the Isaurian, the leader of the Iconoclasts and persecutor of the faithful. Under his son Constantine Copronymus, who inherited his heresy and violence as well as his crown, the faithful in the East offered only their patience in opposition to his persecution. But during the decline of the Empire, when the Caesars were barely able to defend the Orient into which they had retreated, Rome was forced to separate itself from the emperors, after having been abandoned for two hundred years to the fury of the Lombards, and having been forced to seek the protection of the Franks.

Rome endured her sufferings for long before taking this extreme course, and only embraced it after the emperors had come to regard the capital of their empire as a land open to spoliation and exposed to invasion.

Proposition VI: That subjects must oppose the violence of their princes only with respectful remonstrances, without defiance or murmuring, and with prayers for their conversion.

*   *   *

Article III. Two problems posed by the scriptures: David and the Maccabees

Proposition II: That the wars of the Maccabees do not sanction rebellion.

After being conquered by the Assyrians, the Jews were subject in turn to the power of the Persians, of Alexander the Great and finally of the Kings of Syria.

They remained in this condition for about three hundred and fifty years, and for one hundred and fifty of these they accepted the kings of Syria, until the persecution of Antiochus IV Epiphanes caused them to take up arms against him under the leadership of the Maccabees. For a long time they maintained the struggle, during the course of which they treated with the Romans and Greeks against the kings of Syria, their lawful sovereigns, whose rule they finally overthrew and established princes of their own nation.

Here is a clear case of rebellion: if it is not, this instance would seem to show that a tyrannical government and above all a violent persecution for the sake of true religion releases a people from their duty of obedience to their rulers.

It is not to be doubted that the war of the Maccabees was just, for God Himself approved it: but if we examine the actual circumstances of the event, we see that this example does not sanction later revolts for reasons of religion.

The true religion until the coming of the Messiah was to be preserved in the race of Abraham and by succession through the blood line.

It was to be preserved in Judaea in the temple of Jerusalem, the place chosen by God for the offering of sacrifices and for rites not permitted anywhere else.

The very essence of this religion thus required that the sons of Abraham should continue for ever, and in the land given to their fathers, to live there according to the law of Moses, the observances of which had been freely allowed by the kings of Persia and the other rulers down to the time of Antiochus.

The descendants of Abraham living in the Holy Land were to be removed from there only once, at the express command of God, but not into perpetual exile. On the contrary, the prophet Jeremiah who had brought the people the commandment to go to Babylon, where it was God's will that they should expiate their crimes, at the same time promised that after three score years and ten of captivity they would be restored to their own land, there to observe the law of Moses as before, and to practise their religion as usual in the rebuilt temple in Jerusalem. (Jerem. XXV, 12; XXVII, 11–12; XXIX, 10, 14; XXX, 3 etc.)

The people thus restored to their land were to live there until the coming of Christ, at which time God would cause a new people to arise no longer of the race of Abraham, but of all the nations of the world, and would scatter the Jews unfaithful to their Messiah in captivity throughout the world.

But before this the Messiah was to be born of this people, and was to found among the Jews in Jerusalem that Church which was to fill the whole universe. This great mystery of religion is vouched for by all the prophets, and it is not the place here to rehearse all the passages where they do so.

From this it may be seen that by the extinction of the race of Abraham, or by their expulsion from their country at the time of the kings of Syria, religion would be led astray and the worship of God overthrown.

It only remains now to examine Antiochus' intentions.

He commanded that the Jews should forsake their law to live after the manner of the Gentiles, sacrificing to the same idols and giving up their temple, which he desecrated by erecting the statue of Olympian Zeus on the altar of God. (I Mac. i, 43)

He decreed the punishment of death for those who disobeyed. (*Ibid.*, 52) This he carried out: all Judaea ran with the blood of its sons. (*Ibid.*, 60, 73, 64, etc.)

He marshalled all his forces "to destroy the Israelites and the remains of Jerusalem, and to wipe out from Judaea the memory of the people of God, there to establish strangers, and to parcel out the land by lot." (I Mac. III, 35–36)

He had determined to sell to the Gentiles all who escaped death, and the merchants of the neighbouring peoples flocked with money to buy them. (I Mac. III, 41; II Mac. VIII, 11, 14, 34, 36)

It was in this desperate extremity that Judas Maccabaeus took up arms with his brothers and those of the Jews who survived. When they saw the pitiless king directing all his energies to "the total ruin of the nation, they said to one another: 'let us not suffer our people to be destroyed, but let us fight for our country and our religion, lest it perish with us.'" (I Mac. I, 42–43)

If subjects are no longer bound to obey a king who abdicates his kingship and completely gives up the government, what are we to think of a ruler who would plan to spill the blood of all his subjects and then, once tired of massacres, would sell the rest to strangers? Can he renounce more clearly his intention to hold them for his subjects, or proclaim himself more flagrantly to be no more the king and father, but the enemy of all his people?

This is how Antiochus acted towards the Jews, who saw themselves not only abandoned, but exterminated in a body by their king, although they were innocent of any offence, as Antiochus himself was forced to admit in the end. "I remember the wrongs I did in Jerusalem, and the unjust commandments that I made to annihilate all the inhabitants of Judaea." (*Ibid.* VI, 12)

But the Jews were even better justified, because in accordance with the dispensation of the time and of their people, their religion would perish with them; and for them to give up their land was to give up their religion as well. They could not therefore allow themselves to be sold or carried off or massacred: in this case the law of God manifestly enjoined them to resist.

Nor did God fail to reveal His will to them, by miraculous victories and by the strict command which Judas received when he saw the spirit of the prophet Jeremiah "who placed a golden sword in his hands, saying: 'receive this sacred sword sent of God, in the knowledge that with its aid you shall overthrow the enemies of Israel.'" (II Mac. XV, 15)

It is for God to choose the means by which his people shall be preserved. When Ahasuerus, misled by the wiles of Haman, wished to destroy the whole Jewish people, God prevented this impious design by changing the king's heart by means of his queen Esther, for the king had been drawn into this crime through unfortunate weakness rather than stubborn wickedness. But for the presumptuous Antiochus who openly made war against heaven God prepared a more terrible downfall, and filled His people with a courage against which no wealth, strength or numbers could be more than a forlorn hope.

God granted them so many victories that finally the kings of

Syria made peace with them, recognizing the princes they had chosen from among themselves, and treating them as friends and brothers (I Mac. XI, 24–25 etc.; XIV, 38–39, etc.; XV, 1–2, etc.), so that all the sanctions of legitimate authority combined to establish them.

BK. VII] THE PARTICULAR DUTIES OF ROYALTY:

Article I. General enumeration of princely duties

Subjects have now learned their duties, and we have given kings the first conception of their own. It is now necessary to be more precise, and in order to omit nothing, let us make an exact division of these powers.

The purpose of government is the welfare and preservation of the state.

The preservation of the state requires in the first place the maintenance of a sound internal constitution.

Secondly, the good use of all assistance given to it.

Thirdly, protection from the dangers which menace it.

The human body is preserved in a similar manner, by maintaining a sound constitution; by making use of the aid which human weakness must rely on; by obtaining suitable remedies against the infirmities and sicknesses which may beset it.

The strength of the body politic's constitution rests upon two bases, religion and justice; these are the internal elements which constitute a state. Through the one, God is given what is due to Him; through the other, men receive what is fitting for them.

The essential aids to a monarchy which are necessary for government are arms, counsels, and wealth or finances, under which trade and taxes will be discussed.

We shall conclude by examining the disadvantages which afflict royalty, and the remedies which should be used against them.

The ruler knows all his particular duties when he knows how to perform all these things. This is what we shall teach him in the following books. Let us begin by setting forth his duties in matters of religion.

Article II. Of religion, in that it constitutes the welfare of states and of civil society

Proposition I: That in the ignorance and corruption of the human race some religious principles are always preserved.

It is true that when St. Paul preached to the Lycaonians, he said "that God suffered all nations to walk in their own ways." (Acts XIV, 16) This is as if to say that He had left them entirely to their own devices, and to their own ideas of the proper way to worship God, without giving them any guidance. Yet he adds in the same place: "nevertheless he left not himself without witness, in that he did good, and gave us the rain from heaven, and fruitful seasons, filling our hearts with food and gladness." (*Ibid.*, 17) He would not have addressed these words to that ignorant people, had not some notion of God's power been preserved among them despite their backwardness.

We may observe among these barbarous people an idea of the Deity, to which they wished to offer sacrifice. This type of inherited idea of the Deity, of sacrifices and rites instituted to honor Him is found diffused among the nations from the earliest times, wherever there is some form of polity, so that it can only have come from Noah and his children. . . .

Comparable ideas of the Deity are found in every land from all antiquity, and thus no nation is to be found completely without religion, at least among those which are not completely uncivilised, without civil government or polity.

Proposition II: That these religious concepts have a certain firm and inviolable quality. . . .

Proposition III: That these religious principles, although turned to idolatry and error, sufficed for the foundation of a stable state and government. . . .

Proposition IV: That true religion, being based upon sure principles, makes the constitutions of states more solid. . . .

Although it is true that false religions, since they possess elements of goodness and truth through their recognition of a deity to whom human affairs are subject, may be quite adequate for the foundation of states, nevertheless they always leave a measure of doubt and uncertainty at the back of the mind, which does not permit the state to be established with complete solidity.

We are instinctively ashamed of the fables which make up the false religions, and of what we read in the pagan sages. . . .

This gives rise to a lack of faith: atheism easily takes root in such religions, as may be seen from the example of the Epicureans, with whom St. Paul disputed. . . .

The Stoics who opposed them, and with whom St. Paul also took issue (Acts xvii, 18), had no higher opinion of the deity, for they had made their founder a god, and even honored him above Jupiter.

Thus the false religions were inconsistent. Furthermore they were no more than enthusiasm, blind, seditious, turbulent, partial, sunk in ignorance, confused, lacking order and reason; as may be seen in the stormy and riotous assembly of the Ephesians, and in their insensate clamor in favor of their great Diana. (*Ibid.* XIX, 24, 28, 34, etc.) This is far from the good order and rational stability which form the basis of states, but it is the inevitable consequence of error. We must therefore seek a firm basis for states in the truth, which is the mother of harmony; and truth is only found in the true religion.

Article III

Proposition IX: That the prince should use his power to destroy false religions within the state. . . .

Proposition X: That harsh measures may be taken against observers of false religions, although gentleness is preferable. . . .

Proposition XI: That the prince has no better means of drawing his people to true religion than by setting them a good example. . . .

Proposition XII: That the prince should study the law of God. . . .

Proposition XIII: That the prince is the executor of the law of God. . . .

Proposition XIV: That the prince must see to his people's instruction in the law of God. . . .

* * *

Article V

Proposition IV: That princes have in their care not only the persons devoted to the service of God, but also the property set aside for their subsistence. . . .

Proposition IX: What princes should consider when making grants to the Church, after the example of David; how dangerous it is to seize Church property. . . .

Proposition X: That kings should not encroach upon the rights and powers of the priesthood, and should approve that the priesthood maintain them against all infringement. . . .

Proposition XII: That the regal and sacerdotal powers are separate, but united.

Sacerdotal power in spiritual affairs and regal power in temporal affairs derive from God alone. But the ecclesiastical order acknowledges the regal in matters temporal, just as in spiritual matters kings confess themselves obedient sons of the Church. The whole state of the world turns upon these two powers. That is why they owe one another mutual support. "Zerubbabel (who represented the temporal power) shall be clothed with glory, and shall sit upon the throne and govern; and the priest and the high priest shall sit upon his, and there shall be a counsel of peace (that is perfect concord) between them." (cf. Zech. VI, 13)

Proposition XIII: The dangers threatening kings who choose bad shepherds [for the church]. . . .

Proposition XIV: That the prince should protect piety and favor the righteous. . . .

Proposition XV: That the prince should not suffer the impious, the profane, blasphemers, perjurers or soothsayers. . . .

Proposition XVI: That blasphemies are the ruin of kings and armies. . . .

Proposition XVII: That the prince scrupulously observes his oath.

. . . At his coronation the prince swears to God, as we shall see at greater length [in Prop. 18], to maintain the privileges of the churches; to preserve the Catholic faith received from his fathers; to subdue violence, and to render justice to all his subjects. This oath is the foundation of public tranquillity, and God is all the more obliged by His own truth to make the king observe it, since He is its only guarantor.

There is another form of oath, which sovereign powers make among themselves as equals, which is to uphold treaties. Since every treaty is submitted to an arbiter, those who can only be judged by God have recourse to Him in their treaties, as the ultimate support of public order.

From all this it follows that rulers who fail to observe their oaths to their ultimate ability (which please God may never happen) undermine that which is most solid in human affairs, while at the same time destroying society and making peace impossible for the whole human race. By this act they justly make God and man their implacable enemies, since nothing remains to reconcile them higher than what they have destroyed.

He who cannot feel the full horror of this is cut off from all feeling save that of Hell itself, and the vengeance of the Lord openly and pitilessly declared against him.

*   *   *

Article VI. Religious motives peculiar to kings

Proposition   *I:* That it is God who makes kings and establishes ruling houses. . . .

Proposition   *II:* That God inspires subjects with obedience, and also allows a spirit of insurrection to spread among them. . . .

Proposition   *III:* That God decides the fate of kingdoms. . . .

Proposition   *IV:* That the good fortune of princes comes from God, and is often subject to dramatic reversals. . . .

Proposition   *V:* That there is no element of chance in the government of human affairs, and that fortune is only a word, without real meaning. . . .

Proposition   *VI:* That everything in the world is ordained by God's wisdom, and nothing occurs by chance. . . .

Proposition VII: That there is a special providence acting in human affairs. . . .

Proposition VIII: That kings, more than other men, should resign themselves to the providence of God. . . .

Proposition IX: That no power can escape the hand of God. . . .

Proposition X: That these sentiments produce true piety in the hearts of kings. . . .

Proposition XI: That this is an active piety.

Proposition XII: That the unsuccessful prince should not lose hope, but return to God through penitence. . . .

Proposition XIII: That religion provides princes with particular motives for penitence. . . .

Proposition XIV: That the kings of France have a special duty of loving the Church and of attachment to the Holy See.

. . . A third family [the Capetians] had ascended the throne. A family, if possible, more pious than the other two, under whom France was declared by the Popes [by Alexander III] to be "a realm beloved and blessed by God, whose glory is inseparable from that of the Holy See." A family, too, which alone in all creation can look back on seven hundred years of wearing the crown and ruling without interruption, and what is still more glorious, of being always Catholic, for God in His infinite mercy did not permit that the only prince who ascended the throne a heretic should remain one.

Since it is evident from this survey of our history that the greatest glory of the kings of France is their faith and the continual protection which they have accorded the Church, they will not allow this glory to be diminished: the ruling house will hand it on to its successor until the end of time.

This is the family that produced Saint Louis, the holiest king ever to rule among Christians. All the princes of France who remain today are descended from him. And as Christ said to the Jews: "if ye were Abraham's children, ye would do the works of Abraham" (John VIII, 39), so it only remains for me to say to our princes: if you are the sons of Saint Louis, do the works of Saint Louis.

BK. VIII] THE PARTICULAR DUTIES OF
ROYALTY, CONTINUED: OF JUSTICE:

Article I. That justice is founded on religion

Proposition I: That God is judge of judges and presides over judgments.

"God standeth in the congregation of the mighty; He judgeth among the gods." (Ps. LXXXII, 1)

The gods that God judges are the kings and the judges gathered under their authority to do justice. He calls them gods because the word for 'god' in the language of the scriptures is a word for 'judge': thus the power to judge is a share in the supreme justice of God, with which He has endowed the kings of this earth.

Their principal right to the name of 'god' is the impartiality with which they should dispense justice, without respect of persons, fearing neither great nor small, "for the judgment is God's," as Moses says (Deut. I, 17), in which judgment should be made with god-like impartiality, neither fearing nor favoring any man.

It is written that God judges these earthly gods, for He carries out an unceasing examination of their judgments. . . .

Proposition II: That justice belongs to God, and that He grants it to kings. . . .

Proposition III: That justice is the true quality of kingship, and that which maintains the king firmly on his throne. . . .

Proposition IV: That under a just God there is no purely arbitrary power.

Under a just God there is no power which is by its very nature unrestrained by any law, natural, divine or human.

Nor is there any authority on earth exempt from divine justice. Every judge, even the highest who for this reason are called gods by God Himself, are examined and corrected by a higher judge. "God standeth in the congregation of the mighty; He judgeth among the gods," as has just been said.

Thus all judgments are subject to review by a more august tribunal. God also says for this reason: "When the time shall be fulfilled, I shall judge the justices." (Ps. LXXV, 3) The verdicts of human judges will be passed in review before His eyes.

Consequently even the highest and most absolute judgments are like the others before God, and subject to amendment; but with this one difference, that this is done in a concealed way.

Earthly judges pay little heed to this review of their decisions, for it has no visible result and is reserved for another life; but it is all the more terrible for that, since it is ineluctable. When the hour of the Lord's judgment comes, "you shall find no help, neither from the east nor from the west, nor from the mountains" (and inaccessible places from whence secret aid often comes), "for now God is the judge" (Ps. LXXV, 7), and against Him there is no help.

"For in the hand of the Lord there is a cup of His vengeance and the wine is red," with the fire of justice which shall never be tempered by any infusion of gentleness. Instead it will be "mingled with wormwood," with bitter and poisonous essences. This is a second reason to fear that terrible review of human judgments: it will be conducted in an age of absolutely pure justice, and will be carried through with complete and relentless rigor. "The cup is in the hand of the Lord, and He pours it out for this one and that," to whom he offers it to drink. He presents it to hardened and unregenerate sinners, and above all to unjust judges; "it must be drained, to the very dregs." And there will be no further hope of mercy for them, for this vengeance will be eternal.

Article II. On that form of government which is termed arbitrary

Proposition I: That there is among men a form of government which is called arbitrary, but which is not found among us in well-ordered states.

Four attributes characterise governments of this type.

First: the people are born slaves, that is to say truly serfs, and there are no free men among them.

Second: there is no private property; all sources of wealth belong to the ruler, and there is no right of inheritance, even from father to son.

Third: the ruler may dispose as he wishes, not only of the goods, but also of the lives of his subjects, as though they were slaves.

Fourth and finally: there is no law but the will of the prince.

This is what is termed arbitrary power. I do not wish to examine whether it is lawful or unlawful. There are nations and great empires which are satisfied with this form of government, and it is not for us to awaken their doubts about it. It suffices to say that it is barbarous and odious. These four characteristics are far from our own customs, and so among us there is no arbitrary power.

It is one thing for a government to be absolute, and quite another for it to be arbitrary. (Above, Bk IV, Art I) It is absolute in that it is not liable to constraint, there being no other power capable of coercing the sovereign, who is in this sense independent of all human authority. But it does not follow from this that the government is arbitrary, for besides the fact that all is subject to the judgment of God (which is also true of those governments we have just called arbitrary), there are also [fundamental] laws, in such empires, so that whatever is done contrary to them is null in a legal sense: moreover, there is always an opportunity for redress, either at other times or in other conditions. Thus each man remains the legitimate owner of his property, since no one believes that he can possess anything securely if it is in contravention of the law, whose vigilance and rectification of violence and injustice is perpetual. . . .

This is what is termed legitimate government, by its very nature the opposite of arbitrary government.

Here we shall only discuss the first two attributes of this so-called arbitrary power which we have just described. The last two are so evidently contrary to the dictates of humanity and society that they are quite clearly the opposite of legitimate government.

Proposition II: That under a legitimate government, subjects are free.

It is only necessary to recall the passages in which we have already established that government was paternal, and that kings were fathers: their subjects were thus children, and different from slaves in that they are born free and innocent. (Bk II, Art I; Bk III, Art III)

Government is established to free all men from oppression and violence of every kind, as has been frequently demonstrated. (Bk I, Art I) This constitutes the state of perfect liberty, since there is nothing fundamentally less free than anarchy which destroys all legitimate sanctions between men and leaves no law other than force.

Proposition III: That the ownership of goods is lawful and inviolable.

We have noted how Joshua distributed the lands according to the law of Moses. (Joshua xiii, xiv, 11)

This is the means which ensures their cultivation: experience shows that land which is held not only in common, but also without legitimate and permanent title of ownership, is neglected and left waste. Which is why this order may not be contravened. . . .

*   *   *

Article III. On Legislation and Judgment

Proposition I: Definition of the two subjects.

Law provides the general rule, and judgments apply it to human affairs and to particular cases, as has been said. (Bk I, Art IV)

"Do ye indeed speak righteousness, O congregation? Do ye judge uprightly, O ye sons of men?" (Ps. lviii, 1) If you love the justice required by the law, practise it, and let it be the sole guide of your judgments.

Proposition II: That the first result of justice and laws is the preservation of the rights granted by previous rulers not only to the entire body politic, but also to its component parts. . . .

Proposition III: That praiseworthy customs have the force of law. . . .

Proposition IV: That the duty of the prince is justice, and that he himself is the chief judge. . . .

Proposition V: That the ways of justice are easy to know. . . .

Proposition VI: That the prince establishes tribunals, selects their judges with great care and instructs them in their duties. . . .

*   *   *

Article IV. On the virtues which must accompany justice

Proposition I: That the learned and pious Gerson, in a sermon preached before the king, distinguishes three principal virtues: constancy, prudence and clemency.

Justice must be governed by rules, stable and constant: otherwise it is not equable in its operation and, more capricious than ordered, it follows the whim of its controller.

Justice must be able to distinguish truth from falsehood in the evidence presented to it, or else it is blind in its application. This perspicacity is an advantage which derives from the virtue of prudence.

Finally it must occasionally be relaxed, for otherwise it is extreme and unbearable in its rigor: this mitigation of the harshness of justice comes from the virtue of clemency.

Constancy affirms it in its principles: prudence gives it discernment in questions of fact: clemency enables it to tolerate and pardon weakness. Constancy supports it; prudence applies it; clemency tempers it.

*   *   *

[Books IX and X treat of armed forces, finance, administration and miscellaneous aspects of statesmanship and politics, on all of which the king is given some practical advice.]

12

Constitutionalism

JOHN LOCKE (1632–1704) was the son of a small landowner and attorney who, being a moderate Puritan, fought in the Parliamentary army during the Civil War. Locke was educated at Westminster School and at Oxford, where in 1661–1664 he was a lecturer in Greek, rhetoric, and philosophy. He did not neglect the natural sciences but became competent in chemistry and medicine. The reading of Descartes whetted his appetite for philosophy, though the empiricist epistemology he evolved differed radically from Cartesian rationalism. According to Locke, all knowledge is derived from sensory experience, not from innate ideas. Since different individuals perceive different aspects of the truth, persecution of one's religious opponents is not only useless but sinful. One of the chief roots of evil is passion, or "enthusiasm," which can be defeated only by subordinating everything to reason. Locke thus became the apostle of "sweet reasonableness."

In 1667 Locke became confidential secretary to Lord Ashley (Earl of Shaftesbury), with whom he lived for fifteen years. Most of the late 1670's he spent in France. Having tasted the excitement of English political life in the early 1680's, Locke retired to Holland in 1683, where he came to be on good terms with William III. In February 1689 he accompanied William's wife, Mary Stuart, to England. It was mainly in Holland that Locke wrote his two chief works, the Essay Concerning Human Understanding, and the two Treatises of Government, both of which were first published in 1690. The immediate occasion for the Treatises of Government was the posthumous publication in 1680 of Patriarcha by Sir Robert Filmer (d. 1653), which upheld a divine-right kingship position far more extreme than that of Bossuet.

Locke, The Second Treatise of Government

II] OF THE STATE OF NATURE

4] TO UNDERSTAND political power right and derive it from its original, we must consider what state all men are naturally in, and that is a state of perfect freedom to order their actions and dispose of their possessions and persons as they think fit, within the bounds of the law of nature, without asking leave or depending upon the will of any other man.

A state also of equality, wherein all the power and jurisdiction is reciprocal, no one having more than another; there being nothing more evident than that creatures of the same species and rank, promiscuously born to all the same advantages of nature and the use of the same faculties, should also be equal one amongst another without subordination or subjection; unless the lord and master of them all should, by any manifest declaration of his will, set one above another, and confer on him by an evident and clear appointment an undoubted right to dominion and sovereignty. . . .

6] But though this be a state of liberty, yet it is not a state of license; though man in that state have an uncontrollable liberty to dispose of his person or possessions, yet he has not liberty to destroy himself, or so much as any creature in his possession, but where some nobler use than its bare preservation calls for it. The state of nature has a law of nature to govern it, which obliges every one; and reason, which is that law, teaches all mankind who will but consult it that, being all equal and independent, no one ought to harm another in his life, health, liberty, or possessions; for men being all the workmanship of one omnipotent and infinitely wise Maker — all the servants of one sovereign master, sent into the world by his order, and about his business — they are his property whose workmanship they are, made to last during his, not one another's, pleasure; and being furnished with like faculties, sharing all in one

From John Locke, The Second Treatise of Government, ed. by Thomas P. Peardon (New York, 1952), pp. 4–6, 15–20, 23, 27–29, 54–57, 70–83, 112–115, 119–130, 138–139. Reprinted by permission of the Liberal Arts Press Division of the Bobbs-Merrill Company, Inc.

community of nature, there cannot be supposed any such subordination among us that may authorize us to destroy another, as if we were made for one another's uses as the inferior ranks of creatures are for ours. Every one, as he is bound to preserve himself and not to quit his station wilfully, so by the like reason, when his own preservation comes not in competition, ought he, as much as he can, to preserve the rest of mankind, and may not, unless it be to do justice to an offender, take away or impair the life, or what tends to the preservation of the life, the liberty, health, limb, or goods of another.

7] And that all men may be restrained from invading others' rights and from doing hurt to one another, and the law of nature be observed, which wills the peace and preservation of all mankind, the execution of the law of nature is, in that state, put into every man's hands, whereby everyone has a right to punish the transgressors of that law to such a degree as may hinder its violation; for the law of nature would, as all other laws that concern men in this world, be in vain if there were nobody that in that state of nature had a power to execute that law and thereby preserve the innocent and restrain offenders. And if anyone in the state of nature may punish another for any evil he has done, everyone may do so; for in that state of perfect equality, where naturally there is no superiority or jurisdiction of one over another, what any may do in prosecution of that law, everyone must needs have a right to do.

*　　*　　*

IV] OF SLAVERY

22] THE NATURAL liberty of man is to be free from any superior power on earth, and not to be under the will or legislative authority of man, but to have only the law of nature for his rule. The liberty of man in society is to be under no other legislative power but that established by consent in the commonwealth, nor under the dominion of any will or restraint of any law but what that legislative shall enact according to the trust put in it. Freedom then is not what Sir Robert Filmer tells us "a liberty for every one to do what he lists, to live as he pleases, and not to be tied by any laws"; but freedom of men under government is to have a standing rule to live by, common to every one of that society and made by the legislative power erected in it, a liberty to follow my own will in all things where the rule prescribes not, and not to be subject to the inconstant, uncertain, unknown, arbitrary will of another man; as freedom of nature is to be under no other restraint but the law of nature.

23] This freedom from absolute, arbitrary power is so necessary to, and closely joined with, a man's preservation that he cannot part with it but by what forfeits his preservation and life together; for a man not having the power of his own life cannot by compact or his own consent enslave himself to any one, nor put himself under the absolute arbitrary power of another to take away his life when he pleases. Nobody can give more power than he has himself; and he that cannot take away his own life cannot give another power over it. Indeed, having by his fault forfeited his own life by some act that deserves death, he to whom he has forfeited it may, when he has him in his power, delay to take it and make use of him to his own service; and he does him no injury by it, for whenever he finds the hardship of his slavery outweigh the value of his life, it is in his power, by resisting the will of his master, to draw on himself the death he desires.

V] OF PROPERTY

25] WHETHER we consider natural reason, which tells us that men, being once born, have a right to their preservation, and consequently to meat and drink and such other things as nature affords for their subsistence; or revelation, which gives us an account of those grants God made of the world to Adam, and to Noah and his sons; it is very clear that God, as King David says (Psalm cxv, 16), "has given the earth to the children of men," given it to mankind in common. But this being supposed, it seems to some a very great difficulty how any one should ever come to have a property in anything. I will not content myself to answer that if it be difficult to make out property upon a supposition that God gave the world to Adam and his posterity in common, it is impossible that any man but one universal monarch should have any property upon a supposition that God gave the world to Adam and his heirs in succession, exclusive of all the rest of his posterity. But I shall endeavor to show how men might come to have a property in several parts of that which God gave to mankind in common, and that without any express compact of all the commoners.

26] God, who has given the world to men in common, has also given them reason to make use of it to the best advantage of life and convenience. The earth and all that is therein is given to men for the support and comfort of their being. And though all the fruits it naturally produces and beasts it feeds belong to mankind in common, as they are produced by the spontaneous hand of nature; and nobody has originally a private dominion exclusive of the rest of mankind in any of them, as they are thus in their natural state; yet, being given for the use of men, there must of necessity be a means to appropriate them some way or other before they can be of any use or at all beneficial to any particular man. The fruit or venison which nourishes the wild Indian, who knows no enclosure and is still a tenant in common, must be his, and so his, i.e., a part of him, that another can no longer have any right to it before it can do him any good for the support of his life.

27] Though the earth and all inferior creatures be common to all men, yet every man has a property in his own person; this nobody has any right to but himself. The labor of his body and the work of his hands, we may say, are properly his. Whatsoever then he removes out of the state that nature has provided and left it in, he has mixed his labor with, and joined to it something that is his own, and thereby makes it his property. It being by him removed from the common state nature has placed it in, it has by this labor something annexed to it that excludes the common right of other men. For this labor being the unquestionable property of the laborer, no man but he can have a right to what that is once joined to, at least where there is enough and as good left in common for others.

28] He that is nourished by the acorns he picked up under an oak, or the apples he gathered from the trees in the wood, has certainly appropriated them to himself. Nobody can deny but the nourishment is his. I ask, then, When did they begin to be his? When he digested or when he ate or when he boiled or when he brought them home? Or when he picked them up? And it is plain, if the first gathering made them not his, nothing else could. That labor put a distinction between them and common; that added something to them more than nature, the common mother of all, had done; and so they became his private right. And will anyone say he had no right to those acorns or apples he thus appropriated because he had not the con-

sent of all mankind to make them his? Was it a robbery thus to
assume to himself what belonged to all in common? If such a consent as that was necessary, man had starved, notwithstanding the
plenty God had given him. We see in commons, which remain so
by compact, that it is the taking any part of what is common and
removing it out of the state nature leaves it in which begins the
property, without which the common is of no use. And the taking
of this or that part does not depend on the express consent of all
the commoners. . . .

31] It will perhaps be objected to this that "if gathering the acorns,
or other fruits of the earth, etc., makes a right to them, then any
one may engross as much as he will." To which I answer: not so. The
same law of nature that does by this means give us property does
also bound that property, too. "God has given us all things richly"
(1 Tim. vi. 17), is the voice of reason confirmed by inspiration.
But how far has he given it us? To enjoy. As much as any one can
make use of to any advantage of life before it spoils, so much he
may by his labor fix a property in; whatever is beyond this is more
than his share and belongs to others. Nothing was made by God for
man to spoil or destroy. . . .

32] But the chief matter of property being now not the fruits of
the earth and the beasts that subsist on it, but the earth itself, as that
which takes in and carries with it all the rest, I think it is plain that
property in that, too, is acquired as the former. As much land as a
man tills, plants, improves, cultivates, and can use the product of,
so much is his property. He by his labor does, as it were, enclose it
from the common. Nor will it invalidate his right to say everybody
else has an equal title to it, and therefore he cannot appropriate, he
cannot enclose, without the consent of all his fellow commoners —
all mankind. God, when he gave the world in common to all mankind, commanded man also to labor, and the penury of his condition
required it of him. God and his reason commanded him to subdue
the earth, i.e., improve it for the benefit of life, and therein lay out
something upon it that was his own, his labor. He that in obedience
to this command of God subdued, tilled, and sowed any part of it,
thereby annexed to it something that was his property, which another had no title to, nor could without injury take from him. . . .

34] God gave the world to men in common; but since he gave it
them for their benefit and the greatest conveniences of life they
were capable to draw from it, it cannot be supposed he meant it

should always remain common and uncultivated. He gave it to the use of the industrious and rational — and labor was to be his title to it — not to the fancy or covetousness of the quarrelsome and contentious. . . .

37] . . . Before the appropriation of land, he who gathered as much of the wild fruit, killed, caught, or tamed as many of the beasts as he could; he that so employed his pains about any of the spontaneous products of nature as any way to alter them from the state which nature put them in, by placing any of his labor on them, did thereby acquire a propriety in them; but, if they perished in his possession without their due use, if the fruits rotted or the venison putrified before he could spend it, he offended against the common law of nature and was liable to be punished; he invaded his neighbor's share, for he had no right further than his use called for any of them and they might serve to afford him conveniences of life.

38] The same measures governed the possession of land, too: whatsoever he tilled and reaped, laid up and made use of before it spoiled, that was his peculiar right; whatsoever he enclosed and could feed and make use of, the cattle and product was also his. But if either the grass of his enclosure rotted on the ground, or the fruit of his planting perished without gathering and laying up, this part of the earth, notwithstanding his enclosure, was still to be looked on as waste and might be the possession of any other. . . .

45] Thus labor, in the beginning, gave a right of property wherever anyone was pleased to employ it upon what was common, which remained a long while the far greater part and is yet more than mankind makes use of. Men, at first, for the most part contented themselves with what unassisted nature offered to their necessities; and though afterwards, in some parts of the world — where the increase of people and stock, with the use of money, had made land scarce and so of some value — the several communities settled the bounds of their distinct territories and, by laws within themselves, regulated the properties of the private men of their society, and so, by compact and agreement, settled the property which labor and industry began. And the leagues that have been made between several states and kingdoms either expressly or tacitly disowning all claim and right to the land in the others' possession have, by common consent, given up their pretenses to their natural common right which originally they had to those countries, and so have, by positive agreement, settled a property amongst themselves in distinct parts and parcels of the earth; yet there are still great tracts of ground to be found which — the inhabitants thereof not having joined with the rest of mankind in the consent of the use of their common money — lie waste, and are more than the people who dwell on it do or can make use of, and so still lie in common; though this can scarce happen amongst that part of mankind that have consented to the use of money.

46] The greatest part of things really useful to the life of man, and such as the necessity of subsisting made the first commoners of the world look after, as it does the Americans now, are generally things of short duration, such as, if they are not consumed by use, will decay and perish of themselves; gold, silver, and diamonds are things that fancy or agreement has put the value on, more than real use and the necessary support of life. Now of those good things which nature has provided in common, every one had a right, as has been said, to as much as he could use, and property in all that he could effect with his labor; all that his industry could extend to, to alter from the state nature had put it in, was his. He that gathered a hundred bushels of acorns or apples had thereby a property in them; they were his goods as soon as gathered. He was only to look that he used them before they spoiled, else he took more than his share and robbed others. And indeed it was a foolish thing, as well as dishonest, to hoard up more than he could make use of. If he gave away a part to anybody else so that it perished not uselessly in his possession, these he also made use of. And if he also bartered away plums that would have rotted in a week for nuts that would last good for his eating a whole year, he did no injury; he wasted not the common stock, destroyed no part of the portion of the goods that belonged to others, so long as nothing perished uselessly in his hands. Again, if he would give his nuts for a piece of metal, pleased with its color, or exchange his sheep for shells, or wool for a sparkling pebble or a diamond, and keep those by him all his life, he invaded not the right of others; he might heap as much of these durable things as he pleased; the exceeding of the bounds of his just property not lying in the largeness of his possession, but the perishing of anything uselessly in it.

47] And thus came in the use of money — some lasting thing that men might keep without spoiling, and that by mutual consent men would take in exchange for the truly useful but perishable supports of life. . . .

49] Thus in the beginning all the world was America, and more so than that is now; for no such thing as money was anywhere known. Find out something that has the use and value of money amongst his neighbors, you shall see the same man will begin presently to enlarge his possessions.

50] But since gold and silver, being little useful to the life of man in proportion to food, raiment, and carriage, has its value only from the consent of men, whereof labor yet makes, in great part, the measure, it is plain that men have agreed to a disproportionate and unequal possession of the earth, they having, by a tacit and voluntary consent, found out a way how a man may fairly possess more land than he himself can use the product of, by receiving in exchange for the overplus gold and silver which may be hoarded up without injury to any one, these metals not spoiling or decaying in the hands of the possessor. This partage of things in an inequality of private possessions men have made practicable out of the bounds of society and without compact, only by putting a value on gold and silver, and tacitly agreeing in the use of money; for, in governments, the laws regulate the right of property, and the possession of land is determined by positive constitutions.

* * *

VIII] OF THE BEGINNING OF POLITICAL SOCIETIES

95] MEN BEING, as has been said, by nature all free, equal, and independent, no one can be put out of this estate and subjected to the political power of another without his own consent. The only way whereby any one divests himself of his natural liberty and puts on the bonds of civil society is by agreeing with other men to join and unite into a community for their comfortable, safe, and peaceable living one amongst another, in a secure enjoyment of their properties and a greater security against any that are not of it. This any number of men may do, because it injures not the freedom of the rest; they are left as they were in the liberty of the state of nature. When any number of men have so consented to make one community or government, they are thereby presently incorporated and make one body politic wherein the majority have a right to act and conclude the rest.

* * *

99] Whosoever, therefore, out of a state of nature unite into a community must be understood to give up all the power necessary to the ends for which they unite into society to the majority of the community, unless they expressly agreed in any number greater than the majority. And this is done by barely agreeing to unite into one political society, which is all the compact that is, or needs be, between the individuals that enter into or make up a commonwealth. And thus that which begins and actually constitutes any political society is nothing but the consent of any number of freemen capable of a majority to unite and incorporate into such a society. And this is that, and that only, which did or could give beginning to any lawful government in the world.

100] To this I find two objections made:

First, That there are no instances to be found in story of a company of men independent and equal one amongst another that met together and in this way began and set up a government.

Secondly, It is impossible of right that men should do so, because all men being born under government, they are to submit to that and are not at liberty to begin a new one.

101] To the first there is this to answer: that it is not at all to be wondered that history gives us but a very little account of men that lived together in the state of nature. The inconveniences of that condition, and the love and want of society, no sooner brought any number of them together, but they presently united and incorporated if they designed to continue together. And if we may not suppose men ever to have been in the state of nature, because we hear not much of them in such a state, we may as well suppose the armies of Salmanasser or Xerxes were never children because we hear little of them till they were men and embodied in armies. Government is everywhere antecedent to records, and letters seldom come in amongst a people till a long continuation of civil society has, by other more necessary arts, provided for their safety, ease, and plenty; and then they begin to look after the history of their founders and search into their original, when they have outlived the memory of it; for it is with commonwealths as with particular persons — they are commonly ignorant of their own births and infancies.

* * *

IX] OF THE ENDS OF POLITICAL SOCIETY AND GOVERNMENT

123] IF MAN in the state of nature be so free, as has been said, if he be absolute lord of his own person and possessions, equal to the greatest, and subject to nobody, why will he part with his freedom, why will he give up his empire and subject himself to the dominion and control of any other power? To which it is obvious to answer that though in the state of nature he has such a right, yet the enjoyment of it is very uncertain and constantly exposed to the invasion of others; for all being kings as much as he, every man his equal, and the greater part no strict observers of equity and justice, the enjoyment of the property he has in this state is very unsafe, very unsecure. This makes him willing to quit a condition which, however free, is full of fears and continual dangers; and it is not without reason that he seeks out and is willing to join in society with others who are already united, or have a mind to unite, for the mutual preservation of their lives, liberties, and estates, which I call by the general name 'property.'

124] The great and chief end, therefore, of men's uniting into commonwealths and putting themselves under government is the preservation of their property. To which in the state of nature there are many things wanting:

First, there wants an established, settled, known law, received and allowed by common consent to be the standard of right and wrong and the common measure to decide all controversies between them; for though the law of nature be plain and intelligible to all rational creatures, yet men, being biased by their interest as well as ignorant for want of studying it, are not apt to allow of it as a law binding to them in the application of it to their particular cases.

125] Secondly, in the state of nature there wants a known and indifferent judge with authority to determine all differences according to the established law; for every one in that state being both judge and executioner of the law of nature, men being partial to themselves, passion and revenge is very apt to carry them too far and with too much heat in their own cases, as well as negligence and unconcernedness to make them too remiss in other men's.

126] Thirdly, in the state of nature there often wants power to back and support the sentence when right, and to give it due execution. They who by any injustice offend will seldom fail, where they are able, by force, to make good their injustice; such resistance many times makes the punishment dangerous and frequently destructive to those who attempt it.

127] Thus mankind, notwithstanding all the privileges of the state of nature, being but in an ill condition while they remain in it, are quickly driven into society. Hence it comes to pass that we seldom find any number of men live any time together in this state. The inconveniences that they are therein exposed to by the irregular and uncertain exercise of the power every man has of punishing the transgression of others make them take sanctuary under the established laws of government and therein seek the preservation of their property. It is this makes them so willingly give up every one his single power of punishing, to be exercised by such alone as shall be appointed to it amongst them; and by such rules as the community, or those authorized by them to that purpose, shall agree on. And in this we have the original right of both the legislative and executive power, as well as of the governments and societies themselves.

128] For in the state of nature, to omit the liberty he has of innocent delights, a man has two powers:

The first is to do whatsoever he thinks fit for the preservation of himself and others within the permission of the law of nature, by which law, common to them all, he and all the rest of mankind are one community, make up one society, distinct from all other creatures. And, were it not for the corruption and viciousness of degenerate men, there would be no need of any other, no necessity that men should separate from this great and natural community and by positive agreements combine into smaller and divided associations.

The other power a man has in the state of nature is the power to punish the crimes committed against that law. Both these he gives up when he joins in a private, if I may so call it, or particular politic society and incorporates into any commonwealth separate from the rest of mankind. . . .

131] But though men when they enter into society give up the equality, liberty, and executive power they had in the state of nature into the hands of the society, to be so far disposed of by the legislative as the good of the society shall require, yet it being only with an intention in every one the better to preserve himself, his liberty and property — for no rational creature can be supposed to change his condition with an intention to be worse — the power of the society, or legislative constituted by them, can never be supposed to extend farther than the common good, but is obliged to secure every one's property by providing against those three defects above-mentioned that made the state of nature so unsafe and uneasy. And so whoever has the legislative or supreme power of any common-wealth is bound to govern by established standing laws, promulgated and known to the people, and not by extemporary decrees; by indifferent and upright judges who are to decide controversies by those laws; and to employ the force of the community at home only in the execution of such laws, or abroad to prevent or redress foreign injuries, and secure the community from inroads and invasion. And all this to be directed to no other end but the peace, safety, and public good of the people.

X] OF THE FORMS OF A COMMONWEALTH

132] The majority, having, as has been shown, upon men's first uniting into society, the whole power of the community naturally in them, may employ all that power in making laws for the com-munity from time to time, and executing those laws by officers of their own appointing: and then the form of the government is a perfect democracy; or else may put the power of making laws into the hands of a few select men, and their heirs or successors: and then it is an oligarchy; or else into the hands of one man: and then it is a monarchy; if to him and his heirs: it is an hereditary monarchy; if to him only for life, but upon his death the power only of nominat-ing a successor to return to them: an elective monarchy. And so accordingly of these the community may make compounded and mixed forms of government, as they think good. And if the legisla-tive power be at first given by the majority to one or more persons only for their lives, or any limited time, and then the supreme power to revert to them again — when it is so reverted, the community may dispose of it again anew into what hands they please and so con-stitute a new form of government. For the form of government de-pending upon the placing of the supreme power, which is the legislative — it being impossible to conceive that an inferior power should prescribe to a superior, or any but the supreme make laws — according as the power of making laws is placed, such is the form of the commonwealth.

133] By commonwealth, I must be understood all along to mean, not a democracy or any form of government, but any independent community which the Latins signified by the word *civitas*. . . .

XI] OF THE EXTENT OF THE LEGISLATIVE POWER

134] The great end of men's entering into society being the enjoyment of their properties in peace and safety and the great instrument and means of that being the laws established in that society, the first and fundamental positive law of all commonwealths is the establishing of the legislative power; as the first and fundamental natural law which is to govern even the legislative itself is the preservation of the society and, as far as will consist with the public good, of every person in it. This legislative is not only the supreme power of the commonwealth, but sacred and unalterable in the hands where the community have once placed it. . . .

135] Though the legislative, whether placed in one or more, whether it be always in being, or only by intervals, though it be the supreme power in every commonwealth; yet:

First, it is not, nor can possibly be, absolutely arbitrary over the lives and fortunes of the people; for it being but the joint power of every member of the society given up to that person or assembly which is legislator, it can be no more than those persons had in a state of nature before they entered into society and gave up to the community; for nobody can transfer to another more power than he has in himself, and nobody has an absolute arbitrary power over himself or over any other, to destroy his own life or take away the life or property of another. A man, as has been proved, cannot subject himself to the arbitrary power of another; and having in the state of nature no arbitrary power over the life, liberty, or possession of another, but only so much as the law of nature gave him for the preservation of himself and the rest of mankind, this is all he does or can give up to the commonwealth, and by it to the legislative power, so that the legislative can have no more than this. Their power, in the utmost bounds of it, is limited to the public good of the society. It is a power that has no other end but preservation, and therefore can never have a right to destroy, enslave, or designedly to impoverish the subjects. The obligations of the law of nature cease not in society but only in many cases are drawn closer and have by human laws known penalties annexed to them to enforce their observation. Thus the law of nature stands as an eternal rule to all men, legislators as well as others. The rules that they make for other men's actions must, as well as their own and other men's actions, be conformable to the law of nature — i.e., to the will of God, of which that is a declaration — and the fundamental law of nature being the preservation of mankind, no human sanction can be good or valid against it.

136] Secondly, the legislative or supreme authority cannot assume to itself a power to rule by extemporary, arbitrary decrees, but is bound to dispense justice and to decide the rights of the subject by promulgated, standing laws, and known authorized judges. For the law of nature being unwritten, and so nowhere to be found but in the minds of men, they who through passion or interest shall miscite or misapply it, cannot so easily be convinced of their mistake where there is no established judge. . . . To this end it is that men give up all their natural power to the society which they enter into, and the community put the legislative power into such hands as they think fit with this trust, that they shall be governed by declared laws, or else their peace, quiet, and property will still be at the same uncertainty as it was in the state of nature.

137] Absolute arbitrary power or governing without settled standing laws can neither of them consist with the ends of society and government which men would not quit the freedom of the state of nature for, and tie themselves up under, were it not to preserve their lives, liberties, and fortunes, and by stated rules of right and property to secure their peace and quiet. It cannot be supposed that they should intend, had they a power so to do, to give to any one or more an absolute arbitrary power over their persons and estates and put a force into the magistrate's hand to execute his unlimited will arbitrarily upon them. This were to put themselves into a worse condition than the state of nature wherein they had a liberty to defend their right against the injuries of others and were upon equal terms of force to maintain it, whether invaded by a single man or many in combination. . . . For all the power the government has, being only for the good of the society, as it ought not to be arbitrary and at pleasure, so it ought to be exercised by established and promulgated laws; that both the people may know their duty and be safe and secure within the limits of the law; and the rulers, too, kept within their bounds, and not be tempted by the power they have in their hands to employ it to such purposes and by such measures as they would not have known, and own not willingly.

138] Thirdly, the supreme power cannot take from any man part of his property without his own consent; for the preservation of property being the end of government and that for which men enter into society, it necessarily supposes and requires that the people should have property; without which they must be supposed to lose that, by entering into society, which was the end for which they entered into it — too gross an absurdity for any man to own. Men, therefore, in society having property, they have such right to the goods which by the law of the community are theirs, that nobody has a right to take their substance or any part of it from them without their own consent; without this, they have no property at all, for I have truly no property in that which another can by right take from me when he pleases, against my consent. . . .

140] It is true, governments cannot be supported without great charge, and it is fit every one who enjoys his share of the protection should pay out of his estate his proportion for the maintenance of it. But still it must be with his own consent — i.e., the consent of the majority, giving it either by themselves or their representatives chosen by them. For if any one shall claim a power to lay and levy taxes on the people, by his own authority and without such consent of the people, he thereby invades the fundamental law of property and subverts the end of government; for what property have I in that which another may by right take, when he pleases, to himself?

141] Fourthly, the legislative cannot transfer the power of making laws to any other hands; for it being but a delegated power from the people, they who have it cannot pass it over to others. . . . The power of the legislative, being derived from the people by a positive voluntary grant and institution, can be no other than what that positive grant conveyed, which being only to make laws, and not to make legislators, the legislative can have no power to transfer their authority of making laws and place it in other hands.

XII] OF THE LEGISLATIVE, EXECUTIVE, AND FEDERATIVE POWER OF THE COMMONWEALTH

143] The legislative power is that which has a right to direct how the force of the commonwealth shall be employed for preserving the community and the members of it. But because those laws which are constantly to be executed, and whose force is always to continue, may be made in a little time, therefore there is no need that the legislative should be always in being, not having always business to do. And because it may be too great a temptation to human frailty, apt to grasp at power, for the same persons who have the power of making laws to have also in their hands the power to execute them, whereby they may exempt themselves from obedience to the laws they make, and suit the law, both in its making and execution, to their own private advantage, and thereby come to have a distinct interest from the rest of the community contrary to the end of society and government; therefore, in well ordered commonwealths, where the good of the whole is so considered as it ought, the legislative power is put into the hands of diverse persons who, duly assembled, have by themselves, or jointly with others, a power to make laws; which when they have done, being separated again, they are themselves subject to the laws they have made, which is a new and near tie upon them to take care that they make them for the public good.

144] But because the laws that are at once and in a short time made have a constant and lasting force and need a perpetual execution or an attendance thereunto; therefore, it is necessary there should be a power always in being which should see to the execution of the laws that are made and remain in force. And thus the legislative and executive power come often to be separated.

145] There is another power in every commonwealth which one may call natural, because it is that which answers to the power every man naturally had before he entered into society; for though in a commonwealth the members of it are distinct persons still in reference to one another, and as such are governed by the laws of the society, yet, in reference to the rest of mankind, they make one body which is, as every member of it before was, still in the state of nature with the rest of mankind. Hence it is that the controversies that happen between any man of the society with those that are out of it are managed by the public, and an injury done to a member of their body engages the whole in the reparation of it. So that, under this consideration, the whole community is one body in the state of nature in respect of all other states or persons out of its community. 145] This, therefore, contains the power of war and peace, leagues and alliances, and all the transactions with all persons and communities without the commonwealth, and may be called 'federative,' if anyone pleases. So the thing be understood, I am indifferent as to the name.

147] These two powers, executive and federative, though they be really distinct in themselves, yet one comprehending the execution of the municipal laws of the society within itself upon all that are parts of it, the other the management of the security and interest of the public without, with all those that it may receive benefit or damage from, yet they are always almost united. And though this federative power in the well or ill management of it be of great moment to the commonwealth, yet it is much less capable to be directed by antecedent, standing, positive laws than the executive, and so must necessarily be left to the prudence and wisdom of those whose hands it is in to be managed for the public good. . . .

*   *   *

XVIII] OF TYRANNY

199] As usurpation is the exercise of power which another has a right to, so tyranny is the exercise of power beyond right, which nobody can have a right to. And this is making use of the power any one has in his hands, not for the good of those who are under it, but for his own private separate advantage — when the governor, however entitled, makes not the law, but his will, the rule, and his commands and actions are not directed to the preservation of the properties of his people, but the satisfaction of his own ambition, revenge, covetousness, or any other irregular passion. . . .

201] It is a mistake to think this fault is proper only to monarchies; other forms of government are liable to it as well as that. For wherever the power that is put in any hands for the government of the people and the preservation of their properties is applied to other ends, and made use of to impoverish, harass, or subdue them to the arbitrary and irregular commands of those that have it, there it presently becomes tyranny, whether those that thus use it are one or many. Thus we read of the thirty tyrants at Athens, as well as one at Syracuse; and the intolerable dominion of the *decemviri* at Rome was nothing better.

202] Wherever law ends, tyranny begins if the law be transgressed to another's harm. And whosoever in authority exceeds the power given him by the law, and makes use of the force he has under his command to compass that upon the subject which the law allows not, ceases in that to be a magistrate and, acting without authority, may be opposed as any other man who by force invades the right of another. This is acknowledged in subordinate magistrates. He that has authority to seize my person in the street may be opposed as a thief and a robber if he endeavors to break into my house to execute a writ, notwithstanding that I know he has such a warrant and such a legal authority as will empower him to arrest me abroad. And why this should not hold in the highest as well as in the most inferior magistrate, I would gladly be informed. Is it reasonable that the eldest brother, because he has the greatest part of his father's estate, should thereby have a right to take away any of his younger brother's portions? Or that a rich man who possessed a whole country should from thence have a right to seize, when he pleased, the cottage and garden of his poor neighbor? The being rightfully possessed of great power and riches, exceedingly beyond the greatest part of the sons of Adam, is so far from being an excuse, much less a reason, for rapine and oppression, which the endamaging another without authority is, that it is a great aggravation of it; for the exceeding the bounds of authority is no more a right in a great than in a petty officer, no more justifiable in a king than a constable; but is so much the worse in him in that he has more trust put in him, has already a much greater share than the rest of his brethren, and is supposed, from the advantages of his education, employment, and counselors, to be more knowing in the measures of right and wrong.

203] May the commands, then, of a prince be opposed? May he be resisted as often as any one shall find himself aggrieved, and but imagine he has not right done him? This will unhinge and overturn all polities, and, instead of government and order, leave nothing but anarchy and confusion.

204] To this I answer that force is to be opposed to nothing but to unjust and unlawful force; whoever makes any opposition in any other case draws on himself a just condemnation both from God and man; and so no such danger or confusion will follow, as is often suggested. . . .

* * *

XIX] OF THE DISSOLUTION OF GOVERNMENT

211] He that will with any clearness speak of the dissolution of government ought in the first place to distinguish between the dissolution of the society and the dissolution of the government. That which makes the community and brings men out of the loose state of nature into one politic society is the agreement which everybody has with the rest to incorporate and act as one body, and so be one distinct commonwealth. The usual and almost only way whereby this union is dissolved is the inroad of foreign force making a conquest upon them; for in that case, not being able to maintain and support themselves as one entire and independent body, the union belonging to that body which consisted therein must necessarily cease, and so every one return to the state he was in before, with a liberty to shift for himself and provide for his own safety, as he thinks fit, in some other society. Whenever the society is dissolved, it is certain the government of that society cannot remain. . . .

212] Besides this overturning from without, governments are dissolved from within.

First, when the legislative is altered. Civil society being a state of peace amongst those who are of it, from whom the state of war is excluded by the umpirage which they have provided in their legislative for the ending all differences that may arise amongst any of them, it is in their legislative that the members of a commonwealth are united and combined together into one coherent living body. This is the soul that gives form, life, and unity to the commonwealth; from hence the several members have their mutual influence, sympathy, and connection; and, therefore, when the legislative is broken or dissolved, dissolution and death follows; for the essence and union of the society consisting in having one will, the legislative, when once established by the majority, has the declaring and, as it were, keeping of that will. . . . Everyone is at the disposure of his own will when those who had by the delegation of the society the declaring of the public will are excluded from it and others usurp the place who have no such authority or delegation.

213] This being usually brought about by such in the commonwealth who misuse the power they have, it is hard to consider it aright, and know at whose door to lay it, without knowing the form of government in which it happens. Let us suppose then the legislative placed in the concurrence of three distinct persons:

(1) A single hereditary person having the constant supreme executive power, and with it the power of convoking and dissolving the other two within certain periods of time.

(2) An assembly of hereditary nobility.

(3) An assembly of representatives chosen *pro tempore* by the people. Such a form of government supposed, it is evident,

214] First, that when such a single person or prince sets up his own arbitrary will in place of the laws which are the will of the society declared by the legislative, then the legislative is changed. . . . Whoever introduces new laws, not being thereunto authorized by the fundamental appointment of the society, or subverts the old, disowns and overturns the power by which they were made, and so sets up a new legislative.

215] Secondly, when the prince hinders the legislative from assembling in its due time, or from acting freely pursuant to those ends for which it was constituted, the legislative is altered. . . .

216] Thirdly, when, by the arbitrary power of the prince, the electors or ways of election are altered without the consent and contrary to the common interest of the people, there also the legislative is altered; for if others than those whom the society has authorized thereunto do choose, or in another way than what the society has prescribed, those chosen are not the legislative appointed by the people.

217] Fourthly, the delivery also of the people into the subjection of a foreign power, either by the prince or by the legislative, is certainly a change of the legislative, and so a dissolution of the government; for the end why people entered into society being to be preserved one entire, free, independent society, to be governed by its own laws, this is lost whenever they are given up into the power of another.

218] Why in such a constitution as this the dissolution of the government in these cases is to be imputed to the prince is evident. Because he, having the force, treasure, and offices of the state to employ, and often persuading himself, or being flattered by others, that as supreme magistrate he is incapable of control — he alone is in a condition to make great advances toward such changes, under pretense of lawful authority, and has it in his hands to terrify or suppress opposers as factious, seditious, and enemies to the government. Whereas no other part of the legislative or people is capable by themselves to attempt any alteration of the legislative, without open and visible rebellion apt enough to be taken notice of, which, when it prevails, produces effects very little different from foreign conquest. Besides, the prince in such a form of government having the power of dissolving the other parts of the legislative, and thereby rendering them private persons, they can never in opposition to him or without his concurrence alter the legislative by a law, his consent being necessary to give any of their decrees that sanction. But yet, so far as the other parts of the legislative in any way contribute to any attempt upon the government, and do either promote or not, what lies in them, hinder such designs, they are guilty and partake in this, which is certainly the greatest crime men can be guilty of one toward another.

219] There is one way more whereby such a government may be dissolved, and that is when he who has the supreme executive power neglects and abandons that charge, so that the laws already made can no longer be put in execution. This is demonstratively to reduce all to anarchy, and so effectually to dissolve the government. . . .

220] In these and the like cases, when the government is dissolved, the people are at liberty to provide for themselves by erecting a new legislative, differing from the other by the change of persons or form, or both, as they shall find it most for their safety and good; for the society can never by the fault of another lose the native and original right it has to preserve itself, which can only be done by a settled legislative, and a fair and impartial execution of the laws made by it. But the state of mankind is not so miserable that they are not capable of using this remedy till it be too late to look for any. . . . Men can never be secure from tyranny if there be no means to escape it till they are perfectly under it; and therefore it is that they have not only a right to get out of it, but to prevent it.

221] There is, therefore, secondly, another way whereby governments are dissolved, and that is when the legislative or the prince, either of them, act contrary to their trust.

First, the legislative acts against the trust reposed in them when they endeavor to invade the property of the subject, and to make themselves or any part of the community masters or arbitrary disposers of the lives, liberties, or fortunes of the people. . . .

222] . . .Whenever the legislators endeavor to take away and destroy the property of the people, or to reduce them to slavery under arbitrary power, they put themselves into a state of war with the people who are thereupon absolved from any further obedience, and are left to the common refuge which God has provided for all men against force and violence. Whensoever, therefore, the legislative shall transgress this fundamental rule of society, and either by ambition, fear, folly, or corruption, endeavor to grasp themselves, or put into the hands of any other, an absolute power over the lives, liberties, and estates of the people, by this breach of trust they forfeit the power the people had put into their hands for quite contrary ends, and it devolves to the people, who have a right to resume their original liberty and, by the establishment of a new legislative, such as they shall think fit, provide for their own safety and security, which is the end for which they are in society. What I have said here concerning the legislative in general holds true also concerning the supreme executor, who having a double trust put in him — both to have a part in the legislative and the supreme execution of the law — acts against both when he goes about to set up his own arbitrary will as the law of the society. He acts also contrary to his trust when he either employs the force, treasure, and offices of the society to corrupt the representatives and gain them to his purposes, or openly pre-engages the electors and prescribes to their choice such whom he has by solicitations, threats, promises, or otherwise won to his designs, and employs them to bring in such who have promised beforehand what to vote and what to enact. Thus to regulate candidates and electors, and new-model the ways of election, what is it but to cut up the government by the roots, and poison the very fountain of public security? For the people, having reserved to themselves the choice of their representatives, as the fence to their properties, could do it for no other end but that they might always be freely chosen, and, so chosen, freely act and advise as the necessity of the commonwealth and the public good should upon examination and mature debate be judged to require. This those who give their votes before they hear the debate and have weighed the reasons on all sides are not capable of doing. To prepare such an assembly as this, and endeavor to set up the declared abettors of his own will for the true representatives of the people and the lawmakers of the society, is certainly as great a breach of trust and as perfect a declaration of a design to subvert the government as is possible to be met with. To which if one shall add rewards and punishments visibly employed to the same end, and all the arts of perverted law made use of to take off and destroy all that stand in the way of such a design, and will not comply and consent to betray the liberties of their country, it will be past doubt what is doing. What power they ought to have in the society who thus employ it contrary to the trust that went along with it in its first institution is easy to determine; and one cannot but see that he who has once attempted any such thing as this cannot any longer be trusted.

223] To this perhaps it will be said that, the people being ignorant and always discontented, to lay the foundation of government in the unsteady opinion and uncertain humor of the people is to expose it to certain ruin; and no government will be able long to subsist if the people may set up a new legislative whenever they take offense at the old one. To this I answer: Quite the contrary. People are not so easily got out of their old forms as some are apt to suggest. They are hardly to be prevailed with to amend the acknowledged faults in the frame they have been accustomed to. And if there be any original defects, or adventitious ones introduced by time or corruption, it is not an easy thing to get them changed, even when all the world sees there is an opportunity for it. This slowness and aversion in the people to quit their old constitutions has in the many revolutions which have been seen in this kingdom, in this and former ages, still kept us to, or after some interval of fruitless attempts still brought us back again to, our old legislative of king, lords, and commons; and whatever provocations have made the crown be taken from some of our princes' heads, they never carried the people so far as to place it in another line.

224] But it will be said this hypothesis lays a ferment for frequent rebellion. To which I answer:

First, no more than any other hypothesis. . . .

225] Secondly, I answer, such revolutions happen not upon every little mismanagement in public affairs. Great mistakes in the ruling part, many wrong and inconvenient laws, and all the slips of human frailty will be borne by the people without mutiny or murmur. But if a long train of abuses, prevarications, and artifices, all tending the same way, make the design visible to the people, and they cannot but feel what they lie under and see whither they are going, it is not to be wondered that they should then rouse themselves and endeavor to put the rule into such hands which may secure to them the ends for which government was at first erected, and without which ancient names and specious forms are so far from being better that they are much worse than the state of nature or pure anarchy — the inconveniences being all as great and as near, but the remedy farther off and more difficult.

226] Thirdly, I answer that this doctrine of a power in the people of providing for their safety anew by a new legislative, when their legislators have acted contrary to their trust by invading their property, is the best fence against rebellion, and the probablest means to hinder it; for rebellion being an opposition, not to persons, but authority which is founded only in the constitutions and laws of the government, those, whoever they be, who by force break through, and by force justify their violation of them, are truly and properly rebels. . . .

227] In both the forementioned cases, when either the legislative is changed or the legislators act contrary to the end for which they were constituted, those who are guilty are guilty of rebellion; for if any one by force takes away the established legislative of any society, and the laws of them made pursuant to their trust, he thereby takes away the umpirage which every one had consented to for a peaceable decision of all their controversies, and a bar to the state of war amongst them. . . . They actually introduce a state of war which is that of force without authority. . . . And if those who by force take away the legislative are rebels, the legislators themselves, as has been shown, can be no less esteemed so, when they who were set up for the protection and preservation of the people, their liberties and properties, shall by force invade and endeavor to take them away; and so they putting themselves into a state of war with those who made them the protectors and guardians of their peace, are properly, and with the greatest aggravation, *rebellantes,* rebels.

228] But if they who say "it lays a foundation for rebellion" mean that it may occasion civil wars or intestine broils, to tell the people they are absolved from obedience when illegal attempts are made upon their liberties or properties, and may oppose the unlawful violence of those who were their magistrates when they invade their properties contrary to the trust put in them, and that therefore this doctrine is not to be allowed, being so destructive to the peace of the world; they may as well say, upon the same ground, that honest men may not oppose robbers or pirates because this may occasion disorder or bloodshed. . . .

229] The end of government is the good of mankind. And which is best for mankind? That the people should be always exposed to the boundless will of tyranny, or that the rulers should be sometimes liable to be opposed when they grow exorbitant in the use of their power and employ it for the destruction and not the preservation of the properties of their people?

230] Nor let any one say that mischief can arise from hence, as often as it shall please a busy head or turbulent spirit to desire the alteration of the government. It is true such men may stir whenever they please, but it will be only to their own just ruin and perdition; for till the mischief be grown general, and the ill designs of the rulers become visible, or their attempts sensible to the greater part, the people, who are more disposed to suffer than right themselves by resistance, are not apt to stir. The examples of particular injustice or oppression of here and there an unfortunate man moves them not. But if they universally have a persuasion grounded upon manifest evidence that designs are carrying on against their liberties, and the general course and tendency of things cannot but give them strong suspicions of the evil intention of their governors, who is to be blamed for it? . . . This I am sure: whoever, either ruler or subject, by force goes about to invade the rights of either prince or people and lays the foundation for overturning the constitution and frame of any just government is highly guilty of the greatest crime I think a man is capable of — being to answer for all those mischiefs of blood, rapine, and desolation, which the breaking to pieces of governments bring on a country. And he who does it is justly to be esteemed the common enemy and pest of mankind, and is to be treated accordingly. . . .

232] Whosoever uses force without right, as every one does in society who does it without law, puts himself into a state of war with those against whom he so uses it; and in that state all former ties are canceled, all other rights cease, and every one has a right to defend himself and to resist the aggressor. . . .

*   *   *

240] Here, it is like, the common question will be made: Who shall be judge whether the prince or legislative act contrary to their trust? This, perhaps, ill-affected and factious men may spread amongst the people, when the prince only makes use of his due prerogative. To this I reply: The people shall be judge; for who shall be judge whether his trustee or deputy acts well and according to the trust reposed in him but he who deputes him and must, by having deputed him, have still a power to discard him when he fails in his trust? If this be reasonable in particular cases of private men, why should it be otherwise in that of the greatest moment where the welfare of millions is concerned, and also where the evil, if not prevented, is greater and the redress very difficult, dear, and dangerous?

241] But further, this question, Who shall be judge? cannot mean that there is no judge at all; for where there is no judicature on earth to decide controversies amongst men, God in heaven is Judge. He alone, it is true, is Judge of the right. But every man is judge for himself, as in all other cases, so in this, whether another has put himself into a state of war with him, and whether he should appeal to the Supreme Judge, as Jephthah did.

242] If a controversy arise betwixt a prince and some of the people in a matter where the law is silent or doubtful, and the thing be of great consequence, I should think the proper umpire in such a case should be the body of the people; for in cases where the prince has a trust reposed in him and is dispensed from the common ordinary rules of the law, there, if any men find themselves aggrieved and think the prince acts contrary to or beyond that trust, who so proper to judge as the body of the people (who, at first, lodged that trust in him) how far they meant it should extend? But if the prince, or whoever they be in the administration, decline that way of determination, the appeal then lies nowhere but to heaven; force between either persons who have no known superior on earth, or which permits no appeal to a judge on earth, being properly a state of war wherein the appeal lies only to heaven; and in that state the injured party must judge for himself when he will think fit to make use of that appeal and put himself upon it.

*   *   *

13

Mercantilism

JEAN-BAPTISTE COLBERT (1619–1683) was the son of a cloth merchant of Reims who, in 1630, entered the service of the state. The young Colbert served his apprenticeship in his cousin's trading house in Lyons and then in a notary's office in Paris, before going into government service in a bureau of finance. In 1640 he entered the War Office and soon became chief clerk and then secretary to Michel Le Tellier (1603–1685), the organizer of the French army and Colbert's future colleague as Minister of State in Louis XIV's government. In the 1650's, without breaking with Le Tellier, Colbert joined Mazarin's staff and became virtual manager of the Cardinal's huge personal fortune. He bought the barony of Seignelay in 1658 and thus officially joined the ranks of the nobility. Mazarin appreciated Colbert's financial talents and on his death urged the young Louis XIV to take him into his own service. Colbert gathered information on the malversations of Fouquet, the Superintendent of Finances, with the aim of supplanting him. When Fouquet was arrested in 1661, Colbert was elevated to be Comptroller of Finances. In the next few years he became Secretary of State for the King's Household, Secretary of State for the Navy, Superintendent of Commerce, Director of Royal Buildings, Vice-Protector of the French Academy, and Minister of State (member of the King's inner council of trusted advisors). Despite his cold, unsavory character, no one has ever doubted Colbert's technical competence, tremendous capacity for work, efficiency, and zeal in the King's service. One can judge Colbert's economic views from the fact that the extreme form of "mercantilism" came to be known as "Colbertism." The famous memorandum of 1670, most of which is translated here, reflects some of the main points of Colbert's system.

Colbert, Memorandum to the King on Finances, 1670

Sire,

THE STATE in which I perceive Your Majesty's finances to be at present has led me to consider them well and in their fullest extent, to investigate the causes of changes that I find in them and thus to explain them to Your Majesty, that by your great prudence and foresight you may apply the remedies which seem needful and suitable.

All that I shall say to Your Majesty will be based on the experience of nine consecutive years of reasonably successful administration, and upon demonstrable mathematical truths which cannot be gainsaid, if it please Your Majesty to give the time and patience to hear them.

Your Majesty knows from a proof based on the records of the Council and on the fruits of the loan of 1661 that your revenues were reduced to 23 million livres, and that in that year the unavoidable expenses of State could only be met by further alienations of revenue.

Your Majesty knows furthermore that within two years the revenues rose to 50 million, and later to 70 million.

During these nine years of great abundance, the general conduct of affairs has been on a correspondingly lavish scale, and all useful and advantageous expenses of State have been made with grandeur and magnificence.

In the course of this year I find this state of abundance, which seemed general, to have changed for two very important reasons, both intelligible, though one is easy to understand and the other very difficult.

The first is the increase in expenditure which has reached 75 million, thus exceeding peace-time revenues by 5 million.

The other is the widespread difficulty experienced by the tax-

From J. B. Colbert, "Mémoire au Roi sur les Finances" (1670), in Pierre Clément, Lettres, Instructions, et Mémoires de Colbert, 8 vols in 10 (Paris, 1861–1882), VII, pp. 233–246, 250–256. Trans. by Geoffrey W. Symcox.

farmers and receivers-general in collecting money from the provinces, the delays in their payments to the Treasury, and their continual complaints that the enormous dearth in the provinces leads them to fear general ruin and the inability to maintain payment on their farms and general receipts.

It is increasingly evident that these protests are true, for different reports make it clear that there is great poverty in all the provinces. Although this could be attributed to the poor market for grain, it seems clear that some greater reason for this shortage must be sought, even though the slump in the grain market could well deprive the peasants of the means of paying their taxes. But however this may be, when there is money in the kingdom, the general desire for profit causes it to circulate, and from this movement the public treasury draws its profit. And thus there must be another reason for this scarcity than the failure of the grain market.

I confess that when first I noticed this, I thought to reduce expenditure on the Navy, the galleys, the buildings and trade, and even the payments not absolutely necessary for the good and maintenance of the State, keeping only the expenses of war, the Royal Household and the Palace, which are absolutely essential. But upon reflection I thought it necessary first to inform Your Majesty of all the knowledge that I have acquired in the careful investigation that I have made of this matter, since I have observed the prodigious changes which are about to befall us. For this purpose it will be necessary to review the history of the finances from an earlier date, and before this to lay down their guiding principles and maxims.

The King's revenues consist in a part of the goods and ready money that his subjects amass by their labor, by the fruits of the earth, and the products of their industry.

All that the people can amass falls into three divisions: first, for their subsistance and private fortune; second, for the masters who own the land that they cultivate; third, for the King. This is the natural and legitimate order of distribution. But when the royal authority has reached the point to which Your Majesty has carried it, this order must necessarily change. The people, out of fear and respect for this authority, first pay their taxes, keep little for their own subsistance, and pay little or nothing to their lords. And since the people must have the means to pay before they think of settling their taxes, and must always have that proportion of the money necessary to a private citizen, the financial administration must always take great care, employing all Your Majesty's power to attract wealth into the kingdom and to disperse it through the provinces, thus giving the people the means to live with ease and pay their taxes. The demonstration of this truth is so clear and constant that it presents no difficulty. It is as follows:

Let us assume that there are about 150 million livres in coin circulating constantly in the realm. Of these 150 million, 10 to 12 million are consumed each year either in works of various sorts, or by leaving the realm in return for goods and necessary foodstuffs from abroad.

There is always a proportional ratio between these 150 million and the money which Your Majesty receives in revenue. Thus, for example, if the revenues reach 50 million out of a total of 150, it is certain that if 200 million could be attracted into the realm, Your Majesty's revenues would rise correspondingly. Similarly, if the figure falls below 150 million, the revenues will decrease in proportion.

There is also a special proportion between the provinces, besides this general relation between the revenues and the total currency in the whole kingdom. For example, Limousin normally accounts for one-fortieth of the coin circulating in the realm, and according to this proportion pays 1,500,000 livres every year to the King. But should it continue to pay 1,500,000 livres every year and not receive money in return, its proportion would decrease, so that the province would now account for no more than one-sixtieth of the total money in the kingdom, it could then no longer pay its 1,500,000 livres, but only one million. It is true that this one-third of the ready cash which a province loses does not leave the realm but is found in another province, which can make up for the loss of 500,000 livres' revenue. But this is not so in practice, for the transfer takes place imperceptibly, and it is impossible to trace the flow of money from one province to another. But though the change is very gradual, it is nevertheless felt keenly in the losing province, which initially has great difficulty in paying its taxes, and after two years defaults.

From this a clear and obvious conclusion may be drawn: that both the soundness of the finances and the increase of Your Majesty's revenues depend upon increasing by every possible means the quantity of coin circulating within the realm, and upon maintaining the due proportion between the various provinces.

Three things remain to be considered:

First, whether there is at present more money in private commerce than during the last 20 or 30 years.

Second, if the relation between this sum and the revenues has altered.

Third, the reasons for this change.

For the first it may be said with assurance that there is more money in the kingdom than there has perhaps ever been, but that there is much less in private commerce.

The clear proof that there is more comes from common knowledge that cannot be contradicted. The same amount of money as before remains in Europe, save for a small proportion which is used up. Every two years a very rich supply comes from the West Indies. All the kingdoms and states of Europe, Spain, Italy, England, Germany, Sweden, Denmark, Poland, Hungary, Savoy, and Venice are in pressing need and unable to make any expenditure. In our realm no such scarcity has been observed, and it follows therefore that there is more money here than there has ever been.

At the same time it is easy to see that there is less than ever in private commerce. The chances of profit induce private individuals to invest their money in commerce, so that when there is less opportunity for gain, money circulates much less freely.

Before Your Majesty's administration of the finances, there were three ways by which private citizens could profit from their wealth: through the vast alienation of [state] revenues, the loans to businessmen at high interest, and trade.

Your Majesty has reduced the first two, which were easy and convenient, giving a total profit of 30 to 40 million livres, and has striven to build up and increase the third so that it could provide the same return as the others. But the uncertainty of fortunes during the time of the Chamber of Justice [an extraordinary commission set up in 1661 to investigate financial abuses committed since 1635], which only closed a year ago, combined with the magnitude of the enterprise, which in other countries is the labor of centuries, have so far prevented this great achievement. Consequently, though it is certain that there is much more money than ever in the kingdom, it is equally certain that there is much less in private trade.

This first point being well established, we must consider the second, which consists in examining the proportion that the royal revenues have always had, and can have, to the money invested in commerce.

From the records of the *Espargne* from 1630 to 1660 it can be seen that before the declaration of war in 1635, State expenditure never rose above 20–22 million livres. After 1635 it only reached 45 million livres of necessary and useful expenditure in the most difficult years.

It can also be stated with certainty that while there were 150 million livres of coined money in public use, the people paid with difficulty 45 million for State expenditure, that is about one-third.

But it now appears from what has been said before that there are no more than 120 million livres in public use.

Following the same proportion, the King's revenues should be no more than 40 million livres. But since they remain constant at 70 million, it is necessary to examine why this should be so, and in consequence whether they can remain at this level or whether they will rise or fall.

The reason lies in the deep obedience and respect in which the people hold the King's will, which compels them to the greatest efforts to pay their taxes, thus keeping them in that condition of poverty in which they have remained since the war, and preventing them from paying their masters, the lords and landowners, whose complaints are only too public and general throughout the realm.

In order fully to understand whether this state of affairs can endure for any length of time, and whether the revenues can and should rise or fall, it should be observed that these conditions are too crushing to last long. This is clearly demonstrated by the difficulties encountered by the receivers-general in collecting the taille from the *generalités* [tax districts], the delays in their normal payments, their daily protests of the impossibility of continuing the receipts from the *generalités* on the same level as in previous years, and by the assertions of the tax-farmers that the yields of their areas are beginning to decrease appreciably.

To this source of trouble which is already very great of itself must also be added the various excessive expenditures which this year amount in all to 75 million livres. So that instead of pursuing two policies equally vital in time of peace, that is, giving the people a definite and real respite to allow them to recover and build up the means to bear the greatest burdens in time of war, and, secondly, laying aside certain sums for the urgent needs of State, we take from the people double the proportion between the money normally circulating among the public and taxes that they pay. And even so expenditure surpasses the prodigiously high customary revenue, which is 70 million, by 5 million livres.

The conclusions easily deduced from this are: that the people face certain ruin; that taxes must be reduced considerably; and that since the deficit forces consumption of the next year's revenues in advance to meet current expenses, we shall inevitably fall into the need and scarcity of former times. It is now necessary to examine in detail whether the general conduct of the finances and the policies and methods followed have helped to reduce things to this state.

It has been said that the people pay double the proportion which has always been maintained between the amount of money in circulation and the amount paid in taxes, and that there is at present much less of this money. In consequence of this it was necessary to inform Your Majesty that this state of affairs could not last, and you would certainly have decided to reduce expenditure and relieve the burden on the people. Even though it may be said that in a great State such as this these important effects can only be perceived by accurate research, long experience and deep thought, and that understanding comes only with time, it is nontheless sure that the principles upon which policy has been conducted could in time remedy these faults, and these principles must therefore be given careful examination.

From all that has been said above, it follows that the well-being and strength of the people results from maintaining the proportion between the taxes which they pay to the Treasury and the amount of money circulating in commerce.

This proportion has always been 150 million to 45 million. It is now 120 million to 70 million. It is thus far too high, and as a natural result the people must fall into great poverty.

Either of two solutions could be adopted: either reduce taxes and expenditure or increase the amount of money in trade.

For the first, taxes have been lowered, but the King's authority and the people's great respect for his orders have resulted, despite the great reductions made, in high revenues from sources which hitherto produced little. This appears clearly in the tailles which, estimated at 56 million, formerly realized only 16 million for the Treasury, and now realize 24 million on an assessment yield of 32 million. The farmed taxes, the gabelles, which formerly produced only 1 million, now produce 13 million, even though Your

Majesty abolished the surtax on salt and reduced its price everywhere by one-tenth. So we have seen the State revenues increasing at the same time as the great reliefs granted by Your Majesty to his subjects would seem to have reduced them. And as revenues have risen, so has expenditure.

For the second solution, it includes three points: to raise the amount of money in circulation by attracting it from those countries where it has its source, to keep it in the country and prevent it from being taken out, and to give the people the opportunity to draw profit from it.

Since these three points are the foundation of greatness, of the power of the State, and of the magnificence of the King, through' all the great expenses which large revenues permit him to make, which [pre-eminence] is the greater because at the same time the neighboring countries are brought low; there being but a certain quantity of money circulating in all Europe, which is increased from time to time by what comes from the West Indies, it is certain and demonstrable that if there are but 150 million livres in coin circulating among the public, this figure cannot be raised by 20, 30 or 40 million livres unless this be at the expense of neighboring states, thus producing that double increase which has been so notable of late years: the growth of Your Majesty's power and greatness, and the decline of your enemies and of those who envy you.

In implementing these three principles lies all the labor in the conduct of finances since the beginning of Your Majesty's administration. Because it is commerce alone and what depends upon it, that can bring about this great result, and because it was necessary to introduce it into a realm where neither the public powers nor even particular individuals had ever devoted themselves to it, it being in a way contrary to the genius of the nation, there was perhaps no enterprise at once so difficult and so profitable for the reign of Your Majesty. For from this access of financial power stem all the great deeds which you have already achieved and may yet achieve throughout your life. At the moment it is only a matter of reviewing this work and its results. To this end it is necessary to see what has been done to attract money into the kingdom and to keep it here. But since in the natural order of things saving must always precede the acquisition of wealth, it must first be shown how money left the kingdom, and what measures were taken to retain it.

The Dutch, the English and other nations carried away wines, spirits, vinegars, cloth, paper, mercery, and grain in time of need; the Dutch, it should be noted, took nine parts out of ten of the trade. But they brought us cloth and other woollen and textile goods; sugar, tobacco and indigo from the Americas; all the spices, drugs, (word illegible in ms.), and oils, silk, cotton fabrics, leather and many other goods from the Indies; the same goods from the Levant, by the *Échelles* [Ottoman merchant ports] traffic; all the materials for shipbuilding, such as timber, masts, Swedish and Galician iron, copper, pitch, iron cannon, hemp, cordage, wrought and cast iron, brass, navigational instruments, cannonballs, iron anchors, and generally all the requisites for building ships either for the King or for his subjects. Gunpowder, matches, muskets, balls, lead, tin, cloth, London serge, silk and woollen stockings from England; brocades, damasks, camlets and other stuffs from Flanders; lace from Venice and Holland, and braid from Flanders, camlets from Brussels, moquette from Flanders; sheep and cattle from Germany; leather from all countries; horses from all countries; silks from Milan, Genoa and Holland.

All trade between ports and even within the realm was carried by the Dutch, so that the King's subjects had no part of it.

By these means and by a multitude of others too long to relate the Dutch, the English, the men of Hamburg and of other nations brought into the realm a far greater quantity of merchandise than they took away, taking the balance in cash, thus bringing abundance to themselves and scarcity to the kingdom, and by an indubitable consequence increasing their strength and the kingdom's weakness.

It remains to see what remedies have been used for these ills.

First, in 1662, Your Majesty decided to uphold the tax of 50 sous per ton of cargo on all foreign vessels, which produced such an effect that the number of French vessels has increased every year. In 7 or 8 years the Dutch were almost excluded from the coasting trade between ports, which is now carried on by Frenchmen. The advantages accruing to the State from the increased number of sailors and seamen, and the coin retained in the kingdom by this and other means, would be too long to describe.

At the same time Your Majesty began to abolish all the tolls long established on the rivers of the kingdom, and ordered the surveying of those rivers which could be made navigable, to facilitate the transport of foodstuffs and merchandise from within the kingdom to the sea, and thence to other countries. Although all that now attracts the general admiration of men was in disorder in those first years, and though the work of restoration was an unfathomed depth of unforeseeable extent, Your Majesty did not fail to examine the charges on the Five Great Farms [a customs area covering much of central and northern France], and discovered that the regulation of those taxes bearing upon trade had always been made with the greatest carelessness on the recommendation of the tax-farmers. These, concerned only with their own interests and with increasing the profits from their farms in the time that they enjoyed them, had always laid heavy charges on the foodstuffs, goods and manufactures of the kingdom, which they saw exported in great quantity, while lightly taxing the entry of foreign wares, to encourage the import of larger quantities. They gave no thought to the money which left the kingdom as a result of this action, for it was a matter of indifference to them, provided that their farms gave a good return in the time that they held them.

Finally, after a full investigation of the question, Your Majesty decreed the Tariff of 1664 in which the charges are based on a totally different principle. Charges on all native goods and manufactured products were notably lightened and those on foreign goods increased, though with moderation, particularly since if this raising of tariff had been excessive, there being no industry as yet established in the kingdom, it would have proved a great burden to the people, because of their need of foreign goods and manufactures. But this change began to provide the means for establishing the same manufactures in the kingdom:

[There follows a lengthy and detailed list of manufactures recently established in France.]

In a word, all that is needed for building ships is now so well established in the kingdom that Your Majesty need no longer rely on foreign imports for the Navy and even in a short time may be able to furnish shipping materials to other states and thus win money from them. And to the same end of having all that is necessary for the abundant supply of ships, both your own and your subjects', you ordered work to begin on the general overhaul of administration of all the forests of the realm, which, if they continue to be as carefully conserved as they are now, will provide all the required timber in abundance.

Furthermore, to prevent the Dutch from profiting from the trade with the Americas [i.e., the Caribbean], which they had seized and from which they had shut out the French, this being worth at least a million in gold to them annually, Your Majesty formed and built up the West India Company, in which so far you have invested almost four million livres. But you have also had the satisfaction of taking from the Dutch that million in gold which provided for 4000 of their subjects who sailed continually to the Indies with more than 200 vessels.

To prevent the Dutch from taking out of the kingdom more than 10 million in return for the goods that they bring from the East Indies and the Levant, Your Majesty founded Companies for these same countries, in which already you have invested more than 5 million livres. And to reduce the large sums in cash which must be sent to the Indies in the course of trade, you established in Dauphiné, Lyonnais Languedoc, Picardy and Normandy the manufacture of coarse cloth that is in great demand in the Indies. At the same time you laid down regulations and standards for the finishing and dyeing of these goods, so as to give French cloth the advantage over that of other countries, which is now of very poor quality.

And further, to stimulate trade and navigation, which is the source of all wealth, Your Majesty founded the Company of the North which is intended to carry all our foodstuffs and goods to the northern lands, and to bring back all the materials to build ships for Your Majesty's subjects, especially before all these necessities can be found within the realm. . . . Accordingly, by all the methods which are in use, there is reason to hope that the trade and navigation of your subjects will increase during the next twenty or thirty years at the same rate as they have increased in the last seven or eight. All the abundance of those goods which come from the North will pass from Holland, where it has always remained, to this kingdom, which alone would suffice to attract abundance and money, thereby increasing at once the revenues of Your Majesty and the poverty of your neighbors.

*   *   *

But all these great enterprises and a host of others that are in some way new, which Your Majesty began seven or eight years ago, are still only in their infancy and can be brought to perfection only by diligence and single-minded application, and cannot even endure save by the general prosperity of the State, continual large expenses being essential for the maintenance of these great undertakings.

It is certain that if the State had always been in the same condition of poverty as in the past, all the work of financial administration would have been directed to keeping up payments, and none of these ideas, for whose execution the very first step requires money, would have originated or been pursued. But if all the methods employed have kept money in the kingdom, as is beyond doubt, then it is certain that though they have absorbed some revenue, they have also brought about a far greater abundance; the increase in retail trade has accounted for the retention of at least 8–10 million livres of money in the kingdom every year; so that, on the one hand, if [the measures to promote it] have consumed a certain amount of money, on the other they have helped to raise the revenues by four times the amount that they have consumed.

From this argument one can draw a definite conclusion: to use up 40 or 45 million livres per year, that is if all the royal revenues were reduced to this figure, it is not necessary to continue all these foundations and companies. But to raise the revenues to the level of 71 million which they reached this year, and to ensure that there is as much money in the kingdom as is necessary to maintain the due proportion to the amount paid in taxes, and that the people could thus gain some respite, it is absolutely vital to continue the expenditure necessary to maintain, increase and perfect all these great enterprises.

To achieve this there are but two ways. One is obvious; it is to reduce the expenses so that they do not exceed, and even remain less than the revenues. The other is less easy to understand; it consists in taking care that the expenditure is such as to retain money in the kingdom and to spread it equally and in the correct proportion through the provinces; it would not be enough to employ every infallible means to add to the money in the realm, if payments were made outside or in such a way that they would cause money to leave the country at a greater rate than all these means, however judiciously employed, could bring in.

*   *   *

After all the clear proofs and demonstrations presented in this discussion, it only remains to summarize in a few words the trouble, its cause, its effects and its remedy.

The trouble lies in the diminution of the tax-farms' yield and in the difficulties of collection which also produce a reduction in revenue. Its cause:

The excess of expenditure.

The departure of coin from the realm.

The lack of proportion between the taxes paid by the people and the quantity of money circulating in the realm.

Before going more deeply into the last two points, I pray Your Majesty to let me say that since you undertook the direction of finances, you have engaged in a war of money against all the states of Europe. You have already vanquished Spain, Italy, Germany, England and several others which you have cast into the direst poverty and need, and from whose spoils you have grown rich. This has given you the means to achieve what you have up to now, and continue to achieve every day. Only Holland remains, fighting still with great strength; its northern trade which brings it so many advantages, and such great consideration for its naval strength and all its shipping; its East Indies trade, which brings in 12 million livres in cash annually; its Levant trade, which realises as much; its West Indies trade which still produces 3 or 4 million livres; its industries; its trade with Cadiz, Guinea and a multitude of other places, on which all its strength is founded. Your Majesty has formed Companies which attack it on all fronts like armies. In the North our Company already possesses assets of 1 million and 20 ships. In Guinea six French vessels have begun to trade. In the West, Your Majesty has excluded them from all the islands in your power, and the Company which you have founded now provides the kingdom with all its sugar, tobacco and the other products of that region, and is beginning to export them to North Italy and other foreign countries. In the East, Your Majesty has 20 ships, and two have just arrived laden with goods worth 2 million livres, which is a victory worth that same price in the present [trade] war. The Levant Company similarly has assets of 12 million livres and 12 ships. The industries, the canal between the seas, and all the other new foundations that Your Majesty is creating serve as so many reserve corps that Your Majesty is building up from nothing to do full duty in this war, in which Your Majesty sees notable advantages gained each year, such that even the vanquished cannot conceal their losses, which they proclaim in their merchants' continual complaints of lost trade.

This struggle, which is sustained only by sharp intelligence and hard work, and in which the prize of victory must be the spoils of the most powerful republic since the days of Rome, cannot be brought to a rapid conclusion, or, in other words, must remain one of the main aims of Your Majesty's attention for the rest of your life. Before complete victory can be achieved the ships of the Northern Company must be increased to at least 400. Concerning this may it please Your Majesty to note that without this number of ships, if war should break out against the Dutch, [the yield from] all the foodstuffs and natural resources of the kingdom will decrease; these are Your Majesty's only mines, the more so since they bring in 7 or 8 million livres a year. This is why war against the Dutch would have been impossible two years ago. It is now a little easier to undertake, but if Your Majesty continues to aid and foster the Northern Company, in proportion to your assistance, as the number of its ships increases, the difficulty of such a war will diminish and, in time, it would become positively advantageous. The more the Dutch ships are excluded in this way, the greater will be the inducement to Your Majesty's subjects to acquire vessels to carry goods there, following the Company's ships which will point the way.

In addition, the 80 vessels trading to the West Indies must be raised to 150, the six going to Guinea to 30 or 40, the 20 going to the East to 100, the 12 going to the Levant to 60 or 80, and all the other establishments must increase in due measure. And though these increases may seem extremely difficult of achievement, I make bold to say to Your Majesty that you will find less difficulty in carrying them to a conclusion than in first setting them up and bringing all your enterprises to their present level. It is true that much more time will be necessary, but similarly I dare to assure Your Majesty that you will see by definite and indubitable signs that the power of the Dutch, together with their commerce, will decrease year by year. In twelve or thirteen years' time you will reduce them to the direst straits, so long as all the efforts and diligence at Your Majesty's command are devoted to this end.

The palpable reward for all this will be that by attracting a great quantity of wealth into the kingdom by trade, not only will you soon re-establish that due proportion between the money circulating in trade and the taxes paid by the people, but both will be increased proportionately, so that revenue will rise and the people will be in a condition to assist more effectively in the event of war or other emergency.

After these explanations it is necessary to pass to the effects which the present conditions could produce unless quickly remedied.

It is certain, Sire, that Your Majesty as King, and as the greatest king who has ever ascended the throne, by natural inclination prefers to concern himself with war above all else; and that the administration of finances and all that it involves, which is dull and painstaking, is not the usual and natural occupation of kings. Your Majesty thinks ten times more of war than of finances, and even though by your conscientious labour, which has never been equalled by any previous monarch, however great, you have realized its importance, it is indubitable that all (the expenditure for warlike purposes will not fail to decrease, but will even increase) [the words in parentheses were crossed out in the original manuscript]; your thoughts will be devoted to war, and that you will attend to financial affairs only when extreme scarcity obliges you, and will not be pleased to forestall this need by ordering in advance the measures necessary to turn this scarcity onto your enemies and bring back to your realm and to secure that wealth which seems about to leave it.

It is certain, Sire, that the attention which Your Majesty may give to an affair of such weight, and to reading this memorandum, should reveal clearly that one of two courses must be followed: either to go on spending every year the 4 or 5 million livres by which expenditure exceeds revenue in 1670, or to reduce all expenses save those for the navy, trade, repayment of interest, etc.

The first expedient, that of anticipating future revenue, leads ineluctably to such sure and rapid ruin that it is inconceivable that Your Majesty could tolerate it.

The second interrupts the normal and necessary course of financial administration, and prevents all the great results which it seeks to achieve, which have been explained earlier. But the expenses for the navy, trade, and the repayment of loans are almost the only means by which money paid in taxes into the royal coffers returns to the provinces. The repayment of loans produces two notable effects, the one obvious, which is the increase in revenue, and the other, which, though imperceptible, must in time produce a great effect, for those who receive repayments always seek to put their money to good use. Once trade has made more impression on the public mind, every individual will share in the resultant profit.

These therefore are the results which the present condition of the finances can bring about. Either the revenue of future years will have to be used up in advance, or the execution of all the great enterprises detailed above will be held up, especially since their maintenance entails not only the continuance of expenditure at the same rate as before, but even its augmentation.

And since it is not to be doubted that Your Majesty would wish to avoid all these dire effects, the remedies must be considered.

To escape from the parlous state into which the finances have fallen this year it is necessary to find the 5 million livres that were spent in excess of the revenue, and to return to a balance in which expenses do not exceed revenue.

To this end it would be necessary for Your Majesty to reduce next year's expenditure to 60 million livres, including the 2 million which M. de Louvois tells me could be obtained from Lorraine.

For this, the expenses must be reduced as follows;

The navy	2,000,000
The buildings	3,000,000
Repayments	3,000,000
War	1,000,000
Fortifications, as was stated at the beginning of this year	2,000,000
Total	11,000,000

As far as possible the extraordinary expenses of the Royal Household, Mint, etc. should be reduced.

Expenses for the trading companies must be raised by	1,000,000
Balance	10,000,000
From which must be taken the deficit for 1670	5,000,000
Balance	5,000,000

which could serve for [subsidies to] foreign allies and the accumulation of some reserves. And if Your Majesty would wish to put your subjects in condition to aid you considerably in time of war, if peace should last several more years, it would be necessary to reduce the *tailles,* the first by 2 million and the second by another 2 million. And this relief seems to me so necessary that in the people's present condition I deem it impossible for them to continue [to pay], in the event of war, without great reductions.

For the buildings, if Your Majesty would limit yourself to a definite sum for Versailles, which would not be exceeded for any reason, it would be possible to continue the Louvre, begin the Arc de Triomphe, the Pyramid, the Observatory, the Gobelins factory and in general all Your Majesty's other works.

To continue the increase of wealth in the kingdom it is essential to press on with greater determination, strength and diligence than ever all the companies and enterprises already begun.

To prevent money from leaving the realm it is essential to reduce the expenses for fortifications by 1 million at most, as was stated at the beginning of this year:

Also to reduce the number of troops retained by Your Majesty in the ceded territories, which could perhaps be done by building quarters where they could winter on the borders of the realm, perhaps at La Fère where there is much open country, and on the Moselle, near Verdun.

*   *   *

I do not know if I am mistaken, but all these things seem to me very easy to achieve. Your Majesty will judge of this better than I, but I can assure you that I would be willing to answer for it, and that should you decide upon and not exceed for any reason the 60 million livres in the above outline, that is to say three times what Henri IV ever spent, and a quarter as much again as Louis XIII ever spent, even when he was maintaining the armies in Germany, Italy, Catalonia, Flanders and Champagne, I would be willing to guarantee to Your Majesty that you will see the same abundance throughout your life, and that you will see it increase year by year, while your enemies and those jealous of your glory fall gradually into ruin. But Your Majesty will understand that this general progress must never be interrupted, and that it cannot succeed unless Your Majesty give it your continuous and unfailing support, and unless it be directed according to your orders by one mind alone, which will give account of both general and particular matters not only to Your Majesty but in all the Councils as you may command.

14

Anti-Mercantilism

PIETER DE GROOT (1615–1678), a distinguished Dutch statesman, was the son of Hugo Grotius. In 1660 he became pensionary (legal adviser) to the City of Amsterdam. As could be expected, he was prominent in the circles of the States Party, which was then led by Grand Pensionary John De Witt. From September 1670 until March 1672 he served as the Dutch ambassador to France, trying hard to stop the deterioration in Franco-Dutch relations, but in vain. The memorandum translated here is a good statement of the Dutch States Party view of international trade as resting on older, medieval concepts [cf. 10], in contrast to Colbertian modernism [cf. 13].

After the Orangist revolution of 1672, De Groot was accused of having sold himself to France, and he spent the next several years of his life in exile in the Spanish Netherlands and in Germany. Indicted for high treason in 1674, he hurried home to vindicate himself and succeeded in proving his innocence so that he was acquitted in 1676. De Groot was allowed to live in peace at home until his death two years later. He also made a name for himself as a poet.

The French statesman Hugues de Lionne (1611–1671) was in 1670 a Minister of State and Secretary of State for Foreign Affairs. Simon Arnauld, Marquis de Pomponne (1618–1699) was French ambassador to the Dutch Republic in 1669–1671; in 1671 he succeeded to Lionne's position in the central government.

a.

Memoire of P. de Groot to Louis XIV, 10 October 1670

THE STATES-GENERAL of the United Provinces of the Netherlands, my masters, who desire nothing more than to maintain and improve an alliance that from all time has been so precious, so serviceable and so glorious to them as that of Your Majesty; being mindful that good relations between princes and governments subsist not so much by virtue of treaties between sovereigns as by the mutual friendship of their subjects who, finding satisfaction in their usefulness to one another, and this usefulness in their reciprocal trade, are drawn together all the more closely because common interest generally fortifies their mutual understanding; observing more and more clearly that for some time, and particularly since it has pleased Your Majesty to levy extraordinary duties upon goods and produce coming from their provinces into this kingdom, the harmonious relations and reciprocal affection of their two peoples are diminishing and failing little by little, as trade languishes under the weight of the tariffs with which it is burdened; they have therefore instructed me to submit to Your Majesty, as I most respectfully do in this present, that commerce, which is the very soul of human society, must inevitably come to complete ruin, if Your Majesty, by reason of your accustomed benevolence, and in order to provide for the needs of your own subjects as much as for those of the States-General, should not see fit to restore it to its original freedom by relieving it of all the extraordinary exactions with which it has been burdened in the last few years.

It is indisputable, Sire, that the happiness of peoples consists mainly in the ease with which they obtain their sustenance, and that it may be justly observed that a person who lives comfortably lives happily. This comfort depends primarily upon man's labor and industry, secondly upon the sale of the fruits of this labor, and finally upon the acquisition of that which he lacks in exchange for that of which he enjoys a superfluity. The first of these factors

From François Mignet, Négociations relatives à la Succession d'Espagne sous Louis XIV, 4 vols. (Paris, 1835–1842),III, pp. 621–624. Trans. by Geoffrey W. Symcox.

scarcely acting without the operation of the other two, and these two depending entirely upon the movement of commerce, or rather themselves composing it, it is easy to conclude that there is no more effective way of making the life of man more pleasant and prosperous than to assist the workings of commerce.

If we add to this that God, by His divine Providence, desiring not only to provide all that is necessary for the happiness of His creature, but also to furnish it in such a manner as to establish harmony and universal community in every region of the earth, has so varied the nature of soils and climates that each country bringing forth something peculiar to itself and to no other, and wishing to exchange what it has in abundance for what it lacks, has need of this general intercourse and reciprocal selling which we call commerce. It is thus easy to see that those who foster trade also improve the means by which mankind grows more happy and prosperous, while by contrast those who impede its flow, denying it access by the imposition of duties so excessive as to prevent sale, prohibit their subjects not only from enjoying the products of other lands, but also from selling in exchange what they themselves have; and by this same action they force their subjects to remain at once burdened with a superfluity and unable to acquire what they need.

Their Lordships the States-General foresee that if Your Majesty should persist in this policy of maintaining the duties levied on foreign goods, other princes and states, which enjoy a similar right in their own countries will enact similar measures, and by so doing will reduce commerce to such straits as to necessitate corrective measures and the restoration of conditions originally obtaining; but preferring to owe this benefit to Your Majesty's kindness and generosity rather than to any other motive or necessity, they have instructed me to beseech Your Majesty most earnestly, in consideration of the ancient alliance that they are privileged to enjoy with you, that it should please you so to gratify them as to remove the extraordinary duties levied upon goods coming from their provinces, and to restore them to the same level as they were at the time of the treaty of 1662, assuring Your Majesty that they will consider it a special obligation which they will not fail to acknowledge on any future occasions.

Upon which the undersigned ambassador, praying that Your Majesty will, with your accustomed graciousness, pardon the method which his illness forces him to adopt, before he has paid his re-

spects in a public audience, most humbly beseeches Your Majesty
to return a favorable answer in accord with his masters' request. At
Paris, October 10, 1670.

(Signed) Groot.

*   *   *

b.
Extract from a letter of Lionne
to Pomponne

17 October 1670

... HE [M. de Groot] spoke with emphasis, and stressed this
one particular point: that he was instructed to request that the
King reduce the new tariff on commodities which the Dutch bring
into France. I enquired whether they regarded this as a breach of
the treaty of 1662; he replied that this was not so, but that they
requested the reduction as an act of favor by the King. Upon which,
after suggesting that he should consider whether they could believe
themselves to be in a position to expect acts of favor of His Majesty,
unless they first changed certain principles which had caused all the
misunderstanding, I declared innocently to him, as though by no
means wishing to delude him with false hopes, that the only way
to obtain a revocation, or even just a reduction of the new tariff, was
for him to adduce reasons to show that France loses a little more
than she gains by it. M. de Groot was greatly taken with this, but I
doubt very much whether he will make anything of it; and M.
Colbert, to whom I recounted this conversation, was greatly amused
by it.

15

Diplomacy

FRANÇOIS DE CALLIÈRES (1645–1717), a minor French nobleman, traveled on many diplomatic missions in the 1670's in Poland, Saxony, Holland, and Bavaria. In 1694–1697 he was engaged in secret negotiations with Dutch statesmen, laying the groundwork for the Peace of Ryswick (1697), in which Callières participated as one of the official French plenipotentiaries. Shortly thereafter he was made one of the personal secretaries to the King. After a last diplomatic mission to Lorraine in 1700, he lived quietly at the court of Versailles until his death.

Callières wrote several treatises on literary style and on the war between the Ancients and the Moderns. In 1689, a panegyric on Louis XIV smoothed the way for his election to the French Academy. But Callières' best-known work is his treatise on diplomacy, selections from which are given below. This treatise seems to have been written between 1698 and 1700; when it was first published in 1716, it enjoyed immediate success, and has been regarded ever since as a classic text on diplomacy.

Callières, On International Negotiations

THE ART of negotiation with princes is so important that the fate of the greatest states often depends upon the good or bad conduct of negotiations and upon the degree of capacity in the negotiators employed. Thus monarchs and their ministers of state

From François de Callières, De la manière de négocier avec les souverains (Paris, 1716), pp. 1–19, 29–44, 46–47, 53–58, 64–68, 71–75, 77–81, 87–99, 137–138, 150–152, 163–166, 175–179, 329–331, 334–341, 350–352, 358–361, 367–370, 373–375. Many of the passages printed here are based on the translation by A. F. Whyte, On the Manner of Negotiating with Princes (London, 1919), pp. 7–14, 18–25, 27, 30–31, 35–42, 45–50, 109–110, 115–116. Reprinted by permission of Constable & Co., with alterations by the editor designed to bring the English translation closer to Callières's original text.

cannot examine with too great care the natural or acquired qualities of those citizens whom they despatch on missions to foreign states to entertain there good relations with their masters, to make treaties of peace, of alliance, of commerce or of other kinds, or to hinder other powers from concluding such treaties to the prejudice of their own master; and generally, to take charge of those interests which may be affected by the diverse conjunctures of events. Every Christian prince must take as his chief maxim not to employ arms to support or vindicate his rights until he has employed and exhausted the way of reason and of persuasion. It is to his interest also, to add to reason and persuasion the influence of benefits conferred, which indeed is one of the surest ways to make his own power secure, and to increase it. But above all he must employ good laborers in his service, such indeed as know how to employ all these methods for the best, and how to gain the hearts and wills of men, for it is in this that the science of negotiation principally consists.

Our nation is so warlike that we can hardly conceive of any other kind of glory or of honor than those won in the profession of arms. Hence it is that the greater number of Frenchmen of good birth apply themselves with zeal to the profession of arms in order that they may gain advancement therein, but they neglect the study of the various interests which divide Europe and which are a source of frequent wars. This inclination and natural application in our people result in a rich supply of good general officers, and we need have no surprise that it is considered that no gentleman of quality can receive a high command in the armies of the King who has not already passed through all these stages by which a soldier may equip himself for war.

But, alas, it is not the same with our negotiators. They are indeed rare among us because there has been in general no discipline nor fixed rules of the foreign service of his Majesty by which good subjects destined to become negotiators might instruct themselves in the knowledge necessary for this kind of employment. And indeed we find that instead of gradual promotion by degrees and by the evidence of proved capacity and experience, as is the case in the usages of war, one may see often men who have never left their own country, who have never applied themselves to the study of public affairs, being of meager intelligence, appointed so to speak over-night to important embassies in countries of which they know neither the interest, the laws, the customs, the language, nor even the geographical situation. And yet I may hazard a guess that there is perhaps no employment in all his Majesty's service more difficult to discharge than that of negotiation. It demands all the penetration, all the dexterity, all the suppleness which a man can well possess. It requires a widespread understanding and knowledge, and above all a correct and piercing discernment.

It causes me no surprise that men who have embarked on this career for the sake of titles and emoluments, having not the least idea of the real duties of their post, have occasioned grave harm to the public interest during their apprenticeship to this service. These novices in negotiation become easily intoxicated with honors done in their person to the dignity of their royal master. They are like the ass in the fable who received for himself all the incense burned before the statue of the goddess which he bore on his back. This happens above all to those who are employed by a great monarch on missions to princes of a lower order, for they are apt to place in their addresses the most odious comparisons, as well as veiled threats, which make them too painfully aware of their weakness. Such ambassadors do not fail to bring upon themselves the aversion of the court to which they are accredited, and they resemble heralds of arms rather than ambassadors whose principal aim is ever to maintain a good correspondence between their master and the princes to whom they are accredited. In all cases they should represent the power of their own sovereign as a means of maintaining and increasing that of the foreign court, instead of using it as an odious comparison designed to humiliate and contemn. . . . But before I take my subject in detail it is perhaps well that I should explain the use and the necessity for princes, especially for those who govern great states, to maintain continual negotiation both in neighboring countries and in those more distant, both openly and secretly, in war as well as in peace.

To understand the use of negotiations, we must think of the states of which Europe is composed as being joined together by all kinds of necessary commerce, in such a way that they may be regarded as members of one Republic and that no considerable change can take place in any one of them without affecting the condition, or disturbing the peace, of all the others. The blunder of the smallest of sovereigns may indeed cast an apple of discord among all the greatest powers, because there is no state so great which does not find it useful to have relations with the lesser states and to support one or another party among them. History teems with the results of these conflicts which often have their beginnings in small events, easy to control or suppress at their birth, but which when grown in magnitude became the causes of long and bloody wars which have ravaged the principal states of Christendom. Now these actions and reactions between one state and another oblige the sagacious monarch and his ministers to maintain a continual process of diplomacy in all such states for the purpose of recording events as they occur and of reading their true meaning with diligence and exactitude. One may say that knowledge of this kind is one of the most important and necessary features of good government, because indeed the domestic peace of the state depends largely upon appropriate measures taken in its foreign service to make friends among well-disposed states, and by timely action to resist those who cherish hostile designs. There is indeed no prince so powerful that he can afford to neglect the assistance offered by a good alliance, in resisting the forces of hostile powers which are prompted by jealousy of his prosperity to unite in a hostile coalition.

Now the enlightened and assiduous negotiator serves not only to discover all projects and cabals by which coalitions may arise against his prince in the country where he is sent to negotiate, but also to dissipate their very beginnings by giving timely advice. It is easy to destroy even the greatest enterprises at their birth; and as they often require several springs to give them motion, it can hardly be possible for a hostile intrigue to ripen without knowledge of it coming to the ears of an attentive negotiator living in the place where it is being hatched. . . .

Now if a monarch should wait, before sending his envoys to countries near or far, until important event occur — as for instance, until it is a question of hindering the conclusion of some treaty which confers advantage of an enemy power, or a declaration of war against an ally which would deprive the monarch himself of the assistance of that very ally for other purposes — it will be found that the negotiators, sent thus at the eleventh hour on urgent occasions, have no time to explore the terrain or to study the habits of mind of the foreign court or to create the necessary liaisons or to change the course of events already in full flood, unless indeed they bring with them enormous sums whose disbursement must weigh heavily on the treasury of their master, and which run the risk, in truth, of being paid too late.

Cardinal Richelieu, whom I see before me as the model for all statesmen, to whom France owes a very great debt, maintained a system of unbroken diplomacy in all manner of countries, and beyond question he thus drew enormous advantage for his master. He bears witness to this truth in his own political testament, speaking thus:

"The states of Europe enjoy all the advantages of continual negotiation in the measure in which they are conducted with prudence. No one could believe how great these advantages are who has not had experience of them. I confess that it was not till I had five or six years' experience of the management of high affairs that I realized this truth, but I am now so firmly persuaded of it that I will boldly say that the service which is rendered by a regular and unbroken system of diplomacy, conducted both in public and in secret in all countries, even where no immediate fruit can be gathered, is one of the first necessities for the health and welfare of the state. I can say with truth that in my time I have seen the face of affairs in France and in Christendom completely changed because under the authority of his Majesty I have been enabled to practice this principle which till my time had been absolutely neglected by the ministers of this kingdom." . . .

God having endowed men with diverse talents, the best advice that one can give is to take counsel with themselves before choosing their profession. Thus he who would enter the profession of diplomacy must examine himself to see whether he was born with the qualities necessary for success. These qualities are an observant mind, a spirit of application which refuses to be distracted by pleasures or frivolous amusements, a sound judgment which takes the measure of things as they are, and which goes straight to its goal by the shortest and most natural paths without wandering into useless refinements and subtleties which as a rule only succeed in repelling those with whom one is dealing. The negotiator must further possess that penetration which enables him to discover the thoughts of men and to know by the least movement of their countenances what passions are stirring within, for such movements are sometimes betrayed even by the most practiced negotiator. He must also have a mind so fertile in expedients as easily to smooth away the difficulties which he meets in the course of his duty; he must have presence of mind to find a quick and pregnant reply even to unforeseen surprises, and by such judicious replies he must be able to recover himself when his foot has slipped. An equable humor, a tranquil and patient nature, always ready to listen with attention to those whom he meets; an address always open, genial, civil, agreeable, with easy and ingratiating manners which assist largely in making a favorable impression upon those around him — these things are the indispensable adjuncts to the negotiator's profession. Their opposite, the grave and cold air, a melancholy or rough exterior, is repulsive and apt to produce aversion in the interlocutor. Above all the good negotiator must have sufficient control over himself to resist the longing to speak before he has really thought what he shall say. He should not endeavor to gain the reputation of being able to reply immediately and without premeditation to every proposition which is made, and he should take a special care not to fall into the error of one famous foreign ambassador of our time who so loved an argument that each time he warmed up in controversy he revealed important secrets in order to support his opinion.

But indeed there is another fault of which the negotiator must beware: he must not fall into the error of supposing that an air of mystery, in which secrets are made out of nothing and in which the merest bagatelle is exalted into a great matter of state, is anything but a mark of smallness of mind and betokens an incapacity to take the true measure either of men or of things. Indeed, the more the negotiator clothes himself in mystery, the less he will have means of discovering what is happening and of acquiring the confidence of those with whom he deals. The able negotiator will of course not permit his secret to be drawn from him except at his own time, and he should be able to disguise from his competitor the fact that he has any secret to reveal; but in all other matters he must remember that open dealing is the foundation of confidence and that everything which he is not compelled by duty to withhold ought to be freely shared with those around him. This gradually induces the others to respond with marks of confidence in matters which are perhaps of greater importance. Negotiators carry on a reciprocal trade of information: one must give, if one wishes to receive anything, and the more skilful party derives the greater advantage from such an exchange, for his wider knowledge enables him the better to profit from occasions which may arise.

It is not enough, however, for a negotiator to be skilled, perspicacious, and endowed with sterling mental qualities. He must also share in the ordinary sentiments of the human heart, for there is no employment that demands a greater elevation of mind and a greater nobility of manner. An ambassador indeed resembles in a certain sense the actor placed before the eyes of the public in order that he may play a great part, for his profession raises him above the ordinary condition of mankind and makes him in some sort the equal of the masters of the earth by that right of representation which attaches to his service, and by the special relations which his office gives him with the mighty ones of the earth. He must therefore be able to simulate a dignity even if he possess it not; but this obligation is the rock upon which many an astute negotiator has perished because he did not know in what dignity consisted.

To uphold the dignity of his position the negotiator must clothe himself in liberality and magnificence. Let his magnificence appear in his attendants, in his livery, and in his whole outfit. Let clean linen and appointments and delicacy reign at his table. Let him frequently give banquets and diversions in honor of the principal persons of the court in which he lives, and even in the honor of the prince himself, if he so cares to take part. Let him also enter into the spirit of the diversions offered by the prince, but always in a light, unconstrained, and agreeable manner, and always with an open, good-natured, straightforward air, and with a continual desire to give pleasure. If the custom of the country in which he serves permits freedom of conversation with the ladies of the court, he must on no account neglect any opportunity of placing himself and his master in a favorable light in the eyes of these ladies, for it is well known that the power of feminine charm often extends to cover the weightiest resolutions of state. But let him beware! Let him do all things in his power, by the magnificence of his display, by the polish, attraction, and gallantry of his person, to engage their pleasure, but let him beware lest he engage his own heart. He must never forget that love's companions are indiscretion and imprudence. . . .

Now, as the surest way of gaining the good-will of a prince is to gain the good graces of those who have most influence upon his mind, a good negotiator must reinforce his own good manners, his insight of character, and attraction of person by certain expenses which will largely assist in opening his road before him. But these expenses must be laid out adroitly, so that the recipient of a gift may accept it with propriety and without risk of compromising himself. But it is always to be remembered that there is a certain delicacy to be observed in all commerce of this kind, and that he who gives or procures a gift can increase its value by the manner in which he presents it. There are various established customs in different countries by which occasion arises for making small presents. This kind of expense, though it occasions but a small outlay of money, may contribute largely to the esteem in which an ambassador is held and acquire for him friends at the court to which he is accredited and help him to succeed in his negotiations. And, indeed, the manner in which this little custom is carried out may have an important bearing upon high policy. And, of course, in such a matter the practiced negotiator will soon be aware that at every court there are certain persons of greater wit than fortune who will not refuse a small gratification or secret subsidy which may bring in large results, for the wit of these persons enables them to maintain a confidential position at court. For instance, it has been known to happen at some courts that the musicians and singers, who enjoy an informal *entrée* with the prince or with his ministers, have discovered great secrets of state. Or again, the prince may have about his person certain officers of low rank whom he must entrust with some matters, and who do not rise above the temptation of a timely present. There are even some lax ministers of state who would not refuse it if it were offered with address. . . .

The ambassador has sometimes been called an honorable spy because one of his principal occupations is to discover great secrets; and he fails in the discharge of his duty if he does not know how to lay out the necessary sums for this purpose. Therefore an ambassador should be a man born with a liberal hand ready to undertake willingly large expenses of this kind; and he must be even prepared to do it at his own charges when the emoluments of his master are insufficient. . . .

There are some geniuses born with such an elevation of character and superiority of mind that they have a natural ascendancy over all whom they meet. But a negotiator of this kind must take good care not to rely too much on his own judgment in order to voice that superiority which he has over other men, for it may earn for him a reputation for arrogance and hardness; and just on account of his very elevation above the level of common humanity, events may escape him, and he may be the dupe of his own self-confidence. He must sometimes consent to meet smaller men on their own ground.

The good negotiator, moreover, will never found the success of his mission on promises which he cannot redeem or on bad faith. It is a capital error, which prevails widely, that a clever negotiator must be a master of the art of deceit. Deceit indeed is but a measure of the smallness of mind of him who employs it, and simply shows that his intelligence is too meagerly equipped to enable him to arrive at his ends by just and reasonable methods. True enough, deceit has often proved successful in diplomacy; but the foundation of such success is insecure, for it always leaves a drop of hatred and a desire of vengeance in the deceived party; sooner or later, the negotiator will feel the effect of it on his negotiations. Even if fraud were not as despicable as it is to every man of integrity, the diplomatist should consider that he will have more than one negotiation to carry out in the course of his life, and that it is in his interest to establish his reputation. This reputation he should regard as a real asset, for it will, in the course of time, facilitate the success of his other negotiations, and will make him welcome in all the countries where he is known and where he enjoys esteem. He must therefore establish the reputation of his master's and of his own good faith so well that no one would ever doubt his promises.

If the negotiator must be so meticulous in observing all the promises he makes to those with whom he treats, it is easy to judge of the nature of loyalty he owes to his prince or to the state which employs him. This is a truth so obvious that it seems superfluous to dwell upon it; and yet, there have been some corrupt negotiators who have failed in this point on a number of important occasions. However, one should note that a prince or a minister who is deceived by a disloyal negotiator is himself the author of the harm he sustains, for he has been negligent in his choice. When important interests are at stake, it is not enough to select an able and knowledgeable negotiator: he must also be a man of truth and of recognized probity. . . .

Before his elevation to the cardinalate, Cardinal Mazarin was sent on an important mission to the Duke of Feria, Governor of Milan. He was charged to discover the true feelings of the Duke on a certain matter, and he had the cunning to inflame the Duke's anger and thus to discover what he would never have known if the Duke himself had maintained a wise hold over his feelings. The Cardinal indeed had made himself absolute master of all the outward effects which passion usually produces, so much so that neither in his speech nor by the least change in his countenance could one discover his real thought; and this quality which he possessed in so high a degree contributed largely to make him one of the greatest negotiators of his time.

A man who is master of himself and always acts with *sangfroid* has a great advantage over him who is of a lively and easily inflamed nature. One may say indeed that they do not fight with equal arms; for in order to succeed in this kind of work, one must rather listen than speak; and the phlegmatic temper, self-restraint, a faultless discretion and a patience which no trial can break down — these are the servants of success. Indeed the last of these qualities, namely patience, is one of the advantages which the Spanish nation has over our own; for we are naturally lively, and have hardly embarked on one affair before we desire the end in order to embark on another, thus betraying a restlessness which continually seeks new aims. Whereas it has been remarked that a Spanish diplomatist never acts with haste, that he never thinks of bringing a negotiation to an end simply form *ennui,* but to finish it with advantage and to profit from all the favorable conjunctures which present themselves, amongst which our impatience is his advantage. Italy has also produced a large number of excellent negotiators who have contributed much to the high prestige and temporal power of the court of Rome, even to the point at which we now see it. And we ourselves have the same superiority in the art of negotiation over other northern nations which the Spaniards and Italians have over us, from which it might appear that the degree of intelligence varies in Europe with the degree of warmth of its different climates. Now from all this it follows that a man who by nature is strange, inconstant, and ruled by his own humors and passions, should not enter the profession of diplomacy, but should go to the wars. . . .

. . . It will not always be enough that he should execute the exact letter of his instruction; his zeal and intelligence should combine how he may profit from all favorable conjunctures that present themselves, and even should be able to create such favorable moments by which the advantage of his prince may be served, and which may give rise to new orders being issued to him. There are even pressing and important occasions where he is compelled to make a decision on the spot, to undertake certain *démarches* without waiting for the orders of his master which could not arrive in time. But then he must have sufficient penetration to foresee all the results of his own action; and it were well also if he had acquired beforehand that degree of confidence from his own prince which is commonly founded on a proved capacity of good services. He may thus assure himself in moments of sudden decision that he retains the confidence of his prince and that his past success will plead in favor of his present actions. In the absence of such conditions he would be a bold negotiator indeed who entered into engagements in his master's name without express order on his master's part. But on a pressing occasion he can hold such a thing as eventually to be concluded with advantage to his prince, or at least he may be able to prevent the matter in question from turning to his disadvantage until he shall have received orders from him.

It is well that with all these qualities a negotiator and especially one who bears the title of ambassador, should be rich in order to be able to maintain the necessary expenses of his office; but a wise prince will not fall into the fault common to many princes, namely that of regarding wealth as the first and most necessary quality in an ambassador. Indeed he will serve his own interests much better by choosing an able negotiator of mediocre fortune than one endowed with wealth but possessing a small intelligence, for it is obvious that the rich man may not know the true use of riches, whereas the able man will assuredly know how to employ his own ability. And the prince should further remember that it is within his power to equip the able man with all the necessary means, but that it is not in his power to endow with intelligence one who does not possess it.

It is also desirable that an ambassador should be a man of birth and breeding, especially if he is employed in any of the principal courts of Europe, and it is by no means a negligible factor that he should have a noble presence and a handsome face, which will enable him to please those with whom he has to converse. . . .

A man born to diplomacy and feeling himself called to the practice of negotiation must commence his studies by a careful examination of the state of European affairs, of the principal interests which govern the action of different states and which divide them from one another, of the diverse forms of government which prevail in different parts, and of the character of those princes, soldiers, and ministers who stand in positions of authority. In order to master the detail of such knowledge he must have an understanding of the material power, the revenues, and the whole dominion of each prince or each republic. He must understand the limits of territorial sovereignty; he must inform himself of the manner in which the government was originally established; of the claims which each sovereign makes upon parts which he does not possess; for these claims keep alive in him the desire to seize such lands at the first favorable opportunity; he must also distinguish between rights ceded to a sovereign by treaty and those which have not been so sanctioned. For his own instruction he must read with the most attentive care all public treaties, both general and particular, which have been made between the princes and states of Europe; he should consider the treaties concluded between France and the House of Austria as those which give the principal form to the public affairs of Christendom on account of the network of liaisons with other sovereigns which surrounds these two great powers. And since their disputes took their origin in the relations and treaties existing between the King Louis XI and Charles [the Bold], the last Duke of Burgundy, from whom the House of Austria descends, it is vital that the negotiator should be well acquainted with all the treaties made since that time; but especially all those which have been concluded between the principal powers of Europe beginning with the Treaty of Westphalia right up to the present.

Let him also study with understanding and open eye the modern history of Europe. Let him read the memoirs of great men, the instructions and despatches of all our ablest negotiators, both those which are printed in public books and those which are stored in manuscripts in our Office of Public Records, for these documents treat of great affairs, and the reading of them will convey not only facts which are important for the making of history, but also a sense of the true atmosphere of negotiation, and will thus help to form the mind of him who reads them and give him some clue to guide him in similar occasions on his own career. . . .

In order to understand the principal interest of European princes, the negotiator must add to the knowledge which we have just been describing that of dynastic genealogies, so that he may know all the connections and alliances, by marriage and otherwise, between different princes, for these liaisons are often the principal source of their rights and claims to various states. He must also know the laws and established customs of the different countries, especially in all matters relating to the succession to the throne. The study of the form of government existing in each country is very necessary to the diplomatist, and he should not wait until his arrival in a foreign country to study these questions; otherwise he is like a traveller in unknown lands, where he is apt to lose his way. Our own negotiators, who have never travelled before taking up some foreign post and who therefore know nothing of these questions, are usually so saturated in our own customs and habits as to think that those of all other nations must resemble them; but, as a matter of fact, even where such resemblances exist, they are very superficial; thus the authority of one king differs sensibly from another, though both bear the same title to designate their dignity.

There are, for instance, countries where it is not enough to be in agreement with the prince and his ministers, because there are other parties who share the sovereignty with him and who have the power to resist his decisions or to make him change them. Of this state of affairs we have an excellent example in England, where the authority of Parliament frequently obliges the King to make peace or war against his own wish; or again in Poland, where the general Diets have even more extended power, in which it suffices to persuade one single deputy to protest against the decisions of the King, or of the Senate, or of all the other deputies from the provinces to nullify them. An able and prudent negotiator will study the differences between the various forms of government, and, when occasion arises, he will know how to turn to his advantage the opposition between the different powers within the state.

Besides the general public interests of the state there are private and personal interests and ruling passions in princes and in their ministers or favorites, which often play a determining part in the direction of public policy. It is therefore necessary for the negotiator to inform himself of the nature of these private interests and passions influencing the spirits of those with whom he has to negotiate, in order that he may guide his action by this knowledge either in flattering their passions, which is the easiest way, or by somehow finding means to deflect such personages from their original intentions and engagements and cause them to adopt a new line of policy. Such an enterprise carried to success would indeed be a masterpiece of negotiation.

That great man, the Duc de Rohan,[1] tells us in the treatise which he wrote upon the interests of European sovereigns, that the sovereigns rule the people and that the interest rules the sovereign; but we may add that the passions of princes and of their ministers often overrule their interests. We have seen many cases in which monarchs have entered engagements most prejudicial to themselves and their state under the influence of passion. There need be no surprise on this account, for whole nations commit this error, and are apt to ruin themselves in order to satisfy hatred, vengeance, and jealousy, the satisfaction of which is often antagonistic to their veritable interests. Without recourse to ancient history it would be easy to prove by modern examples that men do not act upon firm and stable maxims of conduct; that as a rule they are governed by passion and temperament more than by reason. . . . Such knowledge is not to be found in books alone; it is more easily to be gathered by personal communication with those engaged in public service and by foreign travel, for, however profoundly one may have studied the customs, the policy, or the passions of those who govern in foreign states, everything will appear differently when examined close at hand, and it is impossible to form a just notion of the true character of things except by first-hand acquaintance.

It is therefore desirable that before entering the profession of diplomacy the young man should have travelled to the principal courts of Europe, not merely like those young persons who on leaving the academy or college go to Rome and see the beautiful palaces and the ancient ruins, or to Venice to enjoy the opera and the courtesans; he should indeed embark on his travels at a somewhat riper age when he is more capable of reflection and of appreciating the form and spirit of government in each country, and of studying the character of the prince and of his ministers — doing all this with the deliberate design of returning to these countries at a future day clothed with diplomatic rank. Travel conducted on these lines obliges the traveller to keep a vigilant eye upon everything that comes under his notice. It would be well that in certain cases they should accompany the King's ambassadors or envoys as travelling companions after the manner of the Spaniards and the Italians, who regard it as an honor to accompany the ministers of the Crown on their diplomatic journeys. . . .

It is desirable that such novices in diplomacy should learn foreign languages, for thus they will be protected from the bad faith or the ignorance of interpreters, as well as from the embarrassment of using them in audiences with the sovereign and of having to confide important secrets to them. Every one who enters the profession of diplomacy should know the German, Italian and Spanish languages as well as the Latin, ignorance of which would be a disgrace and a shame to any public man, for it is the common language of all Christian nations. It is also very useful and fitting for the diplomat, charged with matters of state, upon the conduct of which the fate of entire nations may rest, to have such a general knowledge of the sciences as may tend to the development of his understanding; but he must be master of his learning and must not be consumed by it. . . .

* * *

An ancient philosopher once said that friendship between men is nothing but a commerce in which each seeks his own interest. The same is true or even truer of the liaisons and treaties which bind one sovereign to another, for there is no durable treaty which is not founded on reciprocal advantage, and indeed a treaty which does not satisfy this condition cannot subsist, and contains the seeds of its own dissolution. Thus the great secret of negotiation is to bring out prominently the common advantage to both parties of any proposal, and so to link these advantages that they may appear equally balanced to both parties. . . .

A negotiator can discover secrets of state by frequenting the company of those in authority or of their confidants, and there is not a court in the world where ministers or others are not open to various kinds of approach, either because they are indiscreet and often say more than they should, or because they are discontented or incensed, and are thus ready to reveal secrets in order to give vent to their pique. And even the most practiced and reliable ministers are not always on their guard. I have seen very well intentioned statesmen who none the less in the course of conversation, and by other signs, allowed expressions to escape them which gave important clues to their inclinations and to their most secret transactions. And there are courtiers at every court who, though not members of the Council of State, know by long practice how to discover a secret, and who are always prepared to reveal it in order to show their penetration. It is almost impossible to conceal from an active, observant, and enlightened negotiator any important design of public policy, for no departure of state can be made without great preparation which is apt to reveal it, even if no one in the know breathes a word about it. . . .

*   *   *

There are some envoys who abuse the right of customs exemption accorded to them in certain countries on provisions and goods needed to maintain their households; they use it to cover a quantity of other goods sent in by merchants, who pay them a fee for this procedure which defrauds the sovereign of his revenue. This kind of profit is unworthy of a public minister; it arouses disgust both for him and for his master who appears to condone such activities. . . .

The privileges which the law of nations confers on foreign representatives permit them to strive to discover all that passes in the council chamber of the state to which they are accredited; they may draw into their game persons who can provide this information. But the law of nations does not authorize them to form cabals that may trouble the peace of the state: for the same law of nations which ensures their personal safety also covers the safety of the prince or of the government of the country to which they are sent. They may not form any factions in opposition to the recognized authorities without violating public trust, and should they embark on such an enterprise, they are liable to be treated as enemies. . . .

A minister who receives an order from his master to form dangerous cabals in the state where he is sent is to be pitied; he will need all his skill and all his courage to extricate himself from his plight. True enough, there is no service that a good subject or a faithful minister may refuse to his prince or to his country. But this obedience has its limits: it does not extend to perpetration of acts against the laws of God or justice, which do not allow attempts on the life of a prince, or inciting his subjects to rebellion, or usurping his lands, or disturbing the peace of his state by fomenting civil wars, all under cover of friendship. An ambassador must discourage such designs by his counsel, and should his prince or his state persist in them, he may, and he must, ask for his recall, guarding, nevertheless, his sovereign's secret. In justice to most legitimate sovereigns, let us note that very few of them are inclined, of their own accord, to engage in such machinations. . . .

But there is a great difference between debauching the subjects of a prince in order to entice them into conspiracies against him and attempts to persuade them to give information on what goes on in the state. This last practice has always been allowable to a foreign minister, and in this instance it is only the subject who has let himself be corrupted that deserves blame and punishment.

* * *

The different professions of men may be divided into three principal categories: first, the ecclesiastics, of whom there are several kinds; second, the nobles of the sword, who comprise not only those who serve in the army, but also courtiers and gentlemen who are not employed either in the Church or in the administration of justice; third, men of the law, who in France are called "gentlemen of the robe." There are only a few countries where ecclesiastics can be employed to negotiate; it is not fitting to send them on missions to heretics or infidels. At Rome, which seems to be the center of their activities, their attachment to the Pope and the desire which nearly all of them have to receive honors and benefices which the Papal Curia can bestow may render them suspect of too much partiality and deference for the policy and maxims followed by that court, often to the detriment of the temporal power of other sovereigns.

The wise Republic of Venice is so convinced of the partiality of her prelates and clergy for the Holy See, that she not only debars them from all employment at the Venetian embassy at Rome, but even excludes them from all deliberations that affect the Court of Rome, and they are made to leave the City's assemblies whenever any ecclesistical matter comes up for discussion. . . .

Monks are often appropriate for carrying important secret messages, since they can have easy access to princes or to ministers on various other pretexts; but it would not be appropriate to clothe a monk in the character of a public minister.

Gentlemen of the sword can be employed as negotiators in all kinds of countries, without distinction of religion or form of government. A good general officer can be a successful ambassador in a country which is at war. He can give useful advice to the prince or to the state to which he is sent on matters connected with his profession, which is likely to increase his reputation in the country where he resides if it is an ally of his master. He is also in a better position than anybody else to give a reliable account of the forces of the country he finds himself in. . . .

When it is necessary to send an ambassador to a prince who loves his ease and pleasure, a good courtier is more appropriate than a soldier, for he is usually more insinuating in his manner and more accustomed to seek to please those of whom he has need. A man raised at court is pliant and easily recasts himself for any role; he seeks to discover the passions and weaknesses of those with whom he deals, in order to profit by them for his own ends. Thus, as a rule, he succeeds in making himself agreeable to the prince with greater ease than a man who has spent a large part of his life with the troops; it is difficult for the latter not to contract a certain gruffness of disposition and of manners. But be he a soldier or a courtier, if the negotiator has not taken pains to acquire the knowledge of public affairs and of other matters relevant to his mission, then the experience of the one in military affairs and the address of the other will be of no service to the prince who entrusts him with the conduct of his affairs.

The gentlemen of the robe are usually more learned, more diligent, and more orderly and sober in their lives than either the soldiers or the courtiers. A number of them have succeeded in negotiations, particularly when they were accredited to republics or to general gatherings convened to conclude treaties of peace, of league, or other conventions. But they are not so appropriate for missions to the courts of kings and princes, who prefer to deal with courtiers and soldiers, with whom they have a greater affinity of interest and of manner of life. . . . Gentlemen of the sword are also more apt to introduce themselves into the good graces of the ladies, who enjoy some influence at most courts.

The functions of a negotiator are very different from the ordinary occupations of a magistrate: the one treats with a sovereign or with his ministers, with insinuation and persuasion as his only weapons; the other judges lawsuits between litigants made submissive by fear of losing their property. This habit of sitting in the seat of judgment disposes the magistrate to assume an air of grave superiority, which usually makes his character less supple, his exterior more forbidding, and his manners less ingratiating than those of a man of court who is used to living with his superiors or with his equals. Of course, there are, among gentlemen of the robe, many men of superior caliber who have all the necessary qualities to make themselves well liked at the courts of princes. When we note the faults of a profession we do not pretend to ascribe them to every person who exercises it. For if there are many harsh, ill-mannered soldiers, and a number of ignorant, frivolous courtiers, there are also a great many members of these professions who are well-bred, learned, and able, just as there are a number of gentlemen of the robe who are polite, supple, and pleasant in their dealings. . . .

It is not advisable to send a negotiator who is known for his dissolute way of life. . . . Nevertheless, since there is no general rule which does not admit of some exception, let us note that a good drinker will often succeed better than an abstemious man in treating with ministers of the Northern Crowns, provided that he knows how to drink without losing the use of his reason, while making his interlocutors lose the use of theirs. . . .

Generally speaking, a man of letters will make a much better negotiator than an untutored person. He knows how to speak and how to give the right response to whatever is said to him; he speaks with full awareness of the rights of various sovereigns as he seeks to explain those of his own master; he supports his statements with facts and with well chosen examples. On the contrary, an ignorant person does not know how to cite anything but the will or the power of his master and his orders, none of which have the force of law among the other free and sovereign princes and states, which are, however, amenable to be influenced by skilful representations of a learned and eloquent ambassador. . . . The knowledge of facts and of history is one of the main assets in the equipment of a negotiator: since the reasons on both sides of an argument are often debatable, most men prefer to guide themselves by examples and by what has been done in similar situations before.

A poorly educated negotiator is apt to fall into many traps through the obscurity of his style and through poor structure of his speeches and dispatches. It is not enough that he should think aright about a problem; he must also be able to express his thoughts correctly, clearly, and intelligibly. An envoy should be a good speaker in public and should be able to write well, which is extremely difficult for untutored men, and is very rarely achieved by them. . . .

The great powers do not always fill their embassies with their best men. Instead, they are content to send out mediocrities, who solicit and obtain these appointments, while men of superior talent, who would have been so useful in such positions, avoid employment abroad. They rather seek to attach themselves to the person of the prince, for here recompense for their services is far greater and comes their way more frequently, and also because those who are absent from court tend to be forgotten; all of which makes them look upon an embassy as an honorable exile. To remedy this state of affairs, princes and states who wish to be well served abroad should attach special honors and special recompense in recognition of services rendered them in the employments which are of such consequence to them; they should also consider the expenses which their representatives are obliged to bear in order to sustain the honor of their office and to ensure the success of their negotiations. . . .

The prince must also let it be known that he has full confidence in those whom he sends abroad, if he wishes that full weight be given to the words they utter in his name. It is extremely hard for a negotiator to establish his reputation at a foreign court unless the latter is convinced that he enjoys the confidence of his prince and of his principal ministers.

* * *

Most of the great international issues have been settled by ministers on secret missions. The Peace of Munster, one of the most complex and all-embracing treaties ever to be concluded, was not made solely by that vast assembly of ambassadors who came together to work on it. A confidential agent of Duke Maximilian of Bavaria, who was at the time closely allied with the Emperor, came secretly to Paris and settled its main conditions with Cardinal Mazarin. . . . The Peace of the Pyrenees was concluded by the first ministers of France and Spain on the basis of an agreement drawn up at Lyon between Cardinal Mazarin and Pimentel, the secret envoy of the King of Spain. And the stipulations of the Peace of Ryswick had been worked out and agreed upon in secret negotiations, before it was publicly concluded in Holland in the year 1697.

* * *

NOTES

1. Henri, Duc de Rohan (1579–1638), leader of the French Huguenots, and author of the treatise *On the Interest of Princes and States of Christendom,* published in 1639.

16

A Political Commentary

SAMUEL PUFENDORF (1632–1694), a German jurist, was the son of a Lutheran pastor in the Saxon town of Chemnitz. He studied at the Universities of Leipzig and Jena and then became secretary to Coyet, the Swedish resident minister at Copenhagen. The Swedish attack on Denmark in 1657 caused Pufendorf to be imprisoned. He spent his enforced leisure studying Grotius and Hobbes. He later accepted an invitation to Heidelberg, where the Elector Palatine founded for him a special chair of the law of nature and of nations. But it was at Lund, where he had moved in 1670, that Pufendorf completed his principal work, De jure naturae et gentium libri octo (Eight Books on the Law of Nature and of Nations). From Lund, Pufendorf went to Stockholm as historiographer royal, and in 1688 he entered the service of the Elector of Brandenburg, also as historiographer, receiving the title of Baron.

In addition to theoretical treatises on law and on church government, Pufendorf wrote many works on history and on the contemporary scene: histories of Sweden, of Charles X, of the Great Elector Frederick William of Brandenburg, treatises on Franco-Swedish alliances, on the state of the Holy Roman Empire in 1667 (an attack on the House of Austria), and an introduction to the history of the principal states of Europe, written in the early 1680's. Excerpts from this last work are given below. They represent an intelligent observer's estimate of some of the power relations of his time; his appraisal of relations between churches — from the point of view of a Lutheran layman — is of special interest. The term "monarchy of Europe," as used below, denotes "hegemony."

Pufendorf, Introduction to the History of Principal States

THE PREFACE TO THE READER

THAT HISTORY is the most pleasant and useful study for persons of quality, and more particularly for those who design for employments in the state, is well known to all men of learning. It is therefore requisite, that young gentlemen should be exhorted early to apply themselves to this study, not only because their memory is vigorous, and more capable to retain what they then learn, but also because it may be concluded, that he who has no relish for history, is very unlikely to make any advantage of learning or books. It is a common custom as well in public as private schools, to read to their scholars some ancient historians; and there are a great many who employ several years in reading of Cornelius Nepos, Curtius, Justin and Livy, but never as much as take into their consideration the history of later times. 'Tis true, and it cannot be denied, but that we ought to begin with the ancient historians, they being equally useful and pleasant; but that the history of later times is so much neglected, is a great mistake, and want of understanding in those to whom the education of youth is committed; for I lay down this as a principle, that we are to study those things in our youth, which may prove useful to us hereafter, when we come to riper years, and apply ourselves to business. Now I cannot for my life apprehend, what great benefit we can expect to receive from Cornelius Nepos, Curtius, and the first decade of Livy, as to our modern affairs, though we had learned them by heart, and had, besides this, made a perfect index of all the phrases and sentences that are to be found in them: or if we were so well versed in them, as to be able to give a most exact account, how many cows and sheep the Romans led in triumph, when they had conquered the Æqui, the Volsci, and the

From Samuelis Pufendorff Einleitung zu der Historie der Vornehmsten Reiche und Staaten . . . (Franfurt am Main, 1684), pp. i–iv, 138–150, 869–872, 877–887, 891–895. English translation from An Introduction to the History of the Principal Kingdoms and States of Europe, by Samuel Puffendorf, 2nd ed., with Additions, tr. by J. Crull (London, 1697), Preface (no pagination) and pp. 69–75, 429–443. The spelling has been modernized.

Hernici. But what a considerable advantage it is to understand the Modern History as well of our native country, as also its neighboring nations, is sufficiently known to such as are employed in states' affairs. But it is not so easy a matter to acquire this knowledge, partly because those histories are comprehended in large and various volumes; partly because they are generally published in the native language of each country; so that he who intends to apply himself to this study, must be well versed in foreign languages. To remove in some measure this difficulty, I did some years ago, for the benefit of some young gentlemen in Swedeland, compile a compendium, in which was comprehended the history of such states as seemed to have any reference unto this kingdom, with an intention only to give them the first taste of those histories fitted chiefly for their improvement. But after this rough draught had fallen into other hands, I had some reason to fear, lest some covetous bookseller or another might publish it imperfect, as I have known it has happened to others, whose discourses scarce premeditated, have been published against their will and knowledge. Wherefore I saw myself obliged, notwithstanding I had but little leisure, to revise the said work, and after I had rendered it somewhat more perfect, rather to publish it, such as it is, than to suffer that another should rob me of it. I hope therefore, that the discreet reader will look favorably upon this work, not as a piece designed for men of great learning, but adapted to the apprehensions and capacities of young men, whom I was willing to show the way, and, as it were, to give them a taste, whereby they might be encouraged to make a further search into this study. I must here also advertise the reader, that because I have taken the history of each kingdom from its own historians, a great difference is to be found in those several relations, which concern the transactions of some nations that were at enmity, it being a common observation, that their historians have magnified those factions which have proved favorable to their native country, as they have lessened those that proved unfortunate. To reconcile and decide these differences was not my business, but to give a clearer insight into its history. I have added also such observations as are generally made concerning the good and bad qualifications of each nation, nevertheless, without any intention either to flatter or undervalue any; as also what concerns the nature, strength, and weakness of each country, and its form of government: all which I thought might be an inducement to young gentlemen when they travel or converse with men of greater experience in the affairs of the world, to be more inquisitive into those matters. What I have related concerning the interest of each state, is to be considered as relating chiefly to that time when I composed this work. And, though I must confess, that this is a matter more suitable to the capacity of men of understanding than young people, yet I could not pass it by in silence, since this is to be esteemed the principle, from whence must be concluded whether state affairs are either well or ill managed. I must also mention one thing more, which may serve as an instruction to young men, *viz.* that this interest may be divided into an imaginary and real interest. By the first I understand when a prince judges the welfare of his state to consist in such things as cannot be performed without disquieting and being injurious to a great many other states, and which these are obliged to oppose with all their power: as for example, the monarchy of Europe, or the universal monopoly, this being the fuel with which the whole world may be put into a flame. . . . "If you would be the only masters of the world, doth it thence follow, that all others should lay their necks under your yoke?" The real interest may be subdivided into a perpetual and temporary. The former depends chiefly on the situation and constitution of the country, and the natural inclinations of the people; the latter, on the condition, strength and weakness of the neighboring nations; for as those vary, the interest must also vary. Whence it often happens, that whereas we are, for our own security, sometimes obliged to assist a neighboring nation, which is likely to be oppressed by a more potent enemy; we at another time are forced to oppose the designs of those we before assisted; when we find they have recovered themselves to that degree, as that they may prove formidable and troublesome to us. But seeing this interest is so manifest to those who are versed in state affairs, that they can't be ignorant of it; one might ask, how it often times happens, that great errors are committed in this kind against the interest of the state. To this may be answered, that those who have the supreme administration of affairs, are oftentimes not sufficiently instructed concerning the interest both of their own state, as also that of their neighbors; and yet being fond of their own sentiments, will not follow the advice of understanding and faithful ministers. Sometimes they are misguided by their passions, or by time-serving ministers and favorites. But where the administration of the government is committed to the care of ministers of state, it may happen, that these are not capable of discerning it, or else are led away by a private interest, which is opposite to that of the state; or else, being divided into factions, they are more concerned to ruin their rivals than to follow the dictates of reason. Therefore some of the most exquisite parts of Modern History consists in this, that one knows the person who is the sovereign, or the ministers, which rule a state, their capacity, inclinations, caprices, private interests, manner of proceeding, and the like: since upon this depends, in a great measure, the good and ill management of a state. For it frequently happens, that a state, which in itself considered, is but weak, is made to become very considerable by the good conduct and valor of its governors; whereas a powerful state, by the ill management of those that sit at the helm, oftentimes suffers considerably. But as the knowledge of these matters appertains properly to those who are employed in the management of foreign affairs, so it is mutable, considering how often the scene is changed at court. Wherefore it is better learned from experience and the conversation of men well versed in these matters, than from any books whatsoever. . . .

* * *

II] OF THE KINGDOM OF SPAIN

* * *

19] From what has been said it is evident, that Spain is a potent Kingdom, which has under its jurisdiction rich and fair countries, abounding with all necessaries, not only sufficient for the use of its inhabitants, but also affording a great overplus for exportation. The Spaniards also do not want wisdom in managing their state affairs, nor valor to carry on a war: nevertheless this vast Kingdom has its infirmities, which have brought it so low, that it is scarce able to stand upon its own legs: among those is to be esteemed one, the want of inhabitants in Spain, there being not a sufficient number both to keep in obedience such great provinces, and at the same time to make head against a potent enemy; which want is not easily to be repaired out of those countries which are under their subjection, since it is the interest of Spain, rather to restrain the courage of these inhabitants, for fear they should one time or another take heart, and shake off the Spanish yoke. And whenever they raise some soldiers in these provinces, they cannot trust them with the defense of their native country, but are obliged to disperse them, by sending them into other parts, under the command only of Spaniards: Spain therefore is scarce able to raise within itself a sufficient number of soldiers for the guard and defense of its frontier places: wherefore, whenever Spain happens to have war with other nations, it is obliged to make use of foreign soldiers, and to raise those is not only very chargeable but also the king is not so well assured of their faith as of that of his own subjects. The want of inhabitants is also one reason, why Spain cannot now-a-days keep a considerable fleet at sea, which nevertheless is extremely necessary to support the monarchy of that Kingdom. Another weakness is, that the Spanish provinces are mightily disjoined, they being divided by vast seas and countries: these therefore cannot be maintained and governed without great difficulty; for the governors of the provinces being remote from the sight of the prince, he cannot take so exact an account of their actions; and the oppressed subjects want often opportunity to make their complaints to the king; besides that, men and money are with great charge and danger sent out of Spain into these provinces, without hopes of ever returning into the Kingdom. Their strength cannot be kept together, as being obliged to divide their forces. The more disjoined these provinces are, the more frontier garrisons are to be maintained; all which may be saved in a kingdom, whose parts are not so much disjoined. They are also liable to being attacked in a great many places at once, one province not being able to assist another: besides this America being the treasury of Spain, is parted from it by the vast Ocean, whereby their Silver Fleets are subject to the hazard of the seas and pirates. And if it happens that such a fleet is lost, the whole government must needs suffer extremely by the want of it, the inhabitants of Spain being so exhausted, as not to be able to raise sufficient sums to supply the public necessities. The Spaniards are also mighty deficient in regulating their West India trade, which is so ill managed, that the greatest part of those riches are conveyed to other nations, whereby they are empowered to chastise Spain with its own money. After the death of Philip II it has also proved very prejudical to Spain, that by the carelessness of the succeeding kings, and during the long minority of this present, the nobles have so increased their power, that they are now very backward in duly assisting the king, and by impoverishing the king and commonalty have got all the riches to themselves. It is also a common disease in all governments, where the Popish Religion has got the upper hand, that the Popish clergy is very rich and potent, and yet pretends, by a Divine Right, to be exempted from all public burdens, except that some of them in the utmost extremity vouchsafe to contribute some small portion for the defense of the whole, but that not without consent of the Pope: yet the King of Spain has that prerogative, which he obtained from Pope Hadrian IV, that he has the disposal of all the chief church benefices in his Kingdom; and he is also head and master of all the Ecclesiastical Orders of Knighthood in Spain. And because the kings of Spain have hitherto pretended to be the most zealous protectors of the Papal Chair and religion, they have thereby so obliged the zealots of the Roman Catholic Religion, and especially the Jesuits, that these have always been endeavoring to promote the interest of Spain.

20] Lastly, it is also worth our observation, how Spain does behave itself in relation to its neighbors, and what good or evil it may again expect from them. Spain therefore is opposite to the Coast of Barbary, having also several forts on that side, *viz.* Pegnon de Velez, Oran, Arzilla, and would be better if they had also Algiers and Tunis. From hence Spain need not fear anything now, since it has quite freed itself from the very remnants of the Moors: but the piracies committed by those Corsairs is not so hurtful to Spain, as to other nations, who traffic with Spain, Italy or Turkey; for the Spaniards seldom export their own commodities into the other parts of Europe, but these are exported by other nations. The Turks seem to be pretty near to the islands of Sicily and Sardinia, and to the Kingdom of Naples: yet are they not much feared by the Spaniards; the sea which lies between them being an obstacle against making a descent with a considerable army in any of those parts; and if an army should be landed, its provisions, which must come by sea, might easily be cut off: for in such a case all the States of Italy would be obliged to side with the Spaniards to keep this cruel enemy from their borders, and their naval strength joined together, much surpasses the Turks in every respect. From the Italian States, the Spaniards have little to fear, it being a maxim with them, to preserve the peace of Italy, thereby to take away all opportunity from France to get a footing in Italy, which is also a general maxim among all the States of Italy: nevertheless this is the most certain, that if Spain should endeavor to encroach upon the rest of the Italian States, they would unanimously oppose it; and if they should find themselves too weak to oppose their designs, they might be easily wrought upon to call France to their aid. The Pope, perhaps, might be willing enough to be master of the Kingdom of Naples, Spain holding the same in fief of the Papal Chair, and thereby the Popes might have a fresh opportunity to enrich their kindred: but the Pope wants power to execute such a design, and the rest of the States of Italy would not be forward to see so considerable a country added to the Ecclesiastical State; and the Pope's kindred are more for gathering of riches out of the present ecclesiastical revenues, than to bestow the same upon an uncertain war. On the other side, Spain having found it very beneficial for its interest, to pretend to the chief protectorship of the Roman Religion, and that the Pope's good or bad inclinations towards it, may either prove advantageous or disadvantageous, Spain has always endeavored by all means to keep fair with the Popes. France, on the contrary, having taken part with the Protestants, whom Spain and the House of Austria have sought to oppress, has demonstrated sufficiently to the Roman Court, that it is not so fond of that Religion, as to neglect an opportunity to enrich himself with the possessions of the Protestants, and to make way for attaining to the so long projected design of the universal monarchy; which done, he might easily make the Pope his chaplain: wherefore the chief aim of the wisest Popes has been, to keep the power of Spain and France in an equal balance, this being the most proper method to keep up the authority and provide for the security of the popedom. It being the principal maxim of the Venetians, to [p]reserve their liberty and state, by maintaining the peace of Italy, Spain has no reason to be jealous of them as long as it undertakes nothing against them. It is also the interest, as well of them as of all the other Italian States, that the Spaniards remain in possession of Milan, for fear, if France should become master of this Dukedom, it might thereby be put in a way to conquer all the rest of Italy. On the other side, if Spain should show the least inclination to undertake anything against the liberty of Italy, it cannot expect but that the Venetians, if not by an open war, at least, by their counsels and money would oppose it: for the rest, this state endeavors to remain neuter between France and Spain, and to keep fair with both of them, as long as they do not act against their interest; Genoa is of great consequence to the Spaniards, from which depends in a great measure the security and preservation of the Milanese: wherefore, when Charles V could not effect his intention of building a castle (being opposed therein by Andreas Doria) whereby he intended to make the Genoese dance after his pipe, the Spaniards found out another way to make them dependent on their interest, by borrowing vast sums of money from the Genoese upon the security of the king's revenues in Spain. Besides this, they are possessed of the Harbor of Finale on the coast of Genoa, whereby they have taken away the power from them of cutting off the correspondency between Spain and Milan. Spain has great reason to live in a good correspondency with Savoy; for if that prince should side with France against it, the Milanese would be in eminent danger of being lost. But because it would be very pernicious for Savoy if the King of France would become master of Milan, since Savoy would be then surrounded on all sides by the French, it is easy for Spain to maintain a good correspondency with Savoy. Florence and the rest of the Italian Princes have all the reason to be cautious how to offend Spain, yet, as much as in them lies, they would scarce suffer Spain to encroach upon any of them. It is also of consequence to the Spaniards to live in friendship with the Swiss, partly because they must make use of such soldiers as are listed among them; partly because they may be very serviceable in preserving the Milanese; and their friendship is best preserved by money. But, because the Swiss are of several religions, Spain is in greater authority with the Roman Catholic Cantons, but France with the Protestant Cantons, which being the most potent, yet have, either cajoled by fair words, or money, or out of fear connived at the Frenches becoming masters of the County of Burgundy in the last war [Franche-Comté, ceded by Spain in 1678], whereas formerly they used to take effectual care for its preservation. The Hollanders were before the Peace of Munster the most pernicious enemies to Spain; but since the conclusion of that peace there is no cause that Spain should fear anything from them, since I do not see any reason, why these should attack Spain, or endeavor to take anything from them, having enough to do to maintain what they have already got. And, if they should be tempted to attempt anything against the West Indies, they would not only meet with great resistance from the Spaniards there, but also France and England would not easily suffer that both the East and West Indies, the two fountains from where such vast riches are derived, should be in possession of the Dutch: and the Dutch, are for their own interests, obliged to take care, that France, by swallowing up the rest of the Netherlands, may not become their next neighbor on the land, or that it should obtain any considerable advantage against Spain. The power of Germany, Spain may consider as its own, as far as the same depends on the House of Austria. And it is not long ago, since the States of Germany were persuaded to take upon them afresh the guaranty of the Circle of Burgundy [the Spanish Netherlands]; whereby Spain hoped to have united its interest with that of the German Empire against France; since, whenever a war happens between these two crowns, it is scarce possible, that this Circle should escape untouched, it being the most convenient place where they may attack one another with vigor. England is capable of doing most damage to the Spaniards at sea, and especially in the West Indies: but England, in all likelihood, would be no great gainer by it, since the English have a vast trade with the Spanish seaports, and their trade in the Levant would suffer extremely from the Spanish privateers; but also Holland could not look with a good eye upon these conquests of the English. Portugal, by itself, cannot much hurt Spain, but in conjunction with another enemy, it is capable of making a considerable diversion at home. But the Portuguese could not propose any considerable advantages to themselves thereby; and it might easily happen, that Holland siding with Spain might take from hence an opportunity to drive the Portuguese quite out of the East Indies. The king of France, therefore, is the capital and most formidable enemy to Spain, who wanting not power, not only longs to devour the rest of the Netherlands, but also aims at the conquest of other parts of Spain. But if the old maxims of policy are not grown quite out of date, it is to be hoped, that all who have any interest in the preservation of Spain, will with all their power endeavor to prevent the ruin of Spain, that the liberty and possessions of all the States in Europe may not depend on the pleasure and will of one single person. But what revolution may happen in Spain if the present Royal Family, which has no heirs yet, should fail, is beyond human understanding to determine or foresee; because it is to be feared, that upon such an occasion, not only France would do its utmost to obtain it, but also, because several states which were annexed to Spain, by the Royal Family, might take an opportunity to withdraw themselves from the same.

* * *

XII] OF THE SPIRITUAL MONARCHY OF ROME: OR, OF THE POPE

* * *

37] Though the supreme direction and administration of the Romish Religion, together with their other rules, which serve to uphold it, and have been alleged by us here, are a sufficient awe upon the people; and besides this, the Popish clergy know how to manage their affairs with that dexterity as to give some satisfaction to everyone; so that I am apt to believe, that a great many, who live under the Popish subjection, are verily persuaded, to believe what the priests tell them to be real, since they want means and opportunity of being better instructed; nevertheless it is very probable that a great many of the more learned and wiser sort are sufficiently convinced in what manner things are carried on among them, and that therefore it is in respect of some particular considerations that they do not free themselves from this yoke. I am apt to believe, that most are kept back, because they do not see how to remedy this evil; and yet they are unwilling to ruin their fortunes by going over to the Protestant side, where they are not likely to meet with so plentiful a share. These temptations are not easily to be resisted, wherefore they think it sufficient for the obtaining of salvation if they believe in Jesus Christ and trust upon his merits, but for the rest think it of no great consequence if in some matters, which are the inventions of priests, they by conforming themselves play the hypocrite, and believe as much concerning them as is suitable with their opinions. They suppose it to be of no great consequence, that perhaps the female sex and the vulgar sort of people that are always fond of extravagancies, do believe these things in good earnest. There are also, questionless, not a few, who not having sufficient capacity to distinguish between such points in religion as are commanded by God, and between such as are invented by the clergy for private ends, and perhaps coming afterwards to the knowledge of some of these deceits, they take all the rest for fabulous inventions, only covering their atheistical principles with an outward decent behavior to save themselves the trouble of being questioned and disturbed. Every man of sense may without difficulty imagine how easily a sensible Italian or Spaniard, that never has read the Bible or any other Protestant Book, may fall into this error, if he once has had an opportunity to take notice of the intrigues of the clergy; though it is certain, that since the Reformation of Luther, the Church of Rome has changed her habit, and her garment appears far more decent than before. But besides this, there are a great many persons of quality as well as of a meaner condition, who make their advantage of the Romish Religion, where they have an opportunity to provide for their friends, by putting them either into some Order or other of Knighthood, or into that of monks, or other ecclesiastics, by which means a great many families are eased of a great charge, and sometimes are raised by it. At least the superstitious parents are well satisfied when they see their children are become such saints: and those that cannot make their fortunes otherwise, run into a monastery, where they are sure to be provided for. All these conveniences would be taken away if the Popish Monarchy should fall, and the church revenues were applied to the use of the state. The Popish doctrine also has got so firm footing in those countries where it now rides triumphant, that if any of their princes should endeavor to root it out, he would find it a very difficult task, since the priests would be for raising heaven and earth against him, and not stick to find out another James Clement or Ravilliac [the assassins of Henry III and Henry IV of France] for their purpose. Besides this, most of those princes are tied by a political interest to the Church of Rome, and by introducing a reformation cannot propose any advantage to themselves, but rather cannot but fear very dangerous divisions and innovations.

38] . . . The Pope is heartily afraid of a French Monarchy, being well convinced that it would endeavor a thorough reformation of the Court of Rome, and that his wings would be clipped to that degree, that in effect he would be no more than a Patriarch. Neither ought he to expect any better treatment if the Spanish Monarchy had been brought to perfection; as either of them must needs have been destructive to the Protestant Religion.

It may therefore be taken for granted that one of the main pillars of the Popish Monarchy is the jealousy and balance, which is to be kept up between these two Crowns; and that it is the Pope's interest, as much as in him lies, to take care that one of these Crowns do not ruin the other, and set up for an universal Monarchy. If we look into the transactions of former times, we shall find that the Popes have long since observed this maxim. . . .

39] But as to those who have withdrawn themselves from the Pope's obedience, it is certain the Pope would be glad, if they could be reduced to his obedience, provided it might be done by such means, that thereby one party were not so much strengthened as to become terrible to all Europe. For it is better to let my enemy live, than to kill me and my enemy at one stroke. . . . So Gregory XV during the differences between those of the Valtelins and the Grisons sided with the last, the Protestants, against Spain. Neither was Urban VIII dissatisfied at the success of Gustavus Adolphus against the House of Austria, especially since the latter had given much about the same time an evident instance to the world, as to the business of Mantua, that they used to give no better treatment to Roman Catholics than Protestants. Some have remarked, that when Ferdinand II did desire some subsidies from the Pope, which he had promised before, the Pope sent him plenary indulgences for him and his whole army at the point of death, that they might be prepared to die with the more courage. And some years ago, the Court of Rome was no less concerned at the then prodigious success of France in Holland, when this state seemed to be reduced to the utmost extremity. But the chief aim of the Pope is to reduce by all manner of artifices the Protestants to his obedience. To obtain this end, he sets the Protestants together by the ears, flattereth the Protestant princes, and takes care that many of them may marry Roman Catholic ladies; the younger brothers out of the greatest families he obliges to come over to his party, by bestowing upon them great dignities and church benefices; all that will come over to his side are kindly received and very well used, neither do they write so much against the Protestant divines, but rather endeavor to set up and maintain controversies among them. By these artifices the Popish clergy has got very visible advantages in this age over the Protestants, and are likely to get more every day, since they see with the greatest satisfaction that their adversaries do weaken themselves by their intestine quarrels and divisions.

40] From what has been said it is easily to be judged, whether those differences which are on foot between the Roman Catholics and the Protestants may be amicably composed, either so that both parties should remit something of their pretensions, and agree to one and the same confession of faith, leaving some by-questions to be ventilated in the universities; or so that both parties may retain their opinions, and yet, notwithstanding this difference, might treat one another like brethren in Christ and members of the same Church. Now if we duly weigh the circumstances of the matter, and the Popish principles, such a peace is to be esteemed absolutely impossible; since the difference does not only consist in the doctrine, but both interests are absolutely contrary to one another, for first the Pope is for having the church possessions restored; but the Protestants are resolved to keep them in their possession. The Pope pretends to be the supreme Head of Christendom, but the Protestant States will not part with their prerogative of having their direction *circa Sacra,* which they look upon as a precious jewel belonging to their sovereignty. And to pretend to live in communion and amity with the Pope and not to acknowledge his sovereignty in ecclesiastical affairs, is an absolute contradiction. In the same manner, as if I would be called a subject in a kingdom, and yet refuse to acknowledge the king's authority. Besides this, the infallibility of the Pope is the foundation stone of the Popish sovereignty, and if that is once removed, the whole structure must needs fall, wherefore it is impossible for the Pope, and that for reasons of state, to abate anything from his pretensions wherein he differs from the Protestants. For if it should be once granted that the Pope had hitherto maintained but one single erroneous point, his infallibility would then fall to the ground; since, if he has erred in one point, he may be erroneous in others also. But if the Protestants should allow the Pope's infallibility, they at the same time must deny their whole doctrine. And it seems not probable that the Protestants can ever be brought to contradict and at once to recall their doctrine concerning the vanity of the Popish tenets. Nay, if it might be supposed that the laity should do it, what must become of the clergy? Where will they bestow their wives and children? Wherefore, how good soever the intention may have been of those that have proposed a way of accommodation between the Papists and Protestants, which is commonly called syncretism, they are certainly nothing else but very simple and chimerical inventions, which are ridiculed by the Papists; who in the meanwhile are well satisfied to see that the Protestant divines bestow their labor in vain as to this point, since they (the Papists) are no losers, but rather the gainers by it. For this syncretism does not only raise great animosities among the Protestants, but also does not a little weaken their zeal against the Popish Religion: it is easy to be imagined, that some, who do not throughly understand the differences, and hear the divines talk of an accommodation between both religions, are apt to persuade themselves, that the difference does not lie in the fundamental points; and if in the meanwhile they meet with an advantageous proffer from the Roman Catholics, are sometimes without great difficulty prevailed upon to bid farewell to the Protestant Religion. It is taken for a general rule, that a fortress and a maidenhead are in great danger, when once they begin to parley.

41] But if the question were put, whether the Pope with all his adherents be strong enough to reduce the Protestants under his obedience by force; it is evident enough that the joint power of the Papists is much superior to the strength of the Protestants. For Italy, all Spain and Portugal, the greatest part of France and Poland, adhere to the Pope, as also the weakest part of the Swiss cantons. In Germany those hereditary countries which belong to the House of Austria, the Kingdom of Bohemia, and the greatest part of Hungary, all the bishops and prelates, the House of Bavaria, the Dukes of Neuburgh, and Marquises of Baden, besides some other princes of less note; some counts, lords and others of the nobility and some Imperial Cities, besides others of the Roman Catholic Communion that live under the jurisdiction of the Protestant States; all which according to my computation make up two thirds of Germany. There are also a great many Papists in Holland, neither is England quite free from them. But of the Protestant side are England, Sweden, Denmark, Holland, most of the secular Electors and Princes, and the Imperial Cities in Germany. The Huguenots in France are without strength, and the Protestants in Poland being dispersed throughout the Kingdom are not to be feared. Courland and the cities of Prussia may rest satisfied, if they are able to maintain the free exercise of their religion; neither is Transylvania powerful enough to give any considerable assistance to the Protestant Party. The Papists also have this advantage above the Protestants, that they all acknowledge the Pope for the supreme Head of their Church, and at least to outward appearance, are unanimous in their faith; whereas on the contrary, the Protestants are not joined under one visible spiritual head, but are miserably divided among themselves. For not to mention here those sects of lesser note, *viz.* the Arminians,

Socinians, Anabaptists and such like, their main body is divided
into two parties, of very near equal strength, *viz.* into the Lutherans
and those of the Reformed Religion, a great many of which are so
exasperated against one another, that they could not be more against
the Papists themselves.

Neither are the Protestants united under one church government
or liturgy, but each of these states regulate the same according as
they think fit. Neither can it be denied, but that the Roman Catholic
clergy in general is more zealous and industrious in propagating their
religion than the Protestants; a great many of these making no other
use of the church benefices, than to maintain themselves out of
them, just as if it were a mere trade; and the propagating of the
Christian faith is the least of their care, or at least only their by-work.
Whereas the monks and Jesuits gain great applause by their missions
in the East and West Indies; and though perhaps they brag more
than is true of their great success there, yet is this institution in the
main very praiseworthy. Besides this, there is such an implacable
jealousy between some of the Protestant States, that it is not probable
that they will be one and all against the Papists: not to mention
others here, such a jealousy is between Sweden and Denmark, as
likewise between England and Holland. Though on the other hand,
there is as great a jealousy between France and Spain, which will
always be an obstacle to any union between these two Crowns
against the Protestants. So that notwithstanding the unequality between the Papists and Protestants, these need not fear the Pope's
power. . . .

The best way then to preserve the Protestant Religion is, that each
of these states take effectual care, how the same may be well preserved in their several states. And this may be done without any
crafty inventions, as the Roman Catholics are obliged to make use
of, but only by plain and simple means. One of the main points is,
that both the churches and schools may be provided with persons
fitly qualified for that purpose; that the clergy by their wholesome
doctrine and a good life, may show the way to the rest. That the
people in general, but more especially such as in all likelihood one
time or another may have a great sway in the state, be well instructed
in the true and fundamental principles of the Protestant Religion,
that thereby they may be proof against the temptations of the Court
of Rome, especially when they are to travel in Popish countries. That
the clergy may be so qualified as to be able to oppose the devices

and designs of their enemies, who every day busy themselves in finding out new projects against them.

Some are of opinion, that the Protestant Party would be mightily strengthened, if the two chief factions among the Protestants, that besides the difference in their doctrine are also of a different interest, which seems to flow from their various opinions, could be reconciled to one another; and they believe this not impracticable, if the old hatred, animosities, pride, and self-conceited opinions could be laid aside. But if we duly take into consideration the general inclinations of mankind, this seems to be a hard supposition. For those who peruse the writings of both parties without partiality, cannot but admire how their authors are often obliged to rack themselves, that they may maintain their opinions whether they be consonant to the Scriptures or not: as likewise how they bring to light again the old arguments, which have been refuted a thousand times before. Neither will this do the business, if one opinion should be supposed as good as the other; since such an indifferency would be a shrewd sign that the whole must needs be very indifferent to us. Neither can we without danger declare some points in which we differ, problematical, since I do not see how we can pretend to have a power to declare a certain article either necessary or fundamental, or problematical. Some therefore have thought upon this expedient to make a trial, whether out of the articles, wherein both parties agree, could be composed a perfect System of Divinity, which might be linked together like one chain, according to art. . . . But before a true judgment can be given of this proposition, it would be requisite that such a system composed according to art, were proposed to the world. For my part I know no better advice, than to leave it to the direction of God Almighty, who perhaps one time or another will put us in the way of finding out a good expedient. For untimely remedies may prove the occasion of new divisions. In the meanwhile it behooves both parties notwithstanding these differences to be mindful of their joint interest against their common enemy, since they may verily believe that the Pope has no more kindness for the Lutherans than for those of the Reformed Religion.

But as for the other sects of less note, *viz.* the Socinians, Anabaptists, and such like, it is evident that their principles cannot possibly be reconciled with our religion; for those who adhere to the first, do not consider the Christian doctrine otherwise than a moral philosophy, and the latter scarce know what to believe themselves.

Besides this, the Anabaptists have hatched out I know not what rules of policy, which, if not suppressed in time, must prove destructive to the state. But whether the Socinians also have any such projects in their heads, I am not able to determine, since hitherto they have not been powerful enough to raise any disturbances in the state.

17

Louis XIV's Letters—1661 and 1700—1715

ONLY a small fraction of the writings of Louis XIV has been published. Yet the King's Mémoires, virtually completed by 1671, and his many letters give an insight not only into the royal mind but also into the functioning of his administration. Given below are translations of several of Louis's letters selected from the beginning and from the end of his reign. Most of them are self-explanatory, but a few comments may be in order:

The King of France addresses all dukes, princes, cardinals, marshals, governors of provinces, and persons of equivalent rank as "My cousin." He addresses all kings and sovereign princes as "My brother" (hence the form of address in Letter F, below, is a studied insult). The heir to his throne he addresses as "My son," even if he is his great-grandson, as in the case of the future Louis XV.

Letter A: Nicolas Fouquet (1615–1680?), the Superintendent of Finances arrested in 1661, was, among other things, Marquis of Belle-Isle, which he held as a virtually sovereign master; hence the King's worry about a possible rising there.

Letter C: This letter is the first indication of the decision to accept the will of Charles II of Spain. The several drafts of an earlier letter to Briord (in the Archives of the Foreign Ministry in Paris) indicate that the King and his Council had originally decided to reject this will and to abide by the Second Partition Treaty.

Letter I: François de Neufville, Duc de Villeroy (1644–1730), Marshal of France, had been a personal friend of Louis XIV since childhood. At the end of his reign the King made him Minister of State, governor to the future Louis XV, and named him member of the Council of Regency.

a

To the Queen-Mother

Nantes, 5 September 1661

MADAME my Mother, I have already informed you this morning of the execution of my orders for the arrest of the Superintendent [of Finances, Fouquet], but I am happy to recount the affair to you in detail. You are aware that this has long weighed on my mind, but it was impossible to carry it out sooner, as I wanted him first to see to the payment of thirty thousand écus for the Navy, and besides it was necessary to arrange many things which could not be done in one day. You could not imagine how difficult it was just to arrange for me to speak privately with d'Artagnan [Captain of the Musketeers, well known to the readers of Alexandre Dumas], for I am constantly beset by a host of vigilant observers who, given the slightest sign, would have been able to see far ahead. In spite of this, two days ago I ordered him to be in readiness, and to make use of du Claveau and Maupertuis instead of the noncommissioned officers and corporals of my musketeers, who are for the most part unwell. I was extremely anxious to see an end to this affair, there being no other reason for me to stay in this part of the country.

Finally this morning when the Superintendent arrived to work with me as usual, I detained him by one means or another, pretending to look for documents, until I saw from my study window that d'Artagnan had entered the courtyard. I then allowed the Superintendent to take his leave: after conversing for a moment below stairs with la Feuillade, he disappeared, just as d'Artagnan was greeting M. Le Tellier, so that poor d'Artagnan thought he had missed him, and sent word by Maupertuis that he suspected someone had warned him to escape; but he caught him in the square in front of the great church and arrested him in my name about noon.

D'Artagnan asked for the papers that he had on his person, which I was told would inform me of the true state of affairs at Belle-Isle, but I have had so many other things to do that I have not yet been able to look at them. I did however instruct the Sieur Boucherat to

From Lettres de Louis XIV, Ed. by Pierre Gaxotte (Paris, 1930), pp. 3–12, 113–117, 119–123, 127–131, 149–152, 170–174, 184–186. Translated by Geoffrey W. Symcox and published by permission of the Librairie Jules Tallandier.

place seals on the Superintendent's house, and the Sieur Pellot to do likewise with Pellisson's, whom I have also had arrested. I had let it be thought that I planned to go hunting this morning, and on this pretext had had my carriages made ready and my musketeers mounted. I had also ordered that the Guards stationed here should exercise in the open country, so as to have them all ready to march on Belle-Isle. Immediately [after his arrest] the Superintendent was put in one of my carriages, and escorted by my musketeers who are taking him to the castle of Angers to await me there, while his wife, at my instructions, is on her way to Limoges. Fourille set out at once with my companies of Guards under orders to march to the Strait of Belle-Isle, where he will leave Captain Chavigny with one hundred French Guards and sixty Swiss in command of the fort; if by chance the man left in charge there by the Superintendent wishes to offer resistance, I have ordered them to use force. I had first intended to wait for news of the outcome, but the orders have been devised so well that to all appearances the affair cannot go wrong: in consequence, I shall return at once, and this will be the last letter I shall write to you on this journey.

I later discussed this affair with the gentlemen attending me here. I told them frankly that I had laid my plans four months ago, that you alone had any knowledge of them, and that I did not inform the Sieur Le Tellier until the last two days when he was to draw up the orders. I told them too that I wanted no more Superintendents, but that I should personally administer the finances with the aid of loyal men acting under me, knowing well that this is the true way to assure my financial abundance and to lighten the burdens of my people. You way well believe that many were abashed, but I am happy to let them see that I am not the fool they took me for, and that their best course is to attach themselves to my interest.

I omitted to tell you that I have sent out my musketeers to cover all the roads as far as Saumur, to stop all couriers they find going to Paris, and to prevent any messenger from arriving before the one I have despatched to you. They serve me with such eagerness and promptitude that every day I have fresh cause to be pleased with them. In this latest affair, although I have given various different orders, they have carried them out so well that everything was coordinated without anyone's discovering the secret.

For the rest, I have already begun to savour the pleasure of personally supervising the finances, and have discovered in the short examination I was able to make after dinner several important things that I had not noticed at all, and it is not to be doubted that I shall continue to do so.

Tomorrow I shall have finished all that remains to be done here, and I shall leave at once in the happy expectation of soon embracing you and of personally assuring you of my continuing devotion.

b
To Comte d'Estrades, French Ambassador in London

Fontainebleau, 16 September 1661

MONSIEUR LE COMTE D'ESTRADES, I address this letter to you privately, to open my heart to you on certain matters of great importance touching your employment, which have hitherto been kept from you not through lack of trust, for I have as much confidence in you as in any of my subjects, but for reasons which I shall make clear in the course of this letter.

Immediately upon the death of my cousin Cardinal Mazarin, when I personally assumed the direction of affairs, two questions occupied my attention. First, how vital it was to the peace of all Christian states and to the security of my own that Portugal, which the terms of the peace [of the Pyrenees, 1659] had forced me to abandon, could be saved by some other means, and that this means could only be the arms and aid of England. Second, I observed the Spaniards' lack of good faith in fulfilling their part of the treaty, which has now gone to such lengths that I have been obliged to direct the Archbishop of Embrun, in his instructions, to make formal complaint of twenty-six clauses which they have as yet not implemented, although they cannot complain that there is one clause on my side which I have not regularly observed and carried out.

These two considerations led me to think that, in all justice, my word should bind me no more than theirs did them, but with this difference in my favor, that they had been the first to fail in their obligations, for which they were to blame, while I on the other hand should be fully justified, both before God and in my own conscience, which would not reproach me on that score, should I do no more than follow the example set me by the Spaniards. Moreover, what on their side was a patent lack of good faith would be for me an act of just retaliation which I owed myself, for which no-one could reasonably censure me. I then discussed all that I have just said with the three persons in whom I had the greatest confidence at that time, who declared with one accord that the opinions which had occurred to me were supported by every reason, not only of interest and policy, but also of honor and conscience.

It was therefore decided at that time that the obstacles and intrigues with which the Spaniards, aided by the Emperor, sought to oppose the plan I had formed to win the crown of Poland for my own family constituted a formal breach of the first article of the peace treaty, which lays down that the two kings shall act with all their power, as good brothers, each striving sincerely to secure the other's advancement. In consequence my duty to help restore the crown of Portugal to my brother the Catholic King was no greater than his to obtain that of Poland for my family, since the treaty obliged us both to work sincerely for our mutual advantages. This having been established, some means had to be found to open very secret negotiations with that minister who most enjoys the confidence of the King of England, namely his Chancellor [Clarendon]. Sieur Fouquet informed me that he had in his service a secretary who had served on the embassy of the late Sieur de Bordeaux, who could travel to England on some pretext or other without attracting attention and speak to the Chancellor, to whom he was well known. I agreed to this plan and approved sending the secretary, who made the journey, saw the Chancellor unbeknown to anyone but the King my brother, and established a correspondence between the Chancellor and Fouquet, who kept me informed, by the regular mails. And although the whole negotiation has been handled so far by a person who has given me good cause to be very displeased with his misconduct in other matters, I have been able to make good use of him to encourage the King my brother to overcome various reasons which made him very undecided on the question of [his] Portuguese marriage [to Catherine Braganza], which is the basis of any support which that kingdom can hope for from my said brother.

On your departure for the embassy to England I had intended to inform you of all that had taken place in this negotiation up to that time, and even to instruct you to continue it, rather than to make use of the secretary whose services would have been rendered unnecessary by the presence on the spot of a person in whom I had far greater confidence than in him. But since I knew that this would offend Fouquet, who hoped to improve his standing with me by carrying out as I had charged him an affair of such importance, I wished to take no chances, but wait for another occasion to entrust the matter to you without the fear that he would ruin it out of annoyance at no longer having charge of it, and knowing then that that occasion would not be long delayed. For before your departure I had already decided what to do with him, although various considerations of my own interest made me dissemble and refrain from action until my journey to Nantes.

I therefore now send you a new credential for the Chancellor, to whom you will go to present it on receiving this dispatch, informing him that my being forced to arrest Fouquet changes none of my other decisions, nor my purpose of showing the King my brother every mark of friendship in my power, save only that these will no longer be conveyed by the secretary, whom I have ordered to send no more letters [to the Chancellor], but that I have at the same time entrusted you with the continuance of this negotiation, and that the Chancellor should place complete confidence in what you say to him on my behalf, consequent on this credential.

However, that you may be informed of the current state of the negotiation, I shall inform you that on the condition of the Portuguese marriage and the resultant aid which the King of England will bring to the support of that kingdom, I have let it be hoped that in two or three years I should supply the King my brother with eighteen hundred thousand or two million livres, via the most secret channels which can be devised or imagined so that no-one may know of it. In offering this my sole desire is to be assured of a due recompense, which is that my brother will effectively aid and uphold Portugal with all his forces. I should inform you in this connection that I have all the more reason to make certain of this point, having seen reports from London, from a good source, to the effect that my brother could be well satisfied when the marriage is concluded to receive the sum of money agreed upon for the dowry, together with Tangier, without troubling himself over what subsequently became of the King, Queen and realm of Portugal; by this means he would avoid the breach with which he is threatened by the Spaniards, who would not be greatly concerned by an alliance which offered no serious obstacle to their conquest of Portugal.

I would not willingly believe that my brother the King could be capable of such a sentiment as freely to allow the ruin of princes so intimately allied to him, and for whose safety hardly more is required than his declaration of support for them. But since the report comes from a reliable source, I must at least take care not to supply my money except on the best assurance that it will be used to save Portugal: otherwise, the King my brother would have no cause even to approach me, if he wished only to marry the Portuguese princess for the advantage of the dowry and the fort of Tangier, and not at the same time to espouse the cause of that kingdom and maintain it in its present state.

This is all that I shall say to you at the moment concerning this affair, for in my other letter I grant you leave to come to Gravelines, and to make a journey here, where I shall have further means to explain all my views to you in person. I shall only add here that, as you will have observed from the beginning of this letter, I have judged it expedient that you decipher it yourself, and I require that you should not divulge to any of your secretaries either this letter or any subsequent developments in this negotiation. When you make your reports to me, take care to encipher them yourself in private, on separate sheets [appended to your dispatches], keeping everything in a strongbox to which no one but you has access. On this, I pray God, etc. . . . .

c
To Comte de Briord, Ambassador to the United Provinces

Fontainebleau, 14 November 1700

MONSIEUR LE COMTE DE BRIORD, since I wrote to you on the 10th of this month, the Spanish Ambassador requested an audience, which I granted on the morning of the 11th. He presented a letter signed by the Queen of Spain and the Council appointed by his master the late King [Charles II], containing the clauses of his will settling the succession on my grandsons; failing them, on the Archduke [Charles]; and then [failing him], on the Duke of Savoy. It would be unnecessary to tell you in detail of the urgent entreaties with which he sought to persuade me to accept this will, both for the good of all Europe in general, and of the Spanish monarchy in particular. It will suffice if I tell you that in the two days that I have known of this, I have studied with the minutest attention all the drawbacks and all the advantages of either abiding by the [Partition] Treaty or accepting the will.

In following the first course, I noted the advantage of uniting several important states to my Crown and of weakening a power traditionally hostile to my own. I considered the ties established with the King of England and the States-General, and the aim of preserving the general peace by scrupulously executing the Partition Treaty. On the other hand, I had reason to think that the more my power was increased by the addition of the states assigned [by the treaty] to my son, the more hindrances I should find to the execution of the treaty. The previous negotiations and the present uncertainty of affairs have shown me this only too well. The King of Spain's will added still more difficulties. For since the Archduke was chosen in the event of my grandsons' refusing the succession, the Emperor would have been even more reluctant to agree [to the treaty], and even if he had done so, since the Archduke's refusal would have transferred the right of succession to the Duke of Savoy, the last would have been recognised as legitimate heir to the monarchy by the whole Spanish nation.

Thus in order to execute the treaty it would have been necessary to conquer all the states dependent on the Crown of Spain, so as to distribute them in accordance with the terms of partition. This decision would necessarily entail a war whose end could not be foreseen. Nothing was more contrary to the spirit of the treaty. On the other hand, I say that my acceptance of the will could give no one cause for complaint, if my son is willing to surrender his rights, as he is in fact doing, to the Duke of Anjou. In this way all pretext for war is removed, for Europe will have no reason to fear the engrossing of so many states under a single power; my own strength will not be increased and things will remain as they have been for so many years. It is consequently more to the advantage of Europe as a whole, and even more in accordance with the purpose of the

Partition Treaty, to follow the settlement made by the late King of Spain.

These considerations were decisive, and I had made up my mind to accept the will when I gave [a second] audience to the Ambassador of that Crown. I therefore assured him that I would at once dispatch the Duke of Anjou to Spain. The next day I sent him the letter which I had written to the Council of Regency, warning him that it was necessary to keep the secret for a few days to allow me the time to send word to the King of England and the Grand Pensionary.

Almost the same information has been given to the English Ambassador as to you. You will find it in greater detail in a Memoir which was read to him and of which he was given a copy. He was told that it was dangerous to spend a long time discussing the reply to be given to the Spanish Ambassador, for it could well be that the Ambassador had orders to send an express courier to Vienna as soon as I had refused to accept the will, offering the whole succession to the Archduke.

You will speak in this same vein to the Pensionary. You are also to point out to him that there can never be any certainty of the treaty being carried out, the Emperor not being party to it. And in truth, this difficulty would never have arisen if the King of England and the States-General had pressed the Emperor to subscribe to the treaty, instead of secretly encouraging him to believe that he would not have to do so; if they had acted more vigorously toward the Duke of Savoy; if they had worked in better faith to draw the Northern Crowns and the Princes of the Empire to guarantee the treaty; if finally they had agreed in time to give the aid necessary to secure the execution of the treaty.

But they must not be reproached. It will be enough to speak to the Pensionary as I instruct you in this letter, and to follow the tone of the Memoir that I am sending you. You may even show him the Memoir, but without leaving him a copy. You should however at this juncture redouble your efforts to keep promptly informed of the decisions made by the States-General, and of the orders they may issue for raising troops and fitting out ships. You are to try to ascertain whether they are making overtures to the Elector of Bavaria; what use they intend to make of the forces they maintain in the Spanish Netherlands; if they are meditating some scheme against the Indies or Cadiz, or any stronghold or port in the Spanish Empire, either in the Ocean or in the Mediterranean.

You are to inform the Spanish Ambassador at The Hague that I have instructed you to make known to him the orders I have given you; that the ardour which he has always shown in the service of his master gives me no reason to doubt that he will cooperate with you and furnish you with all the information necessary to the welfare of the Spanish monarchy. You are to inform him that I have no other purpose now than to maintain the complete integrity of all its parts, and you are also to inform him of my reply to the Council of Regency.

d

To Philip V

Marly, 3 March 1702

I HAD in mind your comfort alone when I gave my approval to your plan to bring the Queen with you to Naples, but my regard for you will not permit me to remain silent concerning the disadvantages I foresee as a result of her making the journey. Had I less affection for you, I should have agreed without any reservation; I should have withheld my fatherly advice if it were contrary to your wishes.

Your love for the Queen makes you wish never to be separated from her, but for this very reason you should consider the discomfort to which you expose her by making her undertake a sea voyage as long as the one to Naples. If her affection for you makes her blind to the unfortunate consequences to be feared from this, you should take even greater care and assure your common happiness by giving thought to the preservation of her health. You know how greatly she suffered from the effects of the sea voyage just from Nice to Toulon; you may imagine the effect of a far longer voyage, during which there is absolutely no possibility of landing every day. Instead of the mutual pleasure which you promised each other from this voyage, you are laying up for yourselves continuous misery and anxiety. Among the reasons for this during a sea-voyage I shall mention only the poor health of the Queen; I shall not speak of the dangers, which I hope you will avoid. But once arrived in Naples you will regret many times your decision to bring her with you. If there are still disturbances there, what will you not fear on her behalf? And will you be able to leave her there while you go to command the armies in Lombardy? Or will you remain in Naples for her sake alone, when you are going to Italy to protect your possessions there? If all is calm at Naples it will be unnecessary for you to remain there long. The Queen will thus have made a very arduous journey to remain only a few days at your side; you will then be forced to leave her exposed to every danger you could envisage during your campaign, either from a popular tumult or from the incursions of the Dutch and English in the Mediterranean. Let Your Majesty reflect on the well-founded alarm you would feel if their fleet were to bombard Naples and the Queen were forced to flee; what would you not fear for her from popular disturbance at such a time?

Think of the difficulty you would encounter in returning to Spain with her once the campaign was over. It is impossible to be certain how long you will have to stay in Italy. You will probably not leave the army until after the season for navigation, especially for galleys. It would then be equally difficult for you either to return to Naples to fetch the Queen, or for you to send for her to Milan so as to return together to Spain. Your only course would be to send her back to Spain when you left Naples; you would thus have obliged her to make a journey as wearisome as it would be futile so as to remain just a few days longer in your company, and for her return you will be forced to use the very ships which would be useful to you at Naples.

The undertaking upon which Your Majesty is embarking is too great to be obstructed by further difficulties. For you it is fitting to travel with a small suite when going in person to defend your possessions, but it is not proper that the Queen should travel without the attendance her rank requires. At Madrid your intention of taking her with you is regarded as the consequence of a decision to abandon Spain to the House of Austria. This consideration alone should be enough to make you leave her behind in that kingdom. She will give you far deeper proof of her affection by maintaining the allegiance of the Spanish people by her presence, than by exposing herself to the dangers and hardships of a sea voyage merely to accompany you. She is too reasonable not to understand when you have shown her my letter. You should also have sufficient command of yourself to ask of her, as a natural proof of her affection, what you could require by authority. You will placate your faithful Spanish subjects by leaving among them the person you hold most dear. They will confidently await your return; your enemies' cunning will not avail to dim your glory by representing your departure to defend your Italian possessions as a flight. You are probably aware that this is how they describe it.

It could be asserted without justification that the hope of an heir in the near future obliges you to take the Queen with you, for it is known that she is not yet in a condition to let us believe this to be so. And if she were about to give you children, would it be wise to expose her during her pregnancy to the hardships of a long voyage? And would it be fitting for the heir to your kingdoms to be born outside Spain?

I have gone into all these details in the conviction that the most urgent arguments are necessary to overcome the sorrow that you and the Queen will feel at separating. I could have no hope of persuading her, were her sound understanding not so far in advance of her years. She should draw on it to convince herself that since the two of you may reasonably expect to spend so many years together, it is no great misfortune to be parted for a few months, when your glory, the comfort of your people and the security of your domains are at stake.

During your absence I feel that you should establish the Queen's residence at Saragossa as well as Madrid. Marcin [the French ambassador] will tell you my views on this. I hope that, God favoring your just purposes, she will soon be reunited with you, covered with glory and victorious over your enemies. What I have pointed out to you is purely the result of my affection, and you should follow my advice: it would be better for you not to go to Italy than for you to take the Queen with you. You see the reasons for this; I have weighed and pondered them all. I hope that you will choose the right course and travel alone.

e

To Philip V

Versailles, 1 February 1703

I WAS saddened to read your letter of January 20th, but I must say that the last part made me afraid for you. You have now reigned for two years, but you have not yet, through too much diffidence, spoken out as a master. You have not been able to rid yourself of this shyness even though you scorn the dangers of conspiracies and of the sharpest action in war. And yet you have hardly arrived in Madrid before they succeed in convincing you of your ability to rule alone a monarchy of which, so far, you have felt but the excessive burden. You forget the difficulties of your affairs and congratulate yourself on being able to keep your councils alone. I was far from thinking that such a trap would be set for you and that you could possibly fall into it.

Consider well whether you are justly repaying all the affection I bear you if, the first time you personally exercise your authority, you dismiss from your council Cardinal d'Estrées, him in whom I chose to repose my entire confidence at your court in order to help you bear the burden of your affairs; his devotion to me makes him follow you, when he has nothing more to desire than to enjoy in peace the reputation and the honors which his services have earned him.

But it is not my purpose to upbraid you. I know the secrets of your heart, and the more I feel certain of your feelings, the more concerned I am at the false steps into which you have allowed yourself to be drawn. There is no need to recall all I have done for you, to tell you how I preferred placing you on the throne above my own interests. For there would have been considerable advantages for me in acquiring those states that comprised my portion; they would have offered a weak resistance; you have seen them and can judge this for yourself; you know whether I have ever sought to draw any personal profit from the aid I have given you. Yet I am exhausting my kingdom; all Europe is leagued against me to procure your ruin; Spain, heedless of the misfortunes that threaten her, contributes nothing to her own defense. The trouble, the cost, all fall on me, even though I have no thought but to defend you against the attacks of your enemies.

It is essential that, at the least, your decisions be made in agreement with me; it is asking little that some one person should represent me in your councils; you yourself are percipient enough to desire this. I selected Cardinal d'Estrées as the most versed in affairs of state, the most enlightened man I could place at your side, as the man whose experience and talents would be of most service to you: he is giving up ease, health, perhaps life itself, with no other purpose than to bear witness to his zeal and devotion to me. And when your need for these qualities is greatest, at the moment when it is most vital to make immediate decisions for the safety of yourself and your kingdom, you reveal a lamentable tendency to believe that suddenly you have acquired the ability to govern alone a monarchy that the most capable of your predecessors would have found difficult to direct in its present state. I term indulgence in you what I should have called presumption in another. I know that you are by no means guilty of the latter fault, but the consequences of the former are hardly less serious, and that is what alarms me on your behalf.

I am too much attached to you to bring myself to abandon you. But you will force me into this unfortunate necessity, if I am no longer informed of what is transacted in your councils. I cannot be informed if you restrict Cardinal d'Estrées in the occasions to approach you that you have hitherto granted not only to him, but to the Duc d'Harcourt and Marcin; I shall be forced to recall [the Cardinal], an ordinary embassy being unsuited to a man of his dignity and reputation; but if I recall him, I shall be moved solely by what the interests of my kingdom seem to require of me. It is not right that my subjects should be completely ruined to preserve Spain in spite of herself; and I should be attempting it in vain if I see on her side only uncertainty and indifference, and on yours a lack of confidence in me and in those I send to you: if, in fine, our plans are no longer concerted.

Choose then which you prefer: either the continuance of my aid, or abandonment to the counsels of those who desire your ruin. If the former, instruct Cardinal Porto-Carrero to return to the Despacho even if it is only for six months; continue to allow Cardinal d'Estrées and the President of Castile to have access to it; do not shut yourself up in the shameful indolence of your palace; show yourself to your subjects, listen to their requests, see that they are justly treated, give attention to the safety of your kingdom; in a word, discharge the duties which God has entrusted to you by calling you to the throne. If you choose the second course, I shall be deeply moved by your ruin, which I shall regard as imminent; but at least send me word of your intention, for that would be some small acknowledgement of my past support. It would be a considerable service, for it would give me the opportunity to obtain peace for my subjects.

f
To Victor Amadeus II of Savoy

September 1703

MONSIEUR, Since the bonds of religion, honor, interest, alliance, and your own signature are as nothing between us, I am sending my cousin the Duke of Vendôme, at the head of my armies, to explain my intentions to you. He will allow you no more than twenty-four hours to declare yourself.

g
To All Provincial Governors

Versailles, 12 June 1709

MY COUSIN, the expectation of an imminent peace was so generally diffused throughout my kingdom that I feel that I owe to the loyalty that my people have shown during the course of my reign the satisfaction of learning the reasons which still prevent them from enjoying the peace I had intended to secure for them.

To obtain it I was ready to acquiesce in terms that by no means guaranteed the security of my frontier provinces. But the more I expressed the desire and willingness to allay the suspicions that my enemies profess to retain concerning my power and intentions, the more they increased their claims against me. By adding new demands to their original ones, and by using as a pretext the name of the Duke of Savoy or the interests of the Imperial Princes, they have

revealed that their sole intention is to strengthen the states border-
ing on France at the expense of my Crown, and thus to afford easy
access to the heart of my kingdom on any occasion when it suits
their interests to begin another war.

The war that at present engages me, and which I desire to end,
would not be finished even were I to accept their terms, for they
have given me two months in which to execute my side of the
treaty, and in this time they require that I surrender to them the
fortresses they demand in the Low Countries and Alsace, and
demolish those that they require to be destroyed. For their part they
have refused any other undertaking than to suspend hostilities until
the first of August, reserving to themselves the right of further
military action if the King of Spain, my grandson, persists in his
determination to defend the crown which God has given him, and
to die rather than abandon the faithful subjects who for nine years
have acknowledged him as their lawful sovereign. Such a truce
would be more perilous even than war, and would retard rather
than hasten the conclusion of peace, for it would not only be necessary to continue the expense of maintaining my armies, but after
the expiry of the truce my enemies would have attacked me with the
further advantage of possessing the fortresses into which I myself had
admitted them, while at the same time I should have razed those
which served as a bulwark to some of my frontier provinces.

I shall not mention their suggestions that I should unite my
forces with those of the allies and force the King of Spain, my
grandson, to relinquish his throne, if he will not agree voluntarily
to live henceforth without a state and resign himself to the status
of a private citizen. It is contrary to all humanity to believe that
they really thought to bind me to such an alliance, but even though
my affection for my subjects is no less profound than that which I
bear my own children, and though I share all the privations that
the war inflicts upon such loyal subjects, and have declared to all
Europe that I sincerely desire to let them enjoy peace, I am convinced that they themselves would refuse to accept it on conditions
so unjust and so inimical to the honor of France.

I therefore intend that all those who for so many years have
given me proof of their devotion, giving their labor, their property
and their blood to carry on such a burdensome struggle, should
know that the only reward that the enemy saw fit to offer for the
concessions I was willing to make was a truce which, by being limited

to two months, would obtain for them far greater advantages than they could hope for from reliance on their armies in the field. Since I rely on the protection of God, and I hope that the blamelessness of my intentions will be rewarded by divine favor to my arms, I call upon the archbishops and bishops of my kingdom to stir up still further the ardor of prayer in their dioceses; at the same time I desire that my subjects within your jurisdiction should be told by you that they would be enjoying the benefits of peace if it had depended only upon my will to obtain for them a blessing which they justly desire, but which must be won by fresh exertions, since the vast concessions which I would have made are of no avail in securing general concord. I leave to your judgment the choice of the most suitable means of making public my intentions. With that, my cousin, I pray God that He will keep you in His most holy protection.

h
To the Duc de Saint-Aignan, Ambassador in Spain

28 February 1715

MY COUSIN, I note from your letter of the 11th of this month that Sieur Orry [French financial expert] did not remain long in Madrid after the King of Spain's order that he should prepare to return to my kingdom. You describe his departure, the discussions about the way in which he was dismissed, and the ill-humor which the Spaniards betray at their present subjection to the rule of Italians [of the entourage of Elizabeth Farnese, Philip V's second wife]. You request my orders on the action to be taken in the present circumstances and on the replies which you should make to the questions and complaints of the Spaniards, when they ask you whether I shall abandon them and sacrifice the profit accruing from all that I have done for the welfare and advantage of their country.

That you may be informed of my intentions, you should know that the purpose I set myself in my relations with Spain is the good of my grandson the King, and the upholding of that tender and perfect union which I desire always to maintain with him. If the favor he grants to the Italians should harm one or the other of these, I shall devote all my efforts and shall spare neither advice nor solicitation to open his eyes to his true interests and to deflect him from a course which I should consider dangerous.

If on the other hand I find that the favor shown the Italians does not affect the feeling which my grandson the King should have for me, nor jeopardize the conduct of his affairs, I see no reason obliging me to oppose the trust which the King of Spain appears inclined to place in their opinions. If their advice is preferred before that of the Spaniards, this does not necessarily mean that I am abandoning Spain and sacrificing the profit of all that I have done for that crown so far.

I should wish, both for the good of the King of Spain and for the honor of that nation, that native Spaniards should be preferred for the direction and control of principal affairs. On several occasions I have advised my grandson the King to make use of them rather than foreigners, but he has found out for himself that good men suited for every type of function were even scarcer among them than one could have believed, and for this reason he has placed foreigners in positions which should only have been entrusted to Spaniards. I have found no reason to criticize his appointments. I am even less inclined to do so now that the Italians are protected by the Queen of Spain, and the dearth among the Spaniards of reliable men suitable for employment is as great as ever it was before the arrival of that Princess in Spain.

Finally I have made it clear on several occasions that I had no desire to interfere with the appointments made by the King my grandson to the offices and positions of his monarchy, for he must known better than anyone the persons able to serve him well. I see no reason to do now what I was unwilling to do while Sieur Orry was still in Spain, and while I was far from believing his opinions infallible.

In consequence the course you are to follow is merely to pay careful attention to all that happens, and to listen to what is said to you by the Spaniards and Italians currently in favor; you are to do this, however, in such a manner that the King and Queen will have no cause to suspect that you incline to those who are critical of the government. For above all you must concern yourself solely with the interests of the King my grandson, which I consider in no way separate from my own, and that the information you gather should help you distinguish between what is and what is not to his real advantage.

The first use which you should make of the knowledge you obtain must be to warn him, without compromising those from whom you receive the information, either yourself, if he allows you access and freedom to do this, or if these are not granted you, through intermediaries in whom you know he has the greatest trust.

By virtue of his disposition he will always have especial trust in his confessor, and for this reason I hope that he will always keep Father Robinet, whose integrity and good intentions are known to me. But he is so disliked by Cardinal del Giudice that, if he has any influence over the King of Spain, I am convinced that the confessor will not remain long at Madrid. This Cardinal is so much in my debt for procuring his return that I am sure that he will do his utmost, in his own interest too, to strengthen the close union which I wish to maintain with my grandson the King. The other Italians have the same interest, and I cannot see what they could hope for from acting in opposition to it. Their influence, if it is as great as is reputed, has so far done me no harm and even if it were suspect to me, further confirmation of these suspicions would be necessary before I should openly oppose the course which events may take, which I do not as yet know, and which I could only alter in favor of the Spaniards, whose character, abilities and purposes could arouse the same suspicions. It is highly probable that they will exhibit great enthusiasm for the cause of union so long as they are excluded from the control of affairs, and also that perhaps they would not think and talk similarly if the government were in their charge.

Whoever is given this responsibility by the King of Spain should take particular care to satisfy the complaints of the English over the obstacles raised in the name of my grandson the King against the execution of the terms of the last treaty of peace. Lord Methuen, the English ambassador, should have arrived at Madrid. Before leaving London he informed the Marquis de Monteleon that he would make such reasonable proposals that it was hoped that the King of Spain would be satisfied with them; but that he would leave at once if he found that frivolous objections were being raised, or that he was being gulled; that in this event there would be no treaty of commerce between the two kingdoms.

These words are all the more worthy of attention as the party at present in power in England believes it to be in its interest to find some specious pretext for renewing the war with Spain. And there is no surer way of arousing the English nation than by putting up obstacles to their commercial interests. Therefore make the consequences of this clear to my grandson the King; point them out to the Queen as well; in fine, try to ensure that Lord Methuen's requests are satisfied, and that the reasonable proposals which he is ordered to make are well received.

Furthermore, continue to report anything you learn which may be of service to me. With which, etc....

i

A letter written by Louis XIV a few days before his death and entrusted to Marshal Villeroy to be delivered to Louis XV when he attained the age of seventeen

MY SON, if that Divine Providence in which I place my trust sees fit to preserve your life until that time when reason will enable you to act on your own, respectfully accept this letter from the hands of this faithful subject whom I have caused to swear that he will deliver it to you in person: in this letter you will find the last wishes of your father and your King who, at the moment of departing this life, feels a redoubled tenderness for you, in whom he sees all his children reborn, and at so gentle an age that the disorders which he foresees during your minority trouble him more than the terrors of the death he is about to suffer.

If anything can lessen my sorrow in this present condition, it is, my son, the oath sworn to me by all my faithful subjects to watch over your life and spill their blood for your protection. Reward them, my son, when you come to learn of this, and never forget them, nor my son the Duc du Maine [son of Louis XIV and Madame de Montespan], whom I have judged worthy to be placed near your person, and who will take good care of you. This honor, which I consider necessary because of the love I bear you, will no doubt arouse the enmity of those who find their desire to govern thwarted by this wise precaution; if any harm should come to this prince as a consequence of disorders within your kingdom, or if any change should be made in my arrangements on his behalf, I desire, my son, if God grants you life, that you should restore things to the state in which they are at the time of my death, both in matters of religion and in that which pertains to the Duc du Maine. Put your trust in him; follow his advice; he is well able to guide you, and if death should deprive you of so good a subject, reward his children for all the affection you owe their father by maintaining them in the position which I have given them; [their father] has promised and sworn to me never to abandon you until death.

Let the ties of kinship and affection attach you always to the King of Spain, so that no mistaken considerations of interest or policy may ever divide you from him; herein lies the sole means of preserving the peace and balance of Europe.

Always maintain an unshakeable attachment for the common Father of all the faithful and never cut yourself off, whatever your reason, from the heart and center of the Church. Place all your trust in God, live more as a Christian than a King, and never give Him cause to punish you for any moral shortcoming. Give thanks to His Divine Providence which so manifestly watches over this kingdom. Show to your subjects the same example that a Christian father gives to his family; consider them as your children; make them happy if you would be so yourself; relieve them as soon as possible of all the crushing taxes which the demands of a long war have loaded on them, and which their loyalty has made them bear submissively. Let them enjoy a long peace which alone can restore the affairs of your kingdom; always choose peace before the dubious fortunes of war, and remember that the most glorious victory is too dearly bought when it must be paid for in the blood of your subjects. Never spill this, if it is possible, unless it be for the glory of God; such conduct will draw upon you the blessing of Heaven during the course of your reign; receive mine in this last embrace.